A Conceptual Approach to Moving and Learning

A Conceptual Approach To Moving and Learning

DAVID L. GALLAHUE/Indiana University/*Bloomington, Indiana*

PETER H. WERNER/Miami University/*Oxford, Ohio*

GEORGE C. LUEDKE/Southern Illinois University/*Edwardsville, Illinois*

JOHN WILEY & SONS, INC.
New York   London   Sydney   Toronto

Library of Congress Cataloging in Publication Data:

Gallahue, David L.
  A conceptual approach to moving and learning.

  Bibliography: p.
  Includes indexes.
  1. Physical education for children. 2. Perceptual-motor learning.
I. Werner, Peter H., joint author. II. Luedke, George C.,
joint author. III. Title.

GV443.G23   372.8'6'044   75-2369
ISBN 0-471-29043-2

Printed in the United States of America

10 9 8 7 6 5 4 3 2 1

*To our wives Ellie, Mary, and Sharyn
for their patience and understanding.
Now we know why authors thank their
wives.*

Preface

This textbook is a pioneer effort in the area of improving movement and cognitive abilities through the medium of physical activity. Its developmental approach is soundly based and researched and presents a logical, easy-to-follow rationale for the inclusion of movement as an integral part of the preschool and elementary school day.

The book is directed toward teachers of preschool children, elementary classroom teachers, and physical education specialists who are responsible for the movement education and concomitant learnings of children. It is an outgrowth of the recent surge of interest in the psychomotor, cognitive, and affective development of preschool and elementary school children, and it takes a fresh look at the role of movement in the total spectrum of learning by viewing physical education from a conceptual framework. It combines the best from the newer "movement education" type of programs with the more traditional forms of physical education and views the development of movement and academic concepts as the central focus of physical education at the preschool and elementary school level. The development of movement abilities along with cognitive abilities is expressed as developmental goals of the physical education program.

Instead of a basic resource book for a variety of ill-defined games, rhythms, and self-testing activities, the book is intended to be used as an undergraduate and graduate level textbook that examines how children learn to move and how they learn through movement. A sampling of movement experiences is presented, which will help to achieve clearly stated ends rather than serving as ends in themselves.

There are two major sections: "Learning to Move" and "Learning through Movement." Chapter One is the core of the "Learning to Move" section. It examines movement as a phenomenon that is divided into three major categories: locomotion, manipulation, and stability. A theoretical model is presented for viewing effective and efficient movement in each of these areas as being a developmental process that occurs in six overlapping phases that progress from the simple to the complex. The child's movement abilities are developed and refined in each of these phases through a variety of developmentally appropriate learning experiences that are recognized by the teacher and elaborated on through the use of direct and indirect teaching approaches.

Chapter Two discusses the reflexive behaviors of newborn children. Reflexes are the first form of movement that the developing human being is capable of performing. Therefore, students of human movement will gain a greater understanding of this foundational phase of motor development.

In Chapter Three the development of rudimentary movement abilities in the infant and the influence of both maturation and experience on their acquisition is considered. A distinction is made between movement patterns and movement skills in Chapter Four, which also discusses the mechanical principles that govern man's movement. This discussion of basic mechanics has been included to help the student to conceptualize the three primary classifications of all movement; locomotion, manipulation, and stability.

A variety of fundamental stability, locomotor, and manipulative movements are described and illustrated in Chapters Five to Seven. Common problems that children encounter in the performance of these movements are presented along with concepts that they should know about each; and lists of suggested activities for enhancing each of these fundamental abilities are included.

Chapter Eight deals with the development of higher-level skill concepts in locomotion, manipulation, and stability, and Chapter Nine examines the organization and implementation of the actual lesson in the conceptual curriculum.

Chapter Ten, in the "Learning Through Movement" section, analyzes the contribution of physical education to the cognitive, affective, and perceptual-motor development of children. Chapter Eleven discusses the cognitive development through the application of Piaget's theory of intellectual development, Bloom's cognitive domain, and Montessori's method of teaching children. Perceptual-motor development and the influence of movement on the development of perceptual-motor abilities are discussed in Chapter Twelve.

The integration of language arts, mathematics, science, and social studies through movement experiences in physical education is presented in Chapters Thirteen to Sixteen. Practical examples of integrating each of these classroom subjects with physical education are included.

Chapter Seventeen examines the role of movement in the development of concepts in art and music. An integrated approach is presented in which movement serves as a core to developing knowledge in art and music.

We sincerely thank our students and colleagues who helped to make this book a reality. Their numerous comments and suggestions concerning the conceptual approach were invaluable. We especially thank Clinton Strong, Indiana University, Helen Heitman, University of Illinois, Chicago Circle Campus, and Robert Sweeney, East Stroudsberg State College for their careful review of the text and their many specific contributions. We also thank Christina Brown for her competent typing and Lawrence Manning for his outstanding photography. We are grateful to Andrew Ford, Editor of Wiley, for his interest and enthusiasm in publishing a pioneer textbook. Finally, we thank our families for patience, support, and encouragement and our Creator, who made moving and learning a reality for us all.

David L. Gallahue
Peter H. Werner
George C. Luedke

Contents

PART II   LEARNING THROUGH MOVEMENT

10. Learning Through Movement:

16. Developing Social Studies Concepts

A Conceptual Approach to Moving and Learning

PART I
Learning to Move

Chapter 1
Learning to Move: Introduction

Key Concept: Physical education is that aspect of the total school curriculum that involves children in a series of coordinated movement experiences that are designed to aid them in developing and refining the process of learning to move effectively and efficiently through space.

Content: Why Man Moves
Phases of Motor Development
    Reflexive Behavior
    Rudimentary Movement Abilities
    Fundamental Movement Patterns
    General Movement Skills
    Specific Movement Skills
    Specialized Movement Skills
Categories of Human Movement
    Stability
    Locomotion
    Manipulation
The Content of Physical Education
    Games
    Rhythms
    Self-testing
    Aquatics
The Sequence of Directed Learning Experiences
    Exploration
    Discovery
    Combination
    Selection
    Performance
The Conceptual Model
    Preschool and Primary Grades
    Intermediate Grades and Middle School

Learning to Move: Introduction

WHY MAN MOVES

Man is a moving organism. Without movement he cannot survive, and without life there can be no movement. All of man's covert as well as overt behaviors are reflected through movement to a greater or lesser extent depending on the particular behavior being observed. These movements may be obvious and readily visible to the naked eye as with gross bodily movements, or they may be subtle and detected only through the use of special equipment. For example, the life sustaining movements by the organs of the body are in perpetual motion in order that one's vital life functions may be sustained. If the heart does not beat, or if the lungs do not expand and contract, life will cease within a few short minutes. There is evidence to indicate that the apparent nonmoving act of cortical thought actually involves subtle movements represented by changes in the alpha waves of electroencephalogram recordings. Even the act of standing "completely still" involves subtle but measurable changes in the body's position in space.

Movement is also necessary for survival for somewhat less direct but no less important survival reasons. Man needs to learn how to: (1) adjust and control his environment, (2) understand his environment and (3) communicate within his environment.[1] In other words, man must learn to act, interact, and react effectively and efficiently with his environment. In prehistoric times if one was unable to accomplish the daily tasks of acquiring food, providing shelter, and warding off intruders, his very existence was threatened and he was literally unable to survive. In this respect today's society has not changed markedly from primitive times. Inability to move effectively and efficiently makes it difficult to survive, in both a literal and a figurative sense, without artificial means of support. Man is unable to survive if he cannot meet the demands placed upon him in the countless movement situations that he faces daily and that involve a potential element of danger. The everyday acts of crossing the street, catching a fast moving ball, or balancing on a ladder become dangerous and threatening to survival. The infant entering this world is unable to survive for several years without considerable assistance from those tho take care of his needs. He must develop his movement abilities and learn how to move effectively in order to survive and function purposefully in society. Developing and refining these movement abilities to a point where he is able to act, interact, and react to the demands

4

placed upon him by his environment is a process that begins before birth and does not cease until death. The child must master the basic movement requirements for survival in society before he can concentrate fully on the development of specialized movement skills. Kephart[7] believed that the learning of specific movement skills before basic movement patterns have been adequately developed results in the establishment of "splinter skills." A splinter skill is an isolated skill that is very specialized in nature and is characterized by rigidity of performance rather than adaptability to a variety of movement situations.

If we agree on the importance of developing basic movement abilities before stressing specific and specialized skill development, why then are interscholastic athletics and other forms of highly organized competition permeating the lives of children as low as the first grade? Are we really doing young children a service by teaching them a series of splinter skills to be used in specific activities before they have had an opportunity to more fully develop their basic abilities in a variety of movement situations? Perhaps it would be wise to provide children with a greater variety of movement experiences and more closely ascertain their individual readiness for the rigors of organized athletics before we require them to specialize in the development of skills. Some children, may in fact, be ready

Learning To Move With Skill, Efficiency and Joy.

to develop specific abilities sooner than others, and we need to provide them with opportunities to do so. This must, however, be done as an *outgrowth* of a good physical education program and not in place of it. We must not make the erroneous assumption that all children are ready to specialize in their development of movement skills. The fact is that most young children are not ready to specialize and need to further develop their fundamental movement abilities through a good physical education program *before* embarking on the route of specialization. There is little evidence to support the contention that one must specialize in the development of movement abilities or be involved in organized competition at an early age in order to become a skilled performer in later years. Children that have been involved in the development of fundamental movement patterns and a wide variety of general movement skills have a broad base of movement experience and have at least an equal opportunity of developing the specific and specialized abilities necessary for skilled performance in a *wide variety* of activities.

PHASES OF MOTOR DEVELOPMENT

The development of one's movement abilities occurs in a sequential manner moving from very simple to highly complex movements in a hierarchial manner

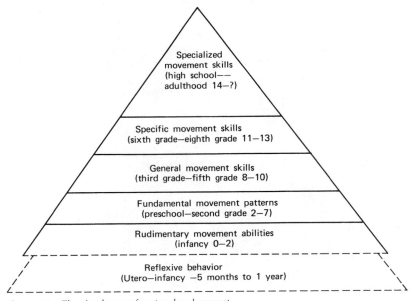

Figure 1-1. The six phases of motor development.

(see Figure 1-1). All children do not necessarily pass through the following phases of motor development in the exact sequence indicated for the development of their various movement abilities. Neither do they adhere exactly to the approximate ages indicated for each phase. Children are multidimensional beings and as such each possesses a unique set of interests, abilities, and motivations that influence the sequence and time of emergence. It is entirely possible, for example, for a nine year old to be at the general or specific movement phase in one area and only at the fundamental movement pattern phase in another. We need only to look at the girl who is adept at rope jumping but terrible in ball throwing, or the boy who performs well with a basketball but is unable to do a basic headstand or cartwheel.

The six phases of motor development outlined in the following pages are designed to indicate where *most* children are in the development of their movement skills. It also serves as an indicator as to when teachers and parents should place emphasis on the development of different degrees of skill that take into account the needs, interests, and capabilities of most children at a certain age.

Reflexive Behavior

The first movements of the developing fetus as well as the neonate are reflexive in nature. That is, they are involuntary movements of the body that are subcortically controlled. Many of these reflexes resemble later voluntary movements and are termed *postural reflexes*. Others are termed *primitive reflexes* because of their resemblance to the movements performed by animals lower on the phylogenetic scale. Primitive reflexes such as the rooting and sucking reflexes are thought to be survival mechanisms. For without them, the newborn would be unable to obtain nourishment. In Chapter Two a discussion of both postural and primitive reflexes with specific concern focused on their possible relationship to voluntary movements that occur during infancy is undertaken.

Rudimentary Movement Abilities

The first voluntary movements of the infant are termed rudimentary movements. Rudimentary movement abilities are those movements that develop during the child's first two years of life. The development of efficient and effective forms of rudimentary movement during infancy helps to form the basic structure for the more difficult movement tasks that lie ahead. Chapter Three discusses these movement abilities, the influence of maturation and learning on their development, and their critical function in serving as the basis for the development of fundamental movement patterns.

Fundamental Movement Patterns

Fundamental movement patterns are an outgrowth of the rudimentary movement abilities developed during the first two years of life. They begin developing around the third year (age 2) and continue through approximately the seventh year (second grade). These are the years in which young children explore and experiment with the movement potentials of their body as they run, jump, throw, catch, and balance their bodies. A movement pattern is characterized by the ability to move in a variety of ways to a given stimulus. Generality of movement is stressed rather than specificity. Fundamental movement patterns allow children to be adaptable in their movements. High degrees of accuracy and precision are not stressed. In order to encourage the development of efficient patterns of movement the environment is structured in such a way that success, inclusion, and a sense of achievement are maximized rather than failure and exclusion. A premium is placed on performing a wide variety of movements in an acceptable manner rather than stressing highly skilled performances in a limited number of skills.

General Movement Skills

The development or refinement of general movement skills forms the fourth phase of motor development. The ability to generalize fundamental abilities begins around the eighth year of life (third grade) and continues through to approximately the tenth year (fifth grade). General movement skills consist of the same elements seen in fundamental performance, but stress now *begins* to be placed by both the students themselves and the teacher on accuracy, form, and skilled performance. It is at this stage of development that children begin to be involved in a wide variety of sport skills that are important in individual, dual, and team activities. The fundamental movement abilities that were developed and refined in the preceding stage are now applied to the learning of sport skills. Sport skills are simply an elaboration of fundamental movements in more complex and specific forms. In Chapter Eight the development of general movement skills is discussed in greater detail. Keep in mind, however, that the thrust of this stage by both the student and teacher is exposure to and development of a *reasonable* degree of skill in *many* sport and dance lead-up activities.

Specific Movement Skills

Specific movement skills are an extension of the movement skills that were stressed in the previous stage. During this phase, however, *increased* emphasis is placed on form, skill, and accuracy. More complex sport skills are refined and

Success Oriented Experiences
Are Important Builders Of
Self-Confidence

utilized in the performance of advanced lead-up activities and the official sport itself. The specific movement skill phase corresponds roughly to the middle school years from age eleven to thirteen (sixth grade through eighth grade) and is a period of more acute refinement of general movement skills in a wide variety of sport activities. The learning situation generally places more emphasis on the product to be learned than on the process of learning that the child is involved in as with movement pattern development. Being more concerned with the product than the process often causes the learning of general movement skills to be structured in such a way that they promote failure rather than success. A model of the particular skill to be learned is presented by the teacher or peer. It is the individual's duty to approximate this model as nearly as possible. The closer the approximation to the model, the greater the feeling of success. The further it is from the model, the greater the sense of failure (see Figure 1-2).

The learning of general movement skills involves experiencing a series of successes and failures in a wide variety of movement activities. The individual develops a final appraisal of his performance in these activities that lies somewhere along a continuum of success and failure that may be similar to the one presented in Figure 1-3. We all tend to rank ourselves somewhere along this continuum according to the model of performance we have established for ourselves

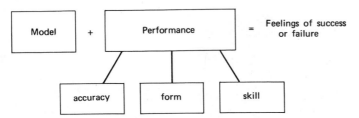

Figure 1-2. The influence of performance on self-concept.

and expect to emulate. If our ratings lie along the positive side of the continuum, our self-concept is enhanced. If it lies on the negative side, our self-concept takes a beating. Movement is the center of life for most preschool and elementary school children. Are we really serving young children's needs if we constantly structure movement experiences in which they must put their self-concept on the line? Is it sufficient to say that "we live in a competitive society and Johnny must learn to compete," or "not everyone can come in first place"? Or is it time for us to reevaluate the place of skill development in our curriculum? Specific skill development is an important phase of the physical education curriculum. However, stress should not be placed on its importance at too early an age. Preschool, primary, and intermediate grade children need to develop and refine their fundamental and general movement abilities before stress is placed on specific and specialized skill development in the high school and adulthood.

Specialized Skill Development

Specialized skill development is the sixth phase of motor development. It begins around the fourteenth year of life and continues into adulthood. It is similar to specific skill development in most ways except that specialized skill development isolates a limited number of *specific* skills to be practiced and perfected for

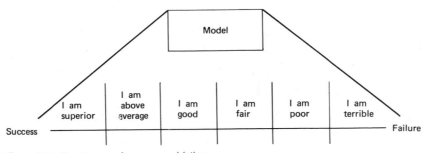

Figure 1-3. Continuum of success and failure.

high levels of performance. The *level* of performance is dependent on the individual's talents and degree of specialization and may range from Olympic, intercollegiate, and interscholastic competition, to personal standards of excellence set forth by the individual in the performance of selected leisure-time activities. As stated earlier, elementary school children are often encouraged to refine the specialized skills involved in a particular sport. Too often this quest for specialization is done at the expense of the development of fundamental movement patterns and general movement skills in many forms of movement. Specialized skill development may be of value to some, if it is not done at the expense of, or in the place of, the regular physical education program. It should only *supplement* the regular program in the form of after school instruction, intramurals or other forms of *informal* competition. If we as educators are aware of the importance of learning to move effectively and efficiently in a variety of ways through our environment and possess an understanding of the developmental characteristics of children, we must then reject the notion that specialized skill development is one of the purposes of the regular physical education program at this level. The scope of this book does not include specialized skill development as a phase of children's motor development.

CATEGORIES OF HUMAN MOVEMENT

The vital importance of learning to move is too important to be left to chance or the whims of untrained persons. The physical education specialist or the classroom teacher with knowledge of: (1) how children learn to move, (2) a keen appreciation of its importance, and (3) the ability to implement programs in motor development, can serve a vital role in developing children's movement abilities.

There are three primary classifications of movement that must be developed in the progression from the rudimentary movement abilities of infancy to the specialized movement skills of adolescence and adulthood. A category of movement is a general classificatory scheme based on common underlying principles of movement. The terms locomotion, manipulation, and stability are used here to represent these underlying principles. They serve as the organizing centers of the conceptual curriculum in the preschool and elementary school. They will be considered more extensively in the chapters that follow. The meaning of the terms will only be explained briefly here.

Stability

Stability refers to the ability to maintain one's balance in relationship to the force of gravity even though the nature of the application of the force may be altered or parts of the body may be placed in unusual positions. The classification of stability extends beyond the concept of balance and includes various axial movements and postures in which a premium is placed on controlling one's equilibrium. Stability is the most basic form of human movement. It is basic to all efficient movement and permeates both the category of locomotion and manipulation.

Locomotion

Locomotion refers to changes in the location of the body relative to fixed points on the ground. To walk, run, hop, jump, slide, or leap is to be involved in locomotion. The movement classification of locomotion develops in conjunction with stability but not apart from it. Fundamental aspects of stability must be mastered before efficient forms of locomotion may take place.

Manipulation

Manipulation is concerned with giving force to objects and absorbing force from objects by use of the hands or feet. The tasks of throwing, catching, kicking, trapping, and striking are included under the dimension of manipulation. Manipulation also refers to the fine motor controls required for tasks such as buttoning, cutting, printing, and writing. The scope of this book, however, is limited to the more gross motor aspects of manipulation. Large muscle manipulative abilities tend to develop somewhat later than stability and locomotor abilities. This is due, in part, to the fact that most manipulative movements incorporate elements of both stability and locomotion.

THE CONTENT OF PHYSICAL EDUCATION

The three categories of human movement that have been outlined briefly may be developed and refined through the four major content areas of physical education: games and sports, rhythms, self-testing, and aquatics. The learning of particular games, rhythms, self-testing, or aquatic skills is a *means* of developing stability, locomotor, and manipulative abilities appropriate to the developmental level of the child. Teachers must not lose sight of this goal. Every activity used in the program should be selected with a conscious awareness that it can contribute to developing and refining certain movement abilities. For children, their primary objective may be *fun*, but the serious teachers of movement have as their objectives LEARNING TO MOVE and LEARNING THROUGH MOVEMENT. The possibility of fun as the motivation to learn is a by-product of any good educational program, and is an important objective. This point cannot be overemphasized, but when fun becomes the primary objective of the program for the *teacher*, then it ceases to be a physical *education* program and becomes a recreation period.

Games

Games are used as a *means* of enhancing movement abilities appropriate to the child's developmental level. They are often classified into three subcontent areas that proceed from the simple to the complex in the following manner:

1. Low organized games and relays.
2. Lead-up games to sports.
3. Official sports.

Rhythms

Rhythms are another content area of the movement program. They are generally categorized into four subcontent areas moving from the simple to the complex within each:

1. Rhythmic fundamentals.
2. Creative rhythms.
3. Folk and square dance.
4. Social dance.

Self-testing

Self-testing, or gymnastic-type activities as they are sometimes called, is the third major content area of the program. This area represents a wide variety of activities in which children work on their own and can improve their performance through their own *individual* efforts. Self-testing activities may be classified in a variety of ways. The following is a common classification scheme for typical self-testing activities.

1. Basic movement patterns and skills.
2. Physical fitness activities
3. Stunts.
4. Tumbling.
5. Small aparatus.
6. Large apparatus.

Aquatics

Aquatics form the fourth and final content area of physical education. Unfortunately, the vast majority of elementary schools do not have the facilities necessary to conduct the aquatic phase of the program. This should not, however, detract from the importance of learning how to control one's body in a different medium, namely water. Because facilities do not exist in most schools at the present time, we must not give up the effort to include aquatics as a portion of the program in the future. This text, however, does not deal with the content area of aquatics due to space limitations. The reader is referred to the excellent book, *The Science of Swimming*, by James Counsilman.

Effectiveness and efficiency in each of the three dimensions of movement is the primary objective of incorporating games, rhythms, and self-testing activities in the program. The degree to which this objective is achieved is dependent on the particular developmental level of the children and the teacher's expertise in structuring developmentally appropriate movement experiences (that appear on the following pages). Games, rhythms, and self-testing activities serve only as the vehicle by which these experiences are applied.

THE SEQUENCE OF DIRECTED LEARNING EXPERIENCES

The content areas of the physical education program mentioned above may be implemented in a variety of ways. The teacher must, however, be fully aware that children pass through a hierarchial sequence of learning experiences in the development of their movement abilities. This sequence is based on two developmental concepts. First, that the acquisition of abilities progresses from the *simple to complex* in a manner similar to the one outlined in Figure 1-1. Second, that children proceed gradually from *general to specific* in the development and refinement of their abilities. Based on these two concepts, it is possible to view learning to move as a phenomenon that occurs from simple to complex and general to specific in the following manner.

1. Exploration.
2. Discovery.
3. Combination.
4. Selection.
5. Competitive performance (see Figure 1-4).

When involved in learning a new stability, locomotor, or manipulative skill that is to be used in a game, rhythm, or self-testing activity, we all generally go through the following sequence of learning experiences:

1. We explore the movements involved in the activity in relative isolation to one another.
2. We discover ways and means of executing each of these movements better through indirect means such as the observation of others performing, pictures, films, or books.

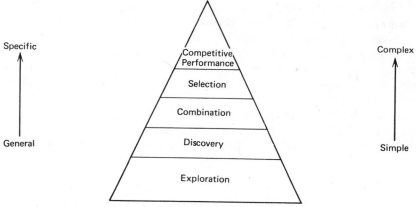

Figure 1-4. Learning experience hierarchy.

3. We combine the isolated movements and experiment with them in various ways.
4. We select "best" ways of combining each of these movements through a variety of lead-up games, and informal means of competition, and presentation.
5. We refine the selected movements to a high degree and perform the particular activity through formal means of competition, presentation, or through leisure-time pursuits.

This sequential progression of learning experiences is the same for adolescents and adults as it is for children, although it may not be as readily apparent. This is because the adolescent and adult are at the specialized skill phase and may spend less time with exploratory, discovery, and indirect combination type experiences, and more time in the selection and performance aspects of the sequence. Preschool and primary grade children at the fundamental motor pattern phase of development spend a great deal of time with exploratory, discovery, and combination experiences, and very little time with selection and performance activities.

Intermediate grade children in the general movement skill phase spend the bulk of their time with combination and selection-type experiences and less time with all others. Those at the specific movement phase spend the greater portion of their time involved with more direct forms of combination and selection experiences. Those at the specialized stage are involved primarily in selection and performance activities.

Remember that this sequence only illustrates the *major emphasis* that is given to the individual's learning experiences based on the appropriate phase of motor development. Because of each individual's unique combination of abilities it is likely that a variety of directed learning experiences ranging from exploration to performance will be incorporaed in each of the phases of motor development. The specific teaching-learning variables operating at the time will be the determining factor as to the types of experiences that are stressed by the teacher.

The teacher who is aware that the emphasis given to certain types of movement experiences is dependent upon the child's level of development will structure the environment and utilize teaching approaches that provide appropriate types of experiences. The following relates each aspect of the sequence of learning experiences and illustrates how teachers may utilize various forms of indirect and direct teaching approaches that are best suited to the developmental level of their students.

Exploration Experiences

Exploration represents the first level of the learning hierarchy (Figure 1-5). In order to take advantage of this level the teacher may utilize an indirect teaching approach that encourages exploration. Movement exploration is a technique of teaching movement that helps children enhance knowledge of their body and its potential for movement in space. The children are encouraged to explore and

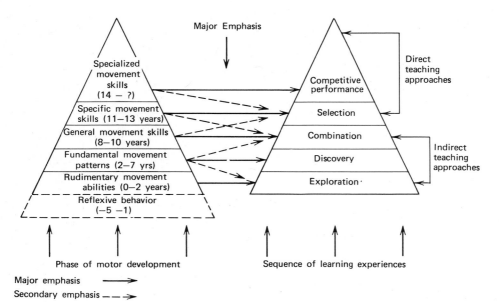

Figure 1-5. Interaction between the phases of motor development, the sequence of learning experiences, and teaching approaches.

Exploration Is A Basic Tool For Learning About Ourself and Our World.

experiment in each of the three classifications of movement. Accuracy and skill in performance are not stressed. This is accomplished by the teacher refraining from establishing a model of performance for the particular movement being explored. Instead, the children are presented with a series of movement questions or challenges posed by the teacher and given an opportunity to solve these problems as they see fit. Any reasonable solution to the problem is regarded as correct. At this time, there is no single "best" method of performance that the teacher attempts to elicit from the children. The teacher is more concerned with their creative involvement in the learning process.

Exploratory experiences are not particularly concerned with the product of the movement act other than acceptable execution of fundamental movements. They are, however, vitally concerned with the process of learning that children are involved in during the act. In other words, the *teacher* is not particularly concerned whether the ball goes in the hoop, the distance David can jump, or if Jennifer can execute a handstand with "perfect" form, but is interested in all achieving some degree of success within the level of their own particular abilities. The teacher also places importance and value on the ability to think and act as an individual. He is concerned that the children are expanding their knowledge of the movement potentials of their body in relation to the five movement qualities that permeate each of the three classifications movement.

This is not to imply that success or goal directed behavior is not important. On the contrary, movement exploration techniques are particularly appropriate for preschool and primary grade children because they structure the environment for success simply by considering all reasonable solutions to the problems posed by the teacher as correct. Success and goal directed behavior is an individual standard that does not require children to emulate a model of performance or to compete with their peers, but permits success within the limits of one's own abilities. In doing so, the child is continually encouraged to explore and experiment with endless combinations and variations in the five qualities of movement that influence the performance in all locomotor, manipulative, and stability movements.

1. FORCE is the degree of muscular tension required to move the body or its parts from place to place or to maintain its equilibrium. Force may be heavy or light or fall somewhere in between these two extremes.

2. TIME is the speed at which movement takes place. The movement may be fast or slow, erratic or sustained, gradual or sudden.

3. FLOW is the continuity or coordination of movements. Flow may be smooth or jerky, free or bound.

4. SPACE is the area that the body occupies as it moves through the environment. Space refers to the *levels, ranges,* and *directions* that the body may move. The body level may be large or small, high, medium, or low. Its range may be wide, narrow, far, near, long or short. Its direction may be forward, backward, sideward, diagonal, or form a straight, zig-zag, or curvy floor pattern.

5. ENVIRONMENT is the actual sensations that the body or its parts directly experience. Different *surfaces, textures,* and *equipment* are utilized. Wood, concrete, grass, water, and Astroturf are examples of different surfaces. Leather, plastic, rubber and the trampoline, balance beam, and jungle gym are examples of various textures and equipment in the environment.

Discovery Experiences

Discovery represents the second classification of the learning hierarchy. Movement experiences that incorporate discovery may be included into the lesson by the teacher in an indirect manner similar to movement exploration experiences. In fact, several authors consider exploration and directed discovery to be synonymous because of similarities in the use of problem-solving techniques by the two. In both types of experiences the teacher does not establish a model for "correct" performance at the outset of the experience. Problems are stated in the form of questions or challenges that are posed by the teacher. These questions result in emphasis being placed on movement pattern develop-

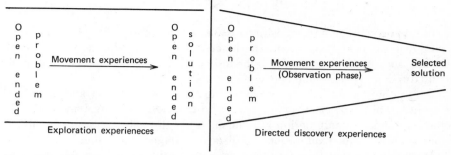

Figure 1-6. Differences between exploratory and discovery experiences utilizing an indirect teaching approach.

ment rather than on skill development. Both exploratory and discovery experiences utilize problem-solving techniques as a common tactic in developing the child's movement abilities. Gilliom has defined problem solving as:

"original thinking, an individual's technique of productive thinking, his techniques of inquiry, which is characterized by (1) a focus on an incomplete situation, (2) the freedom to inquire, and (3) the desire to put together something new to him, on his own, to make the incomplete situation into a complete one."[3]

It is the method employed by the child in the solution of the problems posed by the teacher that causes exploration and directed discovery to be considered separately here. Directed discovery incorporates an observation phase into the total experience, instead of not establishing a model of performance and accepting all solutions as correct as with exploration. The observation phase takes the form of observing the solutions of fellow students, the teacher, or individuals on film in relation to the problem presented. Only after the students have had an opportunity to solve the problem within the limits of their own understanding and ability is the observation phase utilized.

Instead of problems being entirely open-ended, as with exploration, there is a gradual funneling of questions in such a manner that they lead the children to "discovering" for themselves how to perform the particular movement under consideration. There is no single best way to move at this phase of development, and it allows for the performance of several "best" ways. At the end of the process of attempting solutions to the problem at hand, the children have an opportunity to evaluate their interpretations in light of the solutions of others. They are then given an opportunity to reaccess their solutions in light of the performance of others (see Figure 1-6).

Combination Experiences

Combination represents a transitional category in the hierarchial sequence of learning experiences. Movement experiences that utilize combination of movement skills may be incorporated into the lesson by the teacher through both indirect and direct styles of teaching (see Figure 1-7).

Indirect combination is a logical extension of the exploratory and discovery approaches. These experiences differ only in that activities involving stability, locomotion, and/or manipulation are consolidated through the problem-solving approaches used at the exploration and discovery stages of learning.

Direct combination experiences follow a more traditional approach to developing and refining combinations of stability, locomotor, and/or manipulative movements. Direct or traditional teaching approaches, as they are often called, involve establishing a model for correct performance through explanation, and demonstration of the skills to be learned before they are practiced by the students. The children then duplicate the movement characteristics of the model as nearly as possible within the limits of their abilities in a short practice session or drill. The class is generally stopped and the model is presented again along with general comments concerning problems that the class as a whole may be encountering. The class is then involved in an activity that incorporates these skills. The teacher circulates among the students and stops to aid those individuals who may still be having difficulty executing the skills with a general level of proficiency. Direct combination experiences differ from indirect experiences primarily in that they require a model for performance to be established before the movement experience begins while the other does not. This does not mean, however, that the direct form of combination does not permit children to explore and experiment. Establishing a model of performance can also serve as a way of

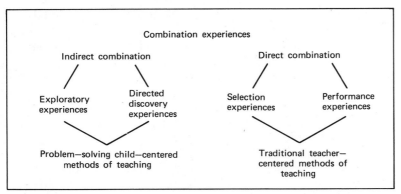

Figure 1-7. Combination experiences may utilize either indirect or direct methods of teaching and may be incorporated at all levels of development.

quickly and efficiently communicating a movement concept to the children that they can then explore.

Selection Experiences

Selection represents the fourth level of the learning hierarchy. In order to take advantage of this level of experience the teacher aids the students in making conscious decisions concerning best methods of performing the numerous combinations of stability, locomotor, or manipulative skills. Rather than merely refining combinations of fundamental movements, children at both the general and specific movement skill stages of motor development begin to select preferred ways of moving in a wide variety of sport, game, and dance activities. Selection experiences follow the same direct progression of explanation, demonstration, and experimentation, followed by general and specific correction and the drill that is used with direct combination experiences. Selection-type experiences, however, utilize more advanced activities than those found in the combination stage. These experiences generally take the form of lead-up activities to dual, team, and individual sports rather than low organized games. Lead-up activities combine two or more selected skills into an approximation of the official sport. They are modified in terms of the quality and quantity of movement skills involved, time, equipment, and facilities required, but are an approximation of the final desired combination of specialized movement skills that will be performed in the final phase.

Competitive Performance Experiences

Competitive performance is the fifth and final level of the learning hierarchy. Individuals at this stage are ready to pit their skills and abilities against those of others. They are engaged in highly organized and competitive sports primarily by adolescents and adults. Competitive performance experiences have no place in a developmentally sound physical education curriculum for the preschool and elementary school child and must not be confused with appropriate forms of informal and low level competition. Competitive performance as used here refers to the actual implementation of activities from the selection stage in interscholastic, intercollegiate, or other forms of recreational competition that involves placing a great deal of importance on winning. Competitive experiences go beyond participating in informal forms of low key competition such as lead-up games or relays that are engaged in by the elementary school child. Considerable stress is placed on winning and the refinement of movements skills is stressed to a high degree. As the performance becomes more refined, greater stress is placed on accuracy and form in performing in a single best way.

To be involved in the movement experiences that stress competitive performance is to be involved in specialized skill development. The job of the preschool and elementary school teacher is to provide children with a series of experiences that contribute to fundamental movement pattern and general movement skill development that forms the basis for specialized skill development in *later* years.

THE CONCEPTUAL MODEL

Unfortunately, programs stressing specialized skill development abound throughout North America. Specialized skill development places primary emphasis on competitive performance-type learning experiences and little or no emphasis on the other aspects of the learning sequence outlined on the preceding pages. There is nothing inherently wrong with skill specialization, but we must ask ourselves if skill specialization in the preschool and elementary school is really in the best interests of most children? If it is considered to be in the child's best interest, it should serve only to supplement the regular program in the form of after school activities. Specialized skill development should *never* overshadow, replace, or serve as the primary purpose of the regular movement program. The regular program in the nursery and elementary school should stress the development and refinement of fundamental movement patterns and general movement skills. And as such, recognize that the sequence of learning experiences must incorporate exploration, discovery, combination, and selection-type learning experiences rather than dealing with specialized skill development through competitive performance experiences.

We must involve children in a series of coordinated movement experiences that go beyond the learning of isolated skills and the in-school playing of specific sports that they would probably learn on their own through some form of organized activity outside of the school, such as the YMCA, YWCA, Boys' or Girls' Clubs, or the Police Athletic League.

> "If physical education is to make a real contribution to the total education of each student it must do more than give him a few isolated skills, most of which can be used only in specific recreational settings."[2]

The conceptual model of physical education is based on the proposition that the development of children's movement abilities occurs in distinct but often overlapping *phases* (rudimentary movement abilities, fundamental movement patterns, general movement skills, specific movement skills, and specialized movement skills) in each of the *categories of human movement* (stability, locomotion, and manipulation) and that this is achieved through participation in the various *content areas* of physical education (self-testing, games and sports, rhythms, and aquatics) and the appropriate sequencing of *learning experiences* (exploration, discovery, combination, selection, competitive performance) that

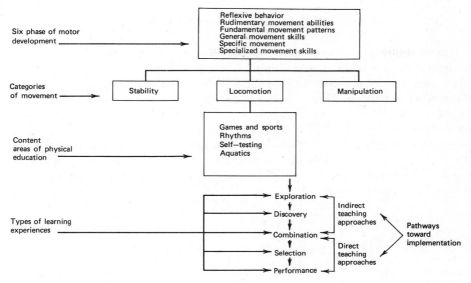

Six phase of motor development → Reflexive behavior / Rudimentary movement abilities / Fundamental movement patterns / General movement skills / Specific movement / Specialized movement skills

Categories of movement → Stability / Locomotion / Manipulation

Content areas of physical education → Games and sports / Rhythms / Self—testing / Aquatics

Types of learning experiences → Exploration / Discovery / Combination / Selection / Performance — Indirect teaching approaches / Direct teaching approaches — Pathways toward implementation

Figure 1-8. A conceptual model for physical education.

are implemented through various *teaching approaches* (indirect and direct). See Figure 1-8.

Stability	Locomotion	Manipulation
1. bending	1. walking	1. throwing
2. stretching	2. running	2. catching
3. twisting	3. jumping	3. kicking
4. turning	4. hopping	4. trapping
5. swinging	5. skipping	5. striking
6. standing	6. sliding	6. volleying
7. inverted supports	7. leaping	7. bouncing
8. rolling	8. climbing	8. rolling
9. landing		
10. stopping		
11. dodging		

Figure 1-9. Some underlying patterns of movement.

Preschool and Primary Grades

The conceptual model recognizes that preschool and primary grade children are involved in developing and refining fundamental movement patterns in the three categories of movement. These categories serve as the organizing centers of the curriculum at this level. This can be done because each pattern of movement found under these three categories can be dealt with in relative isolation of one another (see Figure 1-9). These movement patterns form the basis for all forms of movement. They are developed and refined at the exploration, discovery, and combination levels of learning through indirect and direct styles of teaching, that utilize games, rhythms, and self-testing activities to aid in their development (see Figure 1-10).

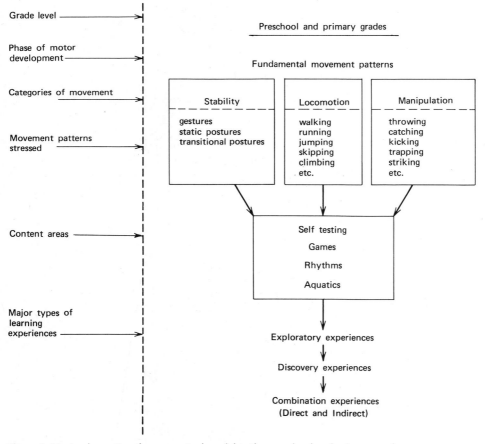

Figure 1-10. Implementing the conceptual model in the preschool and primary grades.

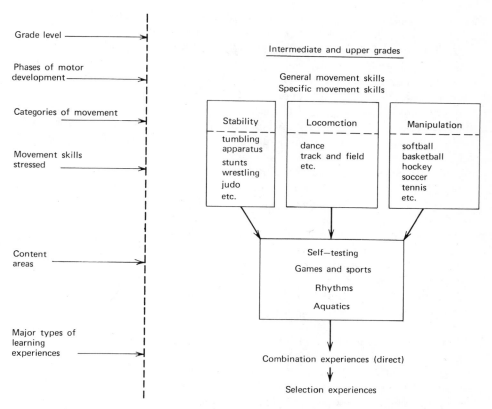

Figure 1-11. Implementing the conceptual model in the upper elementary grades and the middle school.

Intermediate and Upper Elementary Grades

When the conceptual model is applied to intermediate and upper elementary grade children, the teacher is aware that they now are involved in developing general and specific movement skills. At this phase of development, children are constantly combining numerous stability, locomotor and manipulative movements together into various lead-up activities that are approximations of official sports and other forms of competitive performance. Because of this, it becomes exceedingly difficult to separate activities at this level according to one predominant category of movement. The game of softball, for example, involves manipulation (throwing, catching, hitting), locomotion (running, sliding, jumping), and stability (gestures, dodging, stopping) and it would be impossible to categorize it as any one form of movement. The teacher must now make a value judgement as to each activity taught. This decision is based on the teacher's knowledge of the level of skill development of the class, and the particular skills being stressed. The organizing centers of the conceptual curriculum remain the same, but now incorporate movement experiences that generally use combinations of locomotion, manipulation, and/or stability rather than dealing with them in relative isolation of one another. This does not mean that developing and refining general and specific skills in particular concepts of stability, locomotion, and manipulation is any less important at this stage. It means that separating them effectively is impossible. The knowledgeable teacher will still place emphasis on each of the categories of movement and their underlying concepts within the lesson. The movement activities will be chosen to coincide with the levels of learning that are characteristic of children during this time (see Figure 1-11).

The clamor for relevancy and accountability in education brought about in the late 1960s and early 1970s has given rise to *A Conceptual Approach* to *Moving and Learning*. For too many years teachers of physical education, as well as the general population, have had only a vague notion of why balanced motor development and movement education of children is important. The conceptual approach to physical education attempts to provide greater insight to the why and how of movement. The utilization of games, rhythms, and self-testing activities are balanced between the traditional and newer movement education approaches and are viewed as a means to achieving clearly stated ends rather than serving as ends in themself. Developing movement and cognitive concepts through the enhancement of fundamental, general, and specific movement abilities in the areas of locomotion, manipulation, and stability will be considered in detail in the following chapters. The identification of movement and cognitive competencies to be developed through the physical education program is an important first step in an age of accountability.

SELECTED REFERENCES

1. Allenbaugh, N. "Learning About Movement." *NEA Journal*, March 1967.
2. Broer, Marion. *Efficiency in Human Movement*. Philadelphia: W.B. Saunders, 1973.
3. Gilliom, Bonnie. *Basic Movement Education For Children*. Reading, Massachusetts, Addison-Wesley, 1970.
4. Counsilman, James. *The Science of Swimming*. Englewood Cliffs, N.J.: Prentice-Hall, 1968.
5. Gesell, Arnold C. *The First Five Years of Life: A Guide to the Study of The Preschool Child*, New York: Harper and Row, 1940.
6. Godfrey, Barbara, and Kephart, N. C. *Movement Patterns and Motor Education*. New York: Appleton-Century-Crofts, 1969.
7. Kephart, Newell. *The Slow Learner in the Classroom*. 2nd ed. Columbus, Ohio: Charles E. Merrill, 1971.

8. McCandless, Boyd. *Children Behavior and Development*. 2nd ed. New York: Holt, Rinehart, and Winston, 1967.
9. Maier, Henry. *Three Theories of Child Development*. New York: Harper and Row, 1969.
10. Schurr, Evelyn. *Movement Experiences for Children*. New York: Appleton-Century-Crofts, 1967.
11. Siedentop, Daryl. *Physical Education Introductory Analysis*. Dubuque, Iowa: Wm. C. Brown Company Publishers, 1972.
12. Vannier, Maryhelen, Foster, M., and Gallahue, D. L. *Teaching Physical Education in Elementary Schools*. 5th ed. Philadelphia: W. B. Saunders, 1973.

Chapter 2
Reflexive Behavior of the Newborn

Key Concept: Involuntary reflexive behaviors are the first form of movement engaged in by the newborn. These reflexes are classified as primitive and postural in nature and have, at least, an indirect relationship to the performance of later voluntary movements.

Content:

Reflexive Behavior of the Newborn

INTRODUCTION

Reflex movements are evidenced in all fetusas, neonates, and infants to a greater or lesser degree, depending on their age and neurological make-up. Reflex movements are involuntary reactions of the body to various forms of external stimulation. They are subcortical in nature in that they are controlled by the lower brain centers that are also responsible for numerous involuntary life-sustaining processes such as breathing. Voluntary motor control in the normal child is a function of the mature cerebral cortex. Movements that are consciously controlled result from nerve impulses transmitted from the cerebral cortex along afferent (motor) neurons. In the developing fetus and newborn infant the cortex, and even more specifically the motor area of the cortex, is nonfunctional. Thus, movement is of a largely reflexive or involuntary nature.

REFLEXIVE BEHAVIOR AND VOLUNTARY MOVEMENT

As the primitive developmental reflexes are examined, two of their main functions are revealed to be nourishment seeking and protection. It is within these categories that primitive reflexes relate to the movement patterns of the lower primates. The palmar and planter grasping reflexes, for example, have been related to arboreal primates as have the various righting reflexes, which have been associated with the amphibious behavior of the lower life forms. The swimming reflex, which occurs during the second week after birth, provides what appears to be a fascinating link with the past. A coordinated swimming movement is elicited in the infant when he is held in or over the water. One may allow his creative mind to play with each of the primitive reflexes and fit its occurence into a lower order of life.

Several reflexes exist during early infancy that resemble later voluntary movements. These postural reflexes, as they are sometimes called, have been a topic of considerable debate over the past several years. It has been hypothesized and demonstrated by some that these reflex movements form the

30

basis for later voluntary movement. They argue that as the cortex gradually matures, it assumes control over the postural reflexes of walking, climbing, swimming, and the like. Anatomists, on the other hand, argue that there is a recognizable gap of up to several months between the inhibition of a postural reflex and the onset of voluntary movement. This time lag, they contend, clearly illustrates that there is no direct link between postural reflexes and later voluntary movement. Cratty sums up the controversy by stating that:

> "There seems to be no *direct* connection in time between these reflexive movements and the infant's later attempts to assume, voluntarily, an upright position to walk, to swim, and to climb."[2:18]

From this statement, and the research of the anatomists, it *appears* that there is no basis for assuming that the infant's first reflexive movements prepare him for later voluntary movement in any direct way. The possibility does exist, however, that the early reflexive behaviors of the infant are internalized and that this data is stored for future use when attempting similar voluntary movements. This would account for at least an *indirect* link between postural reflexes and later voluntary movement. Because of this it becomes important for those interested in the study of movement to have a clearer understanding of the very first forms of movement behavior.

As the cortex develops, it inhibits some of the functions of the subcortical layers and assumes ever-increasing neuromuscular control. The cortex joins in its ability to store information that is received by way of efferent (sensory) neurons. This phenomenon is evidenced in the phasing-out of reflex behaviors and the assumption of voluntary movements by the infant. Concurrent formation of myelin on nerve fibers prepares the body for the mature neuromuscular state. Movements become more localized as functional neural pathways serve isolated regions of the body with greater precision and accuracy.

The transition from subcortical to cortical neuromuscular control usually involves a period of inactivity. This might manifest itself as a weak or totally absent reflex response during the interim period of change to a higher level of functioning. In many cases, progressive development of the cortex will cause the substitution of one reflex for another. As an example, the body righting reflex appears as the neck righting reflex is inhibited.

DIAGNOSING CENTRAL NERVOUS SYSTEM DISORDERS

It is common procedure for the pediatrician to attempt to elicit primitive and postural reflexes in the neonate and young infant. If the reflex is absent, irregular, or uneven in strength, neurological dysfunction is suspected. The failure of normal reflexive movements to develop or prolonged continuation of various reflexes beyond their normal period may also cause the physician to suspect neurological impairment.

The use of developmental reflexes as a tool for diagnosing central nervous system damage has been widespread. Over the years, scientists have compiled an approximate timetable for the appearance and inhibition of neonatal and infant behaviors. Prechtl, for example, has noted that the resting posture of the newborn is the flexed position. The flexors, in fact, are dominant over the extensors in the early part of life. Shortly, however, cortical control permits the normal neonate to raise his head from the prone position.

"... an absence of the head-lifting response at the third day or later was highly correlated with other signs of neurological abnormalities. We may conclude therefore that normal babies are able to lift their chins when they are in the prone position." [2:83]

Several other meaningful examples of this principal exist. The doll-eye movements of the neonate permit it to maintain constancy of the retinal image. When the head is tilted back, the eyes look down toward the chin, and vice versa. This response is almost always seen in premature infants and during the first day of life in the neonate after which it is replaced by voluntary eye movements. Perseveration of this reflex could indicate delayed cortical maturation.

One means of diagnosing possible central nervous system disorders, therefore, is through perseverating reflexes. It must be noted that complete absence of a reflex is usually less significant than one that remains too long. Other evidence of possible damage may be reflected in a reflex that is too strong or too weak. A reflex that elicits a stronger response on one side of the body than on the other may also indicate damage. An asymmetrical tonic neck reflex, for example, which shows full arm extension on one side of the body and only weak extensor tone when the other side is stimulated may also provide evidence of damage.

PRIMITIVE REFLEXES

Primitive reflexes are closely associated with the obtainment of nourishment and the protection of the infant. They first appear during fetal life and persist well into the first year. The following is a partial list of the numerous primitive reflexes exhibited by the fetus and neonate.

Moro and Startle Reflexes

The Moro and startle reflexes may be elicited in the infant by placing it in a supine position and tapping on the abdomen, or by producing a feeling of inse-curity of support (for instance, allowing the head to drop backward). It may even be self-induced by a loud noise or the infant's own cough or sneeze. In the Moro, there is a sudden extension and bowing of the arms and spreading of the fingers. The legs and toes do the same thing, but less vigorously. The limbs then return to a normal flexed position against the body. The startle reflex is similar in all ways to the Moro reflex except that it involves flexion of the limbs without prior extension.

The Moro reflex is normally present at birth and during the first three months of life. The reaction is most pronounced during the infant's first few weeks. The intensity of the response gradually decreases until it is finally characterized by a simple jerking motion of the body in response to the stimulus (startle reflex). Persistence of the reflex beyond the ninth month may be an indication of neurological dysfunction. An asymmetrical Moro reflex may indicate Erb's palsy or an injury to a limb.

Search and Sucking Reflexes

The search and sucking reflexes enable the newborn to obtain nourishment from its mother. Stimulation of the cheek (search reflex) will result in the infant turning its head toward the source of stimulation. Stimulation of the area above or below the lips will cause a sucking motion (sucking reflex) in an attempt to in-ject nourishment.

Both of these reflexes are present in all normal newborns. The search relfex may persist beyond the first year of life, but the sucking reflex generally disap-pears as a *reflex* by the end of the third month but persists as a voluntary re-sponse.

Hand-Mouth Reflexes

There are two hand-mouth reflexes that are found in the newborn and relate to the neonate's ancestry. The palmar-mental reflex, elicited by scratching the base of the palm, causes contraction of the chin muscles which lift the chin up. This reflex has been observed in newborn infants and may last through the first year of life.

The palmar-mandibular reflex is elicited by applying pressure to the palms of both hands. The responses usually include mouth opening, closing of eyes, and flexing the head forward. This reflex begins decreasing during the first month af-ter birth and usually is not visible after the third month.

Grasping Reflex

During the first two months of life the infant usually has its hands closed tightly. Upon stimulation of the palm, the hand will close strongly around the object without use of the thumb. The grip tightens when force is exerted against the encircling fingers. The grip is often strong enough that the infant is able to support her own weight when suspended. Also, the grip with the left hand is generally stronger than the right.

The grasping reflex is normally present at birth and persists during the first four months of life. The intensity of the response tends to increase during the first month and slowly diminishes after that. Weak grasping or persistence of the reflex after the first year may be a sign of delay in motor development or hemiplegia if it occurs on only one side.

Babinski and Planter Reflexes

In the newborn the Babinski reflex is elicited by pressure on the sole of the foot. The pressure causes an *extension* of the toes. As the neuromuscular system matures, the Babinski reflex gives way to the planter reflex which is a *contraction* of the toes upon stimulation of the sole of the foot.

The Babinski reflex is normally present at birth but gives way to the planter reflex around the fourth month of life and may persist until about the eighteenth month. Persistence of the Babinski reflex beyond the sixth month may be an indication of a developmental lag.

Tonic Neck Reflex

From a supine position the infant's neck is turned so that the head is facing either to the right or to the left. The arms assume a position similar to the fencer's "on-guard." That is, the arm extends on the side of the body that is facing the head and the other arm assumes on acute flexed position. The lower limbs assume a position similar to the arms.

The tonic neck reflex may be observed in most premature infants but it is not an obligatory response in newborns (that is, it does not occur each time the infant's head is turned to one side). However, the three and four month old infant assumes this position about 50 percent of the time and then it gradually fades away. Persistence beyond the ninth or tenth month may be an indication of lack of control over lower brain centers by higher ones.

Approximate Timetable for Appearance and Inhibition of Selected Primitive Reflexive Behaviors

Reflex	Month 0	1	2	3	4	5	6	7	8	9	10	11	12	18	24
Moro and Startle	X	X	X	X	X	X	X								
Search	X	X	X	X	X	X	X	X	X	X	X	X	X		
Sucking	X	X	X	X											
Palmar-mental	X	X	X	X		X	X	X	X	X	X	X	X		
Palmar-mandibular	X	X	X	X											
Babinski	X	X	X	X											
Plantar grasp						X	X	X	X	X	X	X	X	X	
Tonic neck	X	X	X	X	X	X	X	X	X	X					

POSTURAL REFLEXES

Postural reflexes are those that resemble later voluntary movements. They are found in all normal infants during the early months of life and may, in a few cases, persist into the first year. The following is a list of postural reflexes of particular interest to the student of motor development. These reflexes may be indirectly related to later voluntary movement behavior and should be carefully studied by all concerned with the development of voluntary patterns of movement.

Labyrinthine Righting Reflex

The labyrinthine righting reflex may be elicited when the infant is held in an upright position and is tilted either forward, backward, or to the side. It will respond by attempting to maintain the upright position of the head by moving it in the direction opposite to which its trunk is moved.

The labyrinthine righting reflex makes its first appearance around the second month of life and becomes stronger during the middle of the first year. It is a major factor in the infant obtaining and maintaining an upright head and body posture, and contributes to the infant's forward movement during the end of the first year.

Pull-Up Reflex

The pull-up reflex of the arms is an involuntary attempt on the part of the infant to maintain an upright position. When the infant is in an upright sitting position and held by one or both hands, it will flex its arms in an attempt to remain upright when tipped backward. It will do the same thing when tipped forward. The reflexive pull-up reaction of the arms usually appears around the third or fourth month of life and often continues beyond the first year.

Parachute and Propping Reflexes

Parachute and propping reactions are protective movements of the limbs in the direction of the displacing force. These reflexive movements occur in response to a sudden displacing force or when balance can no longer be maintained. Protective reflexes are dependent on visual stimulation and do not occur in the dark.

The forward parachute reaction may be observed when the infant is held vertically in the air and then tilted toward the ground. The arms abduct and extend toward the ground in an apparent attempt to cushion the anticipated fall. The downward parachute reactions may be observed when the baby is held in an upright position and rapidly lowered toward the ground. The lower limbs extend, tense, and abduct. Propping reflexes may be elicited by pushing the infant off balance from a sitting position either forward or backward.

The forward and downward parachute reactions begin to occur around the fourth month. The sideways propping reaction is first elicited between the sixth and eighth month. The backward reaction is first seen between the tenth and twelfth month of life. Each of these reactions tend to persist beyond the first year and are necessary before the infant can learn how to walk.

Rolling Reflex

When the infant is placed in a supine position with the head turned to one side, the remainder of the body moves reflexively in the same direction. First the hips and legs turn into alignment followed by the trunk. The reverse occurs from a prone position when the legs and trunk are turned in one direction, the head will turn reflexively in the same direction.

The rolling reflex begins to appear around the fourth month of life and generally does not persist as a reflex beyond the first year. This reflex forms the basis for voluntary rolling that occurs between the fifth and twelfth months.

Primary Stepping Reflex

When the infant is held erect with its body weight placed forward on a flat surface, it will respond by "walking" forward. This walking movement involves the legs only. The primary stepping reflex is normally present during the first six weeks of life and disappears by the fifth month.

Climbing Reflex

The climbing reflex may be elicited when the infant is held erect and the top of its foot is stimulated. It will respond by flexing the lower leg and swinging it forward and upward. This reflex is usually present during the first six weeks and is inhibited by the fifth or sixth month.

Crawling Reflex

The crawling reflex can be seen when the infant is placed in a prone position and pressure is applied to the soles of the feet. It will reflexively "crawl" using both its upper and lower limbs.

The crawling reflex is generally present at birth and disappears around the fourth month. There is a definite time lag between reflexive and voluntary creeping, which appears between the seventh and ninth months.

Swimming Reflex

When placed in a prone position in or *over* water, the infant will exhibit definite swimming movements of the arms and legs. The movements are well organized and appear more advanced than any of the other locomotor reflexes.

McGraw has filmed reflexive "swimming" movements in the human infant as early as the eleventh day of life.[9] These movements generally disappear around the fifth month.

Approximate Timetable for Appearance and Inhibition of Selected Postural Reflexive Behaviors

Reflex	Month														
	0	1	2	3	4	5	6	7	8	9	10	11	12	18	24
Labyrinthine righting			X	X	X	X	X	X	X	X	X	X	X	X	X
Pull-Up			X	X	X	X	X	X	X	X	X	X	X	X	X
Parachute and Propping				X	X	X	X	X	X	X	X	X	X	X	X
Rolling					X	X	X	X	X	X	X	X			
Stepping	X	X	X	X	X	X									
Climbing	X	X	X	X	X	X									
Crawling	X	X	X	X	X										
Swimming	X	X	X	X	X	X									

In summary, primitive reflexes, which are under the control of subcortical brain layers, are observed in the fetus from about the eighth week of gestation. At approximately eighteen weeks, all the reflexes that will be seen in the neonate are exhibited by the fetus. Generally, reflexes serve the double function of helping the neonate to secure nourishment for itself and for protection. Many of the movements, however, are more closely related to functions in lower primates indicating some ontogenetic link of the human with other forms of life.

As neurological development proceeds in the normal fetus, and later in the normal neonate, reflexes appear and depart on a fairly standard, though informal, schedule. The presence of a primitive or postural reflex is evidence of subcortical control over the movement. Several days after birth, in the normal child, the cortex and myelinated neural pathways should be mature enough to inhibit subcortical control over *some* neuromuscular functions. This is indicated through voluntary control of a movement by the infant reflecting operations at the cortical level. The function of the subcortex is not completely debilitated. Throughout life, it maintains control over such activities as coughing, sneezing, and yawning, as well as the involuntary life processes. The cortex mediates more purposive behavior while subcortical behavior is limited and stereotyped.

Although it is impossible to determine if there is a direct relationship between reflexive behavior and later voluntary movement, it is safe to assume that there is at least an indirect link. This link is associated with the ability of the developing cortex to store information received from the sensory end organs regarding the actual performance of the involuntary movement. The neonate, for example, is able to visually observe its involuntary stepping or grasping behavior and receives tactual and kinesthetic information about it. This information is stored in the association area of the cortex and may aid the infant in the performance of later involuntary stepping or grasping.

Examination of reflex movements in the infant has provided physicians wth a primary means of diagnosing central nervous system damage. Neurological dysfunction may be suspected when any of the four conditions appear.

1. Perseveration of a reflex beyond the age at which it should have been inhibited by cortical control.
2. Complete absence of a reflex (this is oten a less accurate indicator than the others).
3. Unequal reflex responses bilaterally.
4. A response that is too strong or too weak.

SELECTED REFERENCES

1. Breckenridge, M. E., and Murphy, M. N. *Growth and Development of the Young Child*. Philadelphia: W. B. Saunders, 1969.

2. Cratty, Bryant. *Perceptual and Motor Development in Infants and Children*. New York: The MacMillan Company, 1970.

3. Crowell, D. H., "Infant Motor Development" in Brachbill, Y. (ed.) *Infancy and Early Childhood*. New York: The Free Press, 1967.

4. Egan, D. F., Illingworth, R. S., and MacKeith, R. C. *Developmental Screening 0-5 Years*. London: Spastic International Medical Publications, 1969.

5. Espenschade, Anna, and Eckert, H. *Motor Development*. Columbus, Ohio: Charles E. Merrill, 1967.

6. Fiorentino, E. *Reflex Testing Methods for Evaluating Central Nervous System Development*. Springfield, Illinois: Charles C. Thomas, 1963.

7. Illingworth, Robert S. *The Development of the Infant and Young Child*. London: E & S Livingston Ltd., 1967.

8. Landreth, C. *Early Childhood Behavior and Learning*. New York: Alred A. Knopf, 1967.

9. McGraw, Myrtle. *The Neuromuscular Maturation of the Human Infant*. New York: Hafner Publishing Company, 1934.

10. Milner, Ester. *Human Neural and Behavioral Development*. Springfield, Illinois: Charles C. Thomas, 1967.

Chapter 3
Developing Rudimentary Movement Abilities

Key Concept: The normal human infant is involved in the process of achieving voluntary control over its musculature in three areas: stability, locomotion, and manipulation of objects. The sequence of emergence of these rudimentary abilities is controlled mainly by maturation, but the time of their appearance and the extent of development is influenced by learning.

Developing Rudimentary Movement Abilities

INTRODUCTION

The child that comes to us in the preschool or the elementary school is a product of a specific genetic structure and of everything that has ever happened to him (her). He is not a "Tabula Rasa" ready to be molded and shaped to our whims or a precut pattern. Each child is an individual and no two individuals will respond in exactly the same manner. The child's hereditary background as well as his experiential background have a profound effect on the development of his movement abilities. It is important that we study the child beginning with the early movement experiences of infancy in order to gain a better understanding of the development that has taken place *before* he ever enters the nursery or elementary school. It is also important to study infants motor development in order to gain a better understanding of the developmental concept of how man learns to move.

Gaining control over one's musculature, learning to cope with the force of gravity, and controlled movement through space are the major sensory motor tasks facing the infant. During the nine months of fetal life the infant lives in a relatively secure state. He is protected from most outside influences and his needs are satisfied through the umbilical cord. He lives suspended in a fluid environment completely oblivious to the force of gravity. Upon birth he is thrust, rather abruptly, into a totally different environment in which he is at the mercy of those who care for him. His only tools for survival are reflexive movements, many of which will disappear as soon as higher brain centers become more refined.

From the moment of birth the infant is in a constant struggle to gain mastery over the environment in order that he may survive. During the earliest stages of development the infant's primary interaction with the environment is through the medium of movement. There are three primary dimensions of movement that the infant must begin to master for survival as well as for effective and efficient interaction with the world. First, he must establish and maintain the relationship of his body to the force of gravity in order to obtain an upright sitting posture and an erect standing posture (Stability). Second, he must develop basic locomotor abilities in order that he may move through his environment (Locomotion). Third, he must develop the rudimentary manipulative abilities of reach,

42

grasp, and release in order that meaningful contact with objects may be made (Manipulation).

The establishment of these rudimentary abilities in the infant forms the building blocks for more extensive development of the fundamental movement patterns in early and middle childhood and the general motor skills in later childhood. These so-called "rudimentary" movement abilities are highly involved tasks for the infant. The importance of their development must not be overlooked or minimized. The question that arises is; can factors in the environment inhibit or enhance the development of those movement abilities or are they genetically determined and as such not susceptible to modification? The answer to this question has been a topic for debate for many years by psychologists and educators alike, and is discussed in the following section.

MATURATION VERSUS LEARNING

Considerable research has been conducted in an effort to determine the origin of movement abilities in the infant and young child. A controversy has reigned for nearly a century between heritarians and environmentalists on this issue. Heritarians view the emergence and development of movement abilities as a process of maturation unaffected by factors within the environment. Environmentalists on the other hand have attempted to minimize the importance of heredity and stress the role of learning and experience. Historically the nature and the nurture hypotheses of development have each attempted to explain man's development in terms of their own narrow theoretical construct. More recently investigators have come to recognize the interrelatedness of maturation and experience and have tempered their unwavering adherence to one or the other with a quest for a better understanding of the interaction between the two.

Utilization of a dualistic approach to the study of human behavior enables us to view the developing organism more objectively. Within the infant there appears to be a general sequence in the emergence of movement abilities. Specific elements within each of the three dimensions of movement behavior (Stability, Locomotion, Manipulation), which were briefly outlined in the foregoing paragraphs, emerge as if a "biological clock" were ticking off both the time and the order of their appearance. Comparison of the early work of Gesell (1928), McGraw (1940), and Shirley (1931), clearly indicates that differences in the time that certain movement abilities appear to exist, but that there is a very strong tendency for them to surface in a predictable sequence. The fact that infants differ in the time of manifestation of behavior characteristics may be attributed to *inherent* individual differences in their rate of maturation, or differences in *environmental* stimulation between individuals. Both factors probably contribute to this discrepancy. The regular order or sequence in which movement behavior develops is an indication of the cephalocaudal (head and tail) and proximodistal (center to periphery) principles of development in operation. These are factors that do not appear to be greatly modified by situations in the environment unless extreme conditions are present.[4] The reciprocal interaction between maturation and learning plays a major role in determining the onset and extent of development of the movement repertoire of the infant and the young child.

Summary of Research

The investigation conducted by Dennis in 1960 offers an excellent illustration of the interrelatedness of the environment with maturation. This study examined infants reared in three separate institutions in Iran. The infants in two of the institutions were found to be severely retarded in their motor development.[4] In the third little motor retardation was present. The discrepancy between institutions led Dennis to investigate the life styles of the children in each institution. The results of his investigation led to the conclusion that lack of handling, blandness of surroundings, and general lack of movement opportunity or experience was the cause of motor retardation in the two institutions. A similar investigation by Dennis and Najarian revealed like findings in a smaller number of creche infants reared in Beirut, Lebanon.[8] Both of these investigations lend support to the hypothesis that behavioral development cannot be fully accounted for in terms of the maturation hypothesis.

Investigations by Gerber and Dean[10,11] recorded the advanced development in Uganda infants during the first days and months of life. The investigators concluded that the infants motor superiority over infants raised in the United States was due, *in part,* to the enriched environmental stimulation that they received. They were carried on their mother's back much of the time, were fed on demand, and were constantly the center of attention and affection. However, their advanced state at birth (that is, ability to hold head erect, early disappearance of certain reflexes, and so forth) suggests that a genetic maturation factor may also have been the cause of their developmental superiority. Again we see the interrelatedness of maturation and experience.

Due to cultural mores, the humanistic virtues of most investigators, and concerned parents, there are few controlled experiments in which the environmental circumstances of the infant or young child have been intentionally altered in an attempt to determine were serious malfunctioning or atypical behavior will result. Dennis[7,6] did, however, conduct an investigation in which twin infant girls were reared in a very sterile nursery environment (that is, they intentionally received a minimal amount of motor and social stimulation). After fourteen months in this environment their movement behavior was compared with normative data and was found to be retarded beyond the normal limits. Social development, however, was well within the limits of the standard norms, a factor that may suggest a greater need for motor stimulation than social stimulation in the infant.

The child rearing practices of the Hopi Indians was a subject of still another investigation by Dennis.[5] These Indians traditionally restricted their infants' movement by binding them to cradle boards that the mother carries on her back. The infants spend nearly all of their time bound in the cradle board for their first three months of life. As they grow older the number and length of freedom periods is gradually increased. Dennis observed that the movement abilities of these children were *not* retarded as might be expected from the results of the investigations mentioned above. It may be beneficial to consider that perhaps motor activity is not of crucial importance during the first months of life. Being bound securely to the cradle board and the rhythmical movements of the mother carrying the child simulate in many ways life in the womb. The close physical contact with the mother and an opportunity to begin utilizing one's perceptual modalities may have been crucial factors in those first months. One may also consider what the infant observed through his developing visual sense while bound to the cradle board. While on the board the infant was generally on his mother's back in such a position that he was able to view the many new and interesting sights that were going on about him. When not being carried about his was generally propped up by a nearby tree or in a corner and able to observe mother going about her daily chores. In other words the visual and motor stimulation of the Hopi Indian infants was was of considerable higher quality than the sterile environments of the Iranian and Lebanese infants and the two girls investigated by Dennis. This study may serve to point out the close identification of the visual modality with the motor dimension of behavior. It leads one to contemplate the interrelatedness of perceptual and motor functions and the importance of quality stimulation as well as quantity.

The cotwin control studies of human development came into vogue in the thirties as an attempt to assess the affects of maturation and experience on learning. Instead of restricting practice as in the previous investigations one twin was given additional practice in a variety of gross and fine motor activities. The second twin went about his normal daily routine without these benefits. This method of study was much more culturally acceptable than the technique of restricting practice. The now famous T and C twin studies of Gesell and Thompson (1929) and the Johnny and Jimmy studies of McGraw (1935) point out that maturation has a profound effect on learning, by illustrating that both the twin receiving additional training and the control twin developed basically the same movement skills in the same sequence. Espenschade and Eckert reinforced this belief when they stated that:

"There would appear to be little modification of the development of bipedal locomotion through practice, nor is there any evidence that practice will have much influence on the subsequent development of the phylogenetic activities of running, jumping, and throwing. With ontogenetic, or culturally influenced activities such as bicycle riding or roller skating, however, the availability of equipment and the opportunity for practice have a marked influence upon the acquisition of these skills."[9:84]

It should be pointed out, however, that after further investigation (Gesell, 1941, McGraw, 1939), even though the specially trained twin and the control twin were of nearly equal skill, the trained twin did appear to have better control over his musculature and more assurance in his movements. In other words, the enriched movement experiences of the trained twin did have an influence on the *quality* of his movements in that he moved in a more confident and coordinated manner.

Conclusions

It becomes impossible to make a case for either maturation or learning as being the *sole* influence on development. The literature is overwhelmingly in favor of the interaction of one with the other. This compromise view of development may be summed up by Carmichael who as early as 1925 recognized that:

"No real distinction between maturation and learning in the infants' development can be made because hereditary factors are only developed in response to environment, and acquired factors can only be secured through a modification of already existing structure. In all maturation there is learning and in all childhood learning there is hereditary maturation."[11]

Both maturation and learning play important roles in the acquisition of movement abilities. Although experience seems to have little influence on the sequence of their emergence it does appear to affect the time of appearance of certain movements and the extent of their development. The following three sections deal with rudimentary stability, locomotor, and manipulative movements in the sequence that they generally appear in the normal infant. The time range for the emergence of these movement abilities is quite broad and should not be thought of in terms of absolute dates.

STABILITY

The infant is involved in a constant struggle against the force of gravity in his attempts to obtain and maintain an upright posture. Establishing control over the musculature in opposition to gravity is a process that follows a predictable sequence in all infants. The events leading to an erect standing posture begin with gaining control over the head and neck and proceeds down to the trunk and the legs. Operation of the cephalocaudal principle of development is apparent in the infant's sequential progress from a lying position to a sitting posture and eventually to an erect standing posture.

Control of the Head and Neck

At birth the infant has no control over the head and neck muscles. If he is held erect his head will drop forward. Around the end of the first month he gains control over these muscles and is able to hold his head erect when supported at the base of the neck. By the end of the first month of life the infant should be able to lift his chin off the crib when lying in a prone position. By the fifth month he should be able to lift his head off the crib when lying in a supine position.

Control of the Trunk

After the infant has gained mastery of his head and neck muscles he begins to gain control of the muscles in the thoracic and lumbar regions of the trunk. The development of trunk control begins around the infant's second month of life. Control of the trunk muscles may be observed by holding the infant off the ground by the waist and noting his ability to make the postural adjustments necessary to maintain an erect position.

By the end of the second month the infant should be capable of lifting the chest off the floor when placed in a prone position. After the infant is able to lift the chest he begins to draw the knees up toward the chest and then kicks them out suddenly as if swimming. This usually occurs by the sixth month. These are the infant's first futile attempts at purposeful locomotion. Another indication of gaining control over the muscles of the trunk is the infant's ability to turn himself over from a supine to a prone position. This is generally accomplished around the sixth month and is easily done by flexing the hips and stretching the legs out at right angles to the trunk. Mastery of the roll from a prone to a supine position comes somewhat later.

Sitting

Sitting alone is an accomplishment that requires complete control over the entire trunk. The infant of four months is generally able to sit with support. This support comes in the lumbar region. The infant has control over the upper trunk but not the lower portion. During the next month or two the infant gradually gains control over the lower trunk. His first efforts at sitting alone are characterized by an exaggerated forward lean. This is an attempt to gain added support for the lumbar region. Gradually he develops the ability to sit erect with a limited amount of support. By the seventh month the infant is generally able to sit alone completely unsupported. At this juncture he has now gained control over the upper half of his body. It is interesting to note that at the same time the infant is learning to sit alone he is developing control over his arms and hands: a further example of the cephalocaudal and proximaldistal principles of development in operation.

Standing

Achievement of an erect standing posture represents a developmental milestone in the infant's quest for stability. It is an indication that he has gained control over his musculature to an extent that the force of gravity can no longer place such demanding restraints upon his movement. He is now on the verge of achieving upright locomotion (walking), a feat that is universally heralded by parents and pediatricians alike as the child's single most spectacular phase of motor development.

The infant's first voluntary attempts at standing occur around the eighth month. When held under the armpits and brought in contact with a supporting surface the infant will voluntarily extend at the hip, straighten and tense the muscles of the legs and maintain a standing position with considerable outside support. Around the ninth or tenth month the infant is able to stand beside furniture and support himself for a considerable period of time. He gradually begins to lean less heavily on the supporting object and can often be seen testing his balance completely unsupported for a brief instant. Between the eleventh and twelfth month the infant learns to pull himself to a stand by first getting to the knees and then pushing with the legs while his upward extended arms pull

Control of Head and Neck	Held with support . . . . 1st month Lift alone . . . . 5th month
Control of Trunk	Lift head and chest . . . . 2nd month Supine to prone position . . . . 6th month Prone to supine position . . . . . .8th month
Sitting	With support . . . . 4th month Sit alone . . . . 7th month
Standing	Support with hand holds . . . 10th month Pull to supported stand . . . . . 11th month Stand alone . . . . 12th to 15th month

Figure 3–1. Onset of rudimentary stability abilities.

down. Standing alone for extended periods of time generally accompanies walking alone and does not appear separately in most babies. The onset of an erect standing posture normally occurs somewhere between the twelfth and fifteenth months.

At this point the infant has gained considerable control over his musculature. He is able to accomplish the difficult task of rising from a lying position to a standing position completely on his own without any external assistance.

LOCOMOTION

Movement of the infant through space is dependent upon his emerging abilities to cope with the force of gravity. Locomotion does not develop independent of stability, it relies heavily upon it. The infant will not be able to propel himself until he has achieved the rudimentary developmental tasks of stability presented in the previous section. The following are the most frequent forms of locomotion engaged in by the infant while learning how to cope with the force of gravity.

Creeping

The creeping movements of the infant are his first attempts at purposive locomotion. Creeping evolves as the infant gains control of the muscles of his head, neck, and trunk. While in a prone position the infant may reach for an object out in front of him. In doing so he raises his head and chest off the floor. As he comes back down his outstreched arms pull back toward the feet. The result of this combined effort is a slight sliding movement forward. The legs are usually not used in these early attempts at creeping. Creeping generally appears in the infant around the seventh month. It may range in appearance, however, from the fourth to the twelfth months. Its onset and duration is highly variable and depends on the child's vigor, the nature of the supporting surface, and external motivation.[2]

Crawling

Crawling evolves from creeping and often develops into a highly efficient form of locomotion for the infant. Crawling differs from creeping in that the legs and arms are used in opposition to one another. The basic crawling posture is a "hands and knees" position. The infant's first attempts at crawling are characterized by very deliberate movements of one limb at a time. As the infant's proficiency increases his movements become synchronous and more rapid. Most efficient crawlers utilize a contralateral pattern (right arm and left leg), but about twenty percent utilize a homolateral pattern.[2]

Considerable speculation has been raised in the past decade concerning the importance of crawling in the infant's motor development and the "proper" method of crawling. The neurological organization rationale of Carl Delacato (1959, 1966) has placed considerable importance on proper creeping and crawling techniques as a necessary stage in achieving cortical hemispherical dominance. Dominance of one side of the cortex is necessary, according to Delacato, for proper neurological organization. Faulty organization, it is hypothesized, will lead to motor, perceptual, and language problems in the child and adult. It should be pointed out that this hypothesis has come under considerable attack by neurologists, pediatricians, and researchers in the area of child development. Careful evaluation of the pros and cons of Delacato's rationale is necessary before making any definite conclusions.

Upright Gait (Walking)

The achievement of upright locomotion is dependent upon the achievement of stability in the infant. The infant must first be able to control his body in a static position before he can turn attention to the dynamic postural shifts required of upright locomotion. The infant's first attempts at independent walking generally occur somewhere between the tenth and fifteenth month and are characterized by a wide base of support, the feet turned outward, and the knees slightly flexed. These first walking movements are not synchronous and fluid. They are irregular, hesitant, and are not accompanied by reciprocal arm movements. In fact,

Creeping	7th month (range 4th-12th month)
Crawling	9th month (range 6th-12th month)
Upright Gait	Walks with lead .... 9th-12th month Walks alone ....12th-15th month

Figure 3–2. Onset of rudimentary locomotor abilities.

they only vaguely resemble the mature walking pattern of early childhood. The advent of walking and other forms of upright locomotion appear to be primarily influenced by maturation. A child can not move through space until he is developmentally ready. Special training before he is ready is not likely to accelerate his learning. If, however, the child's nervous system and musculature are developed to the point of readiness we may expect to witness slight acceleration in the advent of upright locomotion when the infant receives the benefit of additional environmental supports (that is, encouragement and assistance of parents and furniture hand holds).

Shirley has identified four stages that the infant passes through in learning how to walk unaided.

"(a) an early period of stepping in which slight forward progress is made (3-6 months); (b) a period of standing with help (6-10 months); (c) a period of walking when led (9-12 months); (d) a period of walking alone (12-15 months)."[18]

As the infant passes through each of these stages and progresses toward a mature walking pattern several changes occur. First, the speed of walking accelerates and length of the step increases. Second, the width of the step *increases* until independent walking is well established and then decreases slightly. Third, the eversion of the foot gradually decreases until the feet are pointing straight ahead. Fourth, the upright walking gait gradually smooths out, the length of the step becomes regular, and the movements of the body become synchronous.

MANIPULATION

As with stability and locomotion the manipulative abilities of the infant evolve through a series of stages. In this section, the most basic aspects of manipulation: reach, grasp, and release will be considered. As with the foregoing sections on Stability and Locomotion, the manipulative abilities of the infant may be susceptible to early manifestation even though the process is influenced greatly by maturation. If the child is maturationally ready he will benefit from early opportunities to practice and perfect rudimentary manipulative abilities. Messen et al., have pointed out that:

"The child can be helped to master skills earlier than he ordinarily would through enrichment, but the timing of the enrichment is important. It is almost as bad to present enriching experiences before the child is ready to use them effectively as it is to deprive the child of these stimulations entirely."[16:178]

The following are the three, general stages that the infant engages in in the acquisition of rudimentary manipulative abilities.

Reaching

During the first four months of life the infant does not make definite reaching movements toward objects, although he may attend closely to them visually and make globular encircling motions in the general direction of the object. Around the fourth month the infant begins to make the fine eye and hand adjustments necessary for contact with the object. He often can be observed alternating his glance between the object of regard and his hand in an effort to reduce the gap between the two. The movements are slow and awkward involving primarily the shoulder and elbow. Later the wrist and the hand become more directly involved. By the end of the fifth month the child's aim is nearly perfect. He is now able to reach for and make tactual contact with objects in his environment—an accomplishment necessary before he is able to actually take hold of the object and grasp it in his hand.

Grasping

The newborn will grasp an object when it is placed in the palm of his hand. This action is entirely reflexive, however, until about the fourth month of life. Voluntary grasping must wait until the sensorimotor mechanism has developed to the extent that efficient reaching and meaningful contact can take place. Halverson has identified ten stages in the development of prehension. Briefly summarized and compacted they are: (1) The four month old infant makes no real voluntary effort at tactual contact with objects. (2) The infant of five months is capable of reaching for and making contact with the object. He is able to grasp the object with the entire hand but not firmly. (3) The child's movements gradually refine and by the seventh month he is able to use his palm smoothly. He is still unable to effectively use his thumb and fingers. (4) By the ninth month he begins to use the forefinger in grasping. By the tenth month reaching and grasping are coordinated into one continuous movement. (5) Efficient use of the thumb and forefinger comes into play around the twelfth month. (6) By the time the child is fourteen months old his prehension abilities are very much like an adults.[12]

The developmental progression of reaching and grasping is complex. Landreth (1958) states that there appears to be six component coordinates that are involved in the development of prehension. Espenschade and Ekert have neatly summed up these six developmental acts in the following statement:

"The first of these is the transition from visually locating an object to attempting to reach for the object. Other transitions involve: (2) simple eye-hand coordination, to progressive independence of visual effort with its ultimate expression in activities such as piano playing and typing; (3) initial

maximal involvement of body musculature to a minimum involvement and greater economy of effort; (4) proximal large muscle activity of the arms and shoulders to distal fine muscle activity of the fingers; (5) early crude raking movements in manipulating objects with the hands to the later pincer-like precision of control with the opposing thumb and forefinger; and (6) initial bilateral reaching and manipulation to ultimate use of the preferred hand."
9:94-95

Releasing

A familiar sight when observing an infant about six months old play with a rattle is the frantic shaking. This is a learning activity that is generally accompanied by a great deal of smiling, babbling and obvious glee. Sometimes, however, the same infant may be observed shaking the same rattle but with obvious frustration and apparent rage. The reason for this shift in moods may be attributed to the fact that at six months of age the infant has yet to master the art of releasing an object from his grasp. He has succeeded in reaching for and grasping the handle of the rattle but he is not maturationally able to command the flexor muscles of his fingers to relax their grip on the object on command. Learning to fill a bottle with stones, building a block tower (generally 3 blocks), hurling a ball, and turning the pages of a book are seemingly simple examples of the young child's attempt to cope with the problem of release. But when compared with his earlier attempts at reaching and grasping, it is indeed a remarkable advance. By the time the child is eighteen months old he has mastered the rudimentary elements of releasing objects from his grasp.

Reaching	Gobular ....1st-4th month Definite.............4th month Controlled ....6th month
Grasping	Reflexive............1st-4th month Palmer..............5th-8th month (range) Pincer..............9th-12th month (range)
Releasing	Accomplished by 18th month

Figure 3–3. Onset of rudimentary manipulative abilities.

As the infant's mastery of the rudimentary abilities of manipulation (reach, grasp, and release) are developing, his reasons for handling objects is revised. Instead of simply learning to manipulate objects being the infant's single purpose, he now becomes involved in the process of manipulating objects in order to learn more about the world in which he lives. The manipulation of objects begins to become directed by appropriate perceptions in order that he may achieve meaningful goals.

The development of locomotor, stability, and manipulative movement abilities in the infant is influenced by both maturation and learning. These two facets of development are interrelated and it is through this interaction that the infant develops and refines rudimentary movement abilities. These movement abilities are necessary stepping stones to the development of fundamental movement patterns, general movement skills, and specific movement skills.

SELECTED REFERENCES

1. Carmichael, L., "Heredity and Environment: Are they Antithetical?" *Journal of Abnormal and Social Psychology.* XX:3,257, October, 1925.
2. Cratty, Bryant. *Perceptual and Motor Development in Infants and Children.* New York: The MacMillan Company, 1970.
3. Delacato, Carl. *Neurological Organization and Reading.* Springfield, Illinois: Charles C. Thomas, 1966.
4. Dennis, Wayne, "Causes of Retardation Among Institutional Children: Iran," *Journal of Genetic Psychology,* 96:47-59, 1960.
5. Dennis, Wayne, "Does Culture Appreciably Affect Patterns of Infant Behavior," *Journal of Social Psychology.* 12:307-317, 1940.
6. Dennis, Wayne, "Infant Development Under Conditions of Restricted Practice and Minimum Social Stimulation: A Preliminary Report," *Journal of Genetic Psychology.* 53:149-158, 1938.
7. Dennis, Wayne, "The Effect of Restricted Practice Upon the Reaching, Sitting, and Standing of Two Infants," *Journal of Genetic Psychology,* 47:17-32, 1935.
8. Dennis, Wayne, and Najarion, P. "Infant Development Under Environmental Handicap," *Psychology Monographs.* 71:7, 1957.
9. Espenschade, Anna, and Eckert, H.M. *Motor Development.* Columbus, Ohio: Charles E. Merrill, 1967.
10. Gerber, M., and Dean, R.F.A. "The State of Development in Newborn African Children," *Lancet.* 1:1216-1219, 1957.
11. Gerber, M., and Dean, R.F.A. "Gesell Tests of African Children," *Pediatrics,* 20:1055-1065, 1957.
12. Halverson, H.M., "An Experimental Study of Prehension in Infants By Means of Systematic Cinema Records," *Genetic Psychology Monographs,* 10:107-286, 1931.
13. Landreth, Charles, *The Psychology of Early Childhood.* New York: Alfred A. Knopf Publishing Company, 1958.
14. McCandless, Boyd, *Children Behavior and Development.* New York: Holt, Rinehart, and Winston, 1967.
15. McGraw, Myrtle, *Growth: A Study of Johnny and Jimmy.* New York: Appleton-Century, 1935.
16. Messen, Paul, and Conger, J.J., and Kagan, J. *Child Development and Personality.* New York: Harper and Row, 1969.

17. National Association For the Education of Young Children. *What We Can Learn From Infants.* Washington, D.C., 1970.
18. Shirley, M.M. *The First Two Years.* Minneapolis: University of Minnesota Press, 1931.
19. United States Department of Health, Education, and Welfare. *Prenatal Care.* Washington, D.C., 1962.
20. United States Department of Health, Education, and Welfare. *Infant Care.* Washington, D.C., 1969.
21. White, B.L. and Held, R., "Plasticity of Sensory Motor Development," in *Readings in Child Development and Educational Psychology,* Boston: Allyn and Bacon, 1966.

Chapter 4
Developing Fundamental Movement Patterns and General Movement Skills

Key Concept: Preschool and primary school children are involved in the process of developing and refining fundamental movement patterns, while intermediate and upper elementary grade children are involved in developing general and specific movement skills in a wide variety of movement activities.

Content: Fundamental Movement Patterns
General Movement Skills
Mechanical Principles of Movement
Stability
    Center of Gravity
    Line of Gravity
    Base of Support
Giving Force to the Body and Objects
    Newton's First Law
    Newton's Second Law
    Newton's Third Law
Receiving Force of the Body and Objects

Developing Fundamental Movement Patterns and General Movement Skills

INTRODUCTION

As the child approaches his second birthday a marked change can be observed in how he relates to his environment. By the end of the second year of life he has mastered the rudimentary movement abilities that are developed during the period of infancy. These movement abilities form the basis on which the child develops or refines the fundamental movement patterns of early childhood and the general movement skills of middle childhood. The child is no longer immobilized by his basic inability to move about freely or by the confines of his crib or playpen. He is now able to explore the movement potentials of his body as it moves through space (locomotion). He no longer has to maintain a relentless struggle against the force of gravity but is gaining increased control over his musculature in opposition to gravity (stabilization). He no longer has to be content with crude and ineffective reaching, grasping, and releasing of objects characteristic of infancy, but is rapidly developing the ability to make controlled and precise contact with objects in his environment (manipulation).

FUNDAMENTAL MOVEMENT PATTERNS

We speak of the preschool and primary grade child as being involved in the process of developing and refining fundamental movement patterns in a wide variety of stability, locomotor, and manipulative movements. By this we mean that he is involved in a series of coordinated and developmentally sound experiences that are designed to enhance his knowledge of his body and its potential for movement. Movement pattern development is *not* specifically concerned with developing high degrees of skill in a limited number of movement situations, but rather, is concerned with developing acceptable levels of proficiency in wide variety of movement situations. A movement pattern involves the basic elements of that particular movement only. It does not include such things as the individual's style or personal peculiarities in performance. It does not place emphasis on the combination of a variety of fundamental movements into highly

58

complex skills such as the lay-up shot in basketball, or a floor exercise routine in gymnastics. Each movement pattern is first considered in relative isolation to all others with the young child and then gradually linked with others into a variety of combinations. The locomotor movements of running, jumping, and leaping or the manipulative movements of throwing, catching, kicking, and trapping are all examples of movement patterns that are first considered separately in exploratory and directed discovery experiences. They are then gradually combined in a variety of games, rhythms and self-testing activities. The basic elements of a fundamental movement pattern should be the same for all children.

The development of fundamental movement patterns is basic to the perceptual development of the young child as well as his motor development. A wide variety of movement experiences provide the child with a wealth of information on which to base his perceptions of himself and the world about him. The importance of movement is amplified by numerous educators and psychologists that incorporate physical activities into their programs of readiness and remedial training for schoolwork (see Chapter 12).

When we think of movement pattern development we must extend ourselves beyond the notion that being able to perform a particular stabilizing, locomotor, or manipulative movement necessarily means that the child has mastered that particular pattern. It may simply indicate that he has learned a series of isolated or splinter skills. If this is the case he will be unable to meet the demands of the situation as elements within the environment change. He will not be adaptable in his movements and will be able to move only in prescribed ways to a given set of stimuli. His performance may be compared somewhat to that of an adding machine designed to perform in a specific manner. The adding machine can do only what it has been programmed to do. There is little or no adaptability or flexibility in its performance beyond its stated functions of adding, subtracting, multiplying, and dividing. A computer, on the other hand, can perform an almost unlimited number of related tasks. There is a great deal of flexibility and adaptability in its function and it can be programmed to meet the demands of almost any situation. The same is true for the individual who has participated in a development ally sound physical education program that stresses the development and refinement of fundamental movements through varied activities prior to the development of skilled performance in specific sports activities.

The development and refinement of movement patterns enables the child to move in a variety of ways to a given set of stimuli. They help him gain a thorough knowledge of his movement potential and pave the way for further learning and elaboration of general movement skills.

GENERAL MOVEMENT SKILLS

General movement skill development is based on pattern development and should *follow* it. General movement skills are developed during the intermediate grades. They involve the same movements found in fundamental movement abilities. There are, however, differences in emphasis. Stress now begins to be placed on accuracy, form, and skilled performance. More complex combinations of locomotor, manipulative, and stability movements are dealt with. It is at this point that emphasis begins to be placed on the learning of sport skills. There are fewer exploratory and directed discovery learning experiences and more experiences that involve selection of "best" methods of moving along with the combination of these movements into more complex forms.

When the child is involved in the development and refinement of general movement skills he is involved in a process of applying fundamental movement abilities to the learning of skills that are used in a wide variety of individual, dual, and team sports (see Figure 4-1). These skills are incorporated in lead-up games. A lead-up game is an activity that approximates the official sport that the child will be involved in when he is developmentally ready. Lead-up games are modified to the developmental level of the child. The primary purpose of lead-up activities is to gradually progress from relatively simple activities to more complex ones following the developmental level, needs, and interests of the child. The activity may be highly modified and only vaguely resemble the official sport. It must, however, incorporate two or more skills that are involved in the official sport. The games of circle soccer and line soccer are simple lead-up activities to the official team sport of soccer. They only vaguely resemble the sport, but because they incorporate the skills of kicking and trapping they are classified as lead-up activities to the game of soccer.

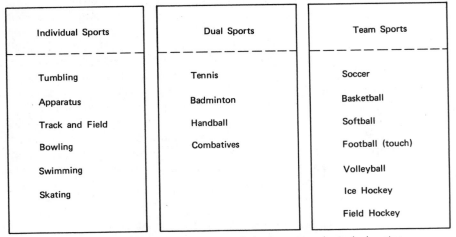

Individual Sports	Dual Sports	Team Sports
Tumbling	Tennis	Soccer
Apparatus	Badminton	Basketball
Track and Field	Handball	Softball
Bowling	Combatives	Football (touch)
Swimming		Volleyball
Skating		Ice Hockey
		Field Hockey

Figure 4-1. Sports in which lead-up games are taught in elementary physical education.

A lead-up game may be only slightly modified and closely approximate the official sport. Half-court basketball, for example, is only a slight modification of the official sport of basketball. This modification is designed to meet the endurance level of the typical upper elementary grade student or anyone else who desires to play. Lane soccer and six man soccer are also slightly modified versions of the official sport, soccer.

Intermediate grade children are involved in a series of developmentally sound movement activities that are designed to enhance their movement abilities in a wide variety of sport skills. Only after they have had an opportunity to develop these general movement skills can we justify placing emphasis on specific skill development in more complex and demanding lead-up activities.

It is not the job of the elementary school physical educator to teach specialized skills in a limited number of activities. This is not meant to imply that properly supervised activities such as intramural competition or activities outside the school, such as Little League Baseball or Biddy Basketball, should not have a place in the life of the child. The development of these specialized skills is justifiable as long as they serve as a supplement to the regular physical education program and do not replace it. This may be analogous to supplementing our regular diet with vitamin pills. If we have an adequate diet the vitamin pills may still do us some good, but if we replaced our regular diet with only vitamin pills, we would not survive long. Many of the necessary minerals and other nutrients found in our diets would be missing. We cannot replace the regular elementary school program with specialized skill development, we can only supplement it with various forms of enrichment.

MECHANICAL PRINCIPLES OF MOVEMENT

Before embarking on a detailed discussion of the three categories of human movement in Chapter 5, 6, and 7 it will prove beneficial to briefly review some mechanical principles of movement as they relate to stability, locomotion, and manipulation respectively. There are a tremendous number of ways in which the human body is capable of moving. At first glance it may appear to be an impossible task to learn all of the skills that are involved in the performance of the numerous game, sport, and dance activities engaged in by the child. Closer inspection of the total spectrum of human movement will reveal, however, that there are fundamental mechanical laws underlying all of man's movement. The mechanical principles of (1) stability (2) giving force to the body and objects and (3) receiving force from the body and objects will be considered in the following sections in order to serve as basic preparation for the chapters that follow.

Stability

All masses that are within the gravitational pull of the earth are subjected to the force of gravity. There are three primary factors of concern in the study of balance principles:

1. Center of Gravity.
2. Line of Gravity.
3. Base of Support.

Center of Gravity

A center of gravity exists within all objects. In geometric shapes it is located in the exact center of the object ⊙ ▫ ╱·╱ △ . In asymmetrical objects (our bodies) it is constantly changing during movement. The center of gravity of our bodies always shifts in the direction of the movement or the additional weight. The center of gravity of a young child standing in an erect position is approximately at the top of the hips between the front and the back of his trunk (see Figure 4-2)

If the center of gravity remains in a stable position as with standing on one foot or performing a headstand we refer to these as being *static balance* activities. If the center of gravity is constantly shifting as with jumping rope, walking, or doing a forward roll we refer to these activities as being *dynamic balance* movements.

Line of Gravity

The line of gravity is an imaginary line that extends vertically through the center of gravity to the center of the earth. The interrelationship of the center of

Figure 4-2. The center of gravity shifts as the body changes position.

Figure 4-3. The line of gravity extends vertically through the center of gravity and the base of support.

gravity and the line of gravity to the base of support determines the degree of stability or instability of the body (see Figure 4-3).

Base of Support

The base of support is the part of the body that comes into contact with the supporting surface. If the line of gravity falls within the base of support the object will balance. If it falls outside the base the object will fall.

1. The larger the base of support the greater the stability of the object as is seen in balancing on two feet as opposed to balancing on one foot.
2. The nearer the base of support to the center of gravity the greater the stability. This may be readily observed by attempting to push someone off balance from an erect standing position and then repeating the act from the referee's position in wrestling or lineman's stance in football.
3. The nearer the center of gravity to the center of the base of support the greater the stability (that is, "distribute your weight evenly").
4. A foot position that allows for a larger base of support in the direction of the movement gives additional stability. This may be readily obsrved by taking notice of how you stop rapidly from a run, or how you place your feet when catching a heavy object that is thrown toward you.

Giving Force to the Body and Objects

Force is one of the basic concepts in the subject of movement and body mechanics. Force is the instigator of all movement and is defined as the effort that one mass exerts on another. The end result may be (1) movement (2) cessation of movement or merely (3) resistance of one body against another. There

Learning About Balance Begins Early in Life

may be force without motion, as is seen in isometric activities, but motion is impossible without some form of force being applied. There are three forces relative to the human body that we are concerned with (1) force produced by muscles (2) force produced by gravitational pull of the earth and (3) momentum.

The entire science of force is based on Newton's three Laws of Motion:

1. The Law of Inertia.
2. The Law of Acceleration.
3. The Law of Action and Reaction.

Newton's First Law

The Law of Inertia states that a body at rest will remain at rest and a body in motion will remain in motion at the same speed in a straight line unless acted upon by an outside force. In other words, in order for a movement to occur a force must act upon a body sufficiently to overcome that object's inertia. If the applied force is less than the resistance offered by the object motion will not occur.

1. Large muscles can produce more force than small muscles as is seen with the amount of force generated by the legs as opposed to the arms.
2. Once an object is in motion it will take less force to maintain its speed and direction (that is momentum). This may be readily observed in such activities as snow skiing, the glide in swimming, or rolling a ball.
3. The heavier the object and the faster it is moving the more force that is required to overcome its moving inertia or to absorb its momentum, as is seen in catching a heavy object as opposed to catching a light object.

Newton's Second Law

The Law of Acceleration states that a change in velocity of an object is directly proportional to the force producing it and inversely proportional to its mass.

1. The heavier the object the more force needed to accelerate of decelerate it. This may be obsrved when throwing a heavy object (shot put) and a light object (softball) a given distance.
2. An increase in speed is proportional to the amount of force that is applied, the greater the amount of force that is imparted to an object the greater the speed that the object will travel.

Application of the Principles of Giving Force to Objects and Receiving Force from Objects is Necessary When Playing With A Ball

3. If the same amount of force is exerted upon two bodies of different mass, greater acceleration will be produced on the lighter or less massive object. The heavier object will, however, have greater momentum once inertia is overcome and will exert a greater force than the lighter object on something that it contacts.

Newton's Third Law

The Law of Action and Reaction states that for every action there is an equal and opposite reaction. This principle of counterforce is the basis for all locomotion and may be observed by the depressions left behind while walking in sand.

Receiving Force of the Body and Objects

In order to stop a moving object we must absorb the force of that object over the greatest distance possible and with the largest surface area possible. This applies to receiving the force of an external object of the body's own weight.

1. The greater the distance over which the force is absorbed the less will be the impact on the part of the body that receives the force. This may be demonstrated by attempting to catch a ball by keeping the arms straight out in front of the body and then repeating the tasks by bending the arms as the ball is being caught. The same thing may be observed in landing with the legs bent from a jump as opposed to landing with the legs straight.
2. Force should be abosrbed over a large a surface area as possible. In this way the impact is reduced in proportion to the size of the surface area and the likelihood of injury is reduced. For example, keeping the arms stiff and trying to absorb the shock of a fall with the hands only will probably result in injury because the small surface area of the hand must receive the entire impact. It is far better to let as much of the body as possible absorb the impact.

Separate discussion of the principles of balance, giving force, and receiving force should not be read to indicate that one is used in isolation of the other. The fact is that most of our movements combine all three of these. An element of balance is involved in almost all of our movements and we both give force to the body and receive force from the body whenever we perform any locomotor or manipulative movement. A gymnast, for example, must maintain his equilibrium when performing a tumbling trick such as a front flip. He also absorbs force from his body (on the landing). A handball player must move to a position of readiness (giving and receiving force to the body), contact the ball (giving force to an object) and maintain his balance throughout the act. Although each of the stability, locomotor, and manipulative movements discussed in the following chapters involve a specific sequence of movements, each of these movements incorporate the basic laws of motion discussed above. These mechanical principles are common to all movement situations.

SELECTED REFRENCES

1. Broer, Marion, *Efficiency of Human Movement*. Philadelphia, W.B. Saunders, 1973.
2. Bunn, John, *Scientific Principles of Coaching*. Englewood Cliffs, N.J., Prentice-Hall, 1955.
3. Cooper, John, and Glassow, R. *Kinesiology*. St. Louis, C.V. Mosby, 1973.
4. Sounder, Marjorie, and Hille, P. *Basic Movement*. New York, The Ronald Press, 1963.

Chapter 5
Developing Fundamental Concepts of Stabilization

Key Concept: Stability is the most fundamental aspect of learning to move. It involves maintenance of balance in relationship to the force of gravity as the body assumes a variety of postures and gestures.

Content: Introduction
Gestures
  Bending
  Stretching
  Twisting
  Turning
  Swinging
Postures
  Static Postures
    Standing
    Inverted Supports
  Transitional Postures
    Rolling
      Forward Roll
      Backward Roll
      Sideward Roll
    Dodging
    Landing
    Stopping
Stability Experiences for Preschool and Primary Grade Children
  Movement Education Experiences
  Games
  Rhythms
  Self-testing

Developing Fundamental Concepts of Stabilization

INTRODUCTION

Stabilization is the most fundamental aspect of learning to move. It is through this dimension that children gain and maintain a point of origin for the explorations that they make in space. Stability involves the ability to maintain one's relationship to the force of gravity. This is true even though the nature of the application of the force may be altered as requirements of the situation demand change, which cause the general relationship of the body parts to the center of gravity to be altered. Movement experiences designed to enhance children's stability abilities enable them to develop flexibility in postural adjustments. As a result they develop the ability to maintain their relationship to gravity even though they move in a variety of different and often unusual ways relative to their center of gravity, line of gravity, and base of support.

The ability to sense a shift in the relationship of the body parts that alter one's balance is required for efficient stability along with the ability to compensate rapidly and accurately for these changes with appropriate compensating movements. These compensatory movements should be adequate to ensure maintenance of balance but they should not be overcompensating. They should be made only with those parts of the body required for compensation rather than readjusting the entire body to restore balance. Children's stability abilities should be flexible in order that they may make all kinds of movements under all sorts of conditions and still maintain their fundamental relationship to the force of gravity.

Gestures and postures are the two major components of stability. *Gestures*, or axial movements as they are often called, are orientation movements of the trunk or limbs while in a static position. The movements of twisting, turning, bending, stretching, and swinging are among those considered to be gestures.

Postures are body positions that place a *premium* on the maintenance of equilibrium while in a position of static or dynamic balance. Standing, sitting, inverted supports, rolling, stopping, dodging, and landing are considered to be the fundamental postures of stability. Development of the following stability abilities is prerequisite to more advanced forms of movement.

70

Solving Movement Problems Involving Fundamental Stability Abilities Is A Valuable Learning Experience

GESTURES

(Axial Movements)

Gestures are movements of the trunk or limbs that serve to orientate the body while it remains in a static position. Gestures are often combined with other forms of movement to create more elaborate movement skills.

Bending

Verbal Description

Bending involves bringing one body part nearer to another through the curling action produced by the body's joints. Bending results in the angle of two bones at a joint being reduced (flexion). The elements of the bending pattern are few and simple:

1. Movement of one body part toward another should be direct and smooth.
2. All bending movements should involve only those parts of the body involved in the movement with no opposing or regressive movements.
3. The child should be able to start and stop the bending movement at any point in the action.

Visual Description

BENDING FORWARD   BENDING SIDEWARD   SQUAT AND BEND

Common Problems

1. Inability to perform the action without visually monitoring the process.
2. Marked lack of speed in the process.
3. Unusual limitation in the extent of the bend possible (this may be due to lack of flexibility rather than a deviation in the movement itself).
4. Wandering jerky movements rather than direct controlled movements.
5. Undue concentration on the movement.

Concepts Children Should Know

1. The terms flex, tuck, and curl are often used to refer to bending movements.
2. The ability to bend a body part depends on the flexibility of the joint.
3. Flexibility is specific to each joint.
4. Boys and girls are usually very flexible when they are young, but often become less so as they grow older from lack of activity.
5. The bending pattern is basic to performing most game, sport, rhythmic and self-testing type activities.

Movement Variations of Bending

Isolated Head and Trunk Movements

1. Bend the neck to the left, right, forward and backward.
   a. "Put your ear close to your sholder" (left and right).

  b. "Put your chin on your chest."
  c. "Look up with your nose pointed at the ceiling."
  2. With the head in a neutral position bend the trunk to the left, right, forward and backward.
  a. "Slide your hand down your side to your knee" (left then right).
  b. "Point your chest toward the floor or bring your chest close to your knees."
  c. "Push your stomach forward and point your chest at the roof."

Isolated Arm Movements

  1. Arms down with elbows at sides—bend lower half of arm forward and upward.
  a. "Point straight ahead."
  b. "Touch your shoulders" (right hand to right shoulder, then left to left).
  c. "Touch your shoulders with the backs of your hands."
  2. Arms outstretched forward—bend lower half of arm upward and backward.
  a. "Point at the ceiling."
  b. "Touch your shoulders."
  c. "Touch your shoulders with the backs of your hands."
  3. Arms outstretched sideward—bend lower half of arm upward and inward.
  a. Repeat cues given for Number 2 above.
  4. Arms outstretched upward—bend lower half of arm backward and downward.
  a. "Point behind you."
  b. "Touch your shoulders."
  5. Arms outstretched sideward—bend arms from the shoulder upward, forward, backward and downward.
  a. "Reach for the sky."
  b. "Reach forward."
  c. "Reach backward."
  d. "Pull your arms in close to your sides."
  6. Wrist and finger flexion can be utilized in any of the above positions.
  a. "Curl your fingers toward your elbows."

Isolated Leg Movements

  1. With support on one leg and the other leg extended forward—bend the lower half of the extended leg downward and backward.
  a. "Point your knee straight forward and let your foot hand down to the floor."
  b. "Point your knee straight forward and try to touch your heel to your seat."

2. With support on one leg and the other leg extended sideward—bend lower half of leg downward and inward.
   a. Repeat cues in Number 1 above.
3. With one leg extended to the rear—bend the lower half of the leg upward and backward.
   a. "Point your foot up to the ceiling."
   b. Touch you heel to your seat."
4. With weight on one leg and the other leg down—bend lower half of the leg backward and upward.
   a. "Point your foot backward."
   b. "Touch your heel to your seat."
5. Ankle and toe flexion can be utilized in any one of the above positions.
   a. "Move your toes up toward your knees."

Combinations of Bending Movements

1. Bend the neck, trunk, hip, knee, ankle, shoulder, elbow and wrist in progressively more complex combinations.
   a. "Bend your arms and legs so that each is bent differently."
   b. "Bend yourself into a small ball."
   c. Etc.
2. Change the body position and the base of support in order to create new bending combinations.
   a. "Bend your arms and legs in as many different ways as you can while resting on your back, your stomach, your hands and knees (back up or chest up), and your knees, etc."
   b. "Using 1, 2, 3, or 4 limbs for support explore as many different ways of bending as you can think of."
3. Combine bending movements with other stability, locomotor or manipulation movements.
   a. "Bend one body part while stretching two other body parts and twisting yet another."
   b. "Bend your trunk a different way each time you take a step."
   c. "Catch a ball and bend your elbows and another body part."

Stretching

Verbal Description

Stretching involves an unfolding motion at the joints. It results in the angle of two bones at a joint being increased to their maximum position and one body part being placed farther from another. To stretch is to move the joints in such a manner that there is a marked upward, outward, or downward movement of the body parts (extension). The elements of the stretching movement are just the opposite of the bending pattern.

Visual Description

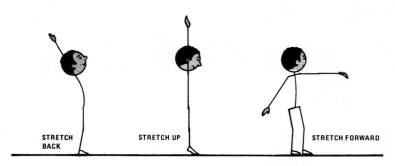

Common Problems

1. As with the bending pattern the amount of stretching possible is determined by the child's flexibility and should not be considered a deviation because of anatomical differences. (Ergo: boys are often less flexible than girls and can not reasonably be expected to stretch as far as girls).[3]
2. The remainder of the common problems are identical to the common problems of bending.

Concepts Children Should Know

1. Stretching is the opposite of bending.
2. Your ability to stretch at a particular joint is dependent on its flexibility just as with bending.
3. Girls are often able to stretch farther than boys.[3]
4. To stretch is to unfold the body or its parts in any direction.
5. The pattern of stretching is used in most sports activities to aid in attaining distance, desired direction, and increased force of the body or object. Stretching is basic to many daily tasks and is fundamental to creative or interpretative dance.

Movement Variations of Stretching

Isolated Head and Trunk Movements

1. Stretch the neck to the left, right, forward, backward and upward.

    a. "Without moving your shoulders and just your head, try to reach your head out past your shoulder" (left, then right).

    b. "Reach as far forward (or backward) as you can with your head."

    c. "Stretch your neck up to the roof."

Isolated Arm Movements

1. Stretch arms sideward, downward, backward and upward.
    a. "Try to stretch your arms to touch two walls."
    b. "Try to reach the floor with your hands without bending."
    c. "While facing me, how far from the wall can you get and still be touching the wall with both hands."
    d. "Keeping your feet flat on the ground, how high up can you reach on the rope?"
2. Stretching of the wrists and fingers may also be utilized.
    a. "How wide can you make your hands?"
    b. "How long can you make your hands?"

Isolated Leg Movements

1. With support on one leg, stretch the free leg forward, sideward and backward.
    a. "Point forward (sideward or backward) with your whole leg. Can you make your leg grow longer?"
2. Ankle and toe extension in the toe raise.
    a. "How tall can you be?"

Combinations of Stretching Movements

1. Stretch the neck, trunk, hip, knee, ankle, elbow and wrist in progressively more complex combinations.
    a. "Stretch another body part with each beat on the drum."
    b. "Stretch your body in as many different directions as you can."
    c. "How many different directions can you make your body by stretching at the same time?"
2. Change the body position and the base of support in order to create new bending combinations.
    a. "Stretch your arms and legs in as many different ways as you can while resting on your back, your stomach, your hands, and knees (back up or chest up), your knees, your seat, etc."
    b. "Using 1, 2, 3, or 4 limbs for support explore as many different ways of stretching as you can think of."
3. Combine stretching movements with other stability, locomotor or manipulative movements.

   a. "Stretch two body parts while bending and twisting two other body parts."
   b. "Jump and stretch."
   c. "Throw the ball and stretch."

Twisting

Verbal Description

Twisting involves the rotation of one body part in relation to another. The body parts are turned in opposite directions or partially rotated while the remainder of the body remains in a fixed position. Twisting is one of the first voluntary movements evidenced in the newborn in his futile effort to propel himself forward and to roll over. The toddler makes great use of twisting in attempting to stand and walk. Twisting is a movement pattern that is almost always seen in conjunction with locomotor and manipulative movements. The essential thing to remember in twisting is that it requires the rotation of one part of the body while the other parts remain immobile.

Visual Description

Common Problems

1. Inability to keep one part motionless while the other twists in relation to it.
2. Exaggerated or inhibited twist when the situation does not call for it.
3. Inability to alter speed.
4. Inability to twist in both directions.
5. Uneven jerky movements.

Concepts Children Should Know

1. When doing a twisting movement one body part must rotate in relation to another body part.

2. A twist is different than a turn. A turn requires the entire body to revolve while the twist requires one part to rotate while the others remain stationary.
3. Twisting movements are basic to most manipulative movements. They are found in most sports, gymnastic and dance activities and are fundamental to numerous daily tasks such as twisting a door knob, or opening a jar.

Movement Variations of Twisting

Isolated Head and Trunk Movements

1. Rotate the head with the head in the neutral position, bent to the left or right, bent forward or backward or in a complete circular motion.
   a. "While standing along side of your partner, move only your head to look at your partner—now look the other way" (repeat varying the rhythm).
   b. "Bend your head forward (backward, to the right or left) and look in both directions."
   c. "Move only your head and neck to draw a circle."
2. Rotate the trunk while in a normal standing position, bent to the left or right, bent forward or backward or in a complete circular motion.
   a. "With your pretend belt facing your partner, rotate your shoulders so that one shoulder is in front of your feet and the other is behind your feet—now put the other shoulder in front."
   b. "Twist your shoulders from side to side while your trunk is bent forward (backward, to the right or left)."
   c. "Move the top part of your body around your hips and waist—can you make your circles small and then larger?"

Isolated Arm Movements

1. Rotate the entire arm while it is held extended at your side, sideward, upward or backward.
   a. "With your arms at your sides (sideward, forward or backward) twist your hands so the palms face forward, backward, sideward or inward."
   b. Other arm position planes may also be utilized.
2. Rotate the lower half of the arm in any of the above positions as well as the bent arm positions described in the "Isolated Arm Movements" section of "Movement Variations of Bending."
   a. "Turn the door knob to open the door to your pretend house."
   b. Again many planes or arm positions may be utilized.

Isolated Leg Movements

1. Rotate the entire leg in any of the numerous movement planes available.

Use the "knee" or "toes" as teaching cues for orienting the child's movements.
2. Rotate the lower half of the leg while the leg is in any knee bent position. Use the "toes" in your teaching areas.

Combinations of Twisting Movements

1. Increase the complexity of the combinations of body parts being twisted.
2. Change the body position and base of support in order to create new twisting combinations.
3. Combine bending movements with other stability, locomotor or manipulation movements.

Note. Refer to "Combinations of Movements" in the bending and stretching movement variation sections.

Turning

Verbal Description

Turning is a movement in which the entire body revolves around its vertical or horizontal axis while in an extended or a flexed position. The flexed turning patterns that are explained in the section on rolling all utilize the fundamental turning pattern and are explained in detail there. The extended turning pattern from the vertical position is explained below.

1. The head serves as the controlling factor for the body. The body will *follow* in the direction of the movement of the head.
2. The eyes are used to maintaining a point of reference in order to avoid a feeling of vertigo.
3. The position of the arms will control the speed of the turn. Arms out— slow. Arms close to the body—fast.
4. The arms as well as the head must be moved in the direction of the turn for maximum efficiency.
5. A preliminary turn in the opposite direction will help develop momentum in the desired direction!

Common Problems

1. Failure to turn the head in the direction desired.
2. Loss of balance (usually due to failure to establish a visual reference point).
3. Awkward jerky movements of the arms.
4. Inability to remain in a small prescribed area.
5. Inability to turn in the opposite direction.

Visual Description

Concepts Children Should Know

1. Twist your head in the desired direction of the turn.
2. Use your arms to speed-up or slow-down your turn.
3. Focus your eyes on a target as you turn so that you do not get dizzy.
4. Turning is used in most games and sports and dances in which a change in direction is involved. It is also found in the sports of ice skating and diving.

Movement Variations of Turning

Whole Body Movements

1. "While standing do 1/4 (1/2, 3/4, full, etc.) turns—do them faster—turn the other way."
2. "Make yourself as tall as possible when you turn."
3. "Make yourself as low as possible when you turn."
4. "How wide can you be when you turn?"
5. "Turn as many different ways as you can on one foot."
6. "Turn as many different ways as you can in a seated position, while on your stomach, your back, your knees or on all fours."

Combinations of Turning Movements

1. Increase the complexity of the combinations of the body being turned. Change the body position and base of support in order to create new turning movements.
   a. "Move from a tall turn down to a short or sitting turn."
   b. "Move from a prone arch turn (on stomach) up to all fours and turn around."

    c. "Move around your hand (foot, elbow, knee) that is 'glued' to the floor."
2. Combine turning movements with other stability, locomotor or manipulative movements.
    a. "Stretch upward and place your foot to your knee as you turn."
    b. "Make two turns around with 1/2 turn jumps."
    c. "Jump, catch the ball and so a 1/4 turn."
    d. "Walk (run, hop, slide, skip, etc.) and do 1/4, 1/2, 3/4 or full turns."
    e. "Face your partner and grasp his hands above your head—bring one set of hands down and turn under raised hands—repeat this moving from face-to-face to back-to-back, etc."

Swinging

Verbal Description

Swinging is a pendulum motion in which one end of the body part remains fixed while the other parts move freely back and forth forming an arc. Swinging is yet another type of gesture that is commonly found in most locomotor and manipulative movements. The following is a brief description of a mature swinging pattern.

1. The movement must be relaxed and rhythmical.
2. The body part (generally the legs or arms) moves in a pendular motion swinging freely about a fixed joint in a smooth arc.
3. The limb remains straight throughout the major portion of the movement.
4. When one limb is swinging forward the other generally swings backward unconsciously (that is, walking, and striking).

Visual Description

Common Problems

1. Loss of balance.
2. Poor rhythmical control.
3. Lack of opposition when required.
4. Inability to swing the limbs efficiently in the less common directions (sideways, overhead).
5. Exaggerated stiffness of the body or the swinging limb.
6. Inability to swing the limbs freely in isolation of the other body parts.

Concepts Children Should Know

1. All motion stops at the front and the back of the swing.
2. When swinging the entire body (on the rings, rope, or ladder) be sure to dismount at the end of your backswing.
3. Adding more force to the downward portion of the swing will cause the body or body part to swing in a greater arc.
4. The swinging pattern is used in all manipulative activities and in the sport of gymnastics on the parallel bars, horizontal bar, rings, and side horse.

Movement Variations of Swinging

Isolated Movements

1. Swing the entire arm, lower arm, the entire leg, lower leg or the upper and lower halves of the body.
    a. "Swing your arms (one forward and one backward)—make your arms stiff—now make your arms like jelly."
    b. "Swing your arms in big circles."
    c. "Swing your arms across your chest and then back out."
    d. "With one arm up and other down, alternately swing arms from your side to a point over your head."
    e. "Swing one leg forward and backward."
    f. "Swing one leg across the body."

Combinations of Swinging Movements

1. Increase the complexity of the combinations of swinging movements.
    a. "Swing one arm and one leg."
    b. "Swing one arm and the opposite leg."
2. Change the body position and the base of support in order to create new swinging movements.
    a. "How many different positions can you be in and still swing your arm?"
    b. "Can you swing any part of your leg while lying on your back?"

3. Combine swinging movements with other stability, locomotor, manipulative movements.
   a. "How many ways can you swing your arms when you bend your trunk forward, sideward or backward?"
   b. "Show how many ways you can swing your arms as you run."
   c. "Hang from a bar and swing."
   d. "Throw a ball in the air and catch it using a little swing and then a lot."

POSTURES

Postures are positions of the body that place a premium on the maintenance of one's equilibrium while in a static or dynamic balance position. All movements of the body involve an *element* of stability for efficient performance, but the *primary* concern of these stability patterns is with maintaining balance in relation to the force of gravity. Each of the following posture patterns place a *premium* on balance.

Static Postures

Static postures are positions of the body in which the individual is required to maintain his stability while the center of gravity remains in a stable position.

Standing

Verbal Description

Achievement of an erect standing posture is one of the major developmental milestones of infancy (see Chapter 3). Standing is a balance posture that requires the body to maintain an erect position over the two feet. Each of the segments of the body are positioned one above the other so that the line of gravity falls within the base of support. The nearer the line of gravity to the center of the base of support the greater the degree of stability. When we speak of the standing pattern we must include standing on one foot as well as both feet with the base of support coming from a variety of surfaces (that is, flat, rounded, wide, narrow).

Good standing posture should be a relaxed position in which the segments of the body are aligned along the natural cervical, thoracic, and lumbar curves of the spine. The following elements are found in a good standing posture.

1. Relaxed, easy alignment of the segments of the body utilizing the natural body curves.
2. Even distribution of the weight over the entire foot.
3. The knees are flexed slightly.
4. The hips are kept level.
5. The chest is kept up and the stomach is held in.
6. The head maintains an erect position.

Visual Description

GOOD POSTURE   POOR POSTURE

Common Problems

1. Maintenance of a rigid straight posture.
2. Weight concentrated on the toes or the heels.
3. Knees locked.
4. Hip pushed to one side.
5. Protruding abdomen.
6. Tilt or forward thrust of the head.
7. Shoulders slumped or uneven.

Concepts Children Should Know

1. Stand tall.
2. Keep your chest up.
3. Keep your seat in.
4. (Avoid using erroneous terms such as "stand up straight" or "keep your shoulders back").

Movement Variations of Standing

Combination Movements

1. The other stability movements of bending, stretching, twisting, turning or swinging can be utilized to vary the child's standing experiences.

2. The isolated movement sections for each of the above movements are stated in terms of a normal standing posture.
3. The base of support for the standing position can be varied.
   a. "Feet close together."
   b. "Toes out."
   c. "Toes in."
   d. "Feet in stride position."
   e. "Feet in straddle position."
   f. "Vary the distance apart and the alignment angles of the feet."
4. The surface to be stood on can be changed.
   a. "Stand on a box, a board, a log, a rope, etc."
   b. "Stand on an incline facing uphill, downhill and sidehill."

Inverted Supports

Verbal Description

Inverted supports involve those postures in which the body assumes an upside-down position for a number of seconds before it is discontinued. Stabilization of the center of gravity and maintenance of the line of gravity within the base of support is the same as for the erect standing posture. An inverted supporting posture, however, utilizes either the head, hands, forearms, or upper arms (or a combination) as the base of support, the shoulders, are *above* the point of support and the feet and legs extend upward.[9]

The following elements are found in an efficient inverted posture.

1. Weight distributed evenly over the supporting surface.
2. Maintain a base of support that is about the length of the distance between the two shoulders.
3. Form a triangular base of support, whenever three points of the body come in contact with the supporting surface, with the head forming the apex of the triangle.
4. Keep the line of gravity as close to the *center* of the base of support as possible.

Common Problems

1. Inability to accurately sense the location and position of the body parts that are not visually monitered.
2. Inability to keep the line of gravity within the base of support.
3. Inadequate or exaggerated base of support.
4. Overbalancing by shifting the body's weight too far forward.

5. Inability to maintain balance as the center of gravity raises or the base of support decreases (that is, progression from tripod to tip-up, headstand and handstand).

Visual Description

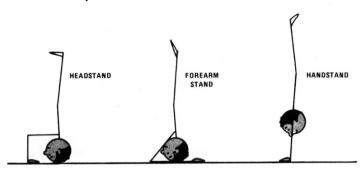

Concepts Children Should Know

1. Make a tripod (3-legged stool) with your hands and head.
2. Keep your body weight low.
3. Raise your legs only after you are balanced in a tucked position.
4. Keep your legs together and arch your back slightly.
5. Tuck your head and roll into a small ball if you overbalance.

Movement Variations of Inverted Supports

Combination Movements

1. The base of support for the inverted support can be varied.
   a. "Kneel and place your head between your hands on the mat" (seven points of contact—toes, knees, hands and head).
   b. "On all fours place your head between your hands on the mat."
   c. Modify the above positions by removing one or more of the contacts or points of support.
   d. "Balance on your head and hands."
   e. "Balance on your hands."
2. The other stability movements of bending, stretching, twisting, turning or swinging can be used with inverted support positions.
   a. "From a tucked or inverted squat stretch (bend, etc.) a leg backward, upward or sideward."
   b. "From a headstand place your legs in a straddle or stride position."

    c. "While in a headstand walk or swing your legs."
    d. "While in an inverted position can you raise or move an arm, an arm and a leg, etc.?"
3. Inverted supports might be combined with manipulative activities.
    a. "Throw a ball with your legs while standing on your head."
    b. "Balance an object on your feet while standing on your head."
    c. "Do a shoulder stand on the parallel bars or some other piece of apparatus."
4. Inverted supports might serve as transitional supports when used in combination with locomotor activities.
    a. "Skip into a cartwheel."
    b. "Jump into a headspring."
    c. "Gallop into a round-off."

Transitional Postures

Transitional postures are positions of the body in which the individual is required to maintain stability while the center of gravity is constantly shifting. These movements are considered to be locomotor movements by some authorities because of the change in the location of the body. They are, however, considered by the authors to be stability movements due to the high degree of importance placed on maintaining equilibrium during their performance.

Rolling

Verbal Descriptions

The roll requires the individual to move through space either forward, backward, or sideward while his body is momentarily inverted. The fundamental rolling patterns of the forward, backward, and sideward rolls incorporate each of the following movements in a coordinated manner.

Forward Roll

1. The hands are placed on the ground from a squat position so that they are shoulder width apart.
2. The body is tucked into a small ball with the chin tucked onto the chest.
3. There is a slight lift and push-off with the legs as the hips raise slightly.
4. As the body inverts, the weight is placed on the child's hands and the shoulders, and the back is kept rounded.

5. The "ball" position is maintained and the child's momentum carries him back to his feet and the original starting position.

Visual Description

Movement Variations of the Forward Roll

Combination Movements

1. The other stability movements of bending, stretching, and so forth can be utilized to vary the forward roll in experiences.
    a. "Bend your body into a small ball as you roll forward."
    b. "Stretch your legs as you do a forward roll to a sitting position."
2. The base of support from which the roll is initiated can be modified.
    a. "Make a triangle with your hands and head on the mat—move from your knees onto your toes and walk up to your hands" (a roll should result).
    b. "Do a forward roll from a straddle."
    c. "Do a forward roll from a squat position."
    d. "How many ways can you perform a forward roll?"
    e. "Balance on one leg and then do a forward roll."
    f. "Roll from a piked stand to a piked sit."
    g. "How many positions can you use to go into a forward roll?"
    h. "Can you change your arm, leg, head or body position as you come out of each forward roll?"
    i. "Do a forward roll into a headstand."
3. Combine rolling movements with locomotor and manipulative movements.
    a. "How high can you jump as you come out of your forward roll?"
    b. "Do a forward roll to a heel click."
    c. "Jump into a forward roll" (dive roll).
    d. "Move as you want to, but when you hear the drum do a roll."
    e. "Can you catch a passed ball after doing a forward roll?"
    f. "Toss a ball in the air, do a forward roll and catch the ball on the first bounce."

Backward Roll

1. The body assumes a squat position. The body rocks slightly forward and is pushed backward by the action of the toes.
2. The body is kept in a small "ball" with the back rounded and chin tucked into the chest.
3. The child sits back on his buttocks and continues in a fluid motion to roll across his back.
4. The hands are placed beside the head with the fingertips facing toward the starting position, and the elbows toward the ceiling.
5. The rolling momentum up the back and the push from the hands guides the child over to a squat position.

Visual Description

Movement Variations of the Backward Roll

Combination Movements

1. Combine backward rolls with other stability movements.
   a. "Do a back roll in a tight tuck."
   b. "Keep your legs straight and do a back roll."
2. The base of support from which the roll is initiated can be modified.
   a. "Lie on your back and grasp your knees—can you rock your boat?"
   b. "Do your back roller and roll back onto your hands (thumbs close to your ears)—now roll hard and bring your knees into your chest." (If the hands and momentum are used a back roll should result).
   c. "Squat on one leg and do a back roll."
   d. "From a straddle position do a back roll into the straddle, squat, knee scale or other position."
   e. "How many ways can you perform a backward roll?"
3. Combine back rolls with locomotor and manipulative movements.
   a. See suggestions listed in the forward roll section (p. 88).
   b. "Do a back roll, jump 1/2 turn and another back roll."
   c. "Do a back straddle roll over a ball and then roll it to your partner."

Sideward Roll

1. The body is stretched out so that it can turn over on itself.
2. The arms are either extended over the head or kept down at the sides.
3. The initial push-off is supplied by either an arm or a leg.
4. The action consists of alternate movements of the hips.

Visual Description

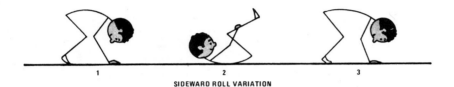

1   2   3

SIDEWARD ROLL VARIATION

Movement Variations of the Sideward Roll

Combination Movements

1. Combine sideward rolls with other stability movements.
   a. "Stretch one arm up above your head and curl the other in close to your chest as you do a side roll."
   b. See suggestions listed in the turning section (p. 80).
   c. "What happens when you arch your back or bend your legs forward? Can you change the direction of your roll?"
2. The base of support from which the roll is initiated can be modified.
   a. "Do a side roll from a hands and knees position."
   b. "Can you do a side roll from a knee scale?"
   c. "Can you do a side roll from a seated position?"
   d. "How many ways can you roll sideways?"
3. Combine side rolls with locomotor and manipulative movements.
   a. "Do an all-fours sideward jump into a sideward roll."
   b. "Can you run, jump, etc. after doing a side roll?"
   c. "Holding a lummi or rhythm stick with both hands do a side roll."
   d. "Hold beanbags in your hands and between your knees and do a side roll."
   e. "Push a ball while doing a side roll."

Common Problems (in all rolls)

1. Failure to move in a straight line.
2. Failure to keep tucked in a small "ball."
3. Failure to keep the limbs close to the body.
4. Failure to use the hands to absorb the body weight and aid in pushing the body over.
5. Placing head on the floor (forward roll).
6. Uneven push-off with hands or legs causing a "lopsided" roll.
7. Inability to utilize the forces of the body in a coordinated manner.

Concepts Children Should Know (in all rolls)

1. Stay tucked-up in a small ball throughout the roll (forward and backward rolls).
2. Use your hands to push-off so that your head does not touch the floor.
3. Keep your chin against your chest.
4. Focus your eyes on an object in front or behind you to help you roll in a straight line.

Inverted Postures Such As The Tripod And Headstand Are Fundamental Stability Abilities

Dodging

Verbal Description

Dodging is a transitional posture in which the body is moved quickly in a direction other than the original line of movement. The fundamental procedures involved in dodging follow.

1. The body stops moving in the original line of direction by using the fundamental stopping pattern (See page 95).
2. The knees are bent and the body weight is shifted in the direction of the dodge (generally to the side).
3. The body moves in the new direction by pushing off on the weight bearing foot of the body.

Concepts Children Should Know

1. Stop your movement suddenly.
2. Shift your body weight to one side quickly.
3. Use your head, shoulders, eyes, or trunk to fake the new direction of your movement.
4. The dodging pattern is used in the tagging games that you play. It is used in any sport in which evading an opponent is important such as football, soccer, hockey or basketball.

Common Problems

1. Failure to stop properly.
2. Inability to shift the body weight in a fluid manner in the direction of the dodge.
3. Slow change of direction.

Movement Variations of Dodging

Combination Movements

1. Combine dodging with other stability movements.
   a. "Dodge by stretching—How many stretching positions can you use to dodge an imaginary ball?"
   b. "Dodge by bending one, two, etc. body parts."
   c. "Combine stretching and bending movements with twisting moves."
2. Change the base of support from which the dodge is initiated.
   a. "Dodge with your feet close together."

    b. "Dodge with your feet in a wide straddle stance."
    c. "Dodge with your feet in a stride position."
    d. "Dodge while standing on one foot."
    e. "Dodge while balanced on one, two, three, etc. parts of your body."
    f. "Dodge as high or as low as possible."
3. Combine dodging with locomotor and manipulative movements.
    a. "Run, walk, jump, hop, etc. and dodge the puff ball."
    b. "Bounce a ball and dodge."
    c. "Jump rope and dodge."

Landing

Verbal Description

Landing is a transitional posture that requires the individual to regain his balance after a brief flight in the air. Landing is a portion of all locomotor movements that require the child to lose contact with the ground with both feet. However, it is most crucial in the various jumping patterns of jumping for distance, jumping for height and jumping from a height (See pages 108-114). The following elements are found in efficient landing:

1. The force of the landing is taken on the balls of the feet. The feet are shoulder width apart and in a stride or straddle position.
2. The ankles, knees, and hip joint bend upon impact. The greater the impact the more flexion that is required.
3. The head and upper body are held erect.
4. The arms extend to the side or forward to aid in maintaining balance.
5. As soon as the force is absorbed the legs straighten in a quick rebounding motion.

Visual Description

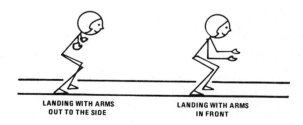

LANDING WITH ARMS
OUT TO THE SIDE

LANDING WITH ARMS
IN FRONT

Common Problems

1. Landing flatfooted.
2. Landing with the knees rigid.
3. Exaggerated or inhibited knee flexion.
4. Landing with feet too close together or too far apart.
5. Failure to keep the head up.
6. Bending forward at the waist.

Concepts Children Should Know

1. Land with your feet apart.
2. Land on the balls of your feet.
3. "Give" with the force of your landing.
4. The greater your impact with the ground the more you must bend in order to absorb it.
5. Rebound quickly.
6. The landing pattern is used in all jumps and is found in basketball in landing from a lay-up shot, jump ball or catching a high pass. It is also found in the jump pass and catch in football and the spike and block in volleyball. Landing is required in any activity in which the body is propelled into the air.

Movement Variations of Landing

Combination Movements

1. Combine the landing with other stability movements.
   a. "Bend your body slowly into a tight tucked position as you land."
   b. "Stretch your arms and head up as you land."
   c. "Jump down as softly as you can."
   d. Explore the other stability movements of twisting, turning, swinging, etc.
   e. "Can you land and fall into a roll?"
2. Change the base of support for the landing.
   a. "Land with your feet close together."
   b. "Land with your feet wide apart."
   c. "Land with one foot in front of the other."
   d. "Land on one foot."
   e. "Land on feet and hands."
   f. "Can you use three limbs when you land?"
   g. "Can you land inside the hoop?"

3. Combine landing with locomotor and manipulative movements.
    a. "Jump forwards, backwards and to the sides."
    b. "Do jump turns."
    c. "Leap and balance on your landing foot."
    d. "Run and jump over a cone."
    e. "Hop with a partner."
    f. "Bounce a ball as you jump up and down."
    g. "How many different ways can you land while using your beanbag?"
    h. "Jump rope at different speeds."

Stopping

Verbal Description

Stopping is a transitional posture that is used in all locomotor activities. The stride stop is most commonly used when coming to an abrupt halt. The fundamentals of the stride stop involve:

1. Come to a halt with the feet in a stride position and the knees bent.
2. The body weight is leaned backward and balance is regained.

Concepts Children Should Know

1. Stop with one foot forward.
2. Bend your knees.
3. Lean back.
4. Keep your head up.
5. Stopping is basic to performing all locomotor activities in games, sports and dance.

Common Problems

1. Stopping with the legs straight.
2. Failure to lean back thus causing the body weight to continue forward and extra steps to be taken.
3. Failure to keep the upper body erect and the head up.

Movement Variations of Stopping

Combination Movements

1. Combine stopping with other stability movements.
    a. "Freeze with arms, legs and body parts in different positions."

b. Since most stopping movements either involve a jump or hop, or a drag or hesitation, landing activities are especially applicable.

c. Explore the stability movements of dodging, pivoting, etc.

2. Change the base of support for stopping.
   a. "Stop with your feet close together."
   b. "Stop with your feet wide apart."
   c. "Stop with one foot in front of the other."
   d. "Stop on your toes or heels."
   e. "Use your hands to help you stop at the padded stage."

3. Combine landing with locomotor and manipulative movements.
   a. "Walk, run, jump, hop, etc. and stop."
   b. "Stop, and throw, roll, catch, push or pull an object."
   c. See suggestions listed in the landing section (p. 93-94).

STABILITY EXPERIENCES FOR PRESCHOOL AND PRIMARY GRADE CHILDREN

Movement Education Experiences

The refining of fundamental movement patterns is constantly being stressed in the preschool and primary grades (see Figure 1-10). Ideally, the teacher is interested in providing exploratory, discovery, and combination experiences for these children. The teaching approach used here would most likely be some form of movement education. Movement education includes exploratory, discovery, and indirect combination learning activities that are organized for teaching purposes around specified themes or concepts. Most frequently these themes center around (1) the fundamental movement patterns in the three categories of movement, (2) the qualities of movement and (3) the principles of body mechanics. Some examples of movement themes that might be encompassed are:

1. Safety[7]*
2. Adding to the Range and Understanding of Movement[7]
3. Understanding Direction[7]
4. Qualities[7]
5. Stretching and Curling[7]
6. Change of Direction[7]
7. Twisting[7]

*The numbers used in this and subsequent chapters refer to textbooks listed in the Selected References in which this information may be obtained.

8. Moving at Different Levels[5]
9. Moving in the Air[5]
10. Moving Different Body Parts[5]
11. Creating Force[5]
12. Absorbing Force[5]
13. Moving at Different Speeds[5]
14. Run, Jump, etc.[8]
15. Moving in Response to Different Rhythms[5]

There are many more themes that are possible through either isolation or combination of movements. If we isolate the theme of bending, the following might be representative of the exploratory, discovery and combination experiences utilized.

Theme—Bending

Exploratory Experiences

The teacher suggests or challenges but refrains from setting a "correct" model for performance.

1. Have a straight and curved line drawings taped to walls or cones—the figures will have one or a combination of angles and/or curves that the children will mimic.
2. A similar idea might use pictures of objects such as trees, triangles, rocket ships, and so forth.
3. Utilize mats and small apparatus that the children can shape their bodies around and which can serve as obstacles to the direct reaching of an object.
   a. A cardboard box with holes in the sides might be used to cause children to reach through and bend the arm(s) in various positions in pursuit of objects within the covered box.
   b. The placement of a hoop or tire on the floor with a beanbag inside might lead a child to utilize his or her feet in retrieving the object.
   c. Obstacle course set-ups can also be incorporated here.

Discovery Experiences

The teacher places qualifications or limitations on movements as the children explore, discover, and share their experiences.

1. The teacher manipulates a rope or hinged stick and asks the children to mimic the figures with their bodies. The teacher with the children points out the different solutions. (Some children will use the entire body and some will use only their limbs or parts of their bodies).
2. The teacher qualifies the body position to be used. Bending movements can be performed with the children on their stomach, backs, sides, and all fours.

---

3. The teacher qualifies the elements of movement to be utilized such as force, time, level and flow. Bending movements can be performed slowly, rapidly, tightly, loosely, forward, sideward, and so forth.

Indirect Combination Experiences

The teacher continues to qualify or limit movements so that previous movements become progressively more difficult to perform.

1. The teacher asks the children to combine several movements to create their own combinations.
   a. "Can you bend two, three or four body parts at once?"
   b. "How many different directions can you bend your body parts?"
2. The teacher may also utilize rhythm patterns or music to guide bending movements.
   a. "Bend a different way each time you hear the drum."
   b. "Bend your knees and walk in place to the music."
   c. "Bend your arms on the heavy beat and straighten your arms on the light beat" (increase or decrease the tempo).

Direct Combination Experiences

The teacher suggests, demonstrates or drills the child in the desired skill form to be used.

1. The teacher combines several fundamental movements into a series of movements or a routine.
2. The teacher demonstrates a routine with regard to movement pattern form.

The exploratory, discovery, and combination experiences often incorporated in a movement education approach do *not* necessarily mean that the child's learning will not be directly guided by the teacher. Depending on the personalities of the teacher and the child and the established level of communication between the two, it may be quite appropriate for the teacher to utilize direct rather than indirect teaching. Conversely indirect teaching is quite appropriate in a typically direct teaching situation. The two approaches must be used to *complement* one another in attempting to communicate effectively with the learner to enhance understanding of the movement or to stimulate thinking concerning one's own interpretation of movement.

The more traditional content areas of games, rhythms, and self-testing are primarily direct combination experiences. Some activities that are representative of these three traditional content areas will be listed with references in a later portion of this chapter.

Games

In a previous chapter the content area of games was subdivided into:

1. Low organization games and relays
2. Lead-up games to sports
3. Official sports

The major game emphasis in the preschool and primary years is the use of low organized games. These games by definition utilize simple class formations and relatively simple skills. To make sure that the use of the term "simple" is understood here, the teacher must be aware of the children's developmental levels in selecting and modifying these activities so the task being performed is a learning experience that challenges the child as well as allows him to succeed. The complexity of the games and the skills used by the teacher are frequently limited by the children's listening and communication skills as well as their physical capabilities. Specific low organizational games that isolate the fundamental movements of stability are far from prevalent. The game element in most stability oriented activities is induced by the teachers creating a game situation through limitations or rules in relation to specific challenges. For instance, a preschool teacher might create a game that we will call "I Can." She might give the children a bending challenge and ask the children to "touch your elbow to your knee while touching your ear with your free hand." Other games that might be used to isolate stability movements at the preschool or primary levels might include Freeze[1] and Simon Says[5] or other line or circle mimicing games. The game of Freeze might have the students moving into various new positions and then holding them when the teacher calls out "Freeze" and turns to see that nobody is moving and how unique some of the positions are. The game Simon Says could be used to isolate any of the stability movements presented. "Simon Says walk around one foot" (Pivot) or "Simon Says swing your arms."

There are numerous games that combine stability movements with locomotor and/or manipulative movements. These games, which will be presented in the locomotor and manipulative sections of this text book, will also be contributing to the development of gestures and postures which comprise the concept of stability.

Relays

The use of relay activities in the preschool and primary years is limited to situations where the children are capable of understanding that each person on their team affects the overall effort of their team. A relay is usually not suitable for preschoolers and is often not suitable for primary age children. Some children do not seem developmentally ready to understand and accept the team effort necessary in relay competition. Relays should normally encompass skills or movements that are within the repertoire of the children. Relays with unfamiliar movements result in too little success and possibly result in a negative learning experience.

Rhythms

The traditional phase of rhythms in the elementary physical education program also lacks numerous specific activities that stress fundamental stability movements in isolation. However, the teacher has the opportunity to create or utilize stability movements in teaching rhythmic fundamentals[6] and creative rhythms[6] (the first two steps in the activities progression under Rhythms). Movements such as swinging, stretching, bending, twisting, turning, and dodging can be performed to the beat of a rhythm drum. Once the children become aware or sense the rhythm in their bodies through the use of drum tempos, musical records can then be utilized. *Childhood Rhythms, Educational Dance Recordings, Elementary Rhythms, Music for Physical Fitness L.P., Linden Rhythmic Activities, Rhythm Band,* and *Rhythm Time* are just a few of the record series that have music to accompany stability movements.[10] Did You Ever See a Lassie[3] is an American folk dance that might be modified by the teacher to stress stability movements. This dance calls for one child to perform a movement in the center of the circle while the other children sing and walk around him. The activity could easily be modified so that the child in the center performs a stability movement such as a prone stretch and the children in the circle mimic that movement rather than walking around in a circle.

Self-Testing

The third phase of the traditional curriculum is self-testing. The self-testing phase is rich with activities that can stress stability movements in either isolation or combination. Some self-testing activities appropriate for preschool and primary age children are recorded in the following chart.

	Gestures	Static Postures	Transitional Postures
Fundamental Movement Patterns	Weather Vane[9] Balancing on the Bean-bag	Dog Stand[9] Shoulder Stand[9] Bridge Stand[9] Balance Stand[9] Snail[9] Stride Stand[9] Incline Stand[9]	
Physical Fitness	Isometrics (a) Pull Across Chest[6] (b) Behind Neck Pull[6]	Arm Fling[9] Toe Pull[9] Double Backleg Push[9]	
Stunts	Thread the Needle[9]	Measuring Worm[9] Push-up[9] Rabbit Jump[9] Turk Stand[9] Horizontal Stand[9] Chinese Get-up[9] Mule Kick[9] Tripod[9] Head Stand[9]	Wring the Dishrag[9]
Tumbling			Log Roll[9] Side Roll[6] Forward Roll[9] Backward Roll[9] Cartwheel[9]
Small Apparatus (Wands, Hoops Chairs, etc.)		Floor Touch[6] Human Bridge[6] Foot Balance[6]	
Large Apparatus (Balance Beams, Benches, Ropes, Stall Bars)		Foot and Knee Balance[6] Side Balance[6] Inverted Hand[6]	

Note. The number after each activity refers to the text book listed in the Selected References, in which detailed explanation of that particular activity is presented.

A repetition of many of the fundamental movements of stability can be performed by the children when using small and large apparatus. The chart shows a sampling of activities that might be included for preschool and primary age children. The child's movement experience and physical development will determine how far he will progress. Grade level suggestions are given in the references cited. It is the teacher's job to select activities that are best suited to the students' capabilities. Strict adherence to grade level recommendations is unfair to most of the children, and the teacher should make every effort to individualize the teaching progression so that each child might reach his or her present developmental level potential.

In this chapter an attempt has been made to isolate fundamental stability movements for the purposes of identifying them for teaching emphasis and relating them to the locomotor and manipulative activities that follow in Chapters Six and Seven.

SELECTED REFERENCES

1. Anderson, Marian, Elliot, M., and La Berge, J. *Play with a Purpose: Elementary School Physical Education*. New York: Harper and Row Publishers, 1972.
2. Andrews, Gladys, Saurborn, J., and Schneider, E. *Physical Education for Today's Boys and Girls*, Boston: Allyn and Bacon, Inc., 1966.
3. Clark, H., Harrison. *Application of Measurement to Health, Physical Education, and Recreation*. Englewood Cliffs, New Jersey: Prentice-Hall, 1968.
4. Fabricus, Helen. *Physical Education for the Classroom Teacher: A Physical Education Curriculum for Elementary School Children*. Dubuque, Iowa: Wm. C. Brown Company Publishers, 1974.
5. Fait, Hollis F. *Physical Education for the Elementary School Child: Experiences in Movement*. Philadelphia: W. B. Saunders Company, 1971.
6. Gilliom, Bonnie. *Basic Movement Education for Children: Rationale and Teaching Units*. Reading, Massachusetts: Addison-Wesley Publishing Company, 1970.
7. Kirchner, Glenn. *Physical Education for Elementary School Children*. Dubuque, Iowa: Wm. C. Brown Company Publishers, 1974.
8. Kirchner, Glenn, Cunningham, Jean, and Warrell, E. *Introduction to Movement Education: An Individualized Approach to Teaching Physical Education*. Dubuque, Iowa: Wm. C. Brown Company Publishers, 1970.
9. Ryser, Otto. *A Teacher's Manual For Tumbling and Apparatus Stunts*. Dubuque, Iowa: Wm. C. Brown Company Publishers, 1968.
10. Schurr, Evelyn. *Movement Experiences for Children: Curriculum and Methods for Elementary School Physical Education*. New York: Appleton-Century-Crofts, 1967.
11. Vannier, Maryhelen, Foster, M., and Gallahue, D. *Teaching Physical Education in Elementary Schools*. 5th ed. Philadelphia: W. B. Saunders Company, 1973.

Chapter 6
Developing Fundamental Concepts of Locomotion

Key Concept: Locomotion is a fundamental aspect of learning to move effectively and efficiently within one's environment that involves projecting the body into external space relative to a fixed point on the ground.

Content: Introduction
Locomotor Movements
   Walking and Running
   Jumping for Distance
   Jumping for Height
   Jumping from a Height
   Hopping
   Skipping
   Sliding
   Leaping
   Climbing
Locomotor Experiences for Preschool and Primary Grade Children
   Exploratory Experiences
   Discovery Experiences
   Indirect Combination Experiences
   Direct Combination Experiences
   Games
   Rhythms
   Self-testing Activities

Developing Fundamental Concepts of Locomotion

INTRODUCTION

Locomotion, like stability, is a fundamental aspect of learning to move effectively and efficiently within one's environment. It involves projection of the body into external space by altering its location relative to fixed points on the ground. Activities such as walking, running, jumping, hopping, sliding, and skipping are considered to be locomotor movements. Performance of these movements must be sufficiently flexible so that they can be altered as the requirements of the environment demand without deflecting attention from the *purpose* of the act. The child must be able to (1) use any one of a number of types of movements to reach the goal, (2) be able to shift from one type of movement to another when the situation demands it, and (3) be able to alter each movement as the conditions of the environment change. Throughout this process of alteration and modification attention must not be diverted from the goal. For example, the locomotor pattern of walking may be used singularly or it may be used in conjunction with manipulative or stability movements. As a result the pattern of walking is elaborated upon by the inclusion of object handling such as bouncing a ball while walking, or by stressing maintenance of balance such as when walking on a balance beam. Development and refinement of the following locomotor patterns and general movement skills in preschool and elementary school children is essential since it is through these movements that they explore the world about themselves.

In the preceding chapter the suggested movement variations listed under each form of movement were expressed in terms of possible teaching cues that may be utilized in an actual teaching situation. The teaching cues given in that chapter were designed to familiarize you with *some* of the ways of communicating with children. There are numerous other verbal and nonverbal forms of communication that you as a teacher can employ in order to develop a meaningful dialogue with students. *The movement variations found in this chapter and in the following chapter emphasize progression, movement qualities, and combination activities with the other categories of movement.*

104

Being A Good Runner Is Important In A Game of Tag

LOCOMOTOR MOVEMENTS

Walking and Running

Verbal Description

Running is an exaggerated form of walking. The walk is composed of moving one foot ahead of the other with the heel of the forward foot touching the ground before the toe of the opposite foot pushes off. The arms move synchronously in opposition to the legs.

The run differs principally from the walk in that there is a brief phase in which the body is out of contact with the ground during each step. Running incorporates each of the following movements in a coordinated manner.

1. The trunk is erect with only slight forward lean.
2. The arms are bent at approximately right angles and swing in synchronized opposition to the leg action.
3. The supporting foot contacts the ground on the forward portion and nearly under the center of gravity.
4. The supporting knee bends slightly after contacting the ground.
5. The supporting leg is extended at the hip, knee, and ankle in order to propel the body forward and up into the nonsupport phase.

6. The recovery leg raises quickly at the knee while the lower portion of the leg flexes so that the heel is brought close to the buttocks.
7. The head remains upright and forward.
8. The entire motion is loose and relaxed with a minimum of wasted motion.

Visual Description

Common Problems

1. Inhibited or exaggerated arm swing.
2. Crossing the arms in front of the body, or failing to lift them.
3. Improper foot placement (that is, flatfooted, heavy landing, toeing in or out).
4. Inhibited or exaggerated forward lean.
5. Twisting of the trunk.
6. Break in flow, and lack of rhythmical alteration of the arms and legs.
7. Landing on the heels first.
8. Flipping of a foot or leg either in or out.

Concepts Children Should Know

1. Keep your head up.
2. Lean into your run *slightly*.
3. Lift your knees.
4. Bend your elbows and swing the arms freely.
5. Run on the balls of your feet.
6. Run lightly.
7. The running pattern is basic to numerous games and sports that you play, and is used in most active ball games, and track and field events.

Movement Variations of Walking and Running

Movements with the Emphasis of the Base of Support

1. Walk or run with the feet wide apart and then close together.
2. Walk or run with the toes out, in and then forward.

3. Walk or run on the sides of the feet.
4. Walk or run on the heels or toes.

Movements with the Emphasis on Body Position

1. Walk or run with the upper body bent forward, sideward, or backward.
2. Walk or run with the knees high.
3. Walk or run and emphasize various arm swing patterns.
4. Walk or run with arms above the head, to the sides, and so forth.
5. Walk or run with the body stretched high.
6. Walk or run with the body at upper and lower levels.

Movements with Emphasis on Speed and Rhythm

1. Walk or run at various speeds.
2. Stride to a musical beat.
3. Walk or run fast or slow with short and then long strides.
4. Marching types of activities.

Movements with Emphasis on Range

1. Walk or run in place.
2. Shuffle the feet.
3. Walk or run with long or normal strides.
4. Walk or run with an exaggerated weight shift from side to side.

Movements with the Emphasis on Direction

1. Walk or run straight, angular, zigzag or some other geometric shape or design.
2. Walk or run and weave between or around and through obstacles.
3. Walk or run letter or number patterns.

Movements with Emphasis on Intensity of Force

1. Walk or run as lightly or quietly as possible.
2. Walk or run with heavy or hard steps.

Movements with the Emphasis on Flow

1. Walk or run like a wooden soldier.
2. Walk or run like a rag doll.

Movements with Emphasis on the Environment

1. Walk or run up and down the stairs or bleachers.
2. Walk or run on the bench or balance beam.
3. Walk or run through obstacle course.

Jumping for Distance

Verbal Description

The jump for distance is an explosive movement that involves the coordinated performance of all portions of the body. The take-off is with one or both feet and the landing is on both feet. Jumping for distance utilizes each of the following movements in a sequential manner.

1. The joints at the hip, knee and ankle are flexed while the arms swing back and upward.
2. The arms swing forward and upward while at the same time the body begins an extension at the hips, knees and ankles (an explosive movement).
3. As the body is propelled into the air the lower legs flex and the hips flex thus bringing the knees forward.
4. The trunk and arms move forward and downward thus placing the trunk and upper legs in close proximity to one another.
5. Just prior to landing the lower portion of the legs extend.
6. Upon impact the knees bend and the body continues forward and downward.
7. The toes are the last portion of the body to lose contact with the ground upon take-off, the heels are first to touch when landing.

Movements with Emphasis on Creative Expression

1. Walk or run like a camel, giraffe, horse, and so forth.
2. Walk or run like your mother, your father, a clown, the boss.
3. Pretend you are walking or running on ice, in snow, sand, mud, and so forth.
4. Pretend you are walking or running against or with a strong wind.
5. Pretend you are walking or running uphill, downhill or on the side of a hill.

Movements with Emphasis on Combination

1. Walk and hop, walk and run, walk and jump and run.
2. Walk or run as many different ways as possible with a partner.
3. Balance a beanbag while walking or running.
4. Kick or roll a ball while walking or running.
5. Toss and catch a beanbag while walking or running.
6. Push a cage ball while walking or running.
7. Pull a partner while walking or running.
8. Bounce a ball while walking or running.

Visual Description

Common Problems

1. Improper use of the arms (that is, failure to use the arm opposite the propelling leg in a down-up-down swing as the leg bends, extends, and bends again).
2. Twisting or jerking of the body.
3. Inability to perform either a one foot or two foot take-off.
4. Poor preliminary crouch.
5. Restricted movements of the arms or legs.
6. Poor angle of take-off (should be about 45 degrees).
7. Failure to extend fully upon take-off.
8. Failure to bend the knees after the take-off causing the feet to touch ground immediately.
9. Failure to extend the legs forward upon landing.

Concepts Children Should Know

1. Crouch halfway down.
2. Swing your arms back, then forward forcefully.
3. "Explode" forward from the coiled position.
4. Lift your knees up.
5. Stretch and reach forward.
6. This jumping pattern is basic to performing the standing and the running long jump and in stopping.

Movement Variations of the Jump for Distance

Movements with Emphasis on the Base of Support

1. Jump with the feet wide apart and then close together.
2. Jump with one foot forward of the other.
3. Jump with toes pointed out, in and then forward.
4. Jump from a kneeling position.

Movements with Emphasis on Body Position

1. Jump with the upper body bent forward, sideward or backward.
2. Jump using no arm movement.
3. Jump with flexed or extended arm swinging movements.
4. Jump from a tight crouch, slight crouch or upright position.
5. Jump emphasizing landing on the toes, heels or flatfooted.
6. Jump emphasizing landings with various degrees of knee flexion.
7. Jump emphasizing various arm swing patterns (above the head, to the sides, across the body, and so forth).
8. Jump with the neck, hips, knees and elbows in flexed and/or extended positions.

Movements with Emphasis on Speed and Rhythm

1. Swing the arms in a rhythmical pattern while moving from the crouch to the height just prior to take-off (repeat).
2. Jump at various speeds (slow to fast).
3. Jump to a musical beat.
4. Jump fast or slow with either long or short jumps.

Movements with Emphasis on Range and Level

1. Jump as short or long as possible.
2. Jump as low or high as possible.

Movements with Emphasis on Direction

1. Jump forward, sideward, backward or in a circular pattern.
2. Jump a straight, angular, zigzag or some other geometric shape or design.
3. Jump letter or number patterns.

Movements with Emphasis on the Intensity of Force

1. Jump as lightly or quietly as possible.
2. Jump as heavily or loudly as possible.
3. Jump at different levels (low or high).

Movements with Emphasis on Flow

1. Jump with the arms, legs, trunk, held stiffly.
2. Jump with one or more of the body parts relaxed.

Movements with Emphasis on the Environment

1. Jump from side to side over a rope.
2. Jump in and out of a hoop or hoops.

3. Teach the step-hurdle (one foot take-off into two foot landing and jump) on the springboard.
4. Jump around obstacles.
5. Jump in and out or through a hoop held at various heights.
6. Clap hands, change body positions or touch body parts while performing jumps using the springboard or trampoline.

Movements with Emphasis on Creative Expression

1. Jump like a frog, kangaroo, rabbit, horse, monkey, and so forth.
2. Jump over an imaginary brook, crevice, mudpuddle, and so forth.
3. Do a happy, sad, tired, energetic, jump.
4. Do as many different jumps as you can by yourself, with a partner or with a group.

Movements with Emphasis on Combination

1. Jump for distance and then jump for height.
2. Jump up on an object and then down.
3. Jump as short and low as possible.
4. Jump as long and high as possible.
5. Throw and/or catch a beanbag or ball while jumping.
6. Toss and catch a beanbag or ball in the air while jumping.
7. Bounce a ball while jumping.
8. Push or pull an object while jumping.
9. Jump while beating rhythm on lummi sticks.

Jumping for Height

Verbal Description

The jump for height or vertical jump as it is often called is composed of the following movements combined in a coordinated manner:

1. The body assumes a semicrouch position in which the hips, knees, and ankles are flexed.
2. The arms initiate the jumping action with a vigorous lift that is both forward and upward.
3. The upward thrust is continued by forcefully extending the hips, knees, and ankles.
4. The body is fully extended and remains so until the forward portion of the feet are ready to touch the ground again. Then the ankles, knees, and hips flex to absorb the shock of landing.
5. The toes should be the last portion of the body to lose contact with the ground and the first to retouch.

Common Problems

1. Improper crouch (i.e., crouch too low or not low enough).
2. Failure to fully extend the body, legs and arms forcefully into the air.
3. Swinging the arms backward rather than upward.
4. Flexion of the legs immediately after take-off causing the trunk to move forward.
5. Landing with straight legs.

Visual Description

Concepts Children Should Know

1. Crouch halfway down.
2. "Explode" upward.
3. Swing your arms forcefully up.
4. Stretch and reach upward.
5. This jumping pattern is used in rebounding a tossed ball, the lay-up shot in basketball, and the block and spike in volleyball.

Movement Variations of Jumping for Height

The jump for height is not much different than a jump for distance. The only major difference is the vertical force component. Therefore, the activities expressed in the previous section on jumping for distance can be utilized again in this section. Some additional activities more specific to the jump for height might include:

1. Jump in place (direction).*
2. Do ¼, ½, full jump turns to the right or left (direction).

*Note. The word in parenthesis indicates the major quality of movement being stressed. See Chapter 1 page 8 for an explanation of the qualities of movement.

3. Do forward and backward rope jumps (speed and rhythm).
4. Jump and touch a rope or chinning bar at a certain height (environment).
5. Jump and strike a ball or a hanging object with the hand (environment).
6. Jump on the trampoline (environment).
7. Jump and throw an object with your feet (combination).
8. Perform long rope jumping skills (combination).

Jumping for a Height

Verbal Description

The movements involved in jumping from a height are similar to those found in jumping for distance and for height. In jumping from a height emphasis is placed on the take-off and the landing phases of the jump. The following is a brief description of the principle movements involved in jumping from a height:

1. The take-off is from both feet with slight flexion at the knees, hips, and ankles.
2. There is a slight forward lean of the trunk at the m oment of take-off.
3. The arms move forward as the ankles, knees, and hip prepare for the landing.
4. The legs contact the ground shoulder width apart.
5. Upon contact the knees and hip joint flex to an acute angle in order to absorb the impact of the landing. The greater the height jumped from the greater the degree of flexion needed to absorb the force of the landing.

Visual Description

Common Problems

1. Inability to take-off with both feet. This is readily observed in toddlers who are developmentally unable to take-off with both feet and must lead with one foot.
2. Exaggerated or inhibited body lean.
3. Failure to land simultaneously on both feet.
4. Landing "flatfooted."
5. Failure to give sufficiently upon impact.

Concepts Children Should Know

1. Push off with both feet.
2. Lean forward slightly.
3. Move the arms forward.
4. Keep your legs apart and bend them sharply upon landing.
5. This jumping pattern is used whenever you jump from something such as a rock, tree, or jungle gym.

Movement Variations of the Jump from a Height

The jump from a height is also mechanically similar to the jump for distance and the jump for height. Because of this similarity, the previous jumping activity variations presented apply to this section as well. Some additional activities more specific to the jump from a height might include:

1. Jump forward, sideward, or backward from a height (direction).
2. Land as lightly or as forcefully as possible (intensity of force).
3. Jump off a box, chair, bench, balance beam, vaulting stand, rolled mat (environment).
4. Jump from a height and perform a shoulder or forward roll after landing (combination).
5. Jump from a height and perform a straddle jump after landing (combination).
6. Also see landing activities in the preceding chapter. (See pages 93-94.)

Hopping

Verbal Description

The hop is similar to the distance and vertical jumps but the take-off and landing are on the same foot rather than on both feet. The fundamental hopping pattern is composed of the following movements combines in a coordinated manner.

1. The arms are more restricted than in the jump and are kept in front of the body in a bent position. There is, however, a slight simultaneous upward and downward motion of the arms synchronized to the rhythm of the hopping leg.
2. The hopping leg (supporting leg) is flexed at the ankle, knee, and hip.
3. The free leg is bent to an acute angle at the knee.
4. The push-off from the supporting leg is either upward or forward (that is hop in place or hop forward). The knees rarely straighten fully but are kept slightly bent.
5. The free leg performs the same action as the hopping leg, but does not contact the ground. It serves as an aid for maintaining balance.
6. The toes of the hopping foot are the last portion of the body to lose contact with the ground and the first to regain contact.

Visual Description

Common Problems

1. Hopping flatfooted.
2. Exaggerated movements of the arms.
3. Exaggerated movements of the free leg.
4. Exaggerated forward lean.
5. Inability to keep the free leg from contacting the ground.
6. Inability to spring from the contacting foot.
7. Inability to alternate the hopping motion from one leg to the other.

Concepts Children Should Know

1. Take off and land on the same foot.
2. Lift your arms slightly.
3. Push off and land on the balls of your feet.
4. Land softly.

5. The hopping pattern is used in combination with jumping or walking in many sport activities such as the triple jump, and the ballestra in fencing. It is also used in many dance steps such as the polka, mazurka, and schottische.

Movement Variations of Hopping

The hop, as stated, is similar to the distance and vertical jumps. The jumping variations presented previously are applicable here as well. Some additional activities specific to hopping include:

1. Balance on one foot and hop (base of support).
2. Hop with the nonsupportive leg forward, sideward or backward (body position).
3. Hop on one foot and then the other (base of support).
4. Hop and carry a beanbag on the free foot (combination).
5. Hop and toss a beanbag up to the hands with the free foot (combination).
6. Hop while jumping rope (combination).
7. Hop like an Indian doing a rain dance (creative expression).
8. Hop and do turns (combination).
9. Hop and bounce a ball under the nonsupportive leg (combination).

Skipping

Verbal Description

The skip combines two fundamental patterns of movement, the step and the hop, into a more advanced pattern. The skip is a continuous flow of the step-hop with rhythmical alternation of the leading foot. Skipping is composed of the following movements coordinated together.

1. The left (or right) foot steps forward placing the body weight on this foot.
2. Hop on the left foot and extend the right foot forward in a walking manner.
3. Weight is placed on the right foot and a hop on the right foot is executed followed by a step on the left.
4. The movement is continued with alternation of each foot.
5. The arms alternate according to the alternation of the feet. The opposite arm is extended to the leading foot and lifts slightly.

Visual Description

Common Problems

1. Stepping on one foot and hopping on the other.
2. Poor rhythmical flow.
3. Failure to lift the leg upward causing too much gain in distance.
4. Inability to use both sides of the body.
5. Heavy stepping or landing.
6. Extraneous movements of the legs or arms.
7. Crossing the feet.
8. Exaggerated or inhibited arm movements.
9. Inability to move in a straight line.

Concepts Children Should Know

1. Step forward then hop *up* on the same foot.
2. Do the same on the other foot.
3. Lift your knees.
4. Swing your arms up in time with your legs.
5. The skipping pattern is often used in the basketball lay-up shot and is basic to developing good footwork. It is also a part of many folk and square dances.

Movement Variations of Skipping

Since the skip consists of a step and a hop, the variations presented in the walking and hopping sections are appropriate for skipping. Some additional activities specific to skipping might include:

1. Step—hops with long steps forward or backward (range, direction).
2. Step—hops with short steps forward or backward (range, direction).
3. Skip on toes (base of support).

4. Skip moving the trunk or head (body position).
5. Skip as many ways as possible with a partner (environment, creative expression).

Verbal Description

The slide is similar to the skip in that it combines both a step and a hop in a rhythmical manner. Only one leg, however, maintains the leading position. Sliding is executed in a sideward direction. When performed forward or backward it is referred to as galloping. Sliding incorporates each of the following movements in a coordinated sequence.

1. Left (or right) foot steps sideward placing the body weight on this foot.
2. The right is drawn to the side of the left.
3. The leading leg repeats the stepping motion as soon as the trailing leg completes the catch phase.
4. The arms may or may not come into use. When used they maintain a slight sideward and upward motion synchronized with the motion of the lead foot.

Visual Description

Common Problems

1. Keeping the legs too straight.
2. Exaggerated forward lean with the trunk.
3. Jerky movements.
4. Overstepping with the trailing leg.
5. Too much elevation.

Concepts Children Should Know

1. Step to the side and draw the other foot up to it quickly.
2. Repeat, leading with the same foot.
3. Lift the arms slightly.

4. Move on the balls of your feet.
5. The sliding pattern is used in a variety of sports, such as tennis, baseball, basketball, and fencing. It is also used in performing many traditional dances.

Movement Variations of Sliding

The similarity of the slide to the skip permits the use of the previously presented variations with this new fundamental movement. Some additional activities specific to sliding and galloping include:

1. Galloping with the right and then left leg leading (body position).
2. Galloping faster and slower with shorter or longer gallop strides (range, speed, rhythm).
3. Gallop sideward or slide (direction).
4. Slide in a circle (direction).
5. Gallop holding a beanbag between the knees (environment).

Leaping

Verbal Description

The leap is similar to the run in that there is a transference of weight from one foot to the other, but the loss of contact with the ground is sustained with greater elevation and distance covered than in the run. Leaping involves each of the following movements.

1. Stand with the body erect, weight on one foot, and with the other foot slightly forward.
2. Bend the weight bearing leg (rear leg).
3. Push upward and forward with the rear leg and extend the forward leg.
4. The arms work in synchronized opposition to the legs.
5. Land on the forward foot, bend the leg to absorb shock and prepare for the next leap.

Common Problems

1. Failure to use the arms in opposition to the legs.
2. Inability to perform the one foot take-off and landing on the opposite foot.
3. Restricted movements of the arms or legs.
4. Lack of spring and elevation in the push-off.
5. Landing flatfooted.
6. Exaggerated or inhibited body lean.
7. Failure to stretch and reach with the legs.

Visual Description

Concepts Children Should Know

1. Push upward and forward with your rear foot.
2. Stretch and reach with your front foot.
3. Keep your head up.
4. Alternate the arm motion with your leg motion.
5. The leaping pattern is used in hurdling and combined with other movements in performing the high-jump. It also used in conjunction with the run to help you get over small obstacles without altering your stride.

Movement Variations of Leaping

The leap may be considered similar to the run as well as the jump since the alternating action of the legs, the distance and the height, are characteristic of the leap.

1. Leap from a slow and than a fast run (speed, flow, rhythm).
2. Perform a series of running leaps while keeping the arms and legs stiff (body position, flow).
3. Leap to a target or series of target areas in some geometric shape (direction).
4. Run and leap and strike a suspended object with the hand or hands (level).
5. Move legs, arms, and trunk into various positions while in flight during the leap (body position).

Climbing

Climbing is a fundamental movement similar to crawling. The primary difference between the two is that climbing requires the body weight to be *pulled* by the limbs in opposition to the force of gravity while crawling requires the body weight to be *pushed* by the limbs at right angles to it. Climbing may be performed with the legs alone, the arms alone, or with the legs and arms working together. The terrain over which the child climbs or the object being climbed (that is, rope, pole, ladder) dictates the exact form to be taken. The following is a description of a vertical climbing pattern in which both the arms and the legs are used, as in climbing a ladder.

1. The hands are placed in a "thumbs around" grasp. This grasp is fundamental to the proper gripping of all objects no matter what their orientation (that is, horizontal, vertical, diagonal) or their function (that is, batting, raking, writing).
2. The feet are placed securely on the supporting surface with the weight of the body on the balls of the feet.
3. The movement begins with one hand and the *opposite* knee lifting. As this is done the body weight is shifted first from the supporting leg then to the supporting arm.
4. The movement repeats itself using the other hand and leg and continues in a rhythmical manner.
5. The entire body weight must be lifted in each phase.

Visual Description

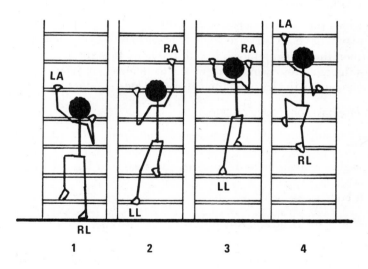

1   2   3   4

Common Problems

1. Improper grasp of the object with the hands.
2. Improper sequencing of the movements of the limbs.
3. Uneven or irregular use of the two sides of the body.
4. Inability to transfer the basic elements of climbing to other objects (that is, horizontal ladder, rope, pole).

5. Inability to alternate use of the hands or the feet such as leading with the same foot when climbing stairs, or with the same hand when climbing a rope.

Concepts Children Should Know

1. Place your thumbs around the bar.
2. Pull with your arms and push with your legs.
3. Move one hand and the opposite leg at the same time.
4. The climbing pattern is used in performing many self-testing activities such as pole and rope climbing, or horizontal and vertical ladder climbing.
5. The climbing movements that you make with your hands and feet are the same as the movements you made when you crawled as a baby except that you are now moving *upward* rather than *forward*.

Movement Variations of Climbing

Movements with the Emphasis on the Base of Support

1. Crawl through a long tube or mat constructed tunnel.
2. Use the hands to pull the body forward while face down on a gym scooter.
3. Use the arms (then the arms and legs) to pull the body forward and backward along a low hanging rope while lying on the back on a gym scooter.
4. Climb up an incline using the legs and then arms and legs.

Movements with the Emphasis on Body Position

1. Climb up, down, or sidewards on an incline on all fours with stomach up or down.
2. Climb in an upright or inverted position using the arms and legs, the legs only or the arms only.
3. Climb with your body parts flexed or extended.

Movements with Emphasis on Speed and Rhythm

1. Crawl as quickly as possible.
2. Climb a ladder and move an arm or leg on each beat of the drum (vary the tempo).
3. Climb to the rhythm of clapping of a tambourine or of a record.

Movements with the Emphasis on Range and Level

1. Climb using any of the climbing variations and make your movements as small or large as possible.
2. Climb with the body in a low, medium or high position.

Movements with Emphasis on Direction

1. Climb forward, backward or sideward on a large piece of apparatus.
2. Climb up or down in an upright or inverted posture.

Movements with Emphasis on Force

1. Climb as vigorously as possible.
2. Climb as slowly and silently as possible.

Movements with Emphasis on Flow

1. Climb with sharp staccato movements.
2. Climb with slow fluid movements.

Movements with Emphasis on the Environment

1. Climb on or around and through the tressel tree or jungle gym.
2. Climb the bleachers or stairs.
3. Climb up a ramp or slide.
4. Climb up or down a rope or pole in an upright or inverted posture.
5. Climb in all directions on the stall bars or cargo net.

Movements with Emphasis on Creative Expression

1. Climb like a monkey, a tiger, a cat, a mountain goat, and so forth.
2. Climb as many different ways as you can on different pieces of apparatus.
3. With climbing as the theme, have the children act out a story play.

Movements with Emphasis on Combination

1. Climb while carrying or balancing an object.
2. Push or pull an object while climbing (e.g., slide a knotted scarf up or down the rope or pole).
3. Climbing and hanging from hands, knees, or other body parts.

Note. The progression of climbing challenges should give children ample opportunities to develop body awareness, climbing coordination, and grip strength.

LOCOMOTOR EXPERIENCES FOR PRESCHOOL AND PRIMARY GRADE CHILDREN

The development and refinement of fundamental movement patterns is our goal when determining locomotor oriented activities for young children. The theoretical position for teaching locomotor movements does not vary from that stated in the previous chapter on stability. The emphasis on locomotor activities should still encompass a movement education approach that progressively exposes children to (1) exploratory, (2) discovery, (3) indirect combination and (4) direct combination experiences. The movement education themes suggested in the stability chapter are suitable here, too. Locomotor movements such as walking, running, and jumping are to be incorporated into these themes for teaching emphasis. Again the teacher utilizes the qualities of movement, movement mechanics and the other categories of movement (stability or manipulation) to vary the nature of locomotor movements. The variations listed for each of the locomotor movements that are presented in this chapter follow this format and provide the basis for the teacher's organization of learning experience. Since the movement variations of each locomotor movement have been elaborated upon in this chapter and the movement education concepts have been elaborated upon in the previous chapter, only a few examples of these types of experiences will be accentuated here. This is done in order that we may reiterate the different teaching approaches and the nature of the activities corresponding to each of the movement experiences.

Exploratory Experiences

The teacher suggests or challenges but refrains from setting a "correct" model for performance.

1. "How many different ways can you walk, run, jump, hop, etc.?"
2. "Can you run, climb, or leap like a dog, monkey, horse, etc.?"
3. "Pretend you are a tight rope walker, or a bouncing ball, or a Mexican jumping bean, or a cowboy at a rodeo, etc."
4. Use small apparatus such as beanbags, ropes, sticks, hoops, etc. in combination with exploratory locomotor activities.
   a. "Hop as many ways as you can with your beanbag."
   b. "How many things can you do with your rope and still be moving about?"
5. Use large apparatus such as balance beams, vaulting stands, cargo nets, hanging ropes, climbing poles, etc. to encourage exploratory locomotor behaviors in relation to these objects.
   a. "Jump as many ways as you can off the vaulting stand."
   b. "Climb in as many ways as you can on the cargo net."

Discovery Experiences

The teacher places qualifications or limitations on movements as the children discover and share experiences. Here the teacher begins to stress the qualities of movement or the mechanics desired.

1. "Skip as many different ways as you can and still not have your head above the tambourine I'm holding in my hand" (raise and lower the tambourine while tapping out the rhythm).
2. Use creative dramatization but allow your narrative to guide or restrict the children's movements as they act out the story.
   a. "Ride your horse at a trot or gallop around the rodeo ring."
   b. "Ride your horse and leap over a wide water hole and then leap over a fence."
3. Use small and large apparatus in guiding children to broaden their locomotor experiences.
   a. "Hop from side to side over a rope."
   b. "Jump over the hoop, onto the box, and so on.

Indirect Combination Experiences

The teacher continues to qualify or limit movements so that previous movements become progressively more difficult to perform. The teacher asks the children to combine several movements in creating their own combinations.

1. "Can you walk and hop and jump around the obstacle course?"
2. "Can you toss and catch a beanbag while walking, running, and jumping?"
3. "Can you jump off the vaulting stand into the hoop and do a roll out of the hoop?"
4. "Change the way you move (locomotor movement) each time you hear the heavy beat on the drum."

Direct Combination Experiences

The teacher suggests, demonstrates, or drills the children in the desired skill form to be used.

1. The teacher combines several fundamental movements into a series of movements or a routine.
   a. "Skip to the first cone, crawl to the second, run to and jump over the third and hop to the finish line."
   b. "Vault into the vaulting stand, jump with a 1/2 turn and do a backward roll."
2. The teacher demonstrates a routine with regard to the movement pattern form.
   a. "Go through this obstacle like this: run to the ladder, climb to the top,

walk across the beam, swing on the rope, land on the mat and do a log roll to the middle of the mat."

b. "Swing your arms back and bend your knees and then thrust your arms forward and up as you push off the floor" (standing long jump drill).

The more traditional curriculum content areas of games, rhythms, and self-testing might be thought of as direct combination experiences since they are primarily teacher directed. Some activities that are representative of these three traditional content areas are summarized. Remember that the teacher might utilize these direct combination experiences intermittently or in conjunction with exploratory, discovery, and indirect combination experiences depending on the communication level that has been established with the children. In other words, direct combination experiences might, therefore, be used to replace or supplement exploratory, discovery, or indirect combination experiences.

Games

The content area of games, as was indicated in the previous chapter, emphasizes low organized games and relays at the preschool and primary grade levels. The following list of games all emphasize fundamental movements. The locomotor movements suggested in the games are in parentheses. However, other locomotor movements may easily be substituted to modify the games as well as its movement emphasis. The game of Dog Catcher,[15] for example, is a running game that requires the children to move from one "kennel" area to another. The two kennels are separated by a zone where the dog catcher ("it") is attempting to catch (tag) any stray dogs and put them in the dog pound. Although the suggested form of locomotion is running, the teacher can vary the form of locomotion to assure that the children receive an opportunity to move in many more ways. Some possible changes in the form of locomotion might include: hopping, galloping, all-fours walk, and lame dog walk. If the dog catcher happens to be a heavy child with little speed, these modifications may help him to be successful. Instead of allowing the child to remain as the dog catcher when he is not fast enough to catch anyone, the teacher can ask the children to hop or do the lame dog walk while the dog catcher is able to maintain a form of locomotion that gives him a speed advantage. The use of other locomotor movements may serve as (1) an equalizing factor, (2) a means of keeping the children interested, (3) a way of requiring more control of their bodies, (4) an avenue to regulate the level of energy expended (physical fitness) and (5) as a technique to broaden the children's locomotor experiences. The relays listed below are only suitable if the children are developmentally ready to handle the team concept, which is the key to relay activities.

Locomotor Low Organization Games and Relays

Game or Activity (fundamental movevent)

1. Automobiles or Airplanes[15] (run)*
2. Back to Back[15] (run)
3. Bird, Beast and Fish[15] (run)
4. Dog Catcher[15] (run)
5. Jump the Creek[15] (jump)
6. Jump the Shot[15] (jump)
7. Loose Caboose[15] (run)
8. Midnight[15] (run)
9. Numbers Change[15] (run)
10. Red Light[15] (run)
11. Skip Tag[15] (skip)
12. Blast Off[15] (jump)
13. Beefsteak[11] (run)
14. Brownies and Fairies[5] (run)
15. Old Mother Witch[11] (run)
16. Simple Tag[11] (run)
17. Poison Tag[11] (run)
18. Back to Back[11] (run)
19. Crab Tag[11] (crabwalk)
20. Red Rover[11] (run)
21. Partner Tag[11] (run)
22. Posture Tag[11] (run)
23. Crows and Cranes[5] (run)
24. Hill Dill[5] (run)
25. Cat and Rat[5] (run)
26. Forest Lookout[5] (run)
27. Chinese Wall[5] (run)
28. Mickey Mouse[5] (run)
29. Fire Engine[5] (run)
30. Trades[5] (run)
31. Hopscotch[2] (hop, jump)
32. Scat[2] (run)
33. Monkey See, Monkey Do[2] (run)
34. Walking Relay[2] (walk)
35. Blast Off[2] (jump, run)
36. Round the Sun[2] (run)
37. Rescue Relay[2] (run)
38. Walk, Run or Hop Relay[11]
39. Shuttle Relay[11] (run)
40. Zigzag Relay[11] (run)
41. Blind Relay[6] (hop)
42. Bronco Relay[6] (gallop)
43. Circle Relay[6] (run)
44. Tightrope Relay[6] (walk)

Rhythms

The locomotor related rhythm activities are quite extensive. Each of the locomotor movements has a distinct rhythmic pattern. Children's discovery of their own rhythm normally must precede the use of an externally set rhythm for these movements. The use of a drum by the teacher, and/or the children tapping the rhythm out probably will be the next step in guiding or improving rhythmical movements. Singing games are often used to attempt to set the external rhythm. The next progressive step would be the use of rhythm instruments and/or records. *The First Book of Creative Rhythms*[16], *Let's Move: A Physical Education Program for Elementary Classroom Teachers*[6], and *Teaching Physical Education*

*Other locomotor movements such as skipping, galloping, hopping, and jumping may be substituted to modify the game and the movement emphasis in this and all subsequent suggested activities.

In Elementary Schools[15] are three texts in which appropriate musical selections for locomotor movements can be found. Suppliers of appropriate records are also indicated. The following rhythmical activities are representative of the preschool and primary grade curriculum.

Locomotor Rhythms

Activity (fundamental movement)

1. Looby Loo[5] (skip)
2. Round and Round the Village[5] (walk, skip)
3. Mulberry Bush[5] (walk, skip)
4. Farmer in the Dell[5] (walk, skip)
5. Did You Ever See a Lassie[5] (walk, stability)
6. Yankee Doodle[5] (gallop)
7. Jolly Is the Miller[5] (skip)
8. Danish Dance of Greeting[15] (side step, run)
9. Chimes of Dunkirk[15] (walk)
10. Seven Jumps[5] (walking, hopping)
11. Jump Jim Jo[5] (jump)

Self-Testing Activities

Basic locomotor movement patterns, skills, and fitness activities related to locomotor movements are the first two subcategories of self-testing. The con-

Riding The "Big Wheelie" Can Be Fun And Educational

tent in these two categories is usually presented in challenge form by the teacher. Specific walking, running, jumping, hopping, skipping, galloping, leaping, or climbing tasks are set forth. The teacher will use progressively more difficult tasks to help make each child aware of his or her improvement. Measurement at this level is primarily to provide the child some meaningful proof of some degree of success. Some physical fitness testing activities that relate directly to locomotor movements are the standing broad jump,[15] the high jump,[15] and the 50 yard dash.[15]

The stunts and tumbling, small manipulative apparatus and large apparatus categories below provide the children with locomotor variations that differ from those used on the floor. The animal walks and movements in relation to or on various pieces of apparatus provide children with a new sensory and environmental media to explore. Some examples of appropriate locomotor oriented self-testing activities are listed below.

1. Stunts and Tumbling
   Camel Walk[6]
   Bouncing Ball[6]
   Wickett Walk[6]
   Crabwalk[6]
   Rabbit Jump[6]
   Measuring Worm[6]
   Seal Walk[6]
   Kangaroo Hop[6]
   Knee Jump[6]
   Bear Walk[5]
   Jump and Click Heels[5]
   Jump and Touch Heels[5]
   Wheelbarrow[5]
   Jump the Stick[5]
   Puppy Run[6]
   Lame Puppy Walk[15]
   Monkey Run[6]
   Under the Bridge[2]
2. Small Manipulative Apparatus
   a. Rope Jumping Skills
      forward jump[6]
      backward jump[6]
      one foot hop[6]
      alternate step[6]
      alternate step—legswing[6]
      rocker step[6]
   b. Hoop Activities
      weave in and out of hoops[6]
      hoop—walk[6]
      hoop—jump[6]
      hoop—run[6]
3. Large Apparatus
   a. Agility Ropes[11] (climbing)
   b. Jumping Boxes, Planks and Sawhorses[11] (climbing, walking, jumping)
   c. Climbing Ropes
      chinning no leg support[11]
      rope hang[11]
      swing[11]
      climb[11]
   d. Stall Bars (climbing)
      pendulum swing[11]
      side lean[11]
      hand walk[11]
   e. Horizontal Ladder (climbing)
      swing and drop[11]
      chin[11]
      side rail trail[11]
   f. Horizontal Bar (climbing)
      hang like a money[11]
      roll over barrow[11]
      skin the cat[11]
      bird's nest[11]

g. Balance Beam and Benches
(walking, running, climbing,
etc.)
forward walk[6]
backward walk[6]

run forward[6]
galloping[6]
side stepping[6]
one foot hop[6]

h. South Hampton Cave[12]

The purpose of this chapter has been to identify and elaborate upon the fundamental locomotor movements. The basic concepts of locomotion have been presented through variations of the fundamentals as well as examples of application of those variations in the movement education and the traditional curricula.

SELECTED REFERENCES

1. Anderson, Marian, Elliot, M., and LaBerge, J. *Play with a Purpose: Elementary School Physical Education.* New York: Harper and Row Publishers, 1972.
2. Andrews, Gladys, Saurborn, J., and Schneider, F. *Physical Education for Today's Boys and Girls.* Boston: Allyn and Bacon, Inc., 1966.
3. Cooper, John, and Glassow, R. *Kinesiology.* St. Louis: C. V. Mosby, 1973.
4. Espenschade, Anna, and Eckert, H. *Motor Development.* Columbus, Ohio: Charles E. Merrill, 1967.
5. Fait, Hollis F. *Physical Education for the Elementary School Child: Experiences in Movement.* Philadelphia: W. B. Saunders Company, 1971.
6. Gallahue, David L., and Meadors, W. J. *Let's Move: A Physical Education Program For Elementary School Teachers.* Dubuque, Iowa: Kendall/Hunt Publishers, 1974.
7. Gilliom, Bonnie. *Basic Movement Education for Children: Rationale and Teaching Units.* Reading, Massachusetts: Addison-Wesley Publishing Company, 1970.
8. Godfrey, Barbara, and Kephart, N.C. *Movement Patterns and Motor Education.* New York: Appleton-Century-Crofts, 1969.
9. Halverson, Lolas. "A Comparison of the Performance of Kindergarten Children in the Take-Off Phase of the Standing Broad Jump." Unpublished doctoral dissertation, University of Wisconsin, 1958.
10. Keogh, Jack. "Motor Performance of Elementary School Children," Department of Physical Education. Los Angeles: University of California, 1965.
11. Kirchner, Glenn. *Physical Education for Elementary School Children.* Dubuque, Iowa: Wm. C. Brown Company Publishers, 1974.
12. Kirchner, Glenn, Cunningham, J., and Warrell, E. *Introduction to Movement Education: An Individualized Approach to Teaching Physical Education.* Dubuque, Iowa: Wm. C. Brown Company Publishers, 1970.
13. Schurr, Evelyn. *Movement Experiences for Children: Curriculum and Methods for Elementary School Physical Education,* New York: Appleton-Century-Crofts, 1967.
14. Scott, Gladys. *Analysis of Human Motion.* New York: Appleton-Century-Crofts, 1963.
15. Vannier, Maryhelen, Foster, M., and Gallahue, D.L. *Teaching Physical Education in Elementary Schools.* Philadelphia: W. B. Saunders Company, 1973.
16. Saffran, Rosanna B. *First Book of Creative Rhythms.* New York: Holt, Rinehart, and Winston, 1963.

Chapter 7
Developing Fundamental Concepts of Manipulation

Key Concept: Gross motor manipulation of objects involves giving force to objects and receiving force from objects through the efficient combination of fundamental locomotor and/or stabilizing movements.

Content: Introduction
Manipulative Movements
    Basic Underhand Toss (2 hands)
    Underhand Throw
    Vertical Toss
    Overhand Throw
    Basket Catch (with arms)
    Underhand and Overhand Catch
    Trapping
    Striking
    Volleying
    Kicking
    Bouncing an Object
    Rolling an Object
Manipulation Experiences for Preschool and Primary Grade Children
    Exploratory Experiences
    Discovery Experiences
    Indirect Combination Experiences
    Direct Combination Experiences
    Games
    Rhythms
    Self-testing Activities

131

Developing Fundamental Concepts of Manipulation

INTRODUCTION

   Gross motor manipulation involves the individual's relationship to objects and is characterized by giving force to objects and receiving force from them. Propulsive movements involve activities in which an object is moved away from the body. Such activities as throwing, kicking, striking, and rolling are involved. Absorptive movements involve activities that are concerned with positioning the body or a body part in the path of a moving object for the purpose of stopping or deflecting that object. Activities such as catching and trapping are involved. Manipulative movements are based on the two primary categories of movement: locomotion and stability. The essence of manipulative movements is that they combine two or more movements from one or both of these categories, and that they are generally used in conjunction with other forms of movement. For example, propulsive movements are generally a composite of stepping—turning—swinging—and stretching. Absorptive movements generally consist of bending and stepping.
   It is through the manipulation of objects that children are able to explore the relationship of moving objects in space. These movements involve making estimates of the path, distance, rate of travel, accuracy, and mass of the moving object. At the point of contact a check on previous estimates is possible. It is through such types of experimentation that children learn the nature and effect of the movement of objects. Because manipulative patterns commonly combine both locomotor and stabilizing movements, efficient use of them should not be expected at the same time that locomotor and stability abilities are developing. Only after these patterns have been fairly well established do we begin to see the emergence of efficient manipulative movements. The following is a description of several manipulative patterns of movement.

132

MANIPULATIVE MOVEMENTS

Basic Underhand Toss
(Two Hands)

Verbal Description

The first evidence of the emergence of the underhand throwing pattern is the child's attempt to throw objects by using his entire body to push them forward. The two handed underhand toss is one of the first manipulative patterns to develop in young children. Whether this is due to particular developmental characteristics or because children are usually required to manipulate large balls is a matter of conjecture. Two hand underhand tossing is composed of the following movements combined in a coordinated manner.

1. The feet are placed in a stride position with one foot slightly ahead of the other.
2. The ball is held with both hands on its sides.
3. There is a slight bend of the knees while the arms simultaneously swing down between the legs.
4. The knees straighten as the ball is brought forward and upward.
5. The ball is released as the hands reach waist height.
6. The arms follow through in the direction of the flight of the ball.

Visual Description

Common Problems

1. Standing with the feet together.
2. Exaggerated or inhibited bend of the legs.
3. Exaggerated or inhibited arm swing.
4. Early or late release of the ball.

5. Lack of follow-through.
6. Poor rhythmical execution of the component parts.

Concepts Children Should Know

1. Face the target.
2. Bend your knees slightly and swing your arms between the knees.
3. Watch the target.
4. Release the ball evenly at waist level.
5. Reach for the target.
6. The underhand tossing pattern is the basic movement that you use whenever throwing a very heavy or bulky object such as a medicine ball or a bale of hay.

Movement Variations of the Underhand Toss (two hands)

Movements with Emphasis on the Base of Support and Body Position

1. Throw with the feet wide apart and then close together.
2. Throw with one foot forward of the other and the feet close or wide apart.
3. Throw from a kneeling, sitting on heels or one knee position.
4. Throw varying the degree of body lean forward and sideward.
5. Throw varying the degree of knee and hip flexion.
6. Throw with the arms bent slightly and fully extended.

Movements with Emphasis on Speed, Rhythm, Flow, and Force

1. Throw an object as slowly, or as quickly as you can (vary the speed).
2. Throw an object as soft or as hard as you can (vary the force).
3. Throw an object with rigid or loose form.
4. Throw to the rhythm of a verbal cue, hand clap, drum beat, or music.

Movements with Emphasis on Range, Level, and Direction

1. Throw moving the arms in a small, medium or large arc.
2. Throw with the arm swing as low or high as possible.
3. Throw to a low, chest high, or high target.
4. Throw emphasizing follow-through to low, medium, or high targets.
5. Vary target challenges so throws require differing arcs.

Movements with Emphasis on Combination, Environment, and Creative Expression

1. Throw an object so it lands between two ropes.
2. Throw an object so it lands in a hoop or a circled rope.

3. Throw an object into a box, through the back of a chair, onto a chair seat, over a balance beam or at an Indian Club.
4. Walk, hop or jump and throw to a target.
5. Throw at a moving target such as a rolled inner tube, tire, or cageball.
6. Throw an object against a wall.
7. Carry an object and climb onto a vaulting stand, throw to a target, jump off and skip to retrieve the object.
8. Throw and catch with a partner on the floor, on a bench, or on a balance beam.
9. Throw like a robot or rag doll.
10. Throw as many ways as you can using "two hands."
11. Throw like a strong or weak man.
12. Throw to show happiness, sadness, and other emotions.

Underhand Throw
(One Hand)

Verbal Description

The underhand throw may be executed with one or two hands depending on the size of the ball used. The one hand underhand throw is composed of the following movements combined in a coordinated manner.

1. The feet are placed in a stride position with the left foot slightly ahead of the other. The body weight is evenly distributed over both feet (right hand throw).
2. The ball is held waist high with the right hand under it (and the left hand lightly on top for control when throwing a large ball).
3. The weight is transferred to the rear foot and the knees bend slightly while at the same time the arm is brought down and back and the body is twisted toward the right.
4. The right arm is swung forward forcefully and the shoulders are rotated to the left while the legs are straightening and the body weight is shifted toward the leading foot.
5. The ball is released approximately at hip level.
6. The throwing arm continues to follow through in the direction of the flight of the ball and the rear foot is brought forward so that it is even with the forward foot.
7. Lack of follow-through with the trailing foot.
8. Failure to rotate the body during the arm swing.
9. Arm crossing in front of the body.
10. Poor rhythmical execution of the component parts.

Visual Description

Common Problems

1. Standing with the feet together.
2. Exaggerated or inhibited bend of the legs.
3. Exaggerated or inhibited arm swing.
4. Early release of the ball.
5. Late release of the ball.
6. Lack of follow-through with the throwing arm.

Concepts Children Should Know

1. Stand with the leg that is on the other side of your throwing arm leading.
2. Twist your trunk to the right as you bring the ball back.
3. Swing the arm(s) quickly forward and step out on the lead foot.
4. Watch the target.
5. Release the ball at waist level.
6. Reach for the target.
7. The underhand throwing pattern is basic to several sports activities such as the pitch-out in football, the pitch in softball, and the shovel pass in basketball.

Movement Variations of the Underhand Throw (one hand)

The one hand underhand toss is similar to the underhand toss with two hands. The two hand underhand toss variations presented previously are applicable here as well. The primary difference between the two types of throws is in the use of the hands and the base of support. In the one hand underhand toss, one hand serves to throw while the other lightly guides the ball. The base of support used for the one hand underhand toss emphasizes opposition with the opposite foot of the tossing hand being forward. Some additional activities specific to the one hand underhand toss might include:

1. Balance on one foot, (same foot as throwing arm) and swing the arm forward and stride with the nonsupporting leg. Repeat this drill emphasizing rhythm and the length of the stride out (base of support).
2. Throw from a kneeling, sitting, or one knee position to target areas at different distances and heights (body support, range, level and direction).
3. Throw an object as hard, soft, quickly, or as slowly as you can (speed and force).
4. Walk, run, jump, or hop and throw an object at a target (combination).
5. Throw at a moving target (environment).
6. Use variations using the right hand, then the left emphasizing coordination of both sides of the body (body position, base of support).
7. Balance the object on one hand and toss back and forth from one hand to the other (combination).
8. Toss an object and have it bounce once before hitting a target area (combination).

Vertical Toss

Verbal Description

The vertical toss is composed of the following movements combined in a coordinated manner.

1. The feet are placed in a stride position with one foot slightly ahead of the other.
2. The ball is gripped on its sides with both hands.
3. The eyes are focused on a target overhead.
4. The knees are bent, the back is kept straight, and the ball is brought down between the knees.
5. As the legs straighten the arms swing vigorously upward. The ball is released as the arms extend overhead.
6. Follow-through with the fingertips in the direction of the ball's path.
7. The eyes are kept on the ball throughout the movement.

Common Problems

1. Failure to keep the back straight.
2. Failure to keep the eyes on the target.
3. Early release of the ball.
4. Late release of the ball.
5. Uneven use of arms.
6. Lack of follow-through.

Visual Description

MODIFIED VERTICAL TOSS: THE UNDERHAND FREE THROW

Concepts Children Should Know

1. Put your hands on the sides of the ball.
2. Keep your back straight when you squat down.
3. Swing the arms up forcefully.
4. Let go of the ball at the top of the swing.
5. Watch the ball.
6. The vertical tossing pattern is basic to performing the bump pass in volleyball, and you use it to set the ball up in many volleyball drills. It is also used in the underhand free throw in basketball, and many of the games that you play, and in ball rhythmics.

Movement Variations of the Vertical Toss

The vertical toss as defined, is a two handed throwing movement that might be executed as a two handed underhand throw. If the vertical toss is basically an underhand pattern, the variations presented for the two handed underhand throw can be utilized here with emphasis being on a target above the child's head. Some additional activities specific to the vertical toss might include:

1. Push an object upward by placing the hands slightly behind and below the object held at chest level (base of support and body position).
2. Use the right or left hand and toss the object above the head (base of support and body position).
3. Throw the object as slowly, as quickly, as soft, as hard, as high, or as low as possible (speed, rhythm, force, range, and level).
4. Toss the ball overhead and let it bounce before catching it (combination).
5. Toss an object through or into an overhead target such as a hula hoop (environment).
6. Do a vertical toss while walking on the floor, a bench, or a low balance beam (environment).

7. Toss the ball up, (high or low) clap the hands, let the ball bounce and then catch it (combination).
8. Throw as if you are putting the ball in orbit (creative expression).

Overhand Throw

Verbal Description

The overhand throw has been studied extensively over the past thirty years with attention being devoted to form, accuracy, and distance. The component parts of this throw will vary depending on which of these three factors the thrower is concentrating on and the starting position that is assumed. However, the general movements of the overhand throwing pattern are performed in the following sequence in a coordinated and overlapping manner.

1. The feet are placed in a stride position with the left foot slightly ahead of the other (right hand throw).
2. The trunk pivots to the right and the body weight shifts to the rear foot.
3. The right arm swings backward and upward while the left arm moves with a forward motion as the body rotates.
4. The left foot steps forward in the direction of the throw.
5. The hips rotate to the left along with the trunk and the shoulders while the throwing arm is retracted to its final position before starting the forward arm action.
6. The right arm is swung forward with the elbow leading. The forearm is extended and the wrist snaps just as the ball is released, and rear foot is brought forward.
7. The exact moment of release of the ball depends on the desired trajectory of the ball.
8. The follow-through is with the finger tips in the direction of the flight of the ball.

Visual Description

The Overhand Throwing Pattern Begins Developing Early And Requires Practice

Common Problems

1. Forward movement of the foot on the same side as the throwing arm.
2. Inhibited back swing.
3. Failure to rotate the hips as the throwing arm is brought forward.
4. Failure to step out on the leg opposite the throwing arm.
5. Poor rhythmical coordination of arm movement with body movement.
6. Inability to release the ball at the desired trajectory.
7. Loss of balance while throwing.

Concepts Children Should Know

1. Stand with the leg that is on the other side of the throwing arm leading.
2. Turn your shoulder toward the target.
3. Raise your free arm and point toward the target.
4. Raise your throwing arm and hold the ball close to your ear.
5. Lead with your elbow on the forward swing.
6. Bring your rear foot forward and follow through.

7. The overhand throwing pattern is used in the sports of baseball, softball, football and on the fast break in basketball. It is also basic to the overhand serves in volleyball and tennis and the smash shot in badminton.

Movement Variations of the Overhand Throw

Movements with Emphasis on Base of Support and Body Position

1. Throw with the feet close together or wide apart and in a normal or stride stance.
2. Throw from various bases of support, sitting or kneeling.
3. With the arm up close to the ear and the elbow flexed, throw and extend the hand out toward a target.
4. Throw with the arm slightly bent or fully extended in an overhead or sidearm pattern.
5. Throw an object across the front of the body to a target.
6. Throw varying the degree of body lean, forward, and sideward.

Movements with Emphasis on Speed, Rhythm, Flow, and Force

1. Throw a small, large, heavy, or light object, as slowly, or as quickly as you can.
2. Throw an object with a long stride and a reach to a target (weight transfer).
3. Accent the coordination of the arm movement and leg stride in throwing to a target by using a verbal cue, hand clap, or drum beat (weight transfer).

Movements with Emphasis on Range, Level, and Direction

1. Throw moving the arm in a small, medium, or large arc.
2. Throw to a low, chest high, or high target.
3. Vary the target challenges so throws require differing arcs.

Movement with Emphasis on Combination,
Environment, and Creative Expression

1. With a two arm overhand pattern, throw an object at the target.
2. Pretend to throw the ball over a tall tree, a wide river, a low fence, or into a mud puddle.
3. Run and throw an object to a target.
4. Throw an object at a moving target such as an old tire or cageball.
5. Throw an object to a target and hop, skip, run, or crawl to retrieve your object.

Basket Catch
(With Arms)

Verbal Description

The basket catch is generally the first absorptive pattern developed by young children. This follows the cephalocaudal and proximoldistal principles of development. The arms and body are used to stop the motion of the ball or thrown object coming toward the child. The object is clasped to the body in order to absorb the force of the ball. The basket catch is composed of the following movements:

1. The feet are apart with one foot slightly ahead of the other. The body weight is placed on the forward foot and the knees are relaxed.
2. The arms are extended in the direction of the ball, waist high, slightly bent, and palms up.
3. The eyes are kept on the ball as it approaches.
4. The arms close around it and bring it to the body.
5. The knees bend slightly, and the weight is shifted to the rear foot in the follow-through phase of the catch.

Visual Description

Common Problems

1. Inability to maintain control of the object.
2. Fingers kept straight rather than slightly flexed.
3. Failure to close the arms around the object.
4. Taking the eyes off the object (looking away).
5. Failure to "give" with the catch and to pull it into the body.

Concepts Children Should Know

1. Make a "basket" with your arms.
2. Watch the ball.
3. Give with the ball as it makes contact.
4. Hug the ball to your chest.
5. The basket catch is used in fielding a punted ball in football and whenever you catch a large, heavy, or bulky object.

Movement Variations of the Basket Catch (with arms)

Movement with Emphasis on the Base of Support and Body Position

1. Catch a large object with the feet in a stride or straddle position with the feet close together or spread wide apart.
2. Catch a large object in an upright, crouched, kneeling, or sitting position.

Movements with Emphasis on Speed, Rhythm, Flow, and Force

1. Catch a large object that is traveling at various speeds and forces.
2. Catch a large object that is thrown and emphasize the smoothness in absorbing the impact. The rhythm and flow here would be dependent on the speed, size, and weight of the object as well as the child's coordination in absorbing the force.

Movements with Emphasis on Range, Level, and Direction

1. Catch an object that is thrown chest high, stomach high, or knee high.
2. Catch an object that is thrown with a high, medium, or slight arc.
3. Catch an object thrown from various angles.
4. Catch an object that has been bounced up or from a distance.

Movements with Emphasis on Combination,
Environment, and Creative Expression

1. Catch an object while hopping, jumping, or running.
2. Toss an object up and catch it on the bounce or in the air.
3. Catch an object while walking forward, sideward, or backward.
4. Catch a balloon, a towel, a pillow, or a playground ball.
5. Toss and catch an object while balancing or moving on a bench or low balance beam.
6. Catch an object like you were a robot or rag doll.

Underhand and Overhand Catch

Verbal Description

The elements of the underhand and overhand catch are essentially the same. The major difference is in the position of the hands upon impact with the object. The underhand catch is performed when the object to be caught is below the waist. The palms of the hands and the wrists are turned upward. When the object is above the waist the palms face away from the individual in the direction of the flight of the object. The fundamental underhand and overhand catching patterns are composed of the following movements.

1. The feet are slightly apart with one foot slightly ahead of the other. The knees are slightly bent and the body weight is shifted in the direction of the object.
2. The arms are extended in the direction of the object but remain slightly bent.
3. The hands are in close proximity to one another.
4. The fingers point either up or down and *away* from the oncoming object (in order to avoid jamming).
5. As the object contacts the hands the fingers wrap around it and the arms and legs "give" in order to absorb its momentum.
6. The weight of the body is shifted backward with the catch.
7. The larger the object and the more force with which it is traveling the more "give" there should be.

Visual Description

OVERHAND CATCH   UNDERHAND CATCH

Common Problems

1. Failure to maintain control of the object.
2. Failure to "give" with the catch.
3. Keeping the fingers rigid and straight in the direction of the object causing jamming

4. Failure to adjust the hand position to the height of the object.
5. Inability to vary the catching pattern for objects of different weight and force.
6. Taking the eyes off the object.
7. Improper stance (that is, a straddle rather than a stride position in the direction of the oncoming object) causing loss of balance when catching a fast moving ball.
8. Closing the hands either too early or too late.
9. Failure to keep the body in line with the ball (that is, reaching out to the side to catch).

Concepts Children Should Know

1. Get directly in the path of the ball.
2. Place one foot ahead of the other.
3. Adjust your hand position for the height of the ball.
   a. Thumbs in—above the waist.
   b. Thumbs out—below the waist.
4. Curve your fingers and keep your eyes on the ball.
5. Pull the ball in toward your body.

Catching A Ball Is A Complex Task Requiring Considerable Coordination Of The Hands And Eyes

6. "Give" with the ball.
7. This catching pattern is used in several sports activities such as football, baseball, basketball and is basic to receiving the force of any object with your hands.

Movement Variations of the Underhand and Overhand Catch

The movement variations mentioned for the basket catch are suitable for these two types of catching also. The greater coordination of the eyes and hands with the underhand and overhand catching patterns allow for more complex variations. Some additional activities more specific to these two forms of catching might include:

1. Catch an object with two hands at the ankles, knees, hips, chest, shoulders, or head (body position level).
2. Catch an object with two hands and emphasize the arm give (rhythm, force, flow).
   a. "Catch the object with your arms straight."
   b. "Catch the object with your arms bent."
   c. "Catch the object with your arms straight and bring the object close to your body" (arm flexion).
3. Catch an object that is thrown to the left or right side of the body and at various heights (body position level).
4. Attempt to catch a small object with one hand, that is rolled, bounced, or thrown at various heights (body position level).
5. Catch a rolling or bouncing ball with two hands (body position level).
6. Catch an object and throw it to a target or partner (environment).
7. Catch an object and walk or skip in a circle (combination).
8. Throw or roll an object against a wall and catch it ont he rebound (environment).

Trapping

Verbal Description

Trapping an object is actually a form of catching in which the feet or body are used to absorb the force of the ball rather than the hands and arms. Trapping is a skill that must be highly refined in order to successfully play the game of soccer. With young children, however, trapping should be viewed in very general terms, namely the ability to stop a ball without use of the hands or arms. Trapping in young children involves the following.

1. The path of the ball is first determined.
2. The body is positioned in such a manner that it is directly in front of the on-coming ball.
3. The eyes are kept on the ball at all times.
4. As the ball contacts the body part it envelops the ball and gives with its force.

Visual Description

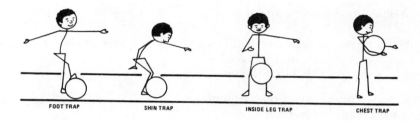

FOOT TRAP   SHIN TRAP   INSIDE LEG TRAP   CHEST TRAP

Common Problems

1. Failure to position the body directly in the path of the ball.
2. Failure to keep the eyes fixed on the ball.
3. Failure to "give" as the ball contacts the body part.

Concepts Children Should Know

1. Get directly in the path of the ball.
2. Keep your eyes on the ball.
3. "Give" with the ball as it touches the body part.
4. The trapping patterns are basic to the sport of soccer and any activity in which your feet are used to stop an object.

Movement Variations of Trapping

Movements with Emphasis on the Base of Support and Body Position

1. Trap an object while standing on both feet, one foot, kneeling, or in a crab position.
2. Using the above positions, trap an object using the feet, knees, shins, thighs, seat, or stomach.

Movements with Emphasis on Speed, Rhythm, Flow, and Force

1. Trap an object traveling at different speeds.
2. Trap an object emphasizing the smoothness of absorbing the force with the body part used.
   a. "Place your foot in front of a rolling object."
   b. "Move your foot back as the object touches your foot and slowly stop the object."

Movements with the Emphasis on Range, Level, and Direction

1. Trap an object by blocking it with very little or a lot of give in the movement.
2. Trap objects thrown at different heights with the feet, knees, or chest.
3. Trap objects thrown from different angles.
4. Trap objects thrown with different arcs.

Movements with the Emphasis on Combination, Environment, and Creative Expression

1. Roll a ball against the wall and trap it with one foot, both feet or the shins.
2. Stop a fleece ball by letting it touch your body very lightly—jump or dodge backward.
3. Trap a rolling ball, bouncing ball, or a ball in flight while moving.
4. Trap a ball rolled by a partner.
5. Trap a ball rolling down an incline board.
6. Trap a ball and pretend your body is a rock, a rubber band, or a pillow.

Striking

Verbal Description

There is a tremendous dearth of information concerning the evolution of striking in children. The first striking movements (other than kicking) appear in young children whenever they hit an object with their hand or an implement. Striking a balloon with the hand or swinging at a ball in flight, or on the ground with an implement is familiar to most children. The sidearm and underhand striking patterns are similar to one another and to the various throwing patterns. Striking is composed of the following fundamental movements coordinated together in a rhythmical fashion.

1. The body is placed in a position with the left side facing the general direction in which the object will travel (right handed striking pattern).
2. The feet are placed a comfortable distance apart (about shoulder width).

3. The striking implement is gripped with a "thumbs around" grasp with both hands touching.
4. The eyes are kept on the ball throughout the movement.
5. The body weight shifts in the direction of the intended hit.
6. The hips turn rapidly in the direction of the weight shift.
7. The arms swing around and the implement contacts the ball when the arms are fully extended and the ball is directly in front of the body.
8. The arms continue to swing in an arc (follow-through).

Visual Description

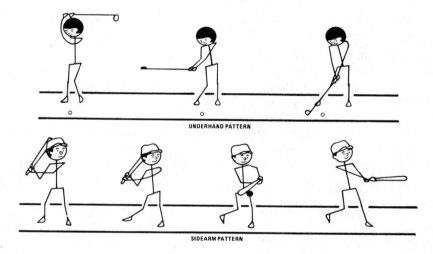

UNDERHAND PATTERN

SIDEARM PATTERN

Common Problems

1. Failure to keep the eyes on the ball.
2. Improper grip.
3. Failure to turn the side of the body in the direction of the intended flight.
4. Inability to sequence the movements in rapid succession in a coordinated manner.
5. Poor backswing.
6. "Chopping" swing.

Concepts Children Should Know

1. Be sure that your hands are touching when you grip the bat and that your right hand is on top of the left (right hand pattern).
2. Keep your eyes on the ball.

3. Shift your weight back then forward as you swing.
4. Make a level swing and hit the ball when your arms are out straight.
5. Follow-through in the direction that the ball is to go.
6. The striking pattern is basic to many sports activities. Some sports use striking with the hand as the implement such as in handball and volleyball. Others use an implement such as in baseball, hockey, golf, tennis, or squash racquets.

Movement Variations of Striking

Movements with Emphasis on Base of Support and Body Position

1. Strike an object with one hand or an implement held by one hand while standing with the feet in a stride or straddle positon and either close together or far apart.
2. Repeat the above using two hands or an implement held with two hands.
3. Utilize the underhand, sidearm or overhand patterns with one or both hands to strike an object.
4. Use the above striking patterns while standing, kneeling, sitting, or lying.
5. Lean the trunk forward, backward and to the sides when utilizing the different striking patterns.

Movements with Emphasis on Speed, Rhythm, Flow, and Force

1. Strike a stationary, resting, rolling, or airborne object lightly, firmly, slowly or quickly.
2. Strike an object and emphasize the follow-through beyond the point of contact.
3. Strike an object so that a verbal cue or drum beat accentuates the point of contact and the transfer of weight.

Movements with Emphasis on Range, Level, and Direction

1. Strike an object rolling on the floor or airborne at different levels with one hand, two hands or with an implement.
2. Strike at an object from above or below, from the right or left and from other angles.
3. Strike at an object from above or below, from the right or left and from other angles.

Movements with Emphasis on Combination,
Environment, and Creative Expression

1. Strike a rolling object with the hand as you walk or run alongside.
2. Strike an airborne object and skip to retrieve the ball.

3. Strike a stationary object on a tee with an implement while balancing on one foot.
4. Use a short striking action and roll or slide an object along a bench or balance beam.
5. Using an implement, strike a vertical or horizontal pole with colored targets.
6. Strike an object into the air and catch it.
7. Toss a beanbag into the air and strike it with a sidearm movement.
8. Strike an object as if you were angry, strong, a jack hammer, a giant, or an elf.

Volleying

Verbal Description

Volleying is a form of striking in which an overhand pattern is used. It is a movement similar to the two handed set shot that used to be popular in basketball, and is similar to the overhead set shot used in power volleyball. The following movements are found in volleying.

1. The feet are placed in a stride position with the knees slightly flexed.
2. The arms are held in front of the face with the elbows facing outward, the thumbs in, and the fingers spread.
3. The fingers are tense, the wrists stiff, and the hands close together.
4. The head is elevated and the eyes are kept on the flight of the ball.
5. As the ball makes contact with the outspread fingers and thumbs the body extends upward to meet the ball.
6. The arms straighten and the fingers and wrist remain stiff.
7. After the ball has been contacted the arms follow through in an upward and outward motion.

Visual Description

Common Problems

1. Failure to keep the eyes on the ball.
2. Inability to accurately judge the flight of the ball and to time the movements of the body properly.
3. Failure to keep the fingers and wrists stiff.
4. Failure to extend all of the joints upon contacting the ball.
5. Lack of follow-through.
6. Inability to contact the ball with both hands simultaneously.

Concepts Children Should Know

1. Get into position directly beneath the ball.
2. Watch the flight of the ball between the opening formed by your two hands.
3. Extend the arms and legs as the ball touches your finger tips.
4. Keep the fingers and wrist stiff throughout.
5. Follow-through in the direction that the ball is to go.
6. Volleying is a striking pattern that is used in many games and in the sport of volleyball.

Movement Variations of Volleying

Volleying essentially is a two hand striking pattern that emphasizes an upward jabbing motion of the hands and arms. The variations mentioned in the striking section may be used as a guide for modifying volleying activities. Some additional activities more specific to volleying might include:

1. By volleying, keep a balloon, or beach ball in the air (rhythm, force, direction).
2. Throw a beach ball in the air and volley it to a wall or over an obstacle (environment).
3. Volley a beach ball or balloon while hopping, jumping, or walking (combination).
4. Volley a balloon while standing, sitting, kneeling, or lying on your back (base of support and body position).
5. Volley the balloon as high or as low as possible (force, direction).

Kicking

Verbal Description

Kicking is a form of striking in which the foot is used to impart force to an object. This is the only form of striking that does not directly involve the use of the arms. Very little research has been conducted into the kicking ability of children. Only the general kicking pattern will be outlined here. Precise variations of the kicking action may be accomplished by making adjustments with the kicking leg and by bringing the arms and trunk into play. The primary factors that influence the type of kick used are: (1) the desired trajectory of the ball, and (2) the height of the ball when it is contacted. The fundamental kicking pattern for a stationary ground ball is composed of the following movements combined in a coordinated manner.

1. The body is stationed one step behind the ball slightly to the left (right footed kick). Keep the eyes on the ball.
2. A step is taken on the left foot placing it to the left of the ball. This serves to rotate the pelvis and to extend the thigh of the kicking leg.
3. The right leg is swung backward while flexing at the hip and knee.
4. The lower portion of the kicking leg is extended forcefully. Contact is made with the instep of the right foot.
5. The arms are used in opposition to one another throughout the kicking motion.
6. The follow-through is with the right leg in the direction of the target.

Visual Description

Common Problems

1. Restricted or absent backswing.
2. Failure to step forward with the nonkicking leg.
3. Tendency to lose balance.
4. Inability to kick with either foot.
5. Inability to alter the speed of the kicked ball.
6. Jabbing at the ball without any follow-through.
7. Poor opposition of the arms and legs.
8. Failure to use a summation of forces by the body to contribute to the force of the kick.
9. Failure to contact the ball squarely or missing it completely (eyes not focused on ball).
10. Failure to get adequate distance (lack of follow-through and force).

Concepts Children Should Know

1. Stand behind and slightly to the side of the ball.
2. Step forward on the nonkicking foot.
3. Keep your eyes on the ball.
4. Swing your kicking leg back then forcefully forward from the knee.
5. Contact the ball with the top portion of your foot (elevated ball) or with the inside portion of your foot (ground ball).
6. Follow-through in the direction that the ball is to go.
7. Use your arms for balance.
8. The kicking pattern is basic to the sport of soccer and is used in kicking games such as kickball.

Movement Variations of Kicking

Movements with Emphasis on the Base of Support and Body Position

1. Kick an object while standing on one foot, in a crab position, in a sitting or lying position.
2. Kick an object while in a stretched or curled position.
3. Kick an object with the arms held overhead, to the sides or in opposition.
4. Kick an object with the toe, heel, instep or inside or outside of the foot.

Movements with Emphasis on Speed, Rhythm, Flow, and Force

1. Kick an object lightly, forcefully, flowly, or quickly.
2. Kick an object with the rhythmical accent or drum beat placed to coincide with contact of the foot with the object.

Movements with Emphasis on Range, Level, and Direction

1. Kick an object using a small, medium, or large kicking motion.
2. Kick an object at the ground, knee, or chest level.
3. Kick an object forward, backward, or to the sides.
4. Kick an object to a near, far, low, or high target.

*Movements with Emphasis on Combination,
Environment, and Creative Expression*

1. Swing the kicking leg forward and back or from side to side with a beanbag balanced on the instep.
2. Toss a beanbag on the instep to a target, over the head or up into the hands.
3. Walk and kick an object through an obstacle course.

4. Pretend you are kicking a soccer goal or punting a football.
5. With a kicking action, slide a beanbag to a partner. Trap the beanbag with the foot when it is kicked back.
6. Kick a large, small, light, or heavy object.
7. Kick an object to or through a target.
8. Kick an object to a target, skip to retrieve it, and carry it back to your kicking area.
9. Repeat the above task only kick the object over or under a large piece of apparatus.

Bouncing an Object

Verbal Description

Bouncing a ball requires the individual to push the ball to the ground with one or both hands in such a manner that it will rebound and can be caught or pushed down again (dribbling). The fundamental bouncing pattern is composed of the following coordinated movements.

1. The feet are placed in a narrow stride position with one foot slightly forward.
2. The ball is held in both hands (or one hand depending on the size of the ball) at waist height.
3. The body weight is placed on the forward foot with a slight forward lean of the trunk.
4. The ball is pushed to the ground with one or both hands and follows through in that direction.
5. As the ball rebounds from the ground it is caught with the hands (as described in the catching section) or it is pushed down toward the ground again (dribbling).
6. When dribbling the ball is pushed with the finger tips.

Visual Description

Common Problems

1. Slapping at the ball rather than pushing it.
2. Irregular bounce and return caused by pushing unevenly with both hands or pushing on an angle.
3. Failure to keep the eyes focused on the ball results in catching problems.
4. Insufficient follow-through on the push causing the ball to fail to return to waist height.
5. Inappropriate force applied to the ball.

Concepts Children Should Know

1. Push the ball down.
2. Keep the wrist stiff.
3. Use your finger tips.
4. Follow-through.
5. The bouncing pattern is used in the sport of basketball and anytime you bounce and catch, or dribble, a ball in a game or rhythmic activity.

Movement Variations of Bouncing an Object

Bouncing an object utilizes a controlled downward striking action against a surface that results in a rebound. The striking and volleying variations may serve as a guide for modifications of bouncing. Some additional activities more specific to bouncing an object might include.

1. Drop the ball from above the head and let it bounce once before catching it (combination).
2. Throw the ball down as hard or as gently as possible to see how high or low the ball can be bounced (force, level, direction).
3. Bounce the ball while standing, sitting or kneeling (base of support and body position).
4. Bounce a ball with two hands at chest, hip, or knee height (level).
5. Using a two hand overhand or underhand throw, bounce a ball into a box on the first bounce (combination, environment).
6. Throw an object against a wall and catch it on the first bounce (combination, environment).
7. Dribble the ball with two hands while walking (combination).
8. Dribble the ball with one hand while moving (combination).
9. Bounce objects of different sizes and weights such as a 14″ or 8″ playground ball, a softball, a rubber ball, and a tennis ball (environment).
10. Bounce a ball on a hard floor or on a mat (environment).

Rolling an Object

Verbal Description

The young child makes many attempts at rolling objects early in life. There is, however, little information available concerning its emergence. Based on the observation of children, the rolling pattern appears to be composed of the following movements.

1. The left foot is placed slightly ahead of the right (rolling with the right hand). The body weight is evenly distributed over both feet.
2. The right hand is placed under the ball and the left on top when rolling a large ball. The ball is grasped from behind with the right hand only when rolling a small ball (right hand roll).
3. The body weight is transferred to the rear foot, the arms swing backward, and the trunk bends forward at the waist all in the same motion.
4. The knees bend slightly, the arms swing forward, and the left foot steps forward all in a coordinated manner.
5. The ball is released close to the ground when the right hand is close to the left foot. Be sure that the left hand is taken off the ball first. It serves only to stabilize a large ball.
6. The right arm follows through in the direction of the target and the right foot is brought forward. The eyes are kept on the target at all times.

Visual Description

Common Problems

1. Failure to transfer the body weight to the rear foot.
2. Placing the hands on the wrong portion of the ball.
3. Releasing the ball too high, causing it to bounce.
4. Releasing the ball at the wrong angle causing it to veer to one side.
5. Lack of follow-through resulting in a weak roll.
6. Swinging the arms too far backward or out to the side.
7. Failure to keep the eyes on the target.
8. Failure to step forward with the left foot.
9. Inability to bring the ball to the side of the body.

Concepts Children Should Know

1. Stand with your right foot leading.
2. Swing your arm straight back as you rock back on your rear foot.
3. Step out on your forward foot as you swing your arm forward.
4. Let go of the ball when it is next to your front foot.
5. Keep your eyes on the target and follow-through in the desired direction.
6. The rolling pattern is basic to the sport of bowling and used in rolling games such as Pin Guard and Guard the Castle.

Movement Variations of Rolling an Object

Rolling an object in most cases utilizes an underhanded throwing pattern. Reference can again be made to the movement variations listed in the previous underhand throwing patterns for one or two hands. Some additional activities specific to rolling an object might include.

1. While lying on the floor, roll the ball around yourself (base of support and body position).

Rolling A Ball With Precision
Takes Practice

2. Roll an object at a target while sitting, kneeling, standing, or in a straddle seat position (base of support and body position).
3. Roll an object softly, smoothly, quickly, slowly, forcefully, or at an angle (force, direction).
4. Initiate rolling movements with a sound of a hand clap, drum beat, or ball skill records (rhythm).
5. Roll an object against a wall, between two boxes, at an Indian Club, over an incline board, or under a wicket (environment).
6. Roll an object on the floor, on a bench, on a beam, and down a slide (environment).
7. Toss the object in the air, let it bounce, catch it, and roll it into a box (combination).
8. Pretend the object you are rolling is very heavy or very light (creative expression).
9. Roll a cageball, basketball, playground ball, soccer ball, softball, wiffle ball, tennis ball, baseball, ping pong ball, or marble (environment).
10. Roll an object on a hard floor, on a mat, up or down an incline board, over a maze of ropes, or on grass or dirt surfaces outside (environment).
11. Pretend you are rolling a boulder or a log. (Pushing an object by placing the hands above and or behind it, is another form of rolling.) (creative expression).

MANIPULATION EXPERIENCES FOR PRESCHOOL AND PRIMARY GRADE CHILDREN

The fundamental movement patterns of manipulation are generally more complex than either the stability or locomotor movements, in isolation or in combination. Manipulation fundamentals rely on previous stability and locomotor experiences to give the child a balanced feeling as the weight is transferred in giving force to, or receiving force from an object. The reliance of manipulative patterns on stability and locomotor experiences suggests an even greater stress on the importance of movement progressions. In addition to being influenced by the child's developmental level and previous movement experiences, fundamental manipulation progressions are greatly influenced by the equipment used, the degree of dynamic balance required of the child and to some degree the order in which the manipulative fundamentals are taught. The equipment used to teach manipulative skills varies in size and weight and sometimes shape. Developmentally we know the young child's movements are gross in nature and gradually become more refined to allow for greater control of the body parts. This fact suggests to teachers that large objects rather than small objects are usually more appropriate in the early stages of learning to catch, throw, roll, or kick. Knowing this fact does not mean that children should not be allowed to explore small objects with their manipulative skills, but it does mean that children might experience success more frequently if the objects used are more appropriate to their developmental level. In the early stages of teaching throwing and catching, the use of scarves or balloons might be very effective. Usually both are colorful and attract the child's attention, but more important than this, is that both of these objects descend very slowly and allow the child to make a successful catch using his or her otherwise inept gross motor movements. The use of scarves and beanbags at the early stages also eliminates the child's distraction or frustration that often times results when a missed ball rolls away. Playground balls of varying sizes can also be used. Ordinarily, a large ball is used first with a smaller ball being used when the child has more control. Selection of a ball that is too large for the child is a possible error also, unless your goal is to teach pushing and striking skills rather than throwing and catching skills. Generally the characteristics of the equipment utilized in the progression suggest moving from (1) large to small, (2) soft to hard, (3) light to heavy, and (4) little rebound to greater rebound qualities.

The degree of dynamic balance required of the child and his or her developmental capabilities will suggest to the teacher the types of activities as well as the fundamental manipulative patterns that should be incorporated into a lesson. The child's static or dynamic balance as well as his coordination will determine his ability to transfer his weight and effectively coordinate the summation of forces into a throw or catch or other manipulative movement.

The recognition by the teacher that balance, weight transfer, and the summation of forces are affected by developmental and experiential variables leads to the third point that possibly the order in which the fundamentals are taught is important. Since several patterns can be developing simultaneously and varied experiences are recommended, a strict manipulative progression cannot be set forth. However, it would seem that on the basis of the child's development of body control that the manipulative movements might progress from pushing and pulling to lifting and carrying, from rolling and stopping to two handed throwing and catching, from kicking and striking to bouncing and trapping, and then to one hand throws and catches. Although the manipulative patterns are largely dependent on the development of stability and locomotor patterns, educators sometimes attempt to teach throwing and catching and other manipulative skills in isolation. The result is a structured learning environment that may cause the child to develop splinter skills and inhibit his passing through the exploratory, discovery, and indirect combination experiences that give the child a broad manipulative movement base. A movement education approach is recommended. The teacher can utilize the movement variations in this chapter and refer to the stability chapter for information concerning movement education themes. Several examples of exploratory, discovery, indirect and direct combination experiences will now be elaborated.

Exploratory Experiences

The teacher suggests or challenges but refrains from setting a "correct" model for performance.

1. "How many different positions can you be in and throw your beanbag?"
2. "How many different directions can you throw your beanbag?"
3. "How many ways can you stop the ball?"
4. "Throw like a robot or rag doll."
5. "How many different ways can you use a beanbag, fleece ball, or playground ball with a cardboard box, target, hoop, tire, or cageball?"

Discovery Experiences

The teacher places qualifications or limitations on movements as the children explore, discover, and share experiences. Here the teacher begins to stress the qualities of movement or the mechanics desired.

1. "Throw the beanbag so it lands between the two ropes."
2. "How many ways can you be moving and use a two hand underhand throw?"
3. "How many different things can you be on and still use a vertical toss?"
4. "What can you do while bouncing a ball?"
5. "How many body parts can you use to hit the cageball?"

Indirect Combination Experiences

The teacher continues to qualify or limit movements so that previous movements become progressively more difficult to perform. The teacher asks the children to combine several movements in creating their own combinations.

1. "Can you walk and kick a ball?"
2. "Can you bounce a ball while bending and turning?"
3. "Can you trap and kick a ball differently each time?"
4. "Can you roll an object so that it begins to bounce?"
5. "What can you do with your beanbag while you are skipping?"

Direct Combination Experiences

The teacher suggests, demonstrates, or drills the children in the desired skill form to be used.

1. "Can you kick or dribble a ball around the markers?"
2. "Roll your ball against the wall, catch it, carry it to and throw it through the hoop and trap it before it passes the black line."
3. "Roll your ball up the incline bench. When it drops off, dribble it to the circle."
4. "Strike the fleece ball with your hand so that it goes to the target."
5. "Field a rolling ball and use a one hand overhand throw to your partner."

The more traditional curriculum content areas of games, rhythms, and self-testing might be thought of as direct combination experiences. As you will recall from the previous chapters, the teacher can use direct or indirect teaching approaches separately or in combination, depending on the communication and physical skills the children possess.

Games

The content area of games emphasizes low organized games and relays for preschool and primary age children. The manipulative games used here might in some cases be considered lead-up games to sports skills. This concept is acceptable since the fundamental patterns being taught often are readily applicable to sports skills when the children eventually begin refining these movements. The isolation of certain sports skills on the other hand, may often serve as the basis for drills. The teacher can utilize these drill type situations by modifying the activity in accordance with the developmental level of the children and by including game or contest elements. The list of games that follows are representative of manipulation oriented games. These games as well as others may be modified to incorporate developmentally suitable manipulative skills. The game of circle soccer for example, calls for a circle of standing children to kick a ball by or between the children on the opposing half of the circle. If these children have had little kicking experience, it might be advisable to first have the children sit in that circle formation and kick a large soft object from this more stable base of support. If their kicking performances are more advanced, the base of support for kicking might become a one leg balanced position, or different types of kicks using the inside and outside of the foot. The game objectives can remain the same, but rolling or throwing skills might be used instead of kicking. The manipulative relays are task oriented in nature and can be used in isolation or in relay situations. As previously mentioned, the teacher must be aware of the children's abilities to understand the team concept that is essential in relay activities.

Manipulative Low Organized Games and Relays

1. Leader Group Ball[12] (rolling and catching)
2. Hit the Pin[12] (rolling)
3. Circle Stride Ball[4] (rolling and catching)
4. Circle Roll Ball[1] (rolling)
5. Sink the Ship (rolling)
6. Shoot the Circle[1] (rolling)
7. Charlie Brown[15] (throwing)
8. Ring Call Ball[3] (vertical toss)
9. Center Base[3] (throwing)
10. Dodgeball[3] (throwing)
11. Run the Gauntlet[3] (throwing)
12. Steal the Bacon[1] (carrying)
13. Teacher in Class[1] (throwing and catching)
14. Race the Ball[1] (throwing and catching)
15. Stop Ball[1] (throwing and catching)
16. Guard the Castle[1] (throwing, rolling and catching)
17. Catch the Bat[15] (catching)
18. Plug[15] (throwing)
19. Poison[15] (kicking or striking)
20. Over and Under[15] (passing)
21. Hot Ball[15] (throwing)
22. Throw It and Run[15] (throwing)
23. Tunnel Ball[8] (rolling and catching)
24. Keep Away[8] (catching and throwing)
25. Beanbag Basket[8] (throwing)
26. Duck on the Rock[8] (throwing)
27. Hit the Basket[4] (throwing)
28. Kneel Ball[4] (throwing and catching)
29. Circle Toss Ball[2] (throwing, rolling and catching)
30. Circle Pole Ball[2] (throwing)
31. Ball Distance Throw[12] (throwing)
32. Back Ball[12] (throwing and catching)
33. Danish Rounders[1] (kicking, catching and throwing)
34. O'Leary[12] (bouncing)
35. Circle Bounce[12] (bouncing)
36. Kick Ball[3] (kicking, throwing and catching)
37. Going Through School[1] (bouncing and catching)
38. Seven Down[1] (tossing, bouncing and catching)
39. Beater Goes Round[15] (striking)
40. Circle Kick Ball[15] (kicking)
41. Shower Ball[15] (volleying)
42. Cageball[15] (volleying)
43. Ball Race[8] (bouncing)
44. Two Squares[9] (bouncing and catching)
45. Bat Ball (throwing or striking)
46. Boundary Ball[3] (throwing, kicking and trapping)
47. Battle Ball[8] (kicking and trapping)
48. Crab Soccer[8] (kicking)
49. Scotter Soccer[8] (kicking)

Relays

50. Fetch and Carry[15] (carrying)
51. Run and Roll Relay[15] (rolling and catching)
52. Zigzag Relay[1] (throwing, rolling and catching)
53. Stick and Ball Relay[8] (manipulation)
54. Line Dribble Relay[8] (manipulation)
55. Shuttle Dribble Relay[8] (kicking)
56. Wall Volley Relay[8] (volleying)

Rhythms

Manipulative related rhythm activities are somewhat dependent on the children's ability to coordinate their movements in giving or receiving force. The child's personal rhythm remains dominant, but musical cues of a verbal or instrumental nature may be utilized to emphasize the preparatory and follow-through rhythms as well as the point of applying or absorbing force. Singing games, drum beats, and records can serve as the musical accompaniment or guide for manipulative activities. Some of the rhythms included in the suggested locomotor activities section can be modified by including a manipulation skill. Jump Jim Jo, for example, can use the bounce in place of the jump. Many activities can be created by the teacher to emphasize the rhythmical aspects of manipulative skills.

Self-Testing Activities

The nature of manipulative activities tends to link some of the subcategories of self-testing activities, namely, fundamental movement patterns, physical fitness and small manipulative apparatus, into one large facet of self-testing. It is difficult to separate these subcategories because fundamental movement patterns relate directly to the small manipulative apparatus and fitness items. However, for the purposes of explanation, the term fundamental movement patterns refers here specifically to manipulative movements. The category of small manipulative apparatus will then be included with the stunts and tumbling and large apparatus categories. The reason for this grouping is that small manipulative apparatus has environmental implications as to the way in which manipulative movements can be used. These two consolidated self-testing categories will now be briefly explained.

The manipulative patterns and skills and physical fitness activities related to manipulative movements are usually presented in the form of a challenge by the teacher. "How far can you throw or kick?" "How many times can you bounce the ball?" "How many times can you hit the target?" These types of challenges give children feedback concerning their skill, form, and accuracy. The teacher can utilize the movement variations suggested in this chapter as a basis for developing appropriate challenge statements.

Small manipulative apparatus, stunts and tumbling and large apparatus emphasizes the fundamentals of manipulation in combination with other forms of movement. Fleece or yarn balls, scarves, beanbags, playground balls, soccer balls, volleyballs, cageballs, medicine balls, rubber balls, tennis or ping-pong balls, lummi sticks, and rhythm sticks are all examples of small manipulative apparatus that can be used as implements in teaching such patterns as throwing, catching, kicking, and striking. Other small manipulative apparatus such as hoops and tires as well as the equipment already mentioned can be used to serve as targets or obstacles in teaching throwing, kicking, or striking movements.

Stunts and tumbling and large apparatus activities related to manipulative skills are also combination type experiences. Performing a forward roll over a ball, a forward roll in the game of Call Ball or throwing and catching a beanbag on a balance beam are all examples of using manipulative movements in combination with stunts and tumbling and large apparatus activities.

The purpose of this chapter has been to identify and elaborate upon several fundamental manipulative movements. The basic concepts of manipulation have been presented through the movement variations of the fundamentals as well as several examples of application of these variations in the movement education and traditional curricula.

SELECTED REFERENCES

1. Anderson, Marian, Elliot, M. E., and LaBerge, J. *Play with a Purpose: Elementary School Physical Education*. New York: Harper and Row Publishers, 1972.
2. Andrews, Gladys, Saurborn, J., and Schneider, E. *Physical Education for Today's Boys and Girls*. Boston: Allyn and Bacon, Inc., 1966.
3. Fabricus, Helen. *Physical Education for the Classroom Teacher: A Physical Education Curriculum for Elementary School Children*. Dubuque, Iowa: Wm. C. Brown Company Publishers, 1974.
4. Fait, Hollis. *Physical Education for the Elementary School Child: Experience in Movement*. Philadelphia: W.B. Saunders Company, 1971.
5. Gallahue, David L., and Meadors, W.J. *Let's Move: A Physical Education Program for Elementary School Teachers*, Dubuque Iowa: Kendall/Hunt Publishers, 1974.
6. Godfrey, Barbara, and Kephart N.C. *Movement Patterns and Motor Education*. New York: Appleton-Century-Crofts, 1969.
7. Keogh, Jack. "Motor Performance of Elementary School Children." Department of Physical Education. Los Angeles: University of California, 1965.
8. Kirchner, Glenn. *Physical Education for Elementary School Children*. Dubuque, Iowa: Wm. C. Brown Company Publishers, 1974.
9. Kirchner, Glenn, Cunningham, J., and Warrell, E. *Introduction to Movement Education: An Individualized Approach to Teaching Physical Education*. Dubuque, Iowa: Wm. C. Brown Company Publishers, 1970.
10. Luedke, George. *Developmental Skills: Progressions and Related Activities*. Unpublished paper. Edwardsville, Illinois: Southern Illinois University, 1970.
11. Moehn, Larry, and Luedke, G. *Methods and Materials in Elementary Physical Education*. Unpublished course syllabus. Edwardsville, Illinois: Southern Illinois University, 1970.
12. Nagel, Charles, and Moore, F. *Skill Development Through Games and Rhythmic Activities*. Palo Alto, California: The National Press, 1966.
13. Plagenhoef, Stanley. *Patterns of Human Motion*. Englewood Cliffs, New Jersey: Prentice-Hall, 1971.
14. Schurr, Evelyn. *Movement Experiences for Children: Curriculum and Methods for Elementary School Physical Education*. New York: Appleton-Century-Crofts, 1967.
15. Vannier, Maryhelen, Foster, M., and Gallahue, D.L. *Teaching Physical Education in Elementary Schools*. Philadelphia: W. B. Saunders Company, 1973.
16. Wickstrom, Ralph. *Fundamental Motor Patterns*. Philadelphia: Lea and Febiger, 1970.

Chapter 8
Developing General and Specific Concepts of Stabilization, Locomotion, and Manipulation

Key Concept: Children in the intermediate and upper elementary grades are in the process of developing and refining their general and specific movement skills primarily through the use of combination and selection type movement experiences.

Content: Introduction

Combination and Selection Experiences Related to Games

    Specific Skill Experiences Related to Basketball

    Specific Skill Experiences Related to Football

    Specific Skill Experiences Related to Soccer

    Specific Skill Experiences Related to Softball

    Specific Skill Experiences Related to Volleyball

Combination and Selection Experiences Related to Rhythms

Combination and Selection Experiences Related to Self-Testing

Developing General and Specific Concepts of Stabilization, Locomotion, and Manipulation

INTRODUCTION

By the third grade most children are beginning to develop *general* and *specific* movement skills in the areas of locomotion, manipulation, and stability. These phases of motor development are most prevalent between the eighth and thirteenth years of life. The emphasis on general and specific movement skills at this time results from the increase in the child's performance level potential. The children as well as the teacher are becoming more concerned with the degree of skill, accuracy, and form that is used in performing a movement. With this concern for refinement, the teacher now relies heavily on direct combination and selection learning experiences. The exploratory, discovery, and indirect combination learning experiences of the preschool and primary years provide children with a solid foundation of movement patterns. It is this solid foundation that will help children reach their developmental potential in the general and specific movement skill phases of motor development. Both the direct combination and selection experiences used in these phases of motor development place a premium on the teacher's direction of the children's movement activities. Direct combination experiences call for the teacher to establish a correct model for performance. The selection experiences then return to a recognition of individual differences, and the teacher helps the children select the best approximations of the model performance based on their body type and capabilities. The result is an improvement of their performance level. This goal of developing skill through combination and selection experiences may take on an emphasis that results in a learning environment that is highly structured. Too much structure and emphasis on the end result can lead to feelings of failure. *The teacher must remember that the learning process still entails progressing through the exploratory, discovery, and indirect combination experiences prior to being ready for the direct combination and selection experiences.* If a child is having difficulty succeeding, a return to these lower order movement experiences might be very helpful to the child's learning as well as his motivation. The emphasis on skill development should not be so great as to sacrifice the effectiveness of the learning process.

168

There Is More Attention To Form, Precision, And Accuracy At The General Movement Skill And Specific Movement Skill Phases Of Development.

When the teacher finds it necessary to return to a lower order movement experience or to modify a higher level experience, the three categories of movement often become more easily identified. Stability, locomotion, and manipulation are still the bases of general and specific movement skill development. Because of the increasing complexity of skills it becomes more difficult to separate activities according to their contribution to any one of the three categories of movement. This does not mean that they are no longer important during this phase. It simply means that separating them effectively is not possible. The informed teacher will still emphasize the stability, locomotor, and manipulative concepts underlying the general and specific movement skills being taught. The modification of an activity or the return to lower order movement experiences are the major avenues by which the teacher can make use of the concepts embodied by the three dimensions of movement.

The general and specific movement skills located in this chapter are related to the content areas of games, rhythms, and self-testing. Suggested general and specific movement skill activities are listed for each of the content areas. These activities have been found to be beneficial to children in Grades 3 through 6. No attempt has been made to subdivide these activity progressions according to grade level. The partial progressions that have been suggested cannot be said to be appropriate to certain age children. Children are developing at different rates and have had different experiences. These individual differences must be taken into consideration by the teacher when selecting class activities. It is the teacher's job to select activities that are best suited to the student's capabilities. The key to a good program is not strict adherence to recommended grade levels for activities. The real *key is the teacher's knowledge of the students' capabilities and knowing how to select and modify activities in accordance with their developmental needs*. The teacher that uses this guideline should make every effort to individualize the teaching progression so that all children might reach their present potential level of development. The teacher's communication with, and observance of, the children provides clues to what activities might be suitable and whether or not an indirect (unstructured) or direct (structured) teaching approach is appropriate. Movement education types of activities, for example, are still acceptable if they are used properly since they can incorporate complex skills and still allow for individualization and creativity.

The overall structure of this chapter is based on the categories of stability, locomotion, and manipulation being stated in the form of fundamentals. Games, rhythms, and self-testing activities are listed with the dominant fundamental being placed in parentheses if the listed activity is not self-descriptive with regard to the fundamental. The numbers after each activity refer to the textbook (see Selected References) in which a detailed explanation of that particular activity is presented.

COMBINATION AND SELECTION EXPERIENCES RELATED TO GAMES

The combination and selection experiences of general and specific movement skills should be an outgrowth of the movement patterns developed through low organizational games and relays that were stressed during the preschool and primary years. These general and specific movement skills are taught and organized around sports skill lead-up activities. A lead-up activity is a modification of an official sport that incorporates elements of that sport into less complex game forms. The purpose of a lead-up game is to refine some of the sport skill fundamentals. Lead-up games usually take the form of a drill, an approximation of a game situation, or a relay. A game such as Pig in the Middle[8] may begin as a drill where the teacher emphasizes passing, catching, and pivoting form. The drill then takes on a competitive element that is designed to motivate the performers to put forth greater effort and concentration in practicing the correct or best way to pass, catch, and pivot. The competitive element in this situation might be the number of interceptions the center man can make in a certain time limit. The game Sideline Basketball[8] utilizes all the fundamentals of basketball and is therefore considered an approximation of the game of basketball. The Weave Dribble[8] is basically a drill, but the teacher may use this skill in a relay situation. Relays should provide a competitive situation that stresses and allows for the *correct* use of fundamentals. The use of relays as well as low organized games is not limited to the preschool and primary years where fundamental patterns are being stressed. Relays are often appropriate for teaching general and specific movement skills. Low organized games may still be used in teaching general and specific movement skills. The skills used in these games can be more heavily emphasized or the game may be modified to utilize more complex skills.

The lead-up games listed below incorporate a variety of general and specific movement skills that are an extension of the fundamental movement skill basis established earlier in the child's movement experiences. Fundamental movement patterns become combinations of movements or specific movements related to the characteristics or requirements of the activity. The equipment or supplies utilized as well as the game restrictions or rules now determines how previous fundamental movement patterns might be modified or incorporated. Throwing, for example, now becomes more specific and requires the child to concentrate on new throwing combinations as well as more precise execution of these new skills. The manipulative activity of throwing becomes a two-hand chest pass or a one-hand push shot in basketball and a forward pass or lateral pass in football. The following charts show the relationship of the fundamental movements to some of the specific skills required for basketball, football, soccer, softball, and volleyball.

Hanging By Your Knees Can Be
A Thrilling And Challenging
Experience

Suggested Game Activities for Developing General Movement Skills

Basketball

Fundamental Movements and Related Specific Movement Skills	Related Lead-Up Activities

MANIPULATION
  Throwing—specific passing skills
  Two-hand chest Pass
  One-hand push pass
  Two-hand overhead pass
  One-hand baseball pass
  Underhand pass
 	
  Throwing—specific shooting skills
  Lay-up shot
  Two-hand push shot
  One-hand push shot
  One-hand jump shot
 	
  Bouncing
  Bounce passes
  Dribbling
 	
  Catching
  Two-hands above waist
  Two-hands below waist
  Two-hands across midline of body
  Rebounding
 	
  Volleying
  Tipping ball to teammate
  Center jump tipping
  Tipping ball into basket
 	
LOCOMOTION
  Walking, Running, Jumping, Leaping, Sliding
 	
STABILIZATION
  Bending, Stretching, Twisting, Turning, Landing, Stopping, Dodging, Pivoting
  *Static, dynamic, or rotational balance are required in specific movement skills.
	1. Birdie in the Cage[3] (passing)
	2. Captain Ball[3] (passing)
	3. Pass and Pass Back[12] (bouncing, passing)
	4. Short Base[12] (two-hand overhead passing)
	5. One Long Pass[12] (one-hand overhead passing)
	6. Bounce Basketball[16] (bouncing, passing)
	7. Five Passes[8] (passing, catching)
	8. Circle Passing[8] (passing, catching)
	9. Pig in the Middle[8] (passing, catching, pivoting)
	10. Skip-One Pass[12] (2-hand underhand tossing)
	11. Dog-Rabbit Basketball[12] (chest passing)
	12. Dribble Shuttle Replay[12] (dribbling)
	13. Shoot and Recover[1] (shooting)
	14. Ten Baskets[12] (basket shooting)
	15. Basketball Golf[12] (basket shooting)
	16. Free Throw Contest[12] (free throwing)
	17. Guard Ball[2] (passing, catching, guarding)
	18. Keep Away[2] (guarding, passing, catching)
	19. Obstacle Dribble and Shooting[12] (dribbling, shooting)
	20. Target Ball[2] (passing, catching, guarding, dribbling)
	21. Fast Break[2] (passing, catching, dribbling, guarding)
	22. Basket Basketball[2] (passing, catching, shooting)
	23. Side Line Basketball[8] (all skills)
	24. Half-Court Basketball[2] (all skills)
	25. Basketball Snatch Ball[3] (passing, shooting, dribbling)
	26. End Ball[3] (passing, catching)

SPECIFIC SKILL EXPERIENCES RELATED TO BASKETBALL

Passing

1. Two-hand chest pass—to a wall target or partner (stress coordination of stride with extension of the arms).
2. One-hand push pass—to a moving target such as a hoop or child.
3. Two-hand overhead pass—over a volleyball net or pole.
4. One-hand baseball pass—from behind a line to a partner on a carpet square.
5. Bounce passes—to stationary and moving targets.

Dribbling

1. Dribble a ball in, around, to, and from self-space area such as a hoop.
2. Mass directional and hand change dribbling drill (move to the right, left, circle forward and backward).
3. Dribble a ball through a human or object obstacle.
4. Dribbling fast, slow, low, or high.

Shooting

1. Stand with the take-off foot on a rubber-backed carpet square and push the ball toward an "X" on the backboard (lay-up).
2. Use one-hand or two-hand push shots from designated distances and angles from the basket.

Catching

1. Child passing to designated hand positions of a partner to utilize two-hand above the waist, two-hand below the waist, and two-hand across the midline catches.
2. Throw a ball above a line on the wall and jump and grab the ball while it is in the air and prior to the landing.

Guarding

1. Side-step drill between cones (sliding).
2. Partner mirror guarding drill where the leader changes directions on command.

Basketball Activities Are Enjoyed By Both Boys And Girls

Running and Pivoting

1. Run and practice the one-foot lead or the stride method of stopping.
2. Run and practice the step-hurdle (one foot take-off to two-foot landing) method of stopping.
3. Place weight on the foot inside of an automobile tire while moving the foot outside the tire with short pushes (pivoting).
4. Combine pivot skills with number 1 and number 2 above.
5. Combine running and pivoting skills with dribbling.

SPECIFIC SKILL EXPERIENCES RELATED TO FOOTBALL

Passing

1. Throw a forward pass through a hoop or to a partner.
2. Throw a forward pass to targets at various distances.
3. Throw a forward pass through a moving hoop.
4. Lateral the ball to a stationary target.
5. Lateral the ball through a rolling tire.
6. Center the ball as a hand-off to the quarterback.
7. Center the ball at increasing distances for accuracy and speed.

Touch Football	
Fundamental Movements and Related Specific Movement Skills	Related Lead-up Activities

MANIPULATION
Throwing
  Forward pass
  Lateral pass
  Centering
 	
Kicking
  Kick-off (place kicking)
  Field goal
  Punting
 	
Catching
  Two-hands at waist
  Two-hands high
  Two-hands low
  Two-hands across midline
  Two-hand over the shoulder
  Hand-off
 	
Carrying
  Two-hand ball carry
  One-hand ball carry
 	
Pushing
  Blocking on the line
  Blocking on the run
 	
LOCOMOTION
Running, Sliding, and Jumping.
 	
STABILIZATION
Stance, Feints, Dodging, Stopping, Landing, Pivoting, Bending, Stretching, and Rolling.
	1. Over and Under[2] (ball handling)
	2. Fumble[2] (carrying the ball)
	3. Open Field Running[2] (dodging)
	4. Kick Over[2] (kicking, catching)
	5. Blocking Practice[8] (blocking)
	6. End Ball[8] (throwing, catching)
	7. Five Step Football[6] (throwing, kicking, catching)
	8. Punt and Catch[8] (punting, catching)
	9. Kickoff Football[2] (kicking, catching, dodging, tagging)
	10. Boundary Ball[2] (passing, catching, kicking)
	11. Field Ball[8] (throwing, catching, kicking)
	12. Steal the Football[2] (dodging, running, tagging)

Catching

1. Stationary partner catching drills to emphasize the basic catching skills listed.

2. Catch a football on the run and in various patterns to learn to receive the ball high or low while moving toward the ball, away from the ball, or at an angle to the ball.
3. Practice hand-offs to the right, to the left, after a fake, or after a pivot.

Ball Carrying

1. Run an obstacle or weave drill using a two-hand or one-hand carry.
2. Carry the ball after catching a pass or through an open field running drill.
3. Carry the ball through a zone of defenders.

Blocking

1. Practice on the line blocking with a partner, stressing proper contact, body position, forward and lateral movements.
2. Practice pass protection blocking techniques.
3. Practice positioning and down field blocking.

Kicking

1. Punt to a partner at varying distances stressing release of the ball and foot contact with the ball.
2. Punt for accuracy or distance contests.
3. Place kick for distance and accuracy (kick-off and field goal).

Running and Dodging

1. Sprint from cone A to cone B.
2. Agility run or weave between cones or tires.
3. Agility run through tires.
4. Run at cone, fake, and go around it.
5. Agility run through a guarded zone stressing dodging, faking, pivoting, and changes of speed.

SPECIFIC SKILL EXPERIENCES RELATED TO SOCCER

Kicking

1. Keep the ball in a designated area and close to you, move the ball with inside and outside of the foot kicks, the toe kick and the heel kick.
2. Dribble the ball to, around, and between cones or other objects.

⚽	Soccer	⚽

Fundamental Movements and Related Specific Movement Skills	Related Lead-up Activities

MANIPULATION
  Kicking
    Inside of the foot kick
    Instep kick
    Outside of the foot kick
    Toe and heel kicks
    Dribbling and passing
    Kick-off
    Corner kick
    Goal kick
    Punt
 	
  Trapping
    Sole trap
    Inside of the foot trap
    Knee or double knee traps
    Thigh or chest traps
 	
  Catching and blocking
    Goalie skills
 	
  Striking
    Heading
 	
  Throwing
    Throw-in
 	
  Tackling
 	
LOCOMOTION
  Running, Jumping, Leaping, Sliding
 	
STABILIZATION
  Bending, Stretching, Twisting, Stopping, Dodging, Pivoting
	1. Circle Soccer[8] (kicking, trapping, passing)
	2. Pin-ball Soccer[2] (kicking, trapping)
	3. Soccer Snatch Ball[3] (tackling, dribbling)
	4. Soccer Touch Ball[3] (kicking, trapping, passing)
	5. Diagonal Soccer[3] (kicking, trapping, passing, dribbling)
	6. Soccer Dodgeball[8] (kicking, trapping, passing)
	7. Sideline Soccer[2] (all specific fundamentals)
	8. Line Soccer[2] (kicking, trapping, passing, dribbling)
	9. Three Line Soccer[3] (all specific fundamentals)
	10. Alley Soccer[12] (all specific fundamentals)
	11. Keep Away[8] (kicking, dribbling, passing, heading, trapping)
	12. Circle Soccer Tag[8] (kicking, passing, trapping, heading)

3. Use an instep kick to attempt to hit specific targets.
4. Pass the ball to a stationary target, a moving target, or to an open space target.
5. Punt the ball for distance.

Trapping

1. Trap a ball rolling directly to you, to the right, or to the left.
2. Trap a ball in flight using the thigh or chest.

Heading

1. Head the ball back to a partner who tossed the ball to you.
2. Head a tossed ball into an upright barrel.
3. Keep the ball up using the headling skill.
4. Head the ball down so the ball may be trapped and passed by a teammate.

Tackling

1. Attempt to take the ball away from an opponent.
2. Attempt to take the ball away from the offensive player dribbling through your zone.

SPECIFIC SKILL EXPERIENCES RELATED TO SOFTBALL

Throwing

1. Use an underhand throw to a stationary or moving target or partner at varying distances.
2. Pitch through a hoop or into a box or a catcher's hand target.
3. Use an overhand throw so the ball bounces once before being caught, so it has a straight flight path, and so it has an arched flight path (also compare distances on these throws).
4. Field a ball and *throw* to a target.

Catching

1. Field ground balls, fly balls, and line drives thrown by the teacher or partner.
2. Field balls thrown against a wall on the fly or on the ground.
3. Catch balls thrown above your head, to your right, and to your left.

	Softball	
Fundamental Movements and Related Specific Movement Skills		Related Lead-up Activities

Fundamental Movements and Related Specific Movement Skills	Related Lead-up Activities

MANIPULATION
  Throwing
    Underhand toss
    Underhand pitch
    Overhand throw
 	
  Catching
    Two-hands above waist
    Two-hands below waist
    Two-hands across midline of body
    Fielding grounders
    Catching fly balls
 	
  Striking (Two-handed with implement)
    Batting ball
    Bunting ball
 	
LOCOMOTION
  Base running, Walking, Jumping, Sliding
 	
STABILIZATION
  Bending, Stretching, Stopping, Pivoting
	1. Target Pitch[2] (pitching)
	2. Kick Ball[2] (throwing, catching, and rules)
	3. Throw It and Run Softball[3] (throwing)
	4. Five Hundred[3] (fungo batting, throwing, catching)
	5. Long Ball or Base[8] (throwing, catching, hitting)
	6. Softball Pop-up[2] (throwing, catching)
	7. Tee Ball[3] (all skills)
	8. Bat Ball[8] (throwing, batting, catching)
	9. Home Run or Out-Softball[1] (batting, fielding, base running)
	10. Circle Softball[2] (batting, pitching, fielding)
	11. Beatball Softball[8] (throwing, catching, running)
	12. Twenty-One Softball[8] (throwing, catching, hitting)
	13. Hit and Run[3] (base running, throwing, catching)
	14. Two-Pitch Softball[3] (all skills)
	15. Baseball Overtake[17] (throwing, catching, base running)
	16. Hit Pin Softball[12] (batting, throwing, catching)
	17. Softball Work-up[1] (all skills)
	18. Home-Run Derby[2] (batting, fielding)

4. Catch fly balls while moving to the right or left or forward or backward.
5. Utilize a pitching and catching drill.
6. Utilize an infield drill.
7. Utilize the above drills with batted balls.

Batting

1. Hit a fleece ball, five-inch playground ball, wiffle ball, or softball off a batting tee.
2. Hit a ball pitched from increasing distances and at varying speeds.
3. Have the batter toss the ball into the air and hit it. (fungo hitting)
4. Stress the grip, stance, and mechanics and have the children bunt a pitched ball into hoop targets or point value areas.

Base Running

1. Practice swinging the bat, placing the bat down on a carpet square, and running past first base. (This can be a timed event to stress the speed of the run as well as the placement of the bat and the overrunning of first base.)
2. Practice rounding the bases going from first base to third base.
3. Practice returning to a base when caught in a "run-down."

SPECIFIC SKILL EXPERIENCES RELATED TO VOLLEYBALL

Two-Hand Volley

1. Volley the ball continuously above a marked line on a wall.
2. Pass the ball to squad members standing in target hoops or restricted space to stress accuracy.
3. Set the ball to a target area stressing the arm and leg extension necessary for a controlled hit.
4. Keep a beachball, balloon, plastic ball, or volleyball up in the air for as many hits as possible within a progressively smaller area.

Underhand Passes

1. Return a low tossed ball using the "bump" or "dig" to the thrower or to a barrel or hoop target.
2. Practice getting in good position to hit low balls hit or thrown to your right or left.
3. Combine the above two activities.

◯ **Volleyball** ◯	
Fundamental Movements and Related Specific Movement Skills	Related Lead-up Activities

MANIPULATION
Striking (One and two hand)
  Two-hand overhead pass or volley
  Two-hand underhand pass ("bump")
  Set-up
  One-hand underhand hit ("dig")
  Underhand serve
  Overhand serve
 	
LOCOMOTION
  Running, Walking, Sliding, Jumping, Leaping
 	
STABILIZATION
  Bending, Stretching, Turning, Swinging, Pivoting
	1. Wall Volley[6]
	2. Bat Dodge Ball[1] (serving, throwing, catching, running)
	3. Battle Ball[2] (throwing, catching)
	4. Backboard Set-up[2] (passing)
	5. Circle Keep-Up[12] (passing)
	6. Keep It Up-Four Square[1] (volleying)
	7. Sit or Stand Volleying[8] (volleying)
	8. Circle Volleying[8] (volleying)
	9. Leader Ball[2] (volleying)
	10. Mass Deck Tennis[2] (throwing, catching)
	11. Net Ball[2] (throwing, catching)
	12. First Fungo[17] (hitting, catching, throwing)
	13. Bounce Serve Volleyball[12] (serving)
	14. Serve Ball[12] (serving)
	15. Alley Serving[8] (serving)
	16. Nebraska Ball[8] (all skills)
	17. Fabric Volleyball[2] (serving, volleying)
	18. One Bounce Volleyball[2] (serving, volleying)
	19. Double Hit Volleyball[12] (serving)
	20. Tether Ball[3] (striking)

Serving

1. Utilize an underhand serve to a partner or against a wall.
2. Serve to targets at varying distances.
3. Serve over the net to specified zones stressing different forces and flight paths.

COMBINATION AND SELECTION
EXPERIENCES RELATED TO RHYTHMS

The rhythmical activities at the general and specific movement skill phases are more complex and require the teacher's use of combination and selection experiences by taking an active role in establishing or modifying the performance model. There is still some emphasis placed on rhythmic fundamentals and creative rhythms categories that were stressed in the child's earlier rhythm experiences. The introduction of new skills or the review and refinement of old skills will constitute the rhythmic fundamentals content. The content of creative rhythms is dispersed over all the rhythm categories. The creative rhythms content is directed toward the use of unique rhythm activities and the individual refinements of rhythm skills. Most of the rhythm activities in the general and specific movement skill phases are categorized as folk, square, or social dance. Each of these categories progressively increases its demands on the child and stresses increased ability to follow directions, to react to music, to perform skills, and to interact socially. The teacher can modify simple folk, square, or social dances to stress refinement or to introduce more complex skills through a familiar activity. The activity of Tinikling[3], for example, stresses the use of a side-step pattern. This activity can be modified to use other locomotor patterns such as the run, hop, or jump. Further complexity can be added by working with a partner or adding a manipulative dimension through the use of balls.

Rhythmical activities such as dances seem to have three areas of specificity. One area accounts for the uniqueness of the movements and gestures. A second area accounts for the formation, sequence, and dance format. The third area accounts for the specific social requirements of the activity. At the elementary school level the greatest emphasis should be placed on learning specific movements through mass movement rhythm activities. Depending on the nature of the activity the formation, sequence, and format can be learned later by the children. The social requirements may be added last to complete the total experience. This approach is suggested as a result of teaching and observing elementary children engage in rhythmical activities. Frequently we teachers tend to reverse the suggested order by making sure the children have a partner of the opposite sex (social requirement). Then we place them in the formation and familiarize them with the structure of the activity (formation, sequence, and format). The last thing we do is what we should do first and that is to stimulate the children's interest and help them learn new ways to move to music. It is suggested that the following rhythm activities be taught with emphasis on children first learning to enjoy the required rhythmical movements.

Suggested Rhythm Activities for
Developing General Movement Skills

F O L K D A N C E	1. Glow Worm Mixer[8] (walking) 2. The Crested Hen[11] (walking) 3. Greensleeves[1] (walking) 4. Bingo[5] (walking) 5. Skip to My Lou[8] (skipping) 6. Paw Paw Patch[8] (walking, hopping, jumping) 7. Norwegian Mountain March[8] (skipping, hopping) 8. Gustaf's Skoal[6] (skipping) 9. Troika[6] (running) 10. Irish Washer Woman[1] (walking) 11. Bleking[8] (bleking) 12. LaRaspa[5] (bleking) 13. Patty Cake Polka[7] (polka) 14. Chimes of Dunkirk[9] (stepping, hopping) 15. Cotton Eyed Joe[7] (polka and 2 step) 16. Cshebogar[8] (sliding) 17. Schottische[8] (running, stepping, hopping) 18. Heel and Toe Polka[8] 19. Horah[11] (schottische) 20. Tinikling[3] (stepping, running, hopping)

1. Sicilian Circle[8] (walking) 2. Texas Star[6] (walking) 3. Take a Little Peek[7] (walking, swinging) 4. Bird in the Cage[7] (hopping, walking) 5. Red River Valley[8] (walking)	SQUARE DANCE

SOCIAL DANCE	1. Waltz[5] 2. Penny Waltz[7] (waltzing) 3. Spanish Circle[3] (waltzing) 4. Little Man in a Fix[3] (running, waltzing) 5. Rye Waltz[3] (waltzing) 6. Fox Trot[5]

**Suggested Rhythm Activities for
Developing General Movement Skills**

1. Swing Across Body[4] 2. Circle Around Body[4] 3. Spiral[4] 4. Bounce and Turn[4] 5. Bounce Under Leg[4] 6. Two Hand Toss[4] 7. Front-swing Toss[4] 8. Partner Tossing[4]	RHYTHMICAL BALL SKILLS

COMBINATION AND SELECTION
EXPERIENCES RELATED TO SELF-TESTING

The self-testing categories of track and field, stunts and tumbling, small manipulative apparatus and large apparatus comprise the majority of the combination and selection experiences in the general and specific movement skill phases. There are still challenge situations where children resort to performing isolated skills, but the program emphasis is not on the fundamental movement or physical fitness categories of self-testing. The fundamental movement patterns have been accentuated in the exploratory, discovery, and combination experiences and now form the basis for greater complexity being attempted and mastered at the general and specific movement skill levels. The physical fitness category essentially consists of stability, locomotion, and manipulation fundamentals in isolation or combination. These isolated or combined movements related to fitness have been included in the movement pattern, general and specific movement skill phases. In the conceptual approach to teaching physical education, physical fitness is a concomitant of a good program. The following list of activities incorporate a variety of general and specific movement skills that are combinations of movements or specific movements related to the characteristics or requirements of the activities and should be an extension of children's earlier fundamental movement experiences.

Suggested Self-Testing Activities for Developing General and Specific Movement Skills

1. Potato Race[8] (starting, running) 2. Number of Jumps[8] (jumping) 3. Baton Passing (starting, running, passing) 4. Start and Pass[8] (starting, running) 5. Starting[8] 6. Running[3] 7. High Jump[8] 8. Standing Long Jump[8] 9. Jogging[17] 10. Long Jump[8] 11. Hurdling[1] 12. Softball Throw[6] 13. Shot Put[8] 14. Triple Jump[8]	TRACK AND FIELD

Stunts and Tumbling Activities

S T U N T S	1. Stride Stand[8] 2. Incline Stand[8] 3. Dog Stand[8] 4. Bear Dance[8] 5. Knee Dip[8] 6. Dead Man's Fall[16] 7. Egg Sit[17] 8. Jump and Reach[17] 9. Seal Slap[8] 10. Knee Spring[16] 11. Hand to Foot Stand[16] 12. Knee Shoulder Balance[16] 13. Leg Wrestle[8] 14. Rooster Fight[8] 15. Crab Fight[8] 16. Bulldog Pull[17] 17. Pin Wheel[16] 18. Squat Through[16] 19. Forearm Balance[16] 20. Pyramids[8]

Stunts and Tumbling Activities

1. Headstand[8]	
2. Cartwheel[8]	
3. Headspring[8]	
4. Dive Roll[16]	
5. Double Roll Forward[16]	T
6. Backward Roll to Head Balance[16]	U
7. Kip[8]	M
8. Round-off[16]	B
9. Round-off into Backward Roll[16]	L
10. Handstand[8]	I
11. Handspring[16]	N
12. One Arm Cartwheel[16]	G
13. Back Handspring[16]	

Small Manipulative Apparatus

	1. Hula Hooping[8]
	2. Twirl Hoop on Body Parts[8]
	3. Do As I Say[3]
	4. Moving the Hoop in Own Space[3]
	5. Moving the Hoop While Moving[3]
	6. Swing and Lean[4]
	7. Ballet Point[4]
HOOPS	8. Back Arch[4]
	9. Forward Jump[4]
	10. Waltz Turn[4]
	11. Run Bowl and Jump Through[8]
	12. Circle Front, Back and Change[4]
	13. Stand and Toss[4]
	14. Roll and Scissors Jump Over[1]

1. Hand Balance[8]	
2. Foot Balance[8]	
3. Jump Through Stick[8]	
4. Mirror Movements[1]	
5. Ankle Toss of Wand[4]	WANDS
6. V Seat and Wand[4]	
7. Kick Over Wand[4]	
8. Crawl Under Wand[14]	
9. Partner Sit and Stand[14]	

Small Manipulative Apparatus

| LONG ROPE JUMPING | 1. Front Door[8] 2. Back Door[8] 3. Hot Pepper[3] 4. High Water[3] 5. Double Dutch[3] 6. Double Irish[3] |

| 1. Two Foot Basic[8] 2. One Foot Hop[8] 3. Forward Variations[8] 4. Backward Variations[8] 5. Overhead Circling[4] 6. Arms Crossed[4] | INDIVIDUAL ROPE JUMPING |

| STRETCH ROPES[3] | 1. Relays 2. Obstacles | SCOOTERS[1] |

| CLUBS | 1. Swinging Movements 2. Circling Movements 3. Forward Swing 4. Sideward Swing 5. Horizontal Circle Outward 6. Step Hop Arm Swing |

Large Apparatus

| 1. Hang[17] 2. Squat[17] 3. Side Lean[17] 4. Pendulum Swing[17] 5. Headstand[17] | STALL BARS |

| HORIZONTAL LADDER | 1. Hang[1] 2. Hang and Drop[1] 3. Side Travel[1] 4. Skip One Rung[1] 5. Skip Two Rungs[1] 6. Backward Travel[1] |

Large Apparatus

1. Lying to Standing[1]
2. Pike Hang[4]
3. Shinny—Up[6]
4. Shinny—Down[6]
5. Inverted Hang and Make Fast[6]

   Double Ropes

6. Straight Arm Hang[3]
7. Bent Arm Hang[3]
8. Inverted Hang[3]
9. Skin the Cat[3]

ROPE CLIMBING

CARGO NET[6]

BENCH ACTIVITIES

1. Animal Walks[3]
2. Locomotor Movements[3]
3. Pulls[3]
4. Pushes[3]
5. Crouch Jumps[3]
6. Forward Roll[3]

STEGEL[3]

BALANCE BOARDS[3]

1. One Knee Mount[10]
2. Squat Mount with a Turn[10]
3. Leap Mount[10]
4. Shoulder Stand Mount[10]
5. Straddle Mount[10]
6. Jumps[10]
7. Leaps[10]
8. Turns[10]
9. Squat Jump Dismount[10]
10. Straddle-Touch the Toes Dismount[10]
11. Cartwheel Dismount[10]

BALANCE BEAM

Large Apparatus

HORIZONTAL BAR

1. Front Pull-Up[16]
2. Arm and Leg Hang[3]
3. Double Leg Hang[3]
4. Front Support Push-Off[3]
5. Skin the Cat[17]
6. Chin[17]
7. Swing Under[1]
8. Underswing Dismount from Support[16]
9. Underswing Dismount with 1/2 Twist[16]
10. Single Knee Swing[3]
11. Hook Swing Dismount[16]
12. Single Knee Mount[1]
13. Double Knee Circle[16] (backward)
14. Single Knee Circle[16] (backward)
15. Front Hip Circle[1]

PARALLEL BARS

1. Hand Walk[1]
2. Straddle Travel[1]
3. Forward Hand Walk, Half Turn and Backward Hand Walk[16]
4. Forward Hand Jump[16]
5. Squat Dismount from Cross Support to Straddle Seat[16]
6. Flank Dismount from Front Leaning Support[16]
7. Flank Dismount from Straight Arm
7. Support[16]
8. Hammock Hang[16]
9. Scissors from Cross Support to Straddle Seat[16]
10. Corkscrew Mount[16]
11. Backward Roll from Straddle Seat to Straddle Seat[16]

Large Apparatus

RINGS

1. Hang and Swing[1]
2. Bent Arm Hang Swing[16]
3. Pull-Up[16]
4. Inverted Squat Hang[16]
5. Inverted Straight Hang[16]
6. Skin the Cat[1]
7. Nest Hang[16]
8. Forward Single Leg Cut and Catch[16]
9. Inlocate from a Jump[16]
10. Ring Sit[1]
11. Backward Double Leg Cut Dismount[16]

SIDE HORSE

1. Front Support[17]
2. Squat Mount, Jump Dismount[16]
3. Squat Mount, Jump Dismounts with Twists[16]
4. Squat Vault[17]
5. Left and Right 1/2 Circle[17]
6. Flank Vault[16]
7. Front Vault[16]
8. Simple Traveling[16]
9. Straddle Mount, Jump Dismount[16]
10. Straddle Vault[16]
11. Single Leg Circles Backward[16]
12. Single Leg Circles Forward[16]

MINI TRAMP, SPRINGBOARD, BOUNCEBOARD[3]

1. Step Hurdle with Claps[17]
2. Tuck Jump[13]
3. Straddle Jump[13]
4. Jump Turns[17]
5. Vault to Knees[13]

Large Apparatus	
1. Break Bounce[16]	
2. Jump, 1/2 Twist[16]	
3. Seat Drop[17]	
4. Tuck Jump[16]	
5. Tuck Jump to Seat Drop[16]	
6. Hands and Knees Drop[17]	TRAMPOLINE
7. Front Drop[16]	
8. Seat Drop—Front Drop[16]	
9. Swivel Hips[16]	
10. Pike Jump[16]	
11. Back Drop[17]	
12. Front Drop to Back Drop[16]	

SELECTED REFERENCES

1. Anderson, Marian H., Elliot, M.E., and LaBerge, J. *Play with a Purpose: Elementary School Physical Education*. New York: Harper and Row Publishers, 1972.
2. Blake, William O., and Volp, A.M. *Lead-up Games to Team Sports*. Englewood Cliffs, New Jersey: Prentice-Hall, Inc., 1964.
3. Dauer, Victor P. *Dynamic Physical Education for Elementary School Children*. Minneapolis, Minnesota: Burgess Publishing Company, 1971.
4. Drury, Blanche Jessen, Schmid, A.B., and Thomson, P. *Gymnastics for Women*. Palo Alto, California: The National Press, 1968.
5. Fabricus, Helen. *Physical Education for the Classroom Teacher: A Physical Education Curriculum for Elementary School Children*. Dubuque, Iowa: Wm. C. Brown Company Publishers, 1972.
6. Gallahue, David L., and Meadors, W.J. *Let's Move: A Physical Education Program for Elementary School Teachers*. Dubuque, Iowa: Kendall/Hunt, 1974.
7. Harris, Jane A., Pittman, A., and Woller, M.S. *Dance a While*. Minneapolis, Minnesota: Burgess Publishing Company, 1968.
8. Kirchner, Glenn. *Physical Education for Elementary School Children*. Dubuque, Iowa: Wm. C. Brown Company Publishers, 1974.
9. Kraus, Richard. *Folk and Square Dances for the Elementary School*. Englewood Cliffs, New Jersey: Prentice-Hall, 1966.
10. Mosston, Muska. *Developmental Movement*. Columbus, Ohio: Charles E. Merrill, 1965.
11. Murray, Ruth. *Dance in Elementary Education*. New York: Harper and Row Publishers, 1963.
12. Nagel, Charles, and Moore, F. *Skill Development Through Games and Rhythmic Activities*. Palo Alto, California: The National Press, 1966.
13. O'Quinn, Garland Jr. *Gymnastics for Elementary School Children*. University Stores, Inc., P.O. Box 1441, Austin, Texas, 1973.

14. Provaznik, Marie, and Zabka, N. B. *Gymnastic Activities with Hand Apparatus for Girls and Boys*. Minneapolis, Minnesota: Burgess Publishing Company, 1965.
15. Richardson, Hazel, *Games for the Elementary School Grades*. Minneapolis, Minnesota: Burgess Publishing Company, 1970.
16. Ryser, Otto *A Manual for Tumbling and Apparatus Stunts*. Dubuque, Iowa: Wm. C. Brown Company Publishers, 1968.
17. Vannier, Maryhelen, Foster, M., and Gallahue, D. L. *Teaching Physical Education in Elementary Schools*. Philadelphia: W. B. Saunders, 1973.

Chapter 9
Organization and Implementation of Movement Experiences

Key Concept: Children's learning experiences, whether they be exploratory, discovery, combination, selection, or performance rest with the teacher's abilities to understand their present capabilities as well as being able to implement those experiences most likely to develop their potentialities.

Content: Introduction
Organizing the Curriculum
    The Yearly and Seasonal Plan
    The Unit and Weekly Plan
    The Daily Lesson Plan
    Concluding Comments on Organizing the Curriculum
Implementing the Curriculum
    Student Needs
    Communicating with Students
    Expression
    Instruction
    Understanding
    Discipline
The Teacher's Role
Implementing Procedures
    Class Management
    Class Formations
The Practical Application of the Conceptual Approach
    The Basis of the Philosophical Construct
    The Philosophical Construct As the Basis for Modifying Learning Experiences
    The Purpose of a Philosophical Construct
    Using the Conceptual Approach to Teach Elementary

Physical Education
   Activities Related to Children's Fundamental
   Movement Patterns
   Activities Related to Children's General and
   Specific Movement Skills
   Activities Related to Children's Total Educational
   Experience

Organization and Implementation of Movement Experiences

INTRODUCTION

As education moves toward an emphasis on the individualization of instruction, the teacher is placed in the position of determining how his or her classes can provide children with meaningful experiences that will challenge each child and meet their individual needs. Many curriculums have been designed with a certain type of child in mind. These curriculums have been geared to average, slow or fast learners and have emphasized content such as games, rhythms, self-testing, physical fitness, relays and small or large group activities. The content, which was subdivided into appropriate grade level activity progressions, was being taught *rather than the child*. The conceptual approach with its three categories of movement (stability, locomotion and manipulation) does not negate or conflict with the content of these other curricular approaches. However, it does attempt to provide the teacher with a basis for analyzing movement experiences with each child's developmental needs in mind. This analysis and the resulting variability that leads to meaningful movement experiences is what is so often lacking in elementary physical education curriculums. The conceptual approach's emphasis on the child rather than the subject matter provides the teacher with a theoretical position that can be an aid to individualizing learning.

ORGANIZING THE CURRICULUM

The conceptual curriculum has as its core the three categories of movement. The concentric rings found in Figure 9-1 emphasize the growth of the child's movement and cognitive concepts in relation to the phases of motor development and the movement experience hierarchy. The movement experiences include a variety of curricular content, which is suitable to the developmental level of the child. The primary purpose of a curriculum is to serve as a guide for planning movement experiences for regular and adapted classes as well as for extra-class or after-school programs. The overall curriculum plan is very general and is directed to the breadth of the program to be offered in a school or school

195

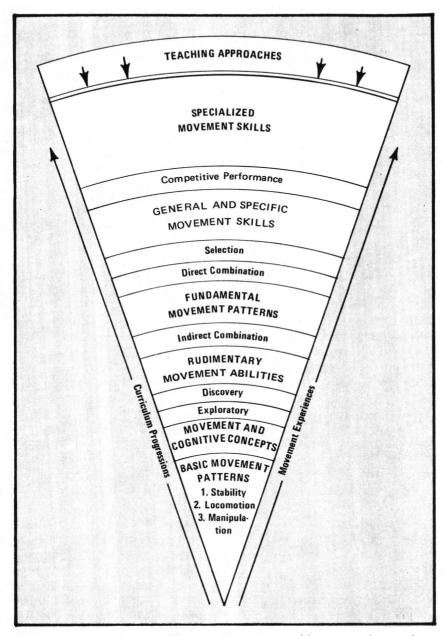

Figure 9-1. A cut from the "pie" of the curricular experiences of the conceptual approach.

system. These curricula are based on general objectives in relation to student needs, teacher personnel, available facilities and equipment as well as the goals of the community. The justification of these overall curriculums is that they provide educators and administrators with a scope and sequence chart that tells them the type of experiences being offered and at what grade level these experiences are occurring. Remember that the progression of experiences that is outlined in the scope and sequence chart only serves as a guide and *is* to be revised frequently, and modified constantly by the teachers of physical education

Yearly plans, unit plans, and daily lesson plans are progressively more detailed aspects of the curriculum. The major components of these plans are briefly dealt with in the following paragraphs. Detailed explanations and examples may be located in many of the basic elementary school physical education textbooks that are available.

The Yearly and Seasonal Plan

There are other stages of planning that take place prior to the teacher presenting the actual lesson. A physical education teacher, the elementary physical education coordinator, or the elementary physical education staff will devise yearly and/or seasonal plans. These plans are more specific than the overall curriculum and take into consideration the children's needs and abilities in a particular school. What was taught last year, the available time, the coordination of indoor and outdoor facilities and equipment as well as teaching personnel are considered.

The Unit and Weekly Plan

The unit plan is again more specific as to the types of movement experiences to be incorporated in the program to teach specific movement patterns or skills. The weekly plan provides the teacher with a means of altering or modifying the unit plan experiences based on how well the children are learning the specified movement patterns or skills. The children may need repetition experiences, or they may be ready for new combination and selection experiences.

The Daily Lesson Plan

The daily lesson plan is a detailed strategy of how the teacher intends to develop the movement experiences for a particular day so the children might reach

SAMPLE LESSON PLAN NO. 1*

I. GENERAL INFORMATION	II. OBJECTIVES	III. EQUIPMENT
A. Date (January 20, 1975) B. Location (multi-purpose room) C. Number of students (33) boys and girls D. Available space (limited) E. Grade level (1st) F. Length of period (20 minutes) G. Previous lesson (movement exploration activities, stressing fall and winter season and Mr. Midnight). H. Today's lesson (movement exploration, stressing different symbols, intensity colors, mechanical [different types of machines]).	A. Develop creative understanding about various symbols. B. Learn to interpret different types of intensity. C. Understand and express types of colors. D. Explore and interpret mechanical objects in our environment. E. Develop and improve agility, coordination and flexibility. F. Develop an attitude that movement is fun.	A. Triangle cut-out B. Square cut-out C. Circle cut-out D. Line cut-out E. Crooked cut-out F. Record player G. Waltz music for background

A. Procedure	B. Class Formation and Movement	C. Skill and/or Teaching Progression and Teaching Cues	D. Evaluation, Modifications, Suggestions
A. Symbol creativity	A. Semicircle formation and/ find your own "space or home." Scattered formation.	A. Feel and talk about different symbols: Explore in your own space the feeling of these symbols. (Make) these shapes with your body: (suggestions). Suggest objects which are in their environment which have these shapes.	A. Observe the students creativity in movement, his sense of knowledge about these shapes.

B. Intensity expression	B. "Own space" (scattered formation)
	Locomotive movement
	Formation—free
		B. Intensity
		Explore large movements
		  small
		  high
		  low
		  heavy
		  light
		  soft
		  noisy
		Suggest or encourage a variation of interpretations.
			B. How well does the student understand these concepts, how creative is his interpretation?

C. Color perception	C. Semicircle formation and/ go back to your own space.	C. Look and discuss various colors: red
		  yellow
		  blue
		  green
		1. Explore in your own space the feeling of these colors:
		2. Suggest various color concepts which are in our environment:
		3. Make your interpretation:
		4. Seek out individual response.
			C. Observe awareness of colors and individual interpretation.

D. Mechanical	D. Your own space	D. Pretend you are an 1. Elevator 2. Popcorn popper 3. Rocket (blast off—orbit—re-entry)	
Game activity Freeze	Vary formations Line Semicircle Scatter	C. March in line—"freeze" a. Work on response to cue word—"freeze" D. "Creep-up" a. Group comes toward instructor when back is turned. b. Instructor calls "freeze" and turns to see position of students.	 D. b.-1—Encourage creativity
Dismissal	Line	c. Take two (2) steps forward d. Stoop and touch floor e. Slap floor four (4) times f. Jump as high as possible "blast-off"	Repeat several times How might the lesson be improved?

SAMPLE LESSON PLAN NO. 2*

I. GENERAL INFORMATION	II. OBJECTIVES	III. EQUIPMENT NEEDED
A. Date January 20, 1975 B. Location: multi-purpose room C. Number of students: 33 (boys and girls) D. Available space per student: limited E. Grade level: 5th F. Length of period: 22 minutes G. Previous lesson: general physical fitness activities H. Today's activity: physical fitness activities and combatives	A. Promote bodily coordination, flexibility, endurance, balance and strength B. To develop an awareness and meaning of warm-up activities and exercises C. Promote student's enjoyment of physical fitness D. Develop an outlet to release tension	A. Record player B. The following records — *La Raspa, Lonely Bull, Kimbo's Ball Gymnastics* C. Whistle

A. Procedure	B. Class Formation and Movement	C. Skill and/or Teaching Progression and Teaching Cues	D. Evaluation, Modifications, Suggestions
A. Warm-up (3 min.)	A. Vertical squad line formation x x x x x x x x	A. 1. Stretching 1. Stretching 2. Bending 3. Getting up from different positions 4. Airplane propellor 5. Wing stretcher	A. Change directions of movements—stress ments—stress
B. Fitness exercise (7 min.)	B. Semi staggered line formation (keep in vertical columns) x x x x x x x x	B. 1. *La Raspa*—move weight on heels 2. Tread mills (to *La Raspa* record) 3. Straddle leg position—stretch out (keep legs straight) 4. Press soles of feet together—push knees down to floor (keep head up) 5. Striding (stress opposition) 6. Flutter kicks—scissor kick and grasp toes and raise heels off the floor (keep legs straight)	5. Alternating jumping jack

C. Combative activities (8 min.)	C. Double line(s)—facing partner
	x x y y
	x x y y
	x x y y
	x x y y
	
	One double line
	x X
	x X
	x X
	x X
		C.
		1. Arms extended overhead
		  a. Face partner—toes to toes
		  b. Keep arms stationary
		  c. Force partner off balance
		2. Arms extended horizontally to sides
		  a. Same procedures
		3. THUNDER CLAP
		  a. Same position—but hands held at shoulder level—palms forward
		  b. Hit hands of opponent and try to knock off balance
		  c. Hands can be moved to avoid contact
		4. SHOULDER PUSH
		  a. Grasp biceps of opponent
		  b. Place one foot to rear and lean upper body toward opponent
		  c. Push past mark
		5. STRADDLE PULL
		  a. Grasp forearms of opponent
		  b. Start in straddle position
		  c. Lower center of gravity and pull opponent across line
		6. LINE PULL GAME
		  a. Team effort using straddle pull
		  b. Time limit—when pulled across become member of opposite team
		7. INDIAN WRESTLE
		  a. Place right foot along side of opponents same foot
		  b. Feet spread for strong base
		  c. Grasp right hands
		  d. Force opponent to move either foot
		8. CHICKEN FIGHT
		  a. Cross arms and balance on one foot
		  b. Hop into opponent and try to force him to place raised foot on floor
		9. ARM WRESTLE
		  a. Lie on stomach facing opponent
		  b. Grasp right hands—elbow to elbow
		  c. Place free hand on lower back
		10. BACK-TO-BACK-PUSH
		  a. Interlock elbows—keep lower backs together
		  b. Push with heels forcing opponent across line
		11. BACK-TO-BACK-PULL
		  a. Same procedure
		  b. Dig heels in and pull opponent across line
		12. CHINESE GET-UP
		  a. Same as Back-to-Back Push
		  b. Keep feet stationary—push and come to a stand
			C. Stress safety—arms straight and stationary
			
			6. Encourage but control competitive excitement
			
			7. Try to use both sides
			
			8. Stress safety
			  a. Arms cannot be raised
			  b. Must stay in your area
			9. Utilize other arm
			
			11. Don't allow students to lower shoulders
			
			12. Stress keeping lower backs together to avoid back injury

D. DISMISSAL (2 min.)	D. Double lines	D. On the command "MOVE" 1. 1/2 turn pivot right to the rear 2. Take two steps forward starting with left foot 3. Squat and touch hands to floor 4. Jump high in the air saying, "— — —"	D. Repeat until class responds as a unit

the skill, social, emotional, and understanding objectives set forth. The daily lesson plan considers the objectives of the unit plan as well as the experiences and modifications of those experiences in the previous weekly and daily plans. This planning process is based on continuous evaluation of whether or not the children are improving and whether or not the movement experiences are appropriate. Here are some things the teacher must consider:

1. What have the previous experiences achieved and at what point are the children now in their learnings?
2. How much time might be devoted to introductory activities, review of skills and the introduction of new experiences?
3. Do the experiences provide a wide range of challenges and are the children experiencing success?
4. Should an indirect or direct teaching approach be used in providing exploratory, discovery, or another level or movement experiences?
5. What information should be learned or reviewed so the game, skill, or movement experience content can be explained and demonstrated concisely as well as developing meaningful teaching cues?
6. What are the class procedures, formations and instructions that will best facilitate the implementations of this lesson?

In responding to these questions the teacher is not only evaluating the effectiveness of how the children are learning, but is also attempting to anticipate the success and failure reactions of children to the next lesson. It is this anticipatory thought that leads the teacher to possible alternative plans that can readily be tried when the class or a child in the class is reacting in such a way as to indicate a need for change in the teaching approach. There are numerous designs for lesson planning. Each design attempts to set forth the *objectives*, *content*, and *class procedures* in a manner that is readily used and understood by the teacher. Several lesson plan designs are illustrated here. The nature and content of the learning experience and whether or not a movement education or teacher directed approach is being utilized are the major reasons for the differences in the formats of these lesson plans. Figure 9–2 presents a general outline that should be followed in developing a lesson plan.

Concluding Comments on Organizing the Curriculum

The planning stages from the overall curriculum down to the daily lesson plan are to help the child to reach his developmental potentialities. Because of inadequate programs and a recognition of the importance of elementary physical

SAMPLE LESSON PLAN NO. 3*

Folk Dancing Skill

I. ACTIVITY
   A. To learn and practice the Schottische Step and use it in a simple folk dance, the Circle Schottische

II. OBJECTIVES
   A. To teach the Schottische Step
   B. To give opportunity for practice of the Schottische Step
   C. To learn a simple dance using the Schottische Step
   D. To develop coordination

III. EQUIPMENT
   A. A record player, suitable recordings of Schottische music to use in practicing the step
   B. Drum
   C. Music of the dance (RCA Circle Schottische) (T.B.) for warm-up

IV. PROCEDURE
   A. Musical warm-up; striding
   B. Have class listen to Schottische music
   C. Clap to music—use loud clap on count one, snap fingers on count four
   D. Do plain running steps to Schottische music (circle formation)
   E. Run three beats or counts, hop on count four
   F. Practice step hops in combination with Schottische step (line drill to music)
   G. Form a single circle of partners—girls on the right of boys
   H. Listen to the music
   I. Teach the step of the dance, one step at a time

V. SUGGESTIONS
   A. If class is having difficulty in doing the dance step, go back to practice the Schottische step and step-hop. Have students help each other.
   B. Review sequence of the steps while just listening to the music
   C. Stimulate interest through background material

VI. EVALUATION
   A. Discuss problems that exist and suggest correction; also have the class make suggestions

SAMPLE LESSON PLAN NO. 4

Ball Skill Activity

I. ACTIVITY—Name of activity—
Guard the Castle
A. Reference where it can be found:
Chapter III, page 65, *Skill Devel-
opment Through Games and
Rhythmic Activities*, by Naegel

II. OBJECTIVES
A. Development and practice of
the two-hand side throw
B. Guarding an object—agility
C. Accuracy in throwing

III. EQUIPMENT
A. Utility ball, Indian club or a
substitute such as a milk carton,
plastic bottle, etc.
B. Facility: indoor or outdoors

IV. PROCEDURE
A. Description of game on
blackboard
B. Questions
Could list some
C. Class proceeds to an activity area
D. Ball skill circuit training
E. Demonstration and explanation
of game on field
F. Discuss safety factors
G. Questions
H. First guard of the castle
selected by the teacher

V. EVALUATION AND DISMISSAL
A. Discuss the problem that
occurred. Suggest solution for
improving game.
B. Teacher determines if objectives
were achieved
C. Did game allow for maximum
class participation?

*Larry Moehn and George Luedke, *Methods and Materials in Elementary Physical Education* Unpublished course syllabus (Edwardsville: Southern Illinois University, 1970).

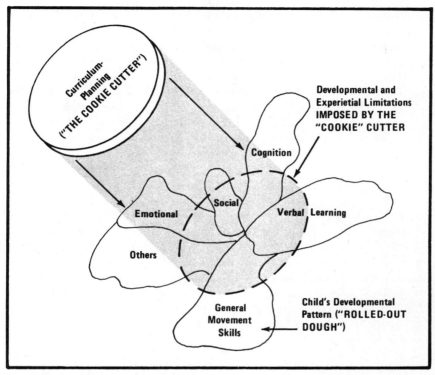

Figure 9-2. The "cookie-cutter effect."

education, educators have invested many hours in the development of curriculum guides filled with appropriate games, rhythms, and self-testing activities so that better programs in physical education would result. Another justification of curriculum guide development with recommended time allotments and suggested grade level placement of activities was to assure the child of receiving a program that was balanced to meet his/her developmental needs. These goals of better programs and meeting the child's developmental needs are certainly commendable. Unfortunately overall curriculums, yearly and seasonal plans, unit and weekly plans, and daily lesson plans have all been developed in advance of their use, have not been evaluated or modified after their use and seemingly perpetuate the very problems for which curriculums and other forms of planning were devised. Planning that does not recognize that children learn at different rates, that instruction needs to be individualized, and that continuous evaluation and modification are essential have a **"cookie-cutter effect"** on the child's developmental and experiential limits (see Figure 9-2). The child's development might be likened to rolled out dough, which has fingers of dough with spaces between them. The fingers might symbolize the areas where the child has developed most. The spaces might symbolize developmental voids. When the standardized "cookie-cutter," which is symbolic of the curriculum is applied to the dough, it removes all possibilities of that child continuing to develop in those areas where he is developmentally most advanced. Hopefully by using the conceptual approach and continuous evaluation in the planning procedures, physical education majors in teacher preparation programs will foster the *individualization of instruction so essential to the inspired learning of children*.

IMPLEMENTING THE CURRICULUM

The manner in which the curriculum is implemented rests primarily with the teacher's understanding of (1) what the students need, (2) of how to communicate with them, (3) of what his role is as the teacher, (4) of what implementation techniques can he employ, and (5) of how to effectively vary activities to meet the students needs. The conscientious and effective teacher will strive to deal with these questions as he evaluates and attempts to improve his teaching performance. Without being overly critical, the effective teacher will be constantly evaluating his or her ability and searching for innovative ways to help students reach their learning potentials.

Student Needs

The reference to student needs in this section will not attempt to deal with the numerous specifics of developmental patterns, interests, or motivations. Student needs will be thought of as general concepts upon which teachers formulate their purposes for teaching. Probably the foremost concept is that the teacher's purpose is to help children *improve*. If the teacher is concerned with children's improvement he is aware of their developmental needs and the developmental potentialities that exist. By condensing the factual knowledge of developmental needs and developmental potentialities into the operational goal of improvement, the teacher does not get bogged down with where the children should be theoretically. The danger with these theoretical concerns is that the teacher teaches theoretical children rather than real children. The operational goal of improvement helps the teacher to see children realistically at whatever level they are performing. The teacher's function then becomes one of evaluating and directing the learning experiences in order to bring about new successes for children.

The operational goal of improvement encompasses three other concepts that guide the teacher in reaching this goal. The first of these concepts is *Movement Control*. Here the teacher is cognizant of the three categories of movement (stability, locomotion, and manipulation) and the phases of motor development (rudimentary movement skills through specialized movement skills). He is also aware of the need for variation and that learning moves from the general to the specific. By condensing this information into the concept of movement control, the teacher again has a basis for analyzing his teaching effectiveness in this area of the child's growth and improvement.

The second concept under the goal of improvement is *Emotional Control*. Here the teacher is concerned with the child's understanding of himself and others. The teacher relys heavily on the ability to communicate with children and to teach them communication skills. These communication skills include discipline as well as experiences through which children can develop responsibility and self-control. The concept of emotional control gives the teacher a guide for evaluating past experiences and designing new experiences.

The third and final concept is *Learning Enjoyment*. This concept also gives the teacher a guide for evaluating and implementing his program with children's improvement in mind. The objective here is for the teacher to develop an eagerness to learn within each child. Success oriented experiences and opportunities to receive praise and recognition reinforce the child's view of learning. By making the development of learning skills enjoyable, the teacher hopes to foster intrinsic (self) motivation within the child.

The overall goal of improvement with its three emphases of (1) Movement Control, (2) Emotional Control, and (3) Learning Enjoyment give the teacher a compact philosophical construct that can serve as an operational guide to teaching action. This construct can and should be modified by the teacher. Its purpose is not to limit the teacher, but to provide operational guidelines to assure that his or her teaching is meaningful to children. Every teacher must rely on some sort of philosophical construct in the teaching situation. A teacher, for example, who has been teaching a number of years in a particular school system has no doubt developed a program that has been designed to meet the student's needs. Because she understands her students' needs and potentialities, she has certain performance expectations for the students. If this teacher would take a new teaching position in another school, she might temporarily lose her perspective of what she could expect of her new students. If she did not rely on her philosophical construct, there is a good chance that she would impose performance expectations on her new students that were based on her knowledge of her former students. The purpose of the suggested philosophical construct is to give the teacher a basis for keeping his or her teaching realistic, practical, and meaningful to the children.

Communicating with Students

Effective communication is the means by which teachers develop in children the necessary understandings that allow them to reach their potentials. Communication takes on different forms and has different goals. The forms of communication are either verbal or nonverbal. Tactual and visual communication are examples of nonverbal communication. The goals of communication include *expression, instruction, understanding,* and *discipline*. Communication is vital to implementing all facets of the program.

Expression

Learning experiences should be designed to allow for the expression of many types of feelings and moods through planned verbal and nonverbal activities. These activities should be adequately supervised since self-control and appropriate response are two objectives of expression. Such activities as creative play, story plays, and dramatization are all excellent activities where the child may express moods, play roles, and engage in fantasy play. The daily class routine should also provide experiences that give children an opportunity to use their communication skills. Facial expressions and the voice qualities of children and teachers, for example, provide children with continual opportunities for learning expressive behavior patterns. Often the approval or disapproval of the child's actions through the facial expression and/or tone of voice of a teacher or classmate have great communicative value and impact. Sometimes these forms of communication are taken lightly by the teacher and are not directed to the understanding and learning of positive forms of communication by children.

Instruction

Effective communication for instructional purposes means that the teacher must develop meaningful verbal and nonverbal forms of corresponding with students. These forms of communication are applied when the teacher explains and/or demonstrates an activity. Explanations should be concise and use vocabulary that is understood by the children. Verbal communication is completed by children listening and the resulting response that indicates understanding. It is often necessary for the teacher to help his students develop listening skills. Making sure that the children are paying attention when the teacher speaks is one way of helping children develop listening skills. If the children are still not understanding, the teacher should rephrase the remarks. Demonstrations can effectively communicate a model for action, but they should be explicit and appropriate to the learning task. Too much demonstration only leads to confusion. Also a heavy reliance on demonstration, or explanation, consumes valuable time in which children could be learning through their involvement.

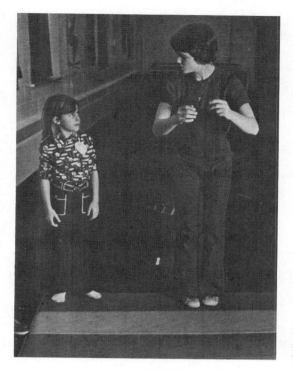

Taking Time For Individual Instruction Is Of Crucial Importance

Understanding

Communication with the child's understanding in mind stresses the importance of feedback. Children must be given an opportunity to interact with the
task to be learned for feedback to be meaningful. Sometimes teachers forget
that children actually pass through the exploratory and discovery experiences to
some degree each time they learn something new. Those teachers who do not
remember this tend to inappropriately give the child feedback information prior
to the child's getting involved with the learning task. The teaching cues used by
the teacher are designed to give the child feedback on his performance. These
cues, if they are to be understood must be meaningful to the child. Since words
are frequently inadequate forms for expressing a physical movement, the
teacher must attempt to develop a meaningful language pattern that does take
on movement meanings. However, the language labels used must frequently be
explained and rephrased in terms that have meaning to each child. If these various teaching cues are not effective, the teacher might rely on visual, tactual or
combinations of feedback to help the child understand. The teaching approach
and level of movement experience being used can also determine the type of

feedback necessary. The feedback information for exploratory and discovery experiences would be general in nature while for selection experiences it would be highly specific. There are several other considerations that contribute to the child's understanding. Among them are the teacher's ability to (1) relate effectively to experiences familiar to the child, (2) to effectively point out the similarities of new movements to past movements and (3) to effectively subdivide complex activities down into meaningful parts.

Discipline

Discipline is a form of communication that includes the expression and instruction as well as the understanding types of communication previously mentioned. The goal of discipline is to help children develop an understanding of acceptable forms of behavior for certain situations and to help them develop self-control rather than relying on external controls set forth by the teacher. Essentially then there are two facets of discipline. One facet is a continuous learning process and the other facet, which may evoke learning, is a control technique used by the teacher. Discipline as a learning process places emphasis on the nature of the teacher-pupil relationship and the class atmosphere that the teacher creates. If the teaching atmosphere is marked by consideration and concern for one another as well as firmness and fairness, the children will be learning discipline by accepting the responsibility for themselves in relation to others. The teacher's approach should emphasize activities that guide the child into accepting more and more of the responsibility for controlling himself. As the child accepts this responsibility, he should be given greater decision making freedom. The nature of the activities presented by the teacher then can become less teacher directed as the child's conscience and social responsibility become more sophisticated. There is a great need for elementary physical education teachers to help children develop conscience and social responsibility. This learning of discipline helps to teach children tolerance, persistence, self-control, and sets the child's base for emotional security.

The continuous learning facet of discipline also includes some guidelines for avoiding the use of control technique forms of discipline and some guidelines for positively redirecting children who are experiencing a momentary loss of control. Here are some of the guidelines for avoiding the use of control techniques.

1. The teachers awareness of the children's developmental needs and the corresponding individualization of instruction.
2. The planning of success oriented activities that provide challenge.
3. The planning of activities that require active participation.
4. The removal of temptation situations that might distract the child from the desired behavior.
5. The teachers enthusiasm and interest in helping students learn.

Discipline Is Sometimes Necessary

6. The teachers recognition and sharing of the students interests.
7. The teachers encouragement and support.
8. The teachers patience and politeness.
9. The teachers setting forth of the operational rules and the expected behaviors prior to participation in an activity.
10. The statement of behavioral and performance directions in positive rather than negative terms.

These are some guidelines for positively redirecting children who are experiencing a momentary loss of control.

1. The teachers ignoring the behavior so as to not reinforce the negative response and thus allow the child to redirect his own behavior.
2. The teachers visual recognition or prompting of the child to control his behavior.
3. The teachers reemphasis on the goals of the task.
4. The teachers redefining the behavioral expectations or limits.
5. The teachers verbalization of his interpretation of the child's behavior to let the child know that he is being understood.
6. The teachers presence in the child's working area may cause the child to control his behavior.

When discipline through a continuous learning process fails, the teacher must resort to control techniques of discipline. The cause of the child's deviant behavior is often not apparent to the teacher. The child may feel frustrated by the learning task, the teacher, other students, a home situation, or a developmental need to assert himself. Regardless of the cause, if the child does not control himself, the teacher must utilize some form of control technique. Kounin in his text, *Discipline and Group Management in Classrooms* refers to "antiseptic control techniques" and the "imposing of external controls" as the two ways in which the teacher can discipline the child. The "antiseptic control techniques" essentially call for the teacher to stop the deviant behavior with as little disruption of the class purpose and rapport as possible. Here the teacher is concerned with emphasizing the learning task and not allowing the disruptive behavior to be reinforced. The "imposing of external controls" might be used by the teacher as a means of protecting the student from harming himself or others or as a form of punishment. The case for imposing external controls for protection is much stronger than the case for punishment. Punishment suppresses behavior but does not stop the behavior since it is the teacher's control and not the child's that is operating. Punishment also has a disruptive effect on the other learners in class.

Although guidelines for the two facets of discipline have been presented, the teacher's ability to use discipline as a learning process or as a means of control must be individually learned. This learning occurs through the teacher's interaction with different types of children in different settings and at different age levels to become familiar with the forms of discipline that are most suitable to his or her personality.

The Teacher's Role

The teacher's role basically is to elaborate upon the concepts of the philosophical construct presented earlier in the chapter. The overall goal of the child's improvement in the areas of movement control, emotional control, and learning enjoyment are now expected to take the form of meaningful movement experiences. There are several other aspects of the teacher's role that are worthy of being mentioned.

1. The teacher should know and understand himself as well as his students so that he can effectively utilize teaching approaches and forms of communication that are suitable to his personality and are meaningful to the students.
2. The teacher should be knowledgeable about the subject matter and be secure enough in his teaching approach to try new approaches that he and/or his students have devised.

3. The teacher should be aware of his effectiveness in the different roles he must play when utilizing the various indirect and direct methods of teaching.
4. The teacher should set a good example, be supportive, and exhibit a positive attitude about himself, the students, and the activities.
5. The teacher should strive to individualize instruction whenever possible to assure each child's success.
6. The teacher should be striving to be a more effective teacher. (An article by Don Hamachek entitled "Characteristics of Good Teachers and Implications for Teacher Education," *Selected Readings in Movement Education*[11] elaborates upon the qualities of the effective teacher.)

Implementing Procedures

The implementing procedures used by the teacher can be categorized into two major subdivisions. The first is class management and the second is class formations. Guidelines for both of these topics are shown on the following page.

Class Management

Class Routine

1. A set procedure should be developed for entering and leaving the activity area.
2. A designated area and procedure for attendance, anouncements, and warm-ups should be developed.
3. If attendance procedures are necessary, number and squad roll techniques often are more efficient.
4. As the children develop self-control, they can assume more of the responsibilities for the class routines of attendance, equipment set-ups, and warm-ups.

Instructional Procedures

1. The implementation of the teacher's plan should result in maximum participation.
2. A routine or set of signals should be established so the children know when they are expected to listen to instructions.
3. A routine for getting and returning equipment as well as for the use of the equipment during instruction should be established.
4. Demonstrations and explanations should utilize class formations that help the child see and hear the instructional comments.

5. Demonstrations and explanations should be concise so that the children can move into the activity as soon as possible.
6. Having the children sitting during demonstrations and explanations is one technique used to control the class and gain their attention.
7. When classes have several groups spread out around the gym, it is a good idea to bring the other students over to one group's area for demonstration and explanation purposes.
8. The teacher should expedite the classes movement from one place to another by giving them a definite place and position to which they are to move.
9. The teacher should handle student questions in an efficient manner so that the class can become involved in the activity sooner.
10. The teacher should be prepared to clarify or modify an activity to make it more meaningful to the children.

Grouping

1. Mass, squad, partner, or individual groupings may be used depending on the nature of the activity, the available equipment, the available space, and the teaching approach being utilized.
2. Homogeneous grouping is most appropriate for teaching children with similar abilities or where similar sizes and strengths are needed for activities.
3. Squad organization gives an opportunity to the child for leadership and provides the teacher with an instructional group that can assume some responsibility for their learning experience.
4. Partner and small group circuits are appropriate for situations that call for the children to experience several different tasks within a class session.
5. Equalizing is a technique that may be used by the teacher in which he attempts to balance the skill abilities of opposing teams.

Safety

1. Mass, squad, partner, or individual activities should emphasize adequate movement space.
2. Where the nature of the activity results in shared space, the teacher should establish a direction into and out of that space.
3. Extra equipment and other items that might clutter the activity area should be removed.
4. A safety check of equipment should occur prior to its use.
5. the students should be made aware of their personal safety with regard to such things as untied shoe laces or the wearing of glasses.
6. The students should be *taught* safety habits.

Dismissal Activities

1. Dismissal activities are designed for the purpose of assuring that each child has been involved in an activity where he has been *successful*.
2. These activities can be of a review nature by incorporating skills that the children have already mastered.
3. These activities can be designed to lead to a group feeling of accomplishment such as in pyramid or marching activities.
4. These activities can be designed to develop a group feeling of responsibility by requiring children to follow a set of directions precisely.
5. Some examples of dismissal activities might include:
    a. "On the command 'Move,' turn around and shake hands with the person behind you in your line."
    b. "On the command 'Move,' take two big steps, turn around, squat down, and touch the floor and then jump up and say that's all!"
    c. "On the command 'Move,' do a forward roll and hop to the end line and sit to remove your gym shoes."
6. These types of dismissals end class on a good note and give a positive feeling of rapport.
7. These activities should be designed to calm and bring the class under control prior to returning to the classroom.

Class Formations

1. A "sepentine run," which is a follow the leader activity where a line of children weave and circle around the gym, can be used to get the children on the traditional straight line.
2. The movement from the line formation to the scatter formation can be accomplished by counting off according to a stated sequence of animals, vegetables, or cars. The children can then move out to their designated spaces in front or behind the line doing a movement characteristic of their category. (A similar approach can be used, only the children will be asked to use different locomotor movements as they move into position.)
3. The success of an activity often depends on the teacher's selection of a formation that is suitable for maximum participation and instructional value. Some of the formations that might be used are:

a. Double line

b. Scatter

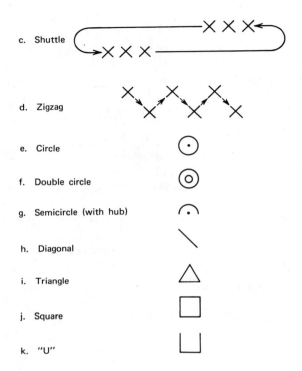

c. Shuttle

d. Zigzag

e. Circle

f. Double circle

g. Semicircle (with hub)

h. Diagonal

i. Triangle

j. Square

k. "U"

THE PRACTICAL APPLICATION OF THE CONCEPTUAL APPROACH

The physical educator now has more information available to him concerning the children's reflexive and rudimentary movement development (Chapters Two and Three), the child's cognitive and perceptual-motor development (Chapters Eleven and Twelve), and other factors concerning children's affective and psychomotor development. The theoretical basis provided by this information has been condensed by the previously introduced philosophical construct of *Improvement* (Figure 9-3) in an attempt to help the teacher handle this information in a useful and practical way. The philosophical construct has been derived from developmental and learning theories. The works of Freud, Piaget, Erikson, Sears, Bruner, Rohwer, Kagan, Fitts, and Skinner have all contributed to the available information on how the child develops and learns. The *Taxonomy of Educational Objectives* set forth by Bloom[1] in 1956 recognized three domains that the child learns and develops. These three domains seem to relate developmental and learning theories to the educational process and are referred to

DOMAINS OF THE TAXONOMY	COGNITIVE	AFFECTIVE	PSYCHOMOTOR
FACETS OF THE PHILOSOPHICAL CONSTRUCT OF IMPROVEMENT	LEARNING ENJOYMENT	EMOTIONAL CONTROL	MOVEMENT CONTROL
PRINCIPLES OF MODIFYING MOVEMENT ACTIVITIES	1. SUCCESS ORIENTED ACTIVITIES a. varied experiences b. child's interests c. child's motivation d. levels of development 2. MAXIMUM PARTICIPATION (INVOLVEMENT) a. individual activities b. dual activities c. group activities 3. ENVIRONMENTAL VARIABLES a. size of space b. type of facility c. available equipment 4. CONCEPTS & STRATEGIES RELATED TO MOVEMENT a. science b. social studies c. mathematics d. language arts e. art and music	5. THE HEIRARCHY OF LEARNING EXPERIENCES & RELATED APPROACHES TO MOVEMENT a. exploratory b. discovery c. combination d. selection e. performance f. movement education g. problem solving h. creative expression 6. THE SENSORY-MOTOR AVENUES a. visual b. auditory c. tactual d. kinesthetic 7. COMMUNICATION a. expression b. instruction c. understanding d. discipline	8. THE THREE CATEGORIES OF MOVEMENT a. stability b. locomotion c. manipulation 9. THE MECHANICS OF MOVEMENT a. base of support b. body position c. production and direction of force d. application of force e. absorption of force or follow-through 10. THE QUALITIES OF MOVEMENT a. force d. space b. time e. environment c. flow 11. THE PERCEPTUAL-MOTOR VARIABLES a. body awareness b. spatial awareness c. directional awareness d. temporal(time) awareness
TEACHER'S GOAL	THE CHILD'S IMPROVEMENT		

Figure 9-3. The philosophical construct of improvement.

as the cognitive, affective, and psychomotor domains. The proposed philosophical construct has resulted from the study of these various developmental and learning theories. Figure 9-3 shows the relationship of the three domains to the facets of the philosophical construct.

The Philosophical Construct as the Basis for Modifying Learning Experiences

If the child's learning experiences were to be modified based on developmental needs and without regard for the philosophical construct, the teacher might find that the extensive information concerning the child's development helped lead in a round-about manner to making the right decisions concerning activity modifications. For example, a teacher might have been attempting to teach first grade children a ball skill relay. Upon observation the teacher noticed that the children seemed to be confused and only interested in their participation with the ball. Based on this observation and the recollection that children at this age tend to be self-centered and oftentimes do not understand their relationship to others in their environment, the teacher determined that these children were not yet ready to understand the teamwork necessary in relay competition. With this realization and awareness of the children's developmental needs, he then decided that instead of teaching ball skills through relays, it would be better to work on rolling and catching skills in a circle game, a partner activity, or better yet an individual activity. The teacher's decision was based on the children's affective development as well as their cognitive development. The children's self-centeredness and lack of understanding of how to share responsibility resulted in their not caring about their relay team member's efforts.

The teacher might find further modifications stemmed from psychomotor considerations. The size of the ball and the prescribed rolling task might not have been suitable to the child's developmental needs. Since the first grader's movements are usually gross in nature, the teacher should select a large ball rather than a small ball. Also, the child's movement control would most likely indicate to the teacher that direct rolling rather than complicated zig zag rolling patterns would be most appropriate for these first graders.

Another factor the teacher might consider is what learning theories suggest in relation to these first graders and the nature of the tasks in which they are engaged. Should the relay or ball skill activity be broken down into parts or should it be presented in its entirety to the children? Should the relay activity be continued until the children learn to do it right? Learning theory indicates that we should teach the whole skill rather than small parts of a task or skill if learning is to take place quickly and accurately. Learning theory also indicates that distributed rather than massed practice would be better for these first graders with their short attention spans. Prolonged incorrect practice would be a waste of time since the correct response desired would be receiving too little reinforcement.

If the teacher's goal was to teach rolling and catching a ball to first graders, the selection of a relay was not good for the aforementioned reasons. However, if the teacher's goal was to familiarize the children with the concept of teamwork in relays, the experience might be modified so that two children make-up one relay team and carry an object together to and from a designated point. In this way the teacher can introduce the need to cooperate as well as the competition between partners (teams). The next meaningful cooperation among team members will be understood and related activities will become more appropriate. An over-emphasis on this concept certainly would not be justified.

This lengthy discourse concerning the hypothetical teacher's thought processes in modifying activities to meet developmental needs was actualizing but very time consuming. The philosophical construct could have been applied to the relay activity situation and yielded the correct modifications with more direct thought. The purpose of the philosophical construct is not to evade the learning of developmental theories, but it is to quickly direct the teacher's attention to those observable guidelines of *movement control, emotional control,* and *learning enjoyment.* Attention to these three things *then* directs the teacher's thinking to call upon this theoretical information to justify their modifications.

In addition to serving as an organizer of learning and developmental knowledges about children, the philosophical construct also serves as an organizer for the expansion and elaboration of these theories through curricula, methodology, or new and related theories or innovation. Figure 9-3 summarizes this expansion and elaboration.

Learning Enjoyment

As stated previously, learning enjoyment is concerned with the child's development of an eagerness to learn. Learning and cognitive theories bring forth the teacher's recognition of the child's interests, motivations, and learning skills. This information must then be translated by the teacher into meaningful guidelines for instructional purposes. Although *there are many overlaps and interrelationships among the facets of the philosophical construct and the proposed principles for modifying activities,* the proposed classification of principles under each of the facets of the philosophical construct have been arbitrarily selected to give further direction and meaning for the teacher's action. Consequently, under the concept of learning enjoyment the teacher is concerned with applying the following principles to the planning and implementation of movement experiences:

1) Success Oriented Activities.
2) Maximum Paticipation (Involvement).
3) Environmental Variables.
4) Concepts and Strategies Related to Movement.
5) Safety.

The teacher is essentially concerned with the child's successes if learning enjoyment is to be achieved. He can help the child succeed by varying the movement experiences so that the child becomes interested and motivated. Interest and motivation are largely dependent on the learner's involvement. The teacher therefore should plan individual, dual, or group activities with an emphasis on maximum participation. The teacher can also maintain the child's interest and motivation by applying environmental variables to the selected movement experiences. By altering the amount of space, the nature of the facility, or the type of equipment being used, the teacher can create opportunities for the child to successfully meet new challenges. The child's desire to learn about his environment also provides an excellent means for teaching the academic concepts of language arts, science, social studies, mathematics, music, and art through movement experiences.

The principles of modifying movement activities under learning enjoyment might be partly illustrated by a situation in which the teacher is teaching rope jumping activities to first or second grade children. Since some of the children are not experiencing success with their individual ropes, the teacher modifies the task to require successful jumps over the rope that is stretched out on the floor. A progressively more difficult challenge might be to have the children swing the rope just slightly forward and then backward and jump over it. The task can be varied also to emphasize counting (mathematics), centripetal and centrifugal forces (science), and learning a rhyme (language arts).

Emotional Control

Emotional control emphasizes the degree of self-direction children assert and the effectiveness of their communication with the environment. Although there are three principles listed under emotional control for the purposes of elaboration and direction for the teacher, all three can be explained through the principle of communication. The heirarchy of learning experiences and related approaches to movement essentially are concerned with the degree of teacher direction or control and the students' responsibility for self-control. The sensory-motor avenues are indicated simply to make the teacher aware of the various ways students communicate. The communication goals of expression, instruction, understanding, and discipline have already been elaborated upon earlier in this chapter under the heading "Communicating with Students."

Movement Control

Movement control incorporates four principles that serve the teacher in modifying movement activities for students. The three categories of movement may aid the teacher in placing emphasis on the child's stability, locomotor, or manipulative movements. For example, a child might be guided to explore various body positions while performing a locomotor and/or manipulative task. This variability can give the child needed movement experiences that may aid his understanding as well as the later performance.

The mechanics of movement complement the three categories of movement by giving the teacher a basis upon which to analyze and modify movement experiences so the child's performance may improve. If a child is having difficulty in effectively causing the necessary summation of forces to occur in throwing a ball, the observant teacher may, for example, be able to relate this to the child's base of support.

The qualities of movement allow for further variation of movement by stressing the speed, rhythm, and force in performing a movement. The child might be guided to move in a certain direction or to accomplish a sequence of tasks that stress variations in the amount of force required.

The perceptual-motor variables are emphasized as a teaching approach that has been derived essentially from the other three principles just mentioned. Body awareness, for example, relates closely to stability, which in turn relates to one's base of support and body position. Spatial, directional, and temporal awareness are closely associated with the qualities of movement. Again there are many overlaps that exist among the elaborated principles.

The Purpose of A Philosophical Construct

The reason for setting forth these principles of modifying activities is that there have been numerous innovative techniques, methods, or curricula developed through the years that have made a contribution to the goal of improving the child. However, many of these innovations have limited the child's learning experiences due to the emphasis or approach being fostered. These modification principles can place the various innovations in perspective by indicating how these approaches might broaden rather than limit the child's movement experiences. The principles of modification in conjunction with the philosophical construct and the conceptual approach seem to offer the teacher the most effective means of individualizng instruction. The philosophical construct and the eleven principles suggested are not to serve as rigid guidelines. Instead, it is hoped that each teacher will add to or reorganize these principles into a workable teaching guide that is suitable to his or her personality.

USING THE CONCEPTUAL APPROACH TO TEACH
ELEMENTARY PHYSICAL EDUCATION

The purpose of this portion of the chapter is to further develop and elaborate the information contained within the two sections of this book: Learning to Move and Learning Through Movement. The following materials are examples from lessons that have been utilized in the elementary school setting and derived basically from the body of knowledge set forth in the conceptual approach to the physical education of young children. The lesson ideas presented are organized into three groups: 1) Activities Related to the Child's Fundamental Movement Patterns, 2) Activities Related to the Child's General and Specific Movement Skills and 3) Activities Related to the Child's Total Educational Experience. Some of the instructional ideas are presented as they were organized when the lessons were implemented. It is suggested that these ideas be restructured and reorganized to best fit the needs and abilities of the children involved.

Activities Related to the Child's Fundamental Movement Patterns

The development of instructional ideas for the child that stress fundamental movement patterns stem primarily from variations of the body of knowledge contained in Chapters Four, Five, Six and Seven, which are concerned with the three categories of movement: stabilization, locomotion, and manipulation. The following are examples of fundamental movement patterns involving stability, locomotion, and manipulation.

Concepts: *Respect for self-space, shared space, and controlled movement are dependent on the establishment of listening skills.*
Organizing Centers: *Stability and Locomotion*
Equipment: *Beanbags or Carpet Squares*
Location: *Large center circle of multipurpose room*
Instructional Ideas:[6]

Place the beanbags in the circle so they are well spaced. There should be a beanbag for each child. The children should be seated outside of the circle as you explain that the line of the circle is actually a high fence. Let the children through the imaginary gate and have them sit on a beanbag. The lesson will proceed to encourage listening and control through the presentation of challenges to the children. The following suggestions are representative of the challenges that might be used.

1. Stand on two feet or one foot while as high or low as you can be.
2. Place two, three, or four body parts on the bean bag.
3. Place designated body parts on the beanbag.

4. Place a body part such as a foot, hand, or knee on the beanbag and move the rest of your body around the beanbag.
5. Walk or hop around your beanbag.
6. On the command "move" jump over your beanbag with high, long, wide, light, or heavy jumps.
7. Move in general space, walk within the boundaries of general space without touching any other person or object. Utilize "freeze" frequently to assure understanding and listening.
8. Walk fast or slow and then return to your self-space.
9. Go to another's self-space and return to your own.
10. Use walking, jumping, hopping, skipping, sliding, and galloping in general space. As more control is developed directional and force changes can be included.
11. Return to your beanbag and make a narrow or wide bridge over it.
12. Place a beanbag on your head, shoulder, knee, back while standing or in crab position.
13. With the beanbag on your head move from a stand to kneeling to stomach, to back and back to a stand.
14. Balance a beanbag while using locomotor movements.
15. Place the beanbag down and place your head, stomach, back, toe or other body parts over the beanbag.
16. Build a beanbag bridge over the fence and have the children walk on the bridge and line up at the door.

Concept: *Environmental variables place new demands on the child's control of locomotor movements.*
Organizing Center: *Locomotion*
Equipment: *Carpet squares, tires, ropes, boxes, benches, hoops, lines, cubes, barrels.*
Location: *Multipurpose room or gymnasium*
Instructional Ideas:[6]

Set the equipment out in designated general space areas. If there is limited equipment students may be assigned to areas and appropriate equipment challenges may be extended to the children within each area. The following suggestions are representative of the challenges that might be used.

1. Jump onto a rubber-backed carpet or into a tire. Then jump so your feet are along the sides of the carpet or on the sides of the tire. Repeat the drill using these cues for the tire "jump in", "jump on" (jumping jack movement).
2. Jump or run on the carpets or in the tires or hoops so that the child has a set number of jumps or running steps in or on each object.

3. Place cones on their sides and have the children jump or leap over them or utilize any or all of the locomotor movements to weave in and out between the cones.
4. Place a row of tires flat on the floor with one next to the other. Have the children jump once or twice on or in each tire.
5. Jump alternately in and on the row of tires.
6. Jump over one, two, or three tires placed flat and edge to edge.
7. Jump over one, two, or three tires stacked one on top of the other.
8. Jump to a target (tire or carpet).
9. Leap to a target. Run and leap to a target.
10. Walk between two outstretched jump ropes approximately four inches apart. Use as a balance area first, then ask child to use long steps, a one foot lead and the other foot lead (gallop movement).
11. Jump to sides, forward, backward, or using turns over an outstretched straight or curved rope.
12. Crawl through a barrel or shape cube using different body parts to first enter and then leave the object.
13. Jump off a bench using the proper landing form.
14. Practice the step-hurdle (one foot take-off to two foot landing) by leaping onto a rubber backed carpet square.
15. Place a carpet square in front of a vaulting table or stand. Using the step-hurdle, vault onto the table on hands and knees, squat, front rest or straddle positions. Dismounts may include stressing the landing form in high, tuck, straddle, or one-half turn jumps onto the mat.
16. Jump or leap over a rolling ball.

Concept: *Environmental variables place new demands on the child's control of manipulative movements.*
Organizing Center: *Manipulation*
Equipment: *Carpet Squares, beanbags, tires, wall targets, cage ball, medicine ball, beachball, playground ball, softball, rhythm ball, fleece ball, hoop, ropes, box, cone, pringle cans, paddles, sticks (paint stirrers).*
Instructional Ideas:[6]

1. Drop a beanbag on your carpet square.
2. Throw the beanbag at the center or corners of the carpet square as soft or hard as you can throw.
3. Sit on your carpet and toss and catch your beanbag. Kneel or stand and toss your beanbag a littler higher so you catch it without moving the carpet square.
4. Take two steps away from your carpet. See if you can throw the beanbag onto the carpet. Increase the distance of the throws. Use high, low, soft, or hard throws.

5. Throw at wall targets and return to your carpet.
6. Throw beanbags into a tire on its side or on its edge.
7. Throw beanbags at a cageball, medicine ball, beachball, or through a hoop, or tire.
8. Roll a ball around your carpet with your hands, hand, feet, foot, knee, or elbow. Keep the ball close to you and be able to "freeze" it.
9. Bounce the ball with both hands or one hand while kneeling or standing in a hoop or circled rope.
10. Bounce a ball into a tire, on a carpet, and into a hoop or box.
11. Slide a beanbag or roll a ball at a pringle can or cone.
12. Hold a beanbag with both hands and drop it onto the kicking foot. Stand outside the hoop and punt the beanbag into the hoop. Increase the distance of the kicks.
13. Push a beanbag, beachball, playground ball, fleece ball and other types of balls with a paddle or stick. Keep the ball under control so that directional and force variations can be used. (This may progress to a mass drill in a general space area if the children are exhibiting good control.)
14. Balance an object on a paddle or stick and then move.
15. Bounce the ball down or up using a paddle.
16. Throw and catch beanbags, fleece balls, or playground balls while balancing on tires at increasing distances. (The base of support is established and allows the child to concentrate on catching the ball coming to him.)

Concept: *Area assignments provide a variety of experiences that encourage the child's creativity within the movement and spatial limitations.*
Organizing Centers: *Stabilization, Locomotion, and Manipulation*
Equipment: *As stated or labeled in examples.*
Instructional Ideas:[6]

The number and the complexity of the movement areas is dependent on the responsibility level, movement control demands, and the equipment, and spatial requirements available. The teacher would be wise to begin with just two areas and increase the areas to what ever number the children are capable of handling.

Area "A" Movement Obstacle Course	Area "B" Scooter Obstacle Challenges

1. Movement Obstacle Course: Rope swing onto a mat, horizontal rope challenges, bench movement challenges and movements through a shaped cone.

2. Scooter Obstacle Challenges: Move through cone obstacle while sitting or lying on the scooter. Move forward or backward using your hands, feet, or both.
3. Crabwalk shuttle changing directions or carrying objects.
4. Crawling, turning, and moving creatively through a barrel or tube.
5. Throw or roll balls to specific targets.
6. Throw a medicine ball at a target on a wall mat.
7. Jump rope with a short rope.
8. Roll or throw a medicine ball to a partner.
9. Dribble a ball through an obstacle course.
10. Push a ball with a paddle or foot or hand through an obstacle course.
11. Jumping and climbing on benches and other small equipment.
12. Carry a medicine ball with a partner.
13. Roll a cageball with a partner.
14. Have a group of children carry a mat or pole.
15. Utilize combination and task sequence activities.

Concept: *Low organizational games provide a variety of movement experiences for the child.*

Organizing Center: *Manipulation and locomotion*

Instructional Ideas:[6]

A game called Rapid Fire calls for a team to be on each side of the gym floor. Players are not permitted to step over the center line or make illegal throws or kicks. Three, five, seven, or nine balls or beanbags may be used. The objective of the game is to have the fewest number of balls on your side when the stopping signal is sounded. Balls thrown after the signal result in an automatic loss for the team throwing the ball. This game activity provides high level participation, fitness, and a variety of movement experiences by changing the legal or correct manipulative task.

1. Roll playground balls or beanbags across line.
2. Utilize one or two hand throws.
3. Utilize playground, fleece, basketball, soccer and other types of balls.
4. Utilize various kicking skills.
5. Require that balls must be trapped with the feet prior to throwing or kicking them across the line.
6. Require different skills for using each of several types of balls. The beachball is hit with the hand. The soccer ball is trapped and kicked with an inside of the foot kick. The playground ball is rolled over the line.

Activities Related to the Child's General and Specific Movement Skills

The elaboration of instructional ideas for the child's general and specific movement skills are an outgrowth of the information contained in Chapter Eight.

The following materials are representative samplings of combination and selection experiences included in the physical education curricular areas of games, rhythms, and self-testing.

Concept: *Basketball skill circuit activities provide for maximum involvement by all of the students.*

Organizing Centers: *Stabilization, Locomotion and Manipulation*

Equipment: *As stated in examples*

Instructional Ideas:[6]

1. Station number 1 - Pivoting: From starting line, run to first tire placing right foot in tire and pivot forward around the tire. Run to the second tire and place right foot in tire and pivot backward around tire. Run to turning line or cone and return placing the left foot in each of the tires and pivoting backward and forward around the tires.

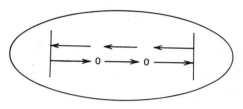

2. Station Number 2 - Obstacle Dribble: The obstacle consists of one cone in the center of a circle and four cones on the line of the circle dividing it into four equal parts. Start at a designated outside cone and dribble to the center cone, out to the next cone, back into the center cone and keep repeating this until stopped. Dribble into the circle using the right hand and dribble out of the circle using the left hand.

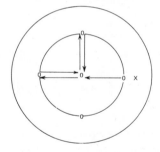

3. Station Number 3 - Rebounding: Toss a partially deflated playground ball above line on wall. Jump and catch ball while ball and jumper are still in the air.

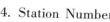

4. Station Number 4 - Guarding: Partner activity where both partners face each other. One is the offensive man who tries to move either to the right or left of a center line and past either of the two side boundaries. If he can cross either of the sidelines without being guarded he scores a point.

5. Station Number 5 - Lay-ups: The objective is to make as many shots within the time limit as possible.

6. Station Number 6 - Wall Chest Pass: Utilizing the proper fundamentals see how many chest passes can be completed in the time allowed.

7. Station Number 7 - Agility Run: Run through patterned obstacle. Each time the runner passes the start, a point is earned.

8. Station Number 8 - Center Jump: Stand with the right and then left side to the wall. Jump and touch above lines on wall with right hand then left. The point value of the highest line touched by the right and left hands is totaled for the score.

9. Station Number 9 - Bounce Pass. Score one point for each pass to your partner that bounces in the hoop between you and is caught.

10. Station Number 10 - Free Throws: Shoot all shots from behind free throw line and rebound quickly. One point for each basket scored.

NOTE: Circuit activities should be introduced prior to their use in a circuit. The number of stations may be increased as the children become capable of handling more responsibility.

Concept: *The lead-up game of Basketball Snatchball is a modification of official basketball*

Organizing Centers: *Manipulation and Locomotion in the form of specific basketball skills.*

Equipment: *Two basketballs, two tires, two lines, and one basket.*

Instructional Ideas:[6] At the command "Go", the first child on team A and team B come out to their team's tires and get the basketball. The ball must be passed to each team member using a designated pass. Dropped balls must be passed again. After all passes have been completed, the active team member is permitted one shot at the basket. He then gets the rebound and quickly dribbles the ball back to the tire and places the ball into the tire. A team gains a point for a basket and for being first to place the ball into the tire. The next person on each team then

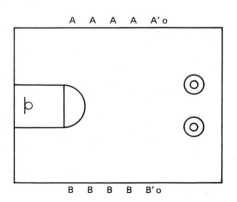

awaits the "GO" signal. A second contest can be run simultaneously at the other end of the court by this method. This game can start out as a drill and then become a competitive game. The game may be varied by requiring different kinds of passes, shots and dribbling techniques, and patterns.

Concept: *Indoor Softball circuit activities enhance general and specific manipulative abilities*

Organizing Centers: *Manipulation in the form of specific softball skills.*

Equipment: *Four soft softballs, one mat, three carpet squares, cones, fleece ball, wiffle bat, five inch rubber ball and small box.*

Instructional Ideas:[6]

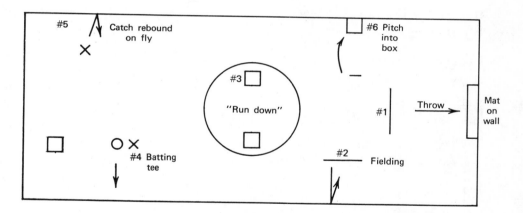

1. Station Number 1 - Throw: Hard overhand throw to mat target stressing opposition and summation of forces.
2. Station Number 2 - Fielding: Throwing ball at line on wall and field grounders getting hands out front and giving with the ball.
3. Station Number 3 - "Run Down": Base runner starts between the bases and basemen and attempts to get to either of the bases without being tagged. (The bases are located to avoid interference with other stations if there is an overthrow—see diagram.)

4. Station Number 4 - Batting Tee: Use stacked cones as a batting tee. Hit a fleece ball off the cones with a wiffle bat stressing the grip, stride, focus, and level swing and putting the bat down prior to retrieving the ball. (Other children must be behind the ondeck batter who will stand on a carpet or in a hoop a safe distance from the batter.)

5. Station Number 5 - Catch Rebound or Fly: Throw a five inch rubber ball against the wall and catch it on the fly.

6. Station Number 6 - Underhand Pitch: Pitch a softball into a box from behind the line. Stress a curved flight and accuracy.

Concept: *Baseball lead-up games are modified to the learner's developmental level*

Organizing Centers: *Manipulation in the form of specific softball skills.*

Equipment: *Stacked cones for a batting tee, fleece ball, wiffle bat, wiffle ball, five inch rubber ball, softball bat, and four sets of markers or lines.*

Instructional Ideas:[6]

The fielding team must stay behind the center line "B". Balls that hit the ceiling or are caught on the fly are outs. The batting team lines up on line "O". The first batter hits the ball off the tee. If the ball hits down beyond line "A", one run is scored for his team. See diagram for other scoring. The batter then goes to line "P" until all of his team has batted and it is their turn to be in the field. The ball and bat selected for this activity will depend somewhat on the skills of the children, the size of the facility, and whether it will be used outside.

Concept: *Physical fitness activities may be performed in a circuit*
Organizing Centers: *Stabilization, Locomotion and Manipulation*
Equipment: *As stated in examples.*
Instructional Ideas:[6]

1. Station Number 1 - 30 foot Shuttle Run
2. Station Number 2 - Medicine Ball Put
3. Station Number 3 - Tire Agility Run
4. Station Number 4 - Rope Climb
5. Station Number 5 - Short Rope Jumping
6. Station Number 6 - Pull-ups

Concept: *Folk dances develop general and specific movement skills*
Organizing Center: *Locomotion in the form of the bleking step.*
Equipment: *Record player, record, and floor space.*
Instructional Ideas:[6] *(La Raspa)*

Have the children stand in a general space area in a scattered formation and show them the step used in the "Mexican Hat Dance". Take them through the dance step move by move using verbal cues such as "kick and kick and kick" or "left and right and left". Use the record and take them through the four repetitions of the bleking step and have them note the change in tone and tempo of the music. Then have them go through the bleking step and turn or move themselves around in various ways when the music is indicating an elbow swing turn. Later have them select *any* partner for this portion of the dance. If uneven numbers are present or as another variation, allow the children to skip or turn in a circle in groups of three, four or more and then return to the bleking steps.

Concept: *A Rhythms circuit is a novel way of ehancing rhythmic skills*
will incorporate hoop activities. Tinikling activities will be in *Zone Two*. In *Zone*
Organizing Centers: *Locomotion and Manipulation*
Equipment: *Hoops, tinikiling poles, long ropes, short ropes, record player and record*
Instructional Ideas:[6]

Utilize a 3/4 or 4/4 time record (depending on the tinikiling step being used). If an appropriate record is not available, these activities can be easily performed to their natural movement rhythms.

Utilizing four zones, or areas, assign squads to each of the zones. *Zone One* will incorporate hoop activities. Tinikiling activities will be in *Zone Two*. In *Zone Three* there will be long rope jumping activities, and in *Zone Four* there will be short rope jumping activities. Each of these activities and their progressions should have been taught previous to this experience. Similar combinations of rhythmical activities may be combined.

ACTIVITIES RELATED TO THE CHILD'S TOTAL
EDUCATIONAL EXPERIENCE

The activities of the elementary physical education curriculum are related to the child's total educational experience. Movement activities provide children with learning experiences associated with the cognitive, affective, and psychomotor domains. This portion of the chapter will emphasize the integration of the three domains of learning in movement activities. The conceptual approach to teaching physical education to young children encompasses the child's perceptual-motor development and the total elementary curriculum subject matter areas of language arts, mathematics, science, social studies, art, and music. For a more comprehensive development and coverage of specific instructional ideas integrating these subject matter areas with physical education experiences, the reader is referred to Chapters Thirteen through Seventeen. Some instructional ideas or activities that have been utilized in the school setting will be suggested but not fully developed here. The purpose of these suggested instructional ideas or activities is to stimulate the reader's awareness of the possibilities for integrating movement activities with the child's total educational experiences.

Activities Related to the Child's Perceptual-Motor Development[6]

1. Place body parts on or over beanbag, move only designated body parts, place one body part on another, change the base of support to feet, foot, back, stomach, or hand and foot. (Body Differentiation)
2. Walk between two pringle cans spaced four inches apart, move through shapes without touching them, make your body tall, long, small, short or wide, or perform jump one-half, one-quarter, or full turns. (Body Image)
3. Balance or stability oriented activities, such as balancing on beanbag stepping stones, directional awareness activities relating to forward, backward, sideward, up and down movements. (Laterality-Directionality)
4. Use scarves, beanbags or balls for throwing and catching activities. (Visual Perception and Eye-Hand Coordination)
5. Hit a drum "X" number of times. The children will then bounce and catch the ball that number of times. (Eye-Hand Coordination, Auditory Discrimination, and Memory)
6. Coordination exercises such as jumping jacks, striding, or various other arm and leg coordination activities. (Rhythmic Patterning, Sequencing, Laterality, Directionality)
7. Tape shapes to the floor and trace them using hands, feet, and various forms of locomotion. See if the child can use a free space and move to outline the shape. Use a jump rope, beanbags, or sticks to make various

shapes. Roll a ball on the lines of shapes. Crawl through or throw an object through standing geometric shapes made from wood. (Form Perception)

8. Use colored flash cards: Green-squat, Yellow-arms overhead, Blue-balance on one foot, and Red-hands to opposite shoulders. (Visual-Motor Match, Color Discrimination)

Activities Related to the Child's Language Arts, Mathematics, Science, Social Studies, and Art and Music Development.[6]

1. Games or activities that stress listening skills. Jump only on the word jump. Substitute other words that are similar and dissimilar in sound. A movement only on the proper word is acceptable. (Language Arts: decoding, encoding, and closure)

2. Movement activities that teach the use or meaning of prepositions. Carpet square, hoops, or tires can be used with various forms of locomotion that stress the child's relationship to that object. Select movements to establish over, under, around, through, between, among, onto, into, and next to. (Language Arts: recognition of prepositions)

3. Devise activities that stress the understanding of vocabulary. Use terms such as big, small, fast, slow, narrow, wide, hard, soft, near, close, up, down, stretched, curled, curved, straight, edge, side, top, and bottom. (Language Arts: vocabulary building and auditory association)

4. The grouping of children for area assignments or the overlapping of general space areas to teach about shared space might help children to realize the relationship of themselves to their group or other groups. (Mathematics: sets)

5. Task sequences for the children that require specific movements performed in a specific order. (Language Arts: auditory memory)

6. Geometric shaped obstacle course where the child must first identify the shape prior to moving through it. Allow children to determine differences in similar shapes of various sizes. (Mathematics: geometric shapes)

7. Take beanbags and stack them up in a self-space area. Take them one at a time to another stacking place and count them. Take your beanbags and make a straight line, triangle, or square. (Mathematics: quantitative ideas and geometric shapes)

8. Combative activities can be utilized to help children become more aware of their base of support, center of gravity, friction, and the application of force. (Science: concepts stated above)

9. Rope jumping activities or Jump the Shot[12]. (Science: centripetal and centrifugal forces)

10. Throw a variety of balls that differ in size, shape, and weight. Why

doesn't the beachball travel as far as the softball? (Science: air resistance and laws pertaining to projectiles)

11. Children are carrying hoops that are their automobiles. They are moving in the general space area of the circle and are subject to the traffic controls of the city. The space outside the circle is subject to country and superhighway traffic controls. (Social Studies: safety)

12. Tap lummi sticks in set patterns. Pass one or two sticks to a partner in set rhythm and pattern. Do the stick pass while marching or jumping. (Music: rhythm and tempo)

13. Play the "Picture Game" where on "freeze" the children all become motionless like a still picture. Concepts that might be stressed include facial expressions, action poses, individual positions, group positions with all separated or touching, statues of famous people, and other posed subject ideas. (Art: expression, line, space and shape)

14. Make animal or object shapes with jump ropes and then move about like that animal or object. Have children identify by the rope shape and then if necessary by the movement what the child has created. (Art: shape, line, space, expression)

SELECTED REFERENCES

1. Bloom, Benjamin S. *Taxonomy of Educational Objectives-Handbook I: Cognitive Domain*. New York: David McKay Co., 1956.
2. Dauer, Victor P. *Dynamic Physical Education for Elementary School Children*. Minneapolis, Minnesota: Burgess Publishing Company, 1971.
3. Kirchner, Glenn. *Physical Education for Elementary School Children*. Dubuque, Iowa: Wm. C. Brown Company Publishers, 1974.
4. Kounin, Jacob S. *Discipline and Group Management in Classrooms*. New York: Holt, Rinehart and Winston, Inc., 1970.
5. Krathwohl, David R.; Bloom, Benjamin S.; and Masia, Bertram B. *Taxonomy of Educational Objectives-Handbook II: Affective Domain*. New York: David McKay Company, Inc., 1964.
6. Luedke, George. *Ideas That Work-An Elementary Physical Education Curricular Guide-Part II*. Unpublished Curriculum Developed and Implemented at the Irving Elementary School Physical Education Learning Center. Alton, Illinois, 1972-1974.
7. Luedke, George. *Physical Education, Educational Psychology and the Affective Domain*. Unpublished Paper. Bloomington: Indiana University, 1972.
8. Luedke, George. *The Principles of Modifying Movement Experiences*. Unpublished Paper. Bloomington: Indiana University, 1972.
9. Moehn, Larry, and Luedke, George. *Methods and Materials in Elementary Physical Education*. Unpublished course syllabus. Edwardsville: Southern Illinois University, 1970.
10. Mosston, Muska. *Teaching Physical Education*. Columbus, Ohio: Charles E. Merrill Books, Inc., 1966.
11. Sweeney, Robert T. *Selected Readings in Movement Education*. Reading, Massachusetts: Addison-Wesley Publishing Company, 1970.
12. Vannier, Mary Helen; Foster, Mildred; and Gallahue, David L. *Teaching Physical Education in Elementary Schools*. Philadelphia: W.B. Saunders Company, 1973.

PART II
Learning Through Movement

Chapter 10
Learning Through Movement: Introduction

Key Concept: The curriculum in preschool and elementary school physical education consists of a series of locomotor, stability, and manipulative experiences designed to aid the child in developing the refining processes of cognitive and affective development through movement.

Content: The Contribution of Physical Education to Human Development Through the Ages

Cognitive Development

Social-Emotional Development

Learning Through Movement: Introduction

THE CONTRIBUTION OF PHYSICAL EDUCATION TO HUMAN DEVELOPMENT THROUGHOUT THE AGES

Throughout the ages philosophers and educators have stressed the importance of physical development and good health as a framework for optimum mental effectiveness. The early Athenian Greeks sought to blend the "man of action" and the "man of wisdom." A prerequisite for developing this ideal citizen was an educational system that would enhance all aspects of a child's physical and mental potential and blend them into a single well-rounded personality. Later, Greek philosophers such as Socrates, Plato, and Aristotle professed "a sound mind in a sound body."

During the Middle Ages stress was placed on the development of the mind at the expense of physical development. The birth of the Renaissance placed a new emphasis on the development of the whole man, mind, and body. Philosophers of the sixteenth century such as Montague, Locke, and Comenius accounted for the necessity of health and physical training although they failed to understand the esthetic and social values of exercise and sports.

The eighteenth century was a period of transition to modern political, social, religious, and educational ideals. Perhaps the French philosopher Rousseau has influenced modern educational ideals more than any other man. The following are some quotations from Rousseau's *Emile* that reveal his views on physical education. "The weaker the body the more it commands; the stronger it is the better it obeys ... A debilitated body enfeebles the soul ... If you would cultivate the intelligence of your pupil, cultivate the power which it is to govern. Give his body continual exercise; make him robust and sound in order to make him wise and reasonable; let him work and move about and run and shout and be continually in motion ... It is a very deplorable error to imagine that the exercise of the body is injurious to the operations of the mind; as if these two activities were not to proceed in concert, and the second were not always to direct the first."[9] Rousseau believed that a sound body makes a sound mind. He understood the comparative educational values of different sports as well as the emotional and social outcomes of physical exercise.

238

The importance of physical development and health as a framework for optimum mental effectiveness is further stressed by other educational philosophers. Kant emphasized the disciplinary value of physical education. A strong, sturdy body and a keen, alert mind were recognized as the results of physical exercise. Pestalozzi believed in the recreational value of play as well as its contribution to the harmonious development of mind, heart, and body. He believed that the strength, skill, endurance, and command of the body in general, derived from physical exercise, warranted an important place for physical education in the total educational curriculum. Froebel theorized that education is most efficiently acquired through activity, self-expression, and social participation. The kindergarten grew out of Froebel's theory of education through play.

Over the past five decades numerous statements have been developed by leading educational organizations that represent the general goals of education. In 1918 the Commission of Reorganization of Secondary Education of the National Education Association issued a report containing the seven cardinal principles of education. The seven cardinal principals were (1) health, (2) command of the fundamental processes, (3) worthy use of leisure time, (4) worthy home membership, (5) vocation, (6) citizenship, and (7) ethical character. In 1938 the Educational Policies Commission outlined four broad objectives that were subsequently used as a basis upon which many state and local organizations structured their educational programs. These were (1) the objectives of self-realization, (2) objectives of human relationships, (3) objectives of economic efficiency, and (4) objectives of civic responsibility. The seven cardinal principles of education and the four objectives of education further point out the need for physical education in the development of the whole child.

Physical educators are perhaps more familiar with the philosophy of physical education proposed by Jesse F. Williams. He proposed that students be educated "through the physical" rather than "of the physical." The concepts of organismic unity (unity of mind and body), interdependence between organism and environment, and social and emotional as well as physiological outcomes of physical activities are outgrowths of this philosophy. As a result, physical education ceases to be merely a gymnastic routine, a series of dance steps, or a coordination exercise; it becomes a rich and varied practice that has its focus not in the muscles but in the "whole" individual. Perspiration and the learning of skills are no longer always the chief outcome. As children learn through movement, they also learn about the cognitive, emotional and social outcomes of physical education.

As the unique contribution of physical education to the total educational curriculum is movement, physical educators must teach children to utilize movement as a means of expressing, exploring, developing, and interpreting themselves and their relationship to the world in which they live (Figure 10-1). The child in the home is family oriented. The parents, particularly the mother, are the greatest influencing factor in a child's development. A good home environment will provide children varied experiences in readiness training for success in school. Each child should receive language stimulation and sensorimotor training involving large muscle activities, body image, fine motor coordination, form perception, and texture, size, and color gradients. A good home environment will also enable children to move along the scale from being egocentrically oriented to where they learn to play alongside and in cooperation with siblings and a few close neighborhood friends. Self-play and parallel play involve many creative and imaginative activities in the home, backyard, and neighborhood. Successful experiences in the home lead toward the development of a good self-concept and an attitude of confidence in preparation for school. If children have a limited amount of experiences in the home or have been unsuccessful in their experiences, it is the job of the school to give them readiness training for success in school. Physical education contributes to readiness for success in school through gross motor activities, perceptual-motor training, and opportunities for emotional-social development.

When children are ready for school, their environment expands to the community and eventually to the state, the nation and the world. Schools, playgrounds, parks, and streets replace the home or immediate neighborhood as the environment for interaction. Children become peer oriented and teachers become the greatest influencing factor in their development. Peers move from small group play to complex social interaction depending on the stage of de-

Children Learn Through
Movement

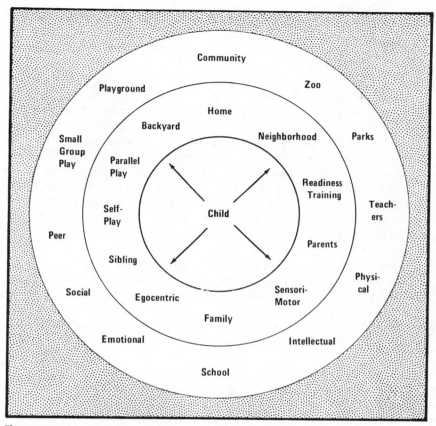

Figure 10-1. The circle of interaction of the developing child and his world.

velopment. In school, teachers introduce children to the rigors of academic learning. Physical education contributes to the total educational curriculum by fostering the physical, cognitive, emotional, and social development of children through movement. Movement becomes a means through which children can express, explore, develop, and interpret themselves and their relationship to the world in which they live.

COGNITIVE DEVELOPMENT

The relationship between motor development and intelligence during the first two years of life is so marked that motor items figure largely in tests of general intelligence. Babies who are slow in sitting, standing, crawling, or walking generally prove to be slow in cognitive development. On the other hand, babies who are advanced in motor development tend to be intellectually precocious. The average difference of the age of walking has been found to be significantly different between babies of high and low intelligence.

Results of research on the relationship between motor skills and academic achievement have indicated that the type of movement activities that children experience may influence their academic achievement. Several perceptual-motor theorists who have worked with low achievers have discovered that perceptual skill deficiencies are prominent factors in poor academic work. Programs of motor therapy have aided these children in developing their symbolic-perceptual systems, and thus have improved their academic achievement.

Ismail, Kephart, and Cowell[4] studied the results of motor aptitude tests, academic success, and intelligence and found that measures of coordination and balance were *fair* predictors of academic achievement. Therefore, experiences designed to enhance the balance and coordination of children should promote, to a certain degree, a better chance for academic success.

Evidence indicates that early exploratory movement and perceptual-motor experiences as initiated through a preventative approach rather than one of remediation will help prepare a child for success in school. Programs designed to enhance the body image, balance, awareness of spatial relationships, space/time relationships, and perception of children through a movement exploration approach will directly affect their cognitive development.

While motor performance and intelligence can be directly related during a child's early years, there is practically no relationship between motor performances and normal intelligence among older children and adolescents. Studies of elementary school children have indicated low correlations between their motor skills and mental growth and reading ability. Children who are mentally deficient, however, are likely to be below the norm for their age in motor development. The more retarded the child is mentally, the more deficient will be his motor development patterns. The differences in motor performance between normal children and mentally retarded children also increase with age.

Although there is practically no relationship between motor performance and normal intelligence, evidence indicates that physical education experiences can be designed to enhance academic learning in the classroom. Werner[11] studied the effects of integration of physical education with selected science concepts upon the science knowledge and selected physical performance skills of boys and girls at the fourth, fifth, and sixth grade levels. Children who received integrated training in the classroom and in physical education on the concepts of levers, Newton's First and Third Laws of Motion, and work performed significantly better on a science knowledge test and on selected motor skills than those who did not receive the benefit of such training. These mechanical principles of movement as well as others can and should be learned by all children. As concepts are learned they can be applied to the learning of new movement patterns. Scientific concepts or applications of them can be made in the exploration and problem solving phases involved in the learning of basic movement patterns in the primary grades. Later, application of efficient movement principles should be transferred to the learning of specific sports skills. As children gain a knowledge of how the body operates and what it is capable of doing, they will understand the cause and effect relationship of exercise and the maintenance of fitness throughout life.

Not only are there opportunities for the integration of mechanical science concepts with physical education, but also many meaningful situations in which physical education can be integrated with mathematics, social studies and language arts to enhance the academic development of children. Number concepts, scoring, records, knowledges involving the background of an activity or sport, terminology, rules governing the activity and strategy of play are but a few examples in which academic concepts can be meaningfully applied in physical education.

Physical education experiences contribute directly to the cognitive development of children early in life through movement exploration and perceptual-motor experiences. Later, there is practically no relationship between motor performance and normal intelligence. However, the integration of physical education with academic concepts increases the possibilities for successful achievement in school.

SOCIAL-EMOTIONAL DEVELOPMENT

The social development and emotional development of children occur simultaneously and interdependently as they interact with their environment and consider their past experiences and present feelings. McCandless[6] has noted that the infant first responds socially and then emotional controls begin to develop. Erikson[5] also links social and emotional growth through a socialization process that depicts developmental psychosocial crises that the child must solve. The child's early experiences of feeling comfort and love in a dependency relationship with his parents, relatives, or caretakers as well as the multiplicity of his environmental stimulation all effect the success of the child's social-emotional development. A good or poor parent, an affluent or culturally deprived environment and the quality and quantity of stimulation for the child will largely determine if he views his world as one that he can control or one that controls him. Since both the social and emotional components are learned, the educator should be encouraged to foster these components within the child's development. If teachers are to foster these developmental components, they must be aware of the powerful influence of early childhood experiences in establishing the child's social and emotional base. Although new experiences can modify the children's social and emotional growth, the childhood base provides the degree of attentiveness and willingness to interact with the environment. This social-emotional foundation, which children carry within them, is one of the major reasons for individual learning differences among children. Two other individual differences related to social-emotional development reported by Davitz[2] include emotional sensitivity and the amount of active emotion the person exhibits. All these interrelated facets of the child's social-emotional development account for such variables as the child's self-concept, the degree of motivation, interests, and eagerness to interact with the environment. It is the teacher's study of the social-emotional developmental process that will provide the necessary understandings to develop meaningful movement experiences. These experiences will be designed to strengthen the child's social-emotional growth and should be in accordance with the child's developmental needs.

Although the scope of this text at this time does not deal in depth with the social-emotional development of the young child, it is recognized that this is an extremely important facet of the total development of the child. For further information concerning the social-emotional behavior of young children the reader is referred to the excellent writings of Espenschade[3], McCandless[6], Mussen[8], Erikson[5], and Sears[5].

SELECTED REFERENCES

1. Cratty, Bryant. *Perceptual and Motor Development in Infants and Children*. New York: Macmillan Company, 1970.
2. Davitz, Joel, *The Communication of Emotional Meaning*. McGraw-Hill Book Company, 1964.
3. Espenschade, Anna, and Eckert, H. *Motor Development*. Columbus, Ohio: Charles E. Merrill, 1967.
4. Ismail, A.H., Kephart, N., and Cowell. C. *Utilization of Motor Aptitude Tests in Prediction of Academic Achievement*. Lafayette, Indiana: Purdue University, 1963.
5. Maier, Henry. *Three Theories of Child Development*. New York: Harper and Row Publishers. 1969.
6. McCandless, Boyd. *Children: Behavior and Development*. New York: Holt, Rinehart, and Winston, Inc., 1967.
7. Miller, Arthur, Cheffers, J.T., and Whitcomb, V. *Physical Education: Teaching Human Movement in the Elementary Schools*. Englewood Cliffs, New Jersey: Prentice-Hall, 1974.
8. Mussen, Paul, Conger, J.J., and Kagan, J. *Child Development and Personality*. New York: Harper and Row Publishers, 1969.
9. Rousseau, J.J. *Emile: or, Treatise on Education*. New York: Translated by W.H. Payne, 1911.
10. Schurr, Evelyn. *Movement Experiences for Children*. New York: Appleton-Century-Crofts, 1967.
11. Werner, Peter. *Effects of the Integration of Physical Education with Selected Science Concepts Upon Science Knowledge and Selected Physical Performance Skills of Boys and Girls at the Fourth, Fifth, and Sixth Grade Levels*. Bloomington, Indiana: Indiana University, Unpublished Doctoral dissertation, 1971.

Chapter 11
Cognitive Concept Development

Key Concept: Knowledge of the intellectual characteristics and needs of children enhances the development of a well rounded and well organized program in elementary school physical education.

Content: Introduction
Piaget's Theory of How Intelligence Develops
   Sensorimotor Phase
      Reflex Stage
      Primary Circular Reactions
      Secondary Circular Reactions
      Secondary Schemata
      Tertiary Circular Reactions
      Invention of New Means
   Pre-Operational Phase
      Preconceptual Stage
      Intuitive Stage
   Phase of Concrete Operations
   Phase of Formal Operations
Bloom's Taxonomy of Educational Objectives
   Knowledge
   Comprehension
   Application
Montessori's Method of Teaching Children
Summary of Intellectual Characteristics and Needs of Children

Cognitive Concept Development

INTRODUCTION

Movement education is valuable in the cognitive development of children. A child's level of achievement is mainly dependent upon innate intellectual capacity, but whether or not this potential is realized depends a great deal upon the physical environment. The child's early contact with the physical environment sets the stage for intellectual, emotional, and social development. As he moves from reflexive behavior to early forms of voluntary movement patterns, he utilizes movement to learn about himself and the environment. Successful movement experiences help him/her gain a positive self-concept (sense of self-worth or worthlessness). The child's movement experiences have also been shown to promote readiness factors for success in school. Physical education provides for challenging opportunities to solve problems and participate in creative experiences. Other situations in physical education offer children opportunities to learn about academic subjects in a practical way through integration of the disciplines.

It is essential that physical educators understand the intellectual characteristics and needs of children so that they can best design the physical education curriculum. In an effort to gain a better understanding of these characteristics and needs of children, we will examine the theories of Piaget, Bloom, and Montessori in the following sections.

PIAGET'S THEORY OF HOW INTELLIGENCE DEVELOPS

Although a zoologist by vocation, Jean Piaget is best known as a psychologist and philosopher for his contribution to the study of intellectual development of children. Piaget views development as an inherent, unchangeable, evolutionary process; yet within this developmental process he locates a series of distinct developmental phases and subphases. A *phase* is a common patterning of an individual's life style for the duration of that particular period of time. Piaget's developmental phases are points of reference designed to help us understand the course of a child's development. They serve only to demonstrate the course of development, and do not represent development itself. Each phase reflects a range of organizational patterns that occur in a definite sequence within an *ap-*

246

proximate age span in the continuum of development. Each phase suggests the potential capacity and probable level of behavior of the child. The completion of one phase provides a passing equilibrium, as well as the beginning of an imbalance for a new phase of development.

Subphases within any one of his major developmental phases are called *stages*. Concern is with the pattern and order of sequence rather than with a quantitative analysis. Piaget intentionally avoids a statistical approach. He deals with a tendency toward patterning without relying upon statistical measures of tendency. An individual's rate of development is not bound by age, but rather by developmental stages and phases in their order of sequence.

Sensorimotor Phase

Piaget's developmental theory begins in the cradle. The first phase, covering the first eighteen months of infant life, is that of sensorimotor intelligence. The major developmental tasks are coordination of his actions or motor activities and his perceptions into a tenuous whole. The sensorimotor phase is broken into several stages.

1. Reflex stage.
2. Primary circular reactions.
3. Secondary circular reactions.
4. Secondary schemata.
5. Tertiary circular reactions.
6. Invention of new means.

Reflex Stage

The use of reflexes prevails during the first stage of the sensorimotor phase. This period is characterized by the neonate's first month of life, although some of the primitive and postural reflexes continue into the infant's first year of life. Examples of primitive reflexes are the Moro, startle, grasping, Babinski, searching and sucking, and tonic neck reflexes. Examples of postural reflexes are the righting reflex, pull-up reflex, rolling reflex, stepping reflex, climbing reflex, and crawling and swimming reflex. The very nature of reflexes, spontaneous repetition through explicit motor activity, provides the necessary experience for their maturation. Repetition of reflexes establishes rhythm and regularity of movement. Further use of reflexes tends to form habits. Gradually, the reflexes evolve into early forms of voluntary behavior (see Chapter 2 for an in depth discussion of reflexes).

Primary Circular Reactions

Primary circular reactions mark the beginning of the second stage of the sensorimotor phase. A primary circular reaction refers to the assimilation of a previous experience and the recognition of the stimulus that triggers the reaction.

At this stage accommodation and assimilation emerge to provide an organizational pattern or schema. A schema is the establishment of a pattern of meaningful behavior. It is a behavioral event that can be repeated and coordinated with others.

Reflexive behavior is slowly replaced by voluntary movements from the first to the third month of development. Neurological maturity is a prerequisite before the infant can understand his own sensations. Although the baby's actions are voluntary, they cannot be described as purposive. Voluntary actions serve to prolong the reflex patterns of the first stage. Gradually more than one sense modality is used at the same time. Accidentally acquired responses become new sensorimotor habits. The baby's voluntary actions of grasping, groping, sucking, or looking and listening bring him into contact with new objects. New sensorimotor functions can be utilized by the growing infant. Vision becomes a continuous experience. Sucking, prehension, and hearing provide experimental situations with newly evolving circular reaction patterns. Objects become closely related with the ongoing behavior pattern. Notions of cause and effect and of time-space awareness find their roots during the stage of primary circular reactions in terms of recognizing a sequence of events.

Secondary Circular Reactions

The stage of secondary circular reactions is marked by a child's efforts to create a state of permanency. Primary circular reactions are repeated and prolonged by new secondary reactions. Through reproduction, repetition, and sequencing of events, established patterns of movement can be repeated and coordinated with other behavioral events. For example, the grasping reflex evolves from a sequence of grasping or holding to a unified activity of shaking or pulling. The sight of the end of a familiar string attached to a mobile may be sufficient to induce an infant to pull the string and cause the mobile to move. The string, the pulling, and the mobile are related to a sequence of events in the universe, although the infant is not yet aware that he belongs to the same universe. The infant widens his scope of activity by relating two or more sensorimotor activities into an experimental sequence of schema. Activity remains the primary motive of experience. Vision becomes the primary coordination of experiences, but other sense modalities are also used.

Many roots for future cognitive understanding are acquired during the stage of secondary circular reactions that can be summarized as follows.

1. The infant reacts to distant objects.
2. The beginning of the differentiation between cause and effect takes place.
3. Qualitative and quantitative evaluation are initiated (more and less, etc.).
4. The coordination of separate reactions and response patterns are unified into one schema.

5. The infant becomes aware that he is part of his environment.
6. The notion of time (before and after) enters a sequence of events.
7. The infant recognizes that a particular stimulus (symbol) is part of an entire action sequence.
8. Variety in available patterns of action, the dawning recognition of symbols, rudimentary projecting of time, as well as increased accommodation stress the intentional aspects of the child's behavior.
9. Imitation, play, and affect (emotion) also appear during this stage of development.

Secondary Schemata

Application of secondary schemata to new situations is the fourth stage of the sensorimotor phase. It begins around the eighth month and continues through the infant's first birthday. The essential characteristic of this stage is the advance in intentional behavior of sensorimotor activities such as the prehensive movements involved in reaching, grasping, and releasing, and can now be applied to new situations. Increased experimentation of the environment is facilitated by greater mobility of the child through crawling and supported walking movements. Ends and means are differentiated through experimentation. For this reason it is important for the infant to experiment with his environment as much as possible. Touching, tasting, smelling, grasping, banging pots and pans together, climbing on top of objects, crawling under objects, and other exploratory movements should be encouraged. Adaptability, or plasticity of response, in the development of good motor patterns will be the result of experimentation.

As perception develops the child can relate increasingly to distant objects. The eyes can work in coordination to fixate on stationary objects or follow a moving target. The eyes and hands can work together to form a matching of perceptual and motor data though at a very rudimentary level. Thus, the child can now move his hands to an object and pick it up quite easily, whereas previously a groping action was evident. During this stage the child also learns to experience action by observation. He allows things to happen and observes the results. For example, a child can watch a toy being manipulated by an adult and then respond with delight or with pained cries.

Tertiary Circular Reactions

The first half of the second year of life introduces the fifth stage of sensorimotor development. It is the stage of tertiary circular reactions and is characterized by discovery of new means through active experimentation. The application of old means to new situations marks the beginning of curiosity and novelty seeking behavior. As children discover new means to perform familiar activities and apply old means to new situations, we should provide an open and enriched environment in an effort to encourage children to explore. All too often play pens are used to corral the child and protect the environment, thereby discouraging exploration and discovery.

As a result of exploration and discovery, imitation and reasoning develop. The child can now grasp an ongoing situation and observe its component parts. Consequently, the child can enter into an activity at any part of the sequence without having to start from the beginning each time.

An awareness of spatial relationships is initiated upon the discovery of objects as objects. The child learns about spatial awareness through activities, such as placing various geometrical forms into corresponding openings or building with blocks. The recognition of spatial relationships between objects leads to an awareness of one's own movements and the movements of other people.

Play becomes an expressive function of the developing child. The action phase of learned behavior is a self-satisfying occupation. Children may play at "going to sleep" or "setting the table," but their actions are repeated as self-satisfying activities, not to learn the concept of "bedtime" or "dinner time." Play is termed *ludic*, as it is an activity calculated to amuse and to excite the playing child. Play is less involved in the context of the existing environment, and tends to have meaning only within the context of the child's own imagined world. Thus, ludic play is a repetition of imitative action phases of real life events or fictitious happenings undertaken without purpose except for the sake of self-amusement and satisfaction.

Invention of New Means

The stage of invention of new means through mental combinations is entered sometime during the second half of the child's second year of life. A gradual shift from *actual* sensorimotor experiences to an increased *reflection* about these experiences occurs during this period. This behavior acts as a stepping stone to the preconceptual phase, an advanced level of intellectual behavior.

Toward the second half of his second year, the child becomes aware of objects as independent, permanent centers with their own properties. Objects take on the property of permanency with their own innate qualities such as color, size, form, and use. Characteristically, however, only one property can be considered at one time.

This period also marks a new relationship of children to the environment. Children begin to experience themselves as one among many. They also understand themselves as a single entity. They can understand the immediate past, present, and immediate future in simple situations. However, they still are confused about the self and the external world. Children still remain egocentric throughout early childhood based on this lack of differentiation between themselves and their environment.

Children's new mental patterns also affect previously learned behavior. Sensorimotor patterns are slowly replaced by semimental functioning. Simple causality is perceived by perception alone. The child can initiate alternatives to most simple forms of action without performing by trial and error. The child has a beginning ability to recall without having to repeat an activity with his sensorimotor system. Still, the child is somewhat dependent upon the sensorimotor approach, as is slow to utilize this new organizational pattern of thinking.

The power of mental representation makes it possible for children to show what we term insight. Correct solutions to problems appear with a suddenness that is familiar from such studies of insight as Kohler's work with chimpanzees. In Piaget's terms, we are witnessing the invention of new means through reciprocal assimilation of schemata, which takes place mentally rather than overtly through trial and error. In other words, children can mentally integrate past experiences with the present situation to solve a problem. For example, if a child wants an object that is placed out of his reach he will use a chair to assist in attaining his goal.

Play begins to take on a new concept. Previously play had been purely functional. It involved repetition of life activities as a pleasurable pursuit for egocentric satisfaction. Play in the form of imitation now proceeds with the attempt to copy either actions or representative symbols of actions. For example, a child may imitate his father's work, or, may imitate a particular action in order to convey the idea that he is going to work. Imitation of riding a horse, driving a car, or moving like an animal are other movements representative of action. Parallel play also becomes one of the child's activities. Children may be seen playing beside each other in the same area and activity, but their goals and objectives are different from each other. For example, when two children are playing side by side with blocks, one may be building a bridge while the other is constructing a tall building. If one child decides he needs some of the other child's blocks to finish his project, egocentrism overtakes the situation. Blocks are taken without consideration and tempers flare. In a while, the children are back playing again. Later, sharing and consideration for others will develop as play concepts.

Preoperational Phase

During this phase of development, children begin to take an interest in the people and things around them, though essentially from their point of view rather than their own. The egocentrism of this phase is an intermediate step between the patterns of purely self-satisfying behavior of the sensorimotor phase and the refined forms of social behavior required in later years. To make this progression, the child requires play, imitation, and the use of langauge, which develop rapidly during the preschool and early school years. The preoperational phase of development is divided into the (1) preconceptual stage from two through four years of age and the (2) intuitive stage from four through seven years of age.

Preconceptual Stage

The life of the child in the preconceptual stage appears to be one of continuous investigation. Play occupies most of the child's waking hours, since this activity serves to consolidate and to enlarge the child's previous acquisitions. He investigates his environment and the possibilities of his activity within it. Every day he discovers new symbols to use in communication with himself and others. Play, with its emphasis on how and why, becomes the primary tool for adaption. For example, the child who has mastered the routine of dressing soon pretends that he is performing real-life tasks and may be seen involved in activities ranging from simple to complicated situations centered around the concept of "dressing." Imaginary and animistic play are prominent activities of the egocentric child. Life is attributed to activity in general, then to movements, to spontaneous movements, and finally, to plants and animals. Thus, it is not surprising to see a young child who is playing with a truck or doll, carrying on a real conversation with the object. As the child pulls the truck behind him on a string, he might say, "Come on truck, we're going to work." To the child, the truck is alive. Playful repetition of actual events brings the child into contact with the questions and objects of everyday life. Gradually the child will move more and more into realistic experiences with his social world.

Although the child is moving into a perceptual world, movement is extremely important to a child at the preconceptual stage. Movement is an important factor in self-discovery. This self-discovery or self-concept ranges from an awareness of and a fascination with his body parts as an infant to an awareness of the limitations of his body when he has climbed to the highest part of a jungle gym and now finds it impossible to climb back down. Through stability experiences he finds a sense of gravity, a zero point or center of balance. Through manipulation he discovers his body parts and their relationship to one another. Through locomotion he discovers independence and achieves a repertoire of body skills that generate pride through movement. Through kinesthetic awareness the child learns to know how it feels to move and the feedback from each movement tells him if he is successful at his performance. Gradually the more intricate patterns of self-propulsion develop. Soon the child discovers how marvelously constructed he is. The emerging self-concept is ego-enhancing as he calls attention to his stunts and tricks. For example, the child may say "Watch me, watch me," as he crosses a balance beam or swings high on a swing.

As the child discovers his self through movement, he also discovers his environment through movement. As a child's world is expanded through his own mobility, new objects are discovered, examined, and named. His vocabulary is increased as he learns the names of his latest discoveries. The fact that he can move from place to place lays the foundation for exploration of an increasingly complicated social as well as physical world. As he moves he crosses the boundaries of other people's rights and possessions. For the first time he must adjust to the fundamental factor of property rights—a concept in learning to socialize in our culture. As the child moves through his environment, he also develops an orientation in space for time and direction. Through his movements the child learns about concepts such as before, after, in front of, in back of, beside, and so forth.

Language also serves as a vehicle of development. The child repeats words, and connects words with visible objects or perceived actions. As in play, the child experiences his world purely from his egocentric vantage point. His language repeats and replaces his sensorimotor development. Communication by verbal and nonverbal language establishes a bond between thought and word, while it negates the autistic world of imagery and ludic play. In the absence of play, language, or imitative behavior, the child is left in his autistic world and is less subject to the impact of his environment. Play, language, and imitation lead to communication with an outside world and to a gradual process of socialization.

The following are characteristics of the child during the preconceptual stage of development.

1. The child is perceptually oriented; he makes judgments in terms of how things look to him.
2. The child centers on one variable only, and usually it is the variable that stands out visually; he lacks the ability to coordinate variables.
3. The child has difficulty in realizing that an object can possess more than one property, and that multiplicative classifictions are possible.
4. The child experiences either the qualitative or quantitative aspects of objects, but not at the same time. He cannot merge concepts of objects, space and causality into temporal interrelationships with a concept of time.
5. The child identifies with those who satisfy his immediate needs. The child's sense of obedience and awe for his model is derived out of a combination of love and fear and provides the foundation for his conscience.
6. As a child moves through a process approach stressing exploration and discovery, he develops his self-concept and gains a sense of achievement.
7. As a child moves he discovers his environment through experiences that involve controlling, rearranging, assembling, constructing, creating, innovating, and manipulating objects.

8. Movement experiences should create an atmosphere for freedom of creative expression—a quality that should be stressed and developed in a humanistic approach rather than stiffled through regulation through conformity.

Intuitive Stage

The life of the child in the intuitive thought stage of development ranges from four through seven years of age. Most important for these children is their widening social interest in the world around them. Repeated contact with other children reduces egocentricity and increases social participation.

The intuitive thought stage marks the first real beginnings of cognition. Speech replaces movement to express thought. The child tries to adjust his new experiences to his previous patterns of thinking. Current development allows a child to generalize his mental experiences. The child can now view two small green blocks and three large red blocks as a collection of five blocks. The wearing of a football helmet—which in the preconceptual stage meant "I am a football player"—now means that he is playing the role that a football player represents. Although the young child can generalize about these mental experiences,

There Is Great Satisfaction In Learning About Yourself And Your Expanding World

it is still difficult for him to entertain two ideas at the same time. He is still preoccupied with parts of the experience, rather than thinking in terms of the whole.

Increasingly, the child employs appropriate language without fully understanding its meaning. Although the child of preschool years often knows his right arm from his left, he has not yet comprehended an internal awareness of right and left. He has not learned to project an inner awareness of right and left into naming the position of objects in the outside world. Another example is that although the child may know how to count, he still has no concept of quantity. A child must master the principles of conservation of quantity, such as permanency and continuity, before he can develop a concept of numbers. For example, when a child counts six pieces of candy and then places them in a paper bag (regrouping), it is not surprising to see him recount the pieces of candy when he takes them out to see if the same amount still exists (permanency). The principle of continuity is illustrated in learning about the number line through the use of number rods. Three rods placed end to end (continuity) equal the length of one different colored rod. In a year or so, the child will be capable of understanding the concept of numbers because he will have mastered these principles.

Intuitive thought introduces a rudimentary awareness of relationships that eventually can be classified into a conceptual hierarchy, but at this early stage are related to concrete events. For example, the family of the child of preschool age consists of all living things in close physical proximity and frequently includes the family pets. It is almost impossible for the child to understand that he belongs to a particular family, community, town, and country all at the same time.

Language at this level serves a threefold purpose. First, it is employed to reflect upon an event and to project into the future. Frequently, the child can be seen in self-conversation or thinking aloud. Second, speech remains primarily a vehicle of egocentric communication. Finally, speech is a means of social communication. It serves as a means to understand the external environment and to adapt to it.

Play reflects much of the evolutionary intellectual development. Play becomes noticeably social although it still has overtones of egocentrism. The child now uses a more extended symbolic imagination. He may play the role of a cowboy, and also plays guessing games and games involving finding a missing object such as in Hide and Seek. Genuine make believe play also emerges, which indicates that the child has achieved a new level of organizational thinking. He can now think in terms of others. (Social disciplines such as collective rules replace individual ludic symbols.) Traditional games of running and tagging become typical of the age group and replace spontaneous games. Most play is now done in relation to other people. The child can also be seen enacting the rules and values of his elders in his play.

Phase of Concrete Operations

At about seven years of age children begin to think in logical ways. They enter the phase of concrete operations that continues until roughly eleven years of age. Now the child can coordinate facts into a logical whole. The cognitive actions of the child during the stage of concrete operations are really systems of action with definite structural properties. They are five in number.

1. *Additive Composition*—It is possible for the child to think of a whole as being made up of the sum of its parts, and to put parts together to form a classification system. He can form classes in hierarchical arrangement.
2. *Reversibility*—A second property of logical thought is that it is reversible. In fact, every cognitive action can be reversed. The child can combine subclasses of animals or toys into a supraclass and he can reverse the process, separating them into the original groups.
3. *Associativity*—Thought is flexible at this stage of cognitive development. The child can put data together in various ways to solve a problem.
4. *Identity*—When comparing two classes of objects or events, the child can establish identity by making a one-to-one correspondence between the elements in each class.
5. *Deductive Reasoning*—In all of his mental operations, his reasoning takes cognition of a larger whole and the logical relationship to it.

It must be stressed that the mental capacities for concrete operations evolve only gradually. The different properties of space are mastered in a definite sequence. First, the child learns about size in terms of length. At about age eight, he thinks of size in terms of weight. Volume is not comprehended until near the end of this phase.

Up to this point, children's concept of time has included only a notion of before and after. Now, time becomes independent of perceptual data. Children can think of time in terms of past, present, and future. The concept of time becomes fully understood with the coordination of the concepts of equal distance and speed.

Thinking can also be equated to mental experimentation with the symbols of relationship within the field of perception. A child's perceptions are more accurate. He moves from egocentric localization to objective localization. Laterality, directionality, position in space, spatial relationships, as well as other perceptual-motor qualities are refined during this period of development.

Play and conversation are no longer primary means of self-expression, but become means for understanding the physical and social worlds. As a child enters school he becomes peer oriented. He becomes emancipated from parental dominance and participates as an equal in his social world. Observation, comparison, and comprehension of others assume an important part in the child's life. A new level of social behavior is learned by understanding others in terms of their social position. Conscience finds its anchoring points in newly acquired centers of mutual respect and awareness for collective obedience.

The imitation of details has an impact upon play. The games that children play take on detailed rules. Neighborhood ball games become highly structured games with some rules that are universal and others that are peculiar to the group playing the game. Play loses its assimilative characteristics and becomes a balanced subordinate process of cognitive thought. This process is further substantiated by the fact that curiosity no longer finds its expression in active play, but in intellectual experimentation.

Phase of Formal Operations

The last phase of intellectual development occurs when the child is between the ages of eleven through fifteen. During this phase childhood ends and youth begins. The youth becomes a person with the capacity to think and to reason beyond his own realistic world and his own beliefs. He enters into the world of ideas and into essences apart from the real world. Cognition begins to rely upon pure symbolism and the use of propositions rather than sole reality. A systematic approach to problems replaces cognitive random behavior.

The ability to reason by hypothesis furnishes the youth with a new tool to understand his physical world and his social relationships within it. Propositional statements of groupings allow the youth to form new concepts. Deduction by implication is at his disposal. Deduction by hypothesis and judgement by implication enable him to reason beyond cause and effect.

Adolescence is known as an age during which youth think beyond the present. They form notions, ideas, and concepts about everything from the past, through the present, and into the future. The youth reflects maturity in cognitive thought, when he can depend solely upon symbolism for operational thought. He thinks by applying symbols of thinking. He develops concepts of concepts. The individual has reached intellectual maturity.

In summary, Piaget recognizes a number of basic trends that concern all developmental processes.

1. All development progresses in identical sequence moving from the simple to the complex in a unilinear manner.
2. Developmental sequences proceed from concrete experiences or problems toward the mastery of abstract concepts.
3. Personality development progresses from contacts with the physical world to contacts with the social world and finally to the ideational world.
4. Children are egocentric at an early age. Gradually, they move through a

period of pure objective appraisal with a sense of relativity emerging at the onset of maturity.

5. Activity without thought to thought with less emphasis on activity is characteristic of the evolution of intellectual behavior.
6. As children learn to manipulate objects in their environment, they move through a sequential pattern. Children learn about objects (1) through their use, (2) through their permanency, (3) through their representative symbols, (4) through their place in space, (5) through their properties, and (6) through their relativity in space, time, and utility.
7. Early in the life of children actions of all objects are attributed to animism (the belief that nonliving things have personality). Gradually, animism is limited to moving objects, and finally, only to self-perpetuating objects.
8. Children learn a sense of ethics and justice (conscience) as they progress toward maturity. First, children adhere completely to adult authority. Adherence to adult authority is replaced by adherence to mutuality, which gives way to social reciprocity, and finally, to social integrity.
9. As children move toward maturity, previous developmental levels of learning are retained throughout life. Various forms of early behavior patterns find their expression at times when individuals face new problems or feel compelled to revert to previous patterns of behavior.

Piaget's theory of intellectual development also has implications for development of children in preschool and elementary school physical education. Several are enumerated as follows.

1. Movement activities such as those involved in reaching, grasping, releasing, pulling, and elementary forms of locomotion should be designed to enhance the development of the child in the sensorimotor phase of development.
2. During the later stages of sensorimotor development, perceptual development may be enhanced through activities involving ocular pursuit; visual-motor coordination involving experiences with the large muscles of the body may also help perceptual development.
3. Experiences involving position in space and spatial relationships can be taught during the last two stages of sensorimotor development although the child should not be expected to go beyond the point of egocentric localization.
4. Imitation and ludic play are primary sources of activity and learning during the last stages of sensorimotor development; parallel play, imaginary play, and role playing become important as the child nears the preconceptual stage of development.
5. Repetition of successful play experiences is a source of enjoyment for the child in the preconceptual stage of development as well as a contributing factor in each child learning a positive self-concept.

6. As the child reaches the intuitive stage of the preoperational phase of development (enters school), his social world expands, and he becomes ready to be involved in playful activities involving small group games having only a few basic rules.
7. During the phase of concrete operations, perceptual and motor development can be refined to a high degree through a quality physical education program that stresses locomotor, stability, and manipulative activities.
8. Children in the phase of concrete operations have expanded their realm of social behavior. They become highly interested in rules and are now interested in more complex play situations such as lead up games to team sports.
9. The adolescent has reached intellectual maturity and is ready for team sports and activities which are highly organized.

In conclusion, it seems evident that sensorimotor experiences of stability, locomotion, and manipulation are essential for maximum development of perceptual, motor, and intellectual patterns of every child through the preschool and elementary school years. A quality program of elementary school physical education adhering to the phases of motor development outlined in Chapter One and Piaget's theory of cognitive development is essential for the sound growth and development of our children.

BLOOM'S TAXONOMY OF EDUCATIONAL OBJECTIVES

Upon learning more about the intellectual development of children such as just reviewed in Piaget's theory of intellectual development, one becomes increasingly aware of the cognitive phases through which children progress. Bloom sheds further light on cognitive development in the Taxonomy of Educational Objectives, Handbook 1, Cognitive Domain (Bloom, 1956). He categorizes phases of learning into six different levels. They are (1) *knowledge*, (2) *comprehension*, (3) *application*, (4) *analysis*, (5) *synthesis*, and (6) *evaluation*. Knowledge, comprehension, and application are levels of learning that are commonly associated with preschool and elementary school children. Knowledge corresponds with the sensorimotor and preoperational phases in Piaget's theory of intellectual development.

Knowledge

Knowledge implies recall or recognition of specific elements in a subject area. Children in this stage of development gain knowledge of their environment through their senses. They touch, taste, smell, listen, visually inspect everything with which they come in contact. They are continually asking questions.

What is this? How does that work? They build and store this knowledge for later use.

The objective of the ability to recall does not in itself suggest either the existence or the nonexistence of the capability of using or applying that knowledge. Although many of the specifics that we learn to recall or recognize during these early years are forgotten, knowledge of them at the time of learning is extremely important for the development of ideas that do stay with us for interpretive and associational uses. Knowledge objectives serve us in this manner throughout life.

Comprehension

Comprehension is the level of learning beyond knowledge and corresponds with the concrete phase in Piaget's theory of intellectual development. Comprehension is described in terms of three different operations. The lowest order is that of translation, in which the known concept or message is put in different words or changed from one kind of symbology to another. Interpretation is the second level of comprehension. Evidence of this behavior is present when a student can go beyond recognizing the separate parts of a communication and see interrelations among parts. In Piaget's theory the child has now mastered the properties of additive composition, reversibility, associativity, identity, and deductive reasoning. The third level of comprehension is extrapolation. In this category the receiver of a communication is expected to go beyond the literal communication and make inferences about consequences of events. Children can also extend time, space, force, and flow dimensions in movement.

Application

At the beginning of the formal operations phase of intellectual development or during the last years of elementary school, children are capable of learning at the applicative level. Application is the use of abstractions in particular and concrete situations. Abstractions may be in the form of general ideas, rules of procedures, or generalized methods. Technical principles, ideas, and theories that must be remembered and applied are also examples of abstraction. The ability to apply principles and generalizations to new situations is important because it makes learning useful in problem solving. It enables a child to gain some degree of control over his environment. It represents one of the learning outcomes that enables a child to cope with conditions and problems in our changing society. The child who can function well at this level of learning has acquired an intellectual independence that frees him from continued dependence of teachers and other adult authorities.

Again, one may draw many inferences between cognitive development and physical education in the preschool and elementary school years. Movement experiences in stability, locomotion, and manipulation in which the child explores space, time, force, and flow are invaluable in helping a child gain knowledge of his environment. Repetition of movement experiences helps a child retain knowledge of his environment. Problem solving and guided discovery experiences in movement enable a child to move through the knowledge, comprehension, and application levels of learning. Experiences in movement should be initiated with simple patterns and through the years move to complex situations involving more than one element of movement such as space, time, force, and flow at one time. Gradually, a child moves through stages of parallel play and small group play to more complex play situations that involve increasing demands upon social competence and in turn greater competence in the comprehensive and applicative levels of learning.

MONTESSORI'S METHOD OF TEACHING CHILDREN

Montessori's system of education evolved after studying under the leading educators in mental retardation. During the French revolution Itard was the first to observe a pupil in the same way the sick are observed in hospitals. For this reason, Itard is sometimes considered the father of scientific education rather than Wundt or Binet. Seguin perfected Itard's methods and established a real educational system for retarded children. Montessori's methods of educating normal preschool children evolved by observing the mentally retarded while studying under Seguin. Seguin believed that the mind and body constitute an organic unity. The function of education is to complement the organic development of the child. He also believed that idiocy was the effect of causes producing retardation of physical and mental development. Seguin believed that children could often be cured of retardation.

Montessori realized that if visual-motor involvement could be utilized by the slow learner, then it should be equally valuable for working with normal children to stimulate them to learn in their early years. She started her first Casa dei Bambini in 1907. The children she worked with were from three to six years of age and from one of the poor sections of Rome. The purpose of the program was to educate the culturally disadvantaged to a level of achievement that the normal child was reaching, much the same as our modern day projects such as Head Start for inner city children. Philanthropists gave her toys and she provided other apparatus with which to work. The teachers were various mothers whom she trained personally.

Several principles from Montessori's program stand out as being important in the education of all children. Education during early childhood is based on the principle of natural development of the child in a Montessori school. A young child is attracted more to stimuli than he is to reason. Education of the senses will lay the foundation for his mental powers. By multiplying sense experiences and developing the ability to evaluate the smallest differences in various stimuli, we refine our senses and appreciate life more thoroughly. The child learns rough, smooth, hot, cold, large, small, thick, thin, and so forth. He also learns gradations of each such as smaller than and larger than.

In a Montessori school the children are free to move. They are free to do their work alone or in groups. They have liberty within limits. They have ground rules for human behavior. They are not allowed to touch another child or his work unless invited. When a child is finished with his work he is free to put it away, to initiate new work, or free to do nothing, but he is not free to bother others.

The Montessori environment also offers freedom from a fear of failure. Tasks are designed so that the child can succeed. The child is free to become. Thus, there is ample opportunity for each child to gain a positive self-concept.

Children learn by doing. As pointed out already, the children learn through their senses in a Montessori class. They move from simple to complex and from concrete to abstract. Typical tasks in a Montessori class are washing tables, polishing shoes, learning colors, manipulating and learning sandpaper letters, working with number rods, learning mathematics symbols, and learning free flow handwriting.

Children seem to enjoy repetition. When motivated, a child has an absence of fatigue. He can often be seen working at a task for two hours. After much repetition, a child becomes an expert at a movement. Repetition is the secret to perfection. This is the way a child learns to button, hook, buckle, and do other manual skills. Situations must be practical and related to real life situations, however.

Motivation is generally no problem in a Montessori class. Children are motivated to imitate adult tasks. When one child knows how to do something, he can hardly wait to show others. A child is motivated to learn an activity to develop a sense of his own worth.

The main job of the teacher in a Montessori class is that of observation and guidance. The teacher must learn from the child the ways and means of his own education. The teacher prepares the environment that ensures certain child responses. Learning comes from the children and not from the teacher. There are no desks in the classroom. The teacher moves about the class and gives guidance where needed. The teacher is not the sole authority and is not the center of dispensing praise, blame, motivation, encouragement, and correction. The child is the center of the learning experience.

These same educational principles that Montessori used so successfully have great merit for utilization in physical education. Physical education in the preschool and elementary school should be built on the principle of natural de-

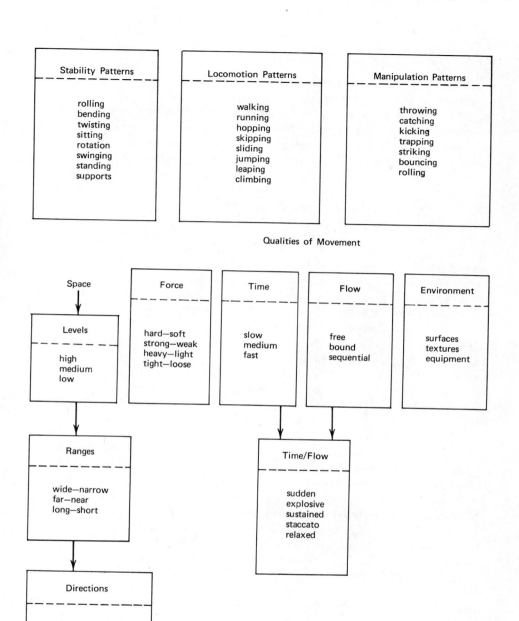

Figure 11-1. Development of basic movement patterns in preschool and primary grades children.

velopment of the child. During the early years (3-7) physical education should be aimed at an education of the senses. Learning experiences in preschool and primary grades should be filled with activities in which children develop the fundamental movement patterns of stability, locomotion, and manipulation (See Figure 11-1). Activities that involve bending, twisting, running, hopping, catching, throwing, striking, and the likehelp children develop a keen awareness of their bodies and their environment. By varying the qualities of movement while exploring the various movement patterns, children develop a plasticity of response. They learn many ways to move, and learn to apply appropriate motor responses to changing environmental conditions. Levels in space (high, medium, low) should be explored. Children should become aware of ranges in movement (wide-narrow, near-far) and directions of movement (forward, backward, sideways, etc.). Experiences in time (slow, medium, fast), force (heavy-light, strong-weak) and flow (free-bound) are also indicative of activities that children need to explore. In short, physical education should help the children learn through multisensorimotor experiences.

Experiences in which children are free to move should be designed by the teacher. Children will accept the ground rules for human behavior. A child should not be allowed to touch another child unless invited. He should be free to experiment in guided discovery situations, but he should not be free to bother others around him. Early school experiences will include individual play and parallel play. Gradually, the children will become ready for small group play, and then for more complex social interaction. When each child is given a ball to manipulate or is free to experiment with various locomotor movement patterns, he will not be attracted toward the end of bothering other children around him. He will be too busy experimenting and learning about how his body moves.

Children learn through the senses by doing. In other words, participation in activities is of utmost importance. Gone is the day where waiting in line or sitting while one child is active is prevalent. Participation through multisensorimotor activities is mandatory in order for each child to perfect his movement patterns and movement skills. Experiences should move from simple to complex and from the concrete to the abstract. Motor experiences should be practical and related to the needs, interests, and social level of the children. For example, whereas it is not recommended to teach a preschool child the intricacies of a basketball hookshot or a complex dance step, it is necessary that we teach him basic ball manipulative patterns and simple locomotor patterns through rhythms. Repetition of patterns is encouraged. After much repetition, a child becomes an expert at movement.

As the children learn through movement experiences that develop movement patterns and movement skills essential to coping with their environment, the physical education curriculum becomes child centered. Just as children in the classroom learn mathematics or science through problem solving and guided discovery, children learn about movement through a set of experiences designed to explore movement patterns and movement skills. Activity becomes a means to an end rather than end in itself. For example, in the past a class being taught a unit in soccer might be taught Circle Soccer or Modified Soccer depending on grade level. This activity was taught as an end, that is to say the games were appropriate for the grade level and unit being taught. To learn how to play soccer was the end objective for the unit. By taking a new look at the same games, we might teach the games because the children are developmentally ready to learn the manipulative patterns of kicking and trapping appropriate for their age and grade level. The games in the soccer unit are no longer the end, but the means to teaching the children about manipulation.

As the physical education curriculum becomes more child centered, the teacher takes on a new role. The physical educator prepares the environment and guides the child's learning experiences. Rather than being concerned only with the *product* of a child's movement, physical education should be directed toward the *process* of learning through which each child explores and discovers many ways to move. In this way, the teacher is not the sole authority. Sources for praise, motivation, encouragement, and correction are both teacher oriented as well as child centered. The child is the center of the learning experience.

SUMMARY OF INTELLECTUAL CHARACTERISTICS AND NEEDS OF CHILDREN

We have examined Piaget's theory of intelligence, Bloom's cognitive domain, and Montessori's method of teaching children. Each gives us some insight about the intellectual characteristics and needs of children. Each has definite application in the field of physical education. Figure 11-2 sums up graphically the cognitive development of children. Knowledge of the phases and stages of development, levels of learning, and characteristics and needs of children should serve as guidelines in the development of the physical education curriculum.

Only three developmental theories have been considered in this context. Many other learning theories are available for investigation concerning the intellectual characteristics and needs of children. Indeed, many volumes have been written and courses in educational psychology have been designed for the purpose of studying such intent. All theories merit consideration as we have much to learn about children and the ways they learn. These three theories were selected for purposes of reference and because of their particular merit toward application in physical education.

With an understanding of the intellectual characteristics and needs of children, attention will now be switched to the role of physical education in the elementary school curriculum. This is not to lend support for justifying physical

APPROXIMATE CHRONOLOGICAL AGE	STAGES	LEVEL OF LEARNING	CHARACTERISTICS AND NEEDS	PHASES
0 to 1 month	Use of reflexes	Reflex	Spontaneous repetition of actions and perceptions into coordinated activities	Sensori-motor
1 to 4½ months	Primary circular reactions		Accomodation and assimilation of experiences into schema	
4½ to 9 months	Coordination of prehension and vision secondary circular reactions		Initiation of cause/effect and qualitative/quantitative experiences	
9 to 12 months	Secondary schemata		Active experimentation of the environment through curiosity and novelty seeking behavior Opportunities for ludic play, imitation, parallel play, and language development	
12 to 18 months	Discovery of new means, tertiary circular reactions	Knowledge	Continuous investigation of the environment	
18 to 24 months	Beginnings of insight and cause/effect relationships		Parallel play, small group play and language development lead to socialization	
2 to 4 years	Perceptually oriented, period from self-satisfying behavior to rudimentary social behavior		Short attention span-good memory Curious, creative, imaginative	Pre-conceptual
4 to 7 years	Awareness of a conceptual hierarchy, first beginnings of cognition		Move from a knowledge of the community to a knowledge of the world	Intuitive thought
7 to 11 years	Additive composition, reversibility, associativity, identity, deductive reasoning	Comprehension	Movement skills develop from movement patterns	Concrete operations
11 years on	Intellectual maturity	Application	Knowledge of right and wrong Understand complex rules and social values Abstract thinking	Formal operations

Figure 11-2. Summary of cognitive development.

education in the elementary school curriculum, but to show that *children learn through movement*. First, a chapter on perceptual-motor development outlines the importance of early movement experiences on the motor, perceptual, and cognitive development of children. Integration of language arts, mathematics, science, social studies, and art and music with physical education are examined in succeeding chapters.

SELECTED REFERENCES

1. Bloom, Benjamin. *Taxonomy of Educational Objectives, Handbook 1, Cognitive Domain*. New York: David McKay Company, 1965.
2. Bloom, Benjamin, Hastings, J.T., and Madaus, G.F. *Handbook on Formative and Summative Evaluation of Student Learning*. New York: McGraw-Hill, 1971.
3. Cratty, Bryant. *Physical Expressions of Intelligence*. Englewood Cliffs, New Jersey: Prentice-Hall, 1972.
4. Educational Policies Commission. *The Central Purpose of American Education*. Washington, D.C.: National Education Association, 1962.
5. Kearney, Newell. *Elementary School Objectives*. New York: Russell Sage Foundation, 1953.
6. Maier, Henry. *Three Theories of Child Development*. New York: Harper and Row Publishers, 1969.
7. Montessori, Maria. *Discovery of the Child*. Notre Dame, Indiana: Fides Publishers, 1967.
8. Mosston, Muska. *Teaching Physical Education*. Columbus, Ohio: Charles E. Merrill, 1969.
9. Piaget, Jean. *The Origins of Intelligence in Children*. New York: International Universities Press, 1952.
10. Piaget, Jean. *To Understand is to Invent*. New York: Grossman Publishers, 1972.
11. Ragan, W.B. *Modern Elementary Curriculum*. New York: Holt, Rinehart, and Winston, 1966.
12. Rambush, N.M. *Learning How to Learn: An American Approach to Montessori*. Baltimore: Helicon Press, 1962.
13. Schwebel, M., and Ralph, J. *Piaget in the Classroom*. New York: Basic Books, Inc., 1973.

CHAPTER 12
Perceptual-Motor Development

Key Concept: Movement plays an important role in the development of perceptual-motor abilities. The link between perceptual and motor functioning is one in which there is a high degree of interdependence of one upon the other.

Perceptual-Motor Development

INTRODUCTION

As an outgrowth of child development, the nature of the perceptual process and the meaning of the term perceptual-motor development have been topics of considerable interest and research in recent years. Questions such as: How does a child learn about his environment? How does the perceptual process operate? How do the various sense modalities interact in the development of a concept? What are the relationships between motor, perceptual, and cognitive development? What are the symptoms of children with learning disabilities problems? What diagnostic tools can be used to test children for perceptual-motor problems? What type of programs can best be effected to help children overcome their perceptual-motor problems? How do normal children develop perceptual-motor abilities? These questions have been asked by leading educators and researchers in the areas of psychology, special education, physical education, and physiology. Although many questions are still unanswered, the results of various studies point out important theories and concepts that have come to serve as the basis or foundation for many perceptual-motor programs today.

What Is Perceptual-Motor Development?

Over the years the term perceptual-motor has connoted different meanings to various people. Historically, writers have devoted individual chapters to the perceptual and motor aspects of the developing child. They have created an artificial division between these two domains that has perpetuated itself in our thinking for many years. On the other hand, others have emphasized the interrelatedness of the two terms as a process of human behavior.[15] For example, human behavior has been thought of as a product of three interrelated processes: 1.) a sensory or afferent input; 2.) a cortical or central process; and 3.) an efferent or motor output (see Figure 12-1). Thus, an overt act of human behavior is initiated by a stimulus (sight, sound, touch, smell, taste) that is received by specialized sensory receptors and transmitted along the neural pathways to the brain. Once at the cortical level, the brain organizes all sensory stimuli at any given point in time from the input cycle and makes it available for future use by collecting, indexing, and storing the information. The cortical process also allows the brain to integrate or match new information with past experiences that have been stored. As a decision to act is made, the message travels along the neural pathways to the muscles at which time a response (read, write, eat, run, throw, etc.) is made. At the time of the response, a feedback mechanism acts as a reinforcer to inform the individual as to whether the response was correct or not. If, for the sake of simplicity, we were to combine the first two processes and call them "perception" and label the efferent process "motor," we can see that all of man's behavior could be thought of as a series of perceptual acts followed by a series of motor acts. In other words, perception is a prerequisite to and necessary for adequate execution of overt motor acts.

If the process of acquiring afferent information through one or more of the senses were inaccurate or slow, the probability of the subsequent motor act being unskilled or inefficient is greater than if the processing of such information is rapid and precise. For example, the terms eye-hand and eye-foot coordination have been used for many years by physical educators as a means of expressing the dependency of efficient movement on the accuracy of one's perceptual information. A youngster in the process of learning to bowl a ball has numerous sensory inputs that must be sorted out in order to roll the ball accurately enough to knock over the pins. If his perceptions are efficient, he is able to move in a coordinated fashion to knock over the pins. If not, the ball misses the pins.

Feedback also plays an important part in the process of perceptual-motor development. It ensures that perceptual and motor learning proceed together. The motor process feeds back information to correct the perception. This altered perception leads to an altered response. The bowler whose ball misses to the

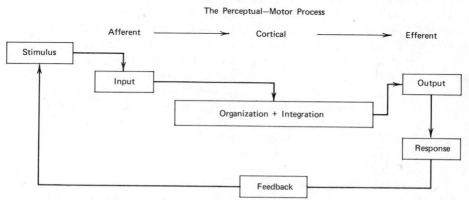

Figure 12-1. The Perceptual-Motor Process

right or left of the pins can correct his effort on the second try. This process continues until the perceptual data and motor response data are congruent or the bowler rolls a strike.

One can readily see the interdependence of the processes of perceptual and motor development, which in essence provide the foundation upon which all behavior is built. It is important to provide all children with multisensory perceptual processing experiences through haptic play so that they become efficient sorters. of information. Experiences involving size, speed, distance, direction, color, temperature, shape, texture, and the like are important so that each child can improve in his capacity to perceive (receive, interpret, and evaluate) increasingly more complex kinds and quantities of information. In turn, overt motor acts will come under greater control. This means that the child will run more efficiently, balance more skillfully, throw more accurately, and draw pictures with greater accuracy and more detail. Thus, we see that as perceptual-motor development progresses the child can exert more and more refined afferent control over his efferent motor behavior. We can also see that all voluntary motor acts are in reality perceptual-motor acts and that in essence physical education programs are perceptual-motor programs.

Refinements in the Perceptual-Motor Process

If perceptual-motor development is linked to efficient sensory-perceptual processing, then we need to know about these processes and the changes that take place in them during childhood. In general, three developmental changes take place with reference to the development of the sensory-perceptual processes. They are evidenced in 1.) a shift in the hierarchy of the dominant sensory systems; 2.) an increase in intersensory communication; and 3.) an accompanying improvement in intrasensory discrimination.[24:111-115]

The first of the developmental changes in sensory-perceptual processing is seen in the shift from the primary use of sensory input from tactile-kinesthetic or proximo receptors to the use of input from telo-receptors (auditory and visual) for modification of behavior. During infancy and early childhood, the tactile-kinesthetic receptors that are relatively crude in terms of processing capacities serve as a basis for regulating the child's motor acts. Later, the visual system that is the most advanced of all sensory systems with regard to the speed and precision with which it can supply information to the individual about his environment becomes the dominant sensory input system.

A good example of this shift in reliance of information from the sensory systems is seen in the development of manipulative abilities in children. During the rudimentary and fundamental movement pattern phases of development the small child relies on his tactile-kinesthetic receptors to gather information. Through the sense of touch the child learns about the shape, size, texture, weight, and taste of objects in his environment. Through crawling and walking the child learns about distance and the relative position of one object to another. With the maturation of the perceptual mechanisms, the child can gather this same information faster and with more precision through visual inspection. A child learning to catch a ball is a case in point. During initial stages, the child cannot estimate the distance from which a ball is thrown, the speed at which the ball travels, or the place where the ball will land. The only type of ball he can catch is one that is rolled slowly to him or one that is thrown right into his arms (basket catch). Later, the child can estimate distance, speed, and projectile of the ball through visual inspection and move to catch balls in many situations. Reliance on visual cues allows the child to make more rapid and precise judgements about his environment. In turn, he can adjust and make more coordinated movements because he can make better use of the sensory information available to him from his environment.

As we study Piaget's developmental stages, we learn that the young child processes only limited amounts of information at a time. The second change in sensory-perceptual processing in the young child is that of improved inter-sensory functioning. This means that as the child develops he is better able to integrate information from several sensory systems at the same time. With this increase in intersensory functioning the child moves away from unimodal or isolated functioning of the sensory systems toward multisensory functioning. The child can now match up what he sees with what he hears. He evaluates what he sees against what he feels. In the example of ball catching abilities, the child integrates sensory inputs by combining visual information (watching the flight of the ball) with what he hears (the sound from the "crack" of the bat hitting the ball). Thus, the child becomes more skilled in using multiple sensory inputs in directing his motor behavior. This factor is important because it is believed to be a reflection of the growing integrative powers of the brain.

At the same time the child's intersensory processing abilities improve, the third major change in sensory-perceptual processing also occurs. This third major change is reflected by an increase in the discriminatory powers of the individual sensory systems. As the child develops each sensory system becomes more refined in its' capacity for discrimination. The child can gradually process more detail in his visual surroundings and detect even small differences or similarities among objects in his environment. For example, with improved intrasensory discrimination the child is able to make more refined decisions about the speed, direction and projection of the batted ball. As a result, he is able to better coordinate his movements to catch the ball.

All three of these changes in sensory-perceptual processing play a vital role in the child's total perceptual-motor development. They are the means by which the child gains greater afferent control over his efferent motor responses. As a result of these changes, the child makes more refined perceptions about his spatial environment and becomes more effective in adapting his behavior to existing environmental circumstances.

AREAS OF STUDY IN LEARNING DISABILITIES

After learning more about the perceptual-motor process, one views the process of learning as a more complex task. As there are many treatises on the subject, the purpose here is not to give a discourse on theories of learning, but to present some basic information about learning disabilities, the stages of learning, the perceptual modalities, and the relationship between perceptual-motor learning and learning disabilities.

What is a Learning Disability?

Upon reviewing the literature, it becomes evident that there are many interpretations of the term "learning disabilities." Children have been classified as learning disabled when having problems in school with hyperactivity, motor coordination, visual perception, speech, reading, writing, and emotional-social adjustment. Children can have one or more of the above problems and be classified as learning disabled. A distinction is made, however, between the retarded child and the learning disabled or slow learner. Whereas, the retarded child has a lower IQ and less learning potential, the learning disabled child is of average and often above average intelligence who for some reason is having trouble learning in school. Thus, the term learning disabilities covers a wide range of children who are having problems learning at one of the stages of perceptual-motor, visual perception, cognitive, or emotional-social development. The term perceptual-motor is a subcategory of learning disabilities and concerns those children who have problems with low level functional deficits or foundational skills, which shall later be discussed as concepts concerning body image, balance, laterality, directionality, spatial awareness, form perception, figure-ground perception, and the like.

Stages of Development

In attempting to learn more about the child and stages of development in the process of learning, it is possible to approach the situation by looking at the stages of development in the "normal" child or to take a remedial approach by looking at the problems learning disabled children have at the various stages of development. In either case all children pass progressively through motor, perceptual-motor, perceptual, and cognitive states of development as outlined by several learning theorists in Figure 12-2. At an early age motor development plays the most important role as the child learns about his environment. The child touches, smells, and tastes everything with which he comes into contact. Early locomotor patterns help develop strength, balance, and estimation of time and distance. Rudimentary manipulative patterns of prehension—reach, grasp, and release—help the child learn about his environment through haptic play experiences involving size, weight, shape, texture, and so forth. Gradually, the child learns about concepts of laterality, directionality, spatial awareness, and form recognition as the perceptual mechanism of vision becomes the primary means of learning about the environment. The child passes from the globular form stage to where he can recognize elements of forms to where he can reproduce forms. Form perception, figure-ground perception, position in space, spatial relationships, tracking, convergence, and eye-hand coordination are other factors that influence the child's development in the perceptual stage. In addition, auditory perception plays an important role in the child's development at the perceptual stage. As the child learns to master his perceptual world, he learns to make generalizations, propositional statements, abstractions and can use symbolic operations in language and mathematics. At this stage of development the child is reaching toward maturity and is functioning at a cognitive level.

All children pass through these developmental stages in somewhat of a spiraling sequence (Figure 12-3) with one phase leading into and overlapping the next. Learning is thus thought of as hierarchial. A strong foundation insures a better chance of a sound structure. But, if the foundation is weak, then the structure built upon the foundation may be weak in accordance with the degree of weakness in the foundation. If a learning sequence is skipped or poorly developed, there may be a greater chance that future learning patterns will not be achieved to their fullest extent.

Children with learning disabilities have experienced a problem with the learning process at one or more of the stages of development. In attempting to determine the child's functional level, several tests are available that can be used as diagnostic tools.* If the child is suspected to have a motor or perceptual-motor problem, the Prudue Perceptual-Motor Survey and Ayres' Southern California Achievement Tests could be used to detect the problem. The Frostig Development Test of Visual Perception, Wepman Auditory Discrimination Test, Beery Developmental Test of Visual Motor Integration and other screening devices can be used to detect perceptual problems. At the cognitive level, the Illinois Test of Psycholinguistic Abilities is the most widely used test to detect problems.

If there is some suspicion that a child is experiencing a learning problem at one of the developmental stages, the diagnostic tests mentioned above or similar

---

*See Selected Tests of Perceptual-Motor Functioning at the end of this chapter.

APPROXIMATE CHRONOLOGICAL AGE	PIAGET'S INTELLECTUAL EVOLUTION	KEPHART'S DEVELOPMENTAL SEQUENCES

0- 6 mo.	Sensorimotor Intelligence
	  Use of reflexes
	  Primary circular reactions
	  Coordination of prehension and
	    vision, secondary circular
	    reactions
		Reflexive Stage
		
		Motor Stage
		  Rudimentary motor pattern
		    development

6-12 mo.	Secondary Schemata Discovery of new means, tertiary circular reactions	Balance Receipt and propulsion Globular Form

1- 2 yrs.	Beginnings of insight and cause/
	  effect relationships
	Egocentric organization
	Perceptive movement
		Motor Perceptual Stage
		  Laterality
		  Hand-Eye coordination
		  Gross motor pattern development
		  Syncretic form

	Intuitive Preoperational Thought	Form recognition

2- 4 yrs.	Perceptually oriented, period from
	  self-satisfying behavior to
	  rudimentary social behavior
	Awareness of a conceptual hierarchy,
	  first beginnings of cognition	

4- 7 yrs.	Beginning abstractions	Perceptual Motor Stage
		  Directionality
		  Eye-hand coordination
		Perceptual Stage
		  Form perception
		  Constructive Form
		  Form reproduction

7-11 yrs.	Concrete Operations
	  Additive composition, reversibility,
	    associativity, identity,
	    deductive reasoning
	  Relationships
	  Classification
	  Permanence
		Perceptual Cognitive Stage
		
		Cognitive Perceptual Stage

11 yrs. on	Formal Operations
	  Intellectual maturity
	  Symbolic operations
	  Abstract thinking
	  Propositional thinking
		Cognitive Stage

FROSTIG'S STAGES OF DEVELOPMENTAL VISUAL PERCEPTION	GETMAN'S DEVELOPMENTAL APPROACH TO VISUAL PERCEPTION	VALETT'S BASIC LEARNING ABILITIES
		Gross Motor Development
		Rudimentary movement patterns
		Self-identification
		Body localization
		Body abstraction
		Muscular strength
		General Physical health
		Sensory-motor integration
		Balance and rhythm
		Body spatial organization
	General Body Movements	Reaction speed - dexterity
	Gross motor locomotor, stability,	Tactile discrimination
	and manipulation patterns	Laterality
		Directionality
Eye-Hand Coordination		Time orientation
	Special Motor Patterns	Perceptual-Motor Skills
Figure Ground Perception	Eye-hand coordination	Auditory acuity
	Eye-foot coordination	Auditory decoding
Perceptual Constancy	Gesture Relationships	Auditoy-vocal association
(Form Perception)		Auditory memory
	Eye Movement Patterns	Auditory sequencing
Position in Space	Tracking	Visual acuity
	Convergence	Visual coordination and pursuit
Spatial Relationships		Visual form discrimination
		Figure-ground differentiation
	Visual Language Patterns	Visual memory
	Classification	Visual motor memory
	Labeling	Fine muscle coordination
	Vocabulary	Visual-motor speed of learning
		Visual-motor integration
	Visualization Patterns	Language Development
		Vocabulary
	Visual Perception	Fluency and encoding
	Abstract thinking	Articulation
	Perception in time and space	Work attack skills
		Reading comprehension
		Writing
		Spelling

Figure 12-2. Stages of development as proposed by leading learning theorists

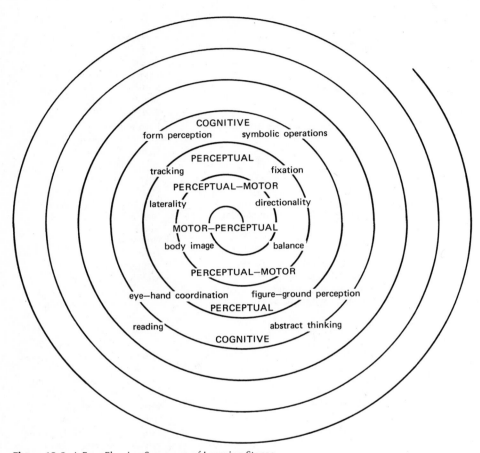

Figure 12-3. A Free Flowing Sequence of Learning Stages

tests should be administered in sequence from the perceptual-motor level through the cognitive level until the problem is pinpointed. It should be remembered that a child could have one or more problems at any of the stages of development, and thus the *whole* child needs to be considered. The child may have a problem with motor coordination, visual perception, auditory perception, language development, reading, emotional development, or any combination of problems. As a result, each child will benefit through a somewhat different approach.

A learning disabilities program with emphasis on teamwork through the cooperative efforts of the classroom teacher, parents, reading teacher, speech therapist, school psychologist, physical educator, and others should be designed to best help each child. In view of this, it is the job of the physical educator to become knowledgeable about perceptual-motor learning and effect programs in movement through a preventative or remedial approach to help children gain a strong foundation for later learning. The physical educator is an integral part of the team helping each child achieve maximum effectiveness in performance at each state of development.

The Perceptual Modalities

The body is a wonderfully equipped organism with sensory transmitters to receive and carry messages to the brain in a variety of modes. Our eyes permit us to see, our ears to hear, our proprioceptors to touch and feel, our nose to smell, and our mouth to taste. A vast network of neurons form a path from these sensory receptors to the brain. At the level of the cortex these messages are organized, categorized, and stored for later use. If a response is required, the cortex initiates the appropriate neural mechanisms and the result is an appropriate manual expression such as speaking, writing, or gross motor movement.

As children progress through the stages of development, they use their perceptual modalities to help them interpret their environment. The use of each of these sensory modes and the ability to organize and interpret messages is the critical point in determining what and how much each child will learn. It is not enough to see, we must interpret what we see so that we may understand (vision). It is not enough to hear, we must be able to discriminate between sounds so that we can understand what we hear. Gradually, our sensory modalities become more adept at differentiating and become more sophisticated. As we grow older we achieve readiness for higher order perceptual tasks, namely schoolwork.

It is at this point that we can distinguish the child who will learn normally in school from the learning disabled child. The normal child learns to organize and interpret messages from the various sense modalities so that he can understand and give meaning to the world around him. Provided he has average or above average intelligence, the learning disabled child may have trouble in one or more of the areas concerning receiving, organizing, interpreting, and responding to stimuli from the various sensory modalities.

For this reason, the various diagnostic tests already cited are administered. If it is found that the child has trouble with auditory perception through discrimination of sounds, sequencing words, and the like, a program stressing learning through the child's strengths, perhaps visual perception, should be recommended. If it is found that a child has trouble with visual perception through spatial awareness, ocular tracking, and the like, a program stressing learning through the child's strengths, perhaps tactile-kinesthetic perception, should be recommended. Through this type of an approach it is possible to teach each child through a program that diagnoses the functional level of the child and draws upon the child's strengths (what he can do) to overcome his weaknesses (what the child cannot do). Thus it is important to find the child's stage of development (perceptual-motor, perceptual, cognitive) and the perceptual modaladities through which he learns best. We should develop the child's perceptual modes, which are functioning properly, and gradually increase the ability of the child to use those perceptual modes that are weak. We should also take the child from his level of performance and move him forward on the continuum toward cognitive development.

The Relationship Between Perceptual-Motor Development and Learning Disabilities

Research efforts are continually being made in an attempt to document the virtues of perceptual-motor training programs on readiness and remedial aspects of perceptual and cognitive development. Each new research effort stimulates new questions and problems and the results that are available are not conclusive, but there is ample evidence to suggest that perceptual-motor training programs are making a positive contribution to the motor, perceptual, and cognitive development of children. After reviewing the literature one may discover several generalizations that lend supportive evidence to and have specific implications for the elementary education and physical education specialist concerned with the prevention and remediation of perceptual-motor learning disabilities. Some of the concepts that arise out of the research follow[10,11,14,23].

1. Not all learning disabilities are perceptual-motor in nature. Some may be due to problems in perceptual functioning. Others may be due to problems in conceptual functioning.
2. Perceptual-motor deficits may or may not lead to learning disabilities in a given child. Despite this fact, diagnosis and remediation of problems is worthwhile if only for the expanded competencies, both physical and emotional (self-concept), that result from such remediation.
3. Our diagnostic tools for assessment are at this time in a rather primitive state. Distinct elements in the perceptual-motor spectrum have yet to be identified. Diagnostic tests cannot yet validly isolate separate factors.
4. Low level functional deficits (perceptual-motor tasks) seem to be associated with high level functional deficits (perceptual-cognitive tasks). This is to say that children who perform poorly on tasks of high level complexity (reading and arithmetic) also tend to perform poorly on low level complexity tasks (laterality, directionality, midline).

5. Intramodal abilities develop before intermodal abilities. This means that children learn to use each of the senses separately before they can interrelate and use more than one mode at a time.

6. The most efficient learning mode seems to be visual perception, although learning is enhanced when information is presented to or processed by two or more modes at the same time. That is the child is likely to learn more if presented information visually and auditorily at the same time than if presented information through only one mode at a time.

7. Not all children are at the same perceptual level on entering the first grade. Perceptual development is a process of both maturation and experience and therefore each child develops at his own individual rate.

8. Adequate perception (auditory, visual, tactile-kinesthetic) is prerequisite to success in school. Inaccurate perceptions lead to difficulties in academic concept formation. Perceptual readiness is an important aspect of total readiness for learning.

9. Perceptual abilities can be improved through specialized training programs.

10. A program of perceptual-motor assessment can be useful at the preschool or kindergarten level to identify potential learning problems in children and to adjust the curriculum to their strengths and weaknesses.

11. Deprivation of perceptual-motor experiences at an early age may hinder the development of the child's perceptual abilities.

12. Perceptual-motor training programs enhance the development of auditory, visual, and tactile-kinesthetic perceptual abilities in young children.

13. Perceptual-motor activities should be included as a part of readiness training programs.

14. Some studies show a relationship between certain perceptual-motor abilities and reading achievement among selected groups of slow, normal, and above average intelligence children.

15. A physical education program that is oriented toward the movement education concept provides many of the movement experiences that contribute to the development of the child's perceptual-motor abilities.

In conclusion, when we say that a child is "ready" to learn, we are in fact referring to a point in time when the child through maturation and learning has sufficiently developed his perceptual and motor abilities to be able to benefit measurably from higher order perceptual and cognitive tasks that is, schoolwork. Movement experiences serve as a vehicle by which these capabilities are refined and developed. Children learn by doing. The physical educator or perceptual-motor specialist plays an important role in the development of the young child's perceptual-motor abilities through a varied program of movement experiences that values the worth of each individual child.

SYMPTOMS OF CHILDREN WITH PERCEPTUAL-MOTOR PROBLEMS

General Symptoms

Children with learning disabilities exhibit a variety of symptoms that may be detected through various informal and formal diagnostic tools. The observant classroom or physical education specialist is able to detect many problems through informal observation of children in the classroom, gymnasium, or playground. The following is a list of emotion, social, cognitive, and physical characteristics that are indicative of behavior patterns of children with learning disabilities. Learning disabled children may possess any one or combination of these characteristics[8,16,22,23].

1. Seems bright; is quiet and obedient, but daydreams and cannot read.
2. Is high strung and nervous; his attention is hard to hold.
3. Has frequent temper outbursts, sometimes for no apparent reason.
4. Will not concentrate for more than a few minutes at a time; he jumps from one thing to another, and minds everyone's business but his own.
5. Lacks self-control; he cannot work with other children; he picks on them constantly; he is very disturbing in the classroom and worse on the playground.
6. Does not work to capacity; he is not learning to read or work with numbers, but has a good vocabulary and uses words correctly.
7. Thinks, speaks, and moves slowly and is a very poor reader, yet in many ways he seems very intelligent.
8. Is unable to perform gross motor movements normally expected of children his age.
9. Has poor eye-hand and eye-foot coordination resulting in the inability to play games and sports well.
10. General clumsiness and hesitancies prevent him from performing simple locomotor movements (jump, skip, hop). He is slow to learn new movement skills.
11. Has difficulty in tying shoes, buttoning buttons or performing similar tasks requiring fine motor coordination.
12. Has difficulty in understanding directional words such as left, right, up, down, in, out, forward, and backward.
13. Is easily distracted by minor audio and visual intrusions into his focus of attention.
14. Appears to be careless, disorganized, and unable to locate objects clearly within his view.
15. Sometimes sees and reproduces letters, words, or numbers backwards, upside down, or rotated upside down and backwards.
16. Has a poor self-concept and has difficulty with peer relations.

If children possess some of these symptoms, it is suggested that formal testing be initiated in an effort to find each child's specific learning disability. As stated before, a series of tests should be administered to determine whether the child's problems are perceptual-motor (Purdue Perceptual-Motor Survey, Ayres' Southern California Achievement Tests), perceptual (Frostig Developmental Test of Visual Perception, Wepman Auditory Discrimination Test, Beery Developmental Test of Visual Motor Integration), or cognitive (Illinois Test of Psycholinguistic Abilities) in nature.

Concepts Related to Perceptual-Motor Learning

The administration of the above diagnostic tools allows the educator to determine the specific nature of each child's problems. As each child is a unique individual, they will differ according to the maturity level, stage of development, and learning experiences with which they come to school. The following is a list of concepts specifically related to perceptual-motor problems. Each concept is related to a low functional deficit. Each child may possess one or more problems related to these concepts. Helping the child overcome these problems will lead to a level of readiness so that the child can achieve a higher functional level.

Acuity—The ability to receive and differentiate meaningfully and accurately auditory and visual stimuli in one's environment.

Balance—The sense of body position and the ability to maintain or regain one's posture or position.

Bilaterality—Using both sides of the body in simultaneous or parallel movement.

Body image or Body Awareness—Awareness of one's own body, knowing the names, movements, functions, and location of body parts; possessing an inner sense that one side of the body is different from the other side of the body; it includes the impressions one receives from internal signals as well as feedback received from others.

Closure—The process of achieving completion in behavior or mental act; the tendency to stabilize or to complete a situation. Closure may occur in any sensory modality.

Convergency-reconvergence—The occular pointing mechanism by which the eyes are "aimed" at a target. It enables one to see a single object at varying distances.

Crawling—Moving in a prone position from one place to another. This movement may be done in homologous, homolateral, or cross pattern movements.

Creeping—Moving on the hands or knees from one place to another. This may be done in homolateral, or cross pattern movements.

Cross-pattern—A movement in which the opposite arm and leg move at the same time.

Decoding—The ability to receive, understand and interpret stimulus messages from one of the sense modalities (auditory, visual, tactile-kinesthetic).

Depth Perception—The aspect of visual perception that deals with the direct awareness of the distance between an object and its observer; the awareness of distance between the front and the back of an object so that it is depicted as three dimensional. The ability to perceive the third dimension that is actually two dimensional.

Directionality—An awareness of laterality and a projection of this awareness into space, such as: up, down, right, left, front, or back.

Dyslexia—Partial inability to read or to understand what one reads either silently or aloud.

Earthbound—Inability to lift the body off the ground when attempting to hop or jump; usually due to a lack of balance and/or coordination.

Encoding—The ability to express one's self through speech, writing, or action.

Eye-hand Coordination—The ability to perceptually organize by joining together in the mind's eye and to reproduce manually.

Figure-ground—Geometrical patterns are always seen against a background and thus appear object-like with contours and boundries. The part seen as the figure tends to appear slightly in front of the background.

Fine-motor—The ability to control the small muscles of the body, primarily the eyes and hands necessary to accomplish academic tasks.

Fixation—The ability of the eyes to maintain focus on an object.

Form Perception—The ability to perceive an arrangement or pattern of elements or parts constituting a unitary whole, wherein the elements are in specific relationship with each other.

Gender Identification—This factor has to do with the child identifying with the appropriate sex. Research has shown that children who have trouble identifying with their appropriate sex have trouble succeeding in learning situations.

Gross-motor—The ability to use the large muscles of the body, primarily the arms and legs, in smooth coordinated movement in order to accomplish certain tasks.

Homolateral—Moving the limbs on one side of the body in unison.

Homologous—Moving the arms in unison, or moving the legs in unison.

Hyperactivity—Excessive activity or output in which the child seems to have a surplus of energy and is unable to control movements for even a short period of time.

Hyperdistractibility—The inability of the child to distinguish the primary stimulus from the background "noise." As a result the child is distracted by various auditory, visual and tactile cues in the environment.

Hypoactivity—Pronounced absence of activity.

Kinesthesia or Kinesthetic—An inner neuromuscular feeling of where the body parts are found and how to move them by recalling previous experiences.

Laterality—An inner sense that one side of the body is different from the other side of the body. Complete motor awareness of both sides of the body.

Listening Skills—A combination of the physical ability to hear, an interpretation of the sounds heard, and a response to that which is heard.

Memory—The ability to recall accurately prior audio, visual, and motor experiences.

Midline—The movement of the eyes, hands, arms, feet, or legs across the midsection of the body without involving any other part of the body, that is, without turning the head, twisting or swaying the trunk, or innervating the opposite limb.

Ocular Pursuits—The ability of the eyes to follow a moving target.

Perceptual-motor Match—The process that integrates the clues provided by the senses with the responses of the neuromuscular system.

Perseveration—The inability to develop a new response to a new or altered stimulus. Continuing to behave or respond in a certain way when it is no longer appropriate.

Position in Space—The direct awareness of the spatial properties of an object, especially in relation to the observer. The perception of position, direction, size, form, and/or distance by any of the senses.

Receipt-propulsion—Involves activities through which a child makes contact with an object moving towards him and in turn the movement that is imparted to an object.

Sequencing—The ability to recall in correct sequence and detail prior auditory, visual, and tactile information.

Spatial Relationships—An understanding of one's relative position in space and the relationship of objects in space to one another. The ability to see similarities in shape, size, and so forth, of two or more objects.

Space-time Relationships—The ability to translate a simultaneous relationship in space to a serial relationship in time or vice versa. For example, the child must recognize the square as a whole when he sees it in space and reproduce it in time as an organized series of lines and angles. This concept also has to do with rhythmical sequencing abilities.

Splinter Skill—A skill developed to solve a specific motor problem and that has little or no carry-over value to other motor activities.

Visual-motor Ability—The ability to visualize and to assemble material from life into meaningful wholes; the ability to see and to perform with dexterity and coordination. The ability to control body or hand movements in coordination with visual perception.

Visual Pursuit—Following a moving object smoothly and continuously. The ability to keep an object in the center of the field of vision and to provide a direct correlation between the movement of the object and the perceptual alterations.

THE PERCEPTUAL-MOTOR PROGRAM

The physical education curriculum should be designed to provide a wealth of sensorimotor experiences through the exploration of locomotion, manipulation, and stability activities. Early school experiences (preschool - grade 2) should provide *all* children with a wide background of haptic play experiences through the exploration of space, force, time, flow, shape, weight, texture, color, design, and the like. If approached in this manner, early play experiences become those of *exploration* and *prevention* rather than *remedial* in nature.

The perceptual-motor program should be a reflection of a well-defined physical education program. During the early school years the movement experiences concerning developmental movement patterns as described in earlier chapters should be a part of each child's background. In addition, the following specialized activities are designed to help children with specific perceptual-motor problems.

Spatial Awareness

1. Body Awareness or Body Image
   a. Ask the child to touch the parts of his body when called out by the teacher. Ask the child to see how many ways he can move the various parts of his body.

Body And Spatial Awareness
May Be Enhanced Through A
Variety Of Movement Activities

b. Have the child look in a mirror and touch body parts on cue from the teacher. Touch the mirror, touch yourself.

c. Keep a balloon in the air by tapping it with various body parts.

d. Set up an obstacle course that stresses directional awareness. Crawl through a tunnel, hop into tires, jump over blocks, crawl under wands, and the like.

e. Have children draw their images on large pieces of paper and allow them to complete missing parts.

f. Have the children alternate contracting and relaxing various muscle groups.

g. Allow the child to draw himself on a mirror with shoe polish.

h. Angels in the Snow - Have the child exercise various unilateral, bilateral, and contralateral movements while on the floor.

i. Get the Message - Child lies on his back while the teacher touches his arms or legs (one at a time) and the child opens the part touched. Touch two body parts at the same time. While the child has his eyes closed, touch a part of the body. Have the child touch exactly where you touched. Give verbal commands and perform the same exercises.

2. Laterality - Directionality
    a. Creep homolaterally while looking at the forward hand or while looking at a target placed at eye level. Creep in various directions.
    b. Creep with cross pattern movement movements looking at the forward hand and at a target placed at eye level. Creep in various directions.
    c. Practice homolateral and cross pattern walking in various directions.
    d. Midair-change - Begin with the left arm forward and the left foot forward with weight evenly distributed on both feet. The right arm should be straight out in back. On the command "Change" the child jumps up in the air reversing the position of his arms and legs. This action is homolateral movement. The eyes should fixate on a target at all times and the child should land on the take-off spot.
    e. Midair-change - Do the above sequence with cross pattern movement.
    f. Ball work - Use one hand with the ball, then repeat the skills with the other hand. Also use the feet to manipulate the ball. Tap a suspended swinging ball. Bounce a ball. Dribble a ball. Throw and catch balls. Kick balls.
    g. Twist board - By using Newton's Law of Action-Reaction move one arm forward while the other arm moves backward. Keep the eyes fixed on a target.

Figure 12-4. Children can indicate the direction in which the arrows are pointing through voice and body action while keeping time to a metronome.

h. Twist board - Use one arm while keeping the other arm at your side. Bring the free arm across the body at waist level and initiate a pushing action across the midline of the body *sneak* the arm back to starting position. This should turn the child in one direction only. Continue this action until the child makes a complete turn.

i. Follow a pattern of arrows that is illustrated on a chalkboard. Move various body parts in the direction in which the arrows are pointing (right, left, up, down). Vocally give the directions in which the arrows are pointing at the same time the body parts are pointing the directions. Perform the above commands while keeping time to the rhythm of a metranome.

j. Scooters - Practice with one leg, then the other.

k. Trampoline activities - Jump on your right foot. Jump on your left foot. Make one-quarter, one-half, and whole turns to the right and left. While jumping touch various body parts to other body parts such as the left hand to the right knee.

l. Perform marching activities stressing right and left.

m. Simon says activities - Have a leader give the children directions to relate one body part to another.

n. Follow the leader activities - Utilize an obstacle course and move to the left, right, over, under, on, through, and around various objects.

3. Midline

a. Chalkboard work - Perform all of the work with the child standing on a raised box so that he cannot move his feet.

   1.) Draw a circle about 24 inches in diameter.
   2.) Draw double circles, one with each hand at the same time.
   3.) Draw a large "lazy eight" (∞) figure.

   In each of the above exercises have the child use both hands, draw in several directions, and change directions upon command.

b. Perform exercises requiring the right side of the body to be coordinated with the left side of the body. For example, touch your right hand to your left toe.

c. Perform jumping jacks.

d. Perform jump rope activities.

e. Follow the leader upon command.

   1.) Touch your right ear with your left hand, then reverse.
   2.) Touch your right shoulder with your left hand.
   3.) Touch your left foot with your right knee.

f. Perform "Angels in the Snow" activities with an emphasis on contralateral movements.

g. Perform ocular pursuit movements to help the eyes cross the horizontal and vertical midlines.

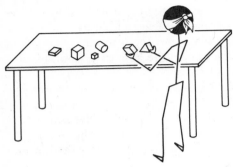

Figure 12-5. Parquetry block exercises help children learn the relationship of one object to another through auditory, visual and tactile cues.

4. Spatial Relationships
   a. Explore space and relate the position of your body to other children and objects in your environment. For example, Mary is standing in front of Amy.
   b. Parquetry Block activities - Reproduce patterns of blocks according to visual, auditory, and tactile cues.

Imitating Body Positions Is An
Excellent Learning Experience

1.) Have a child reproduce a pattern identical to the teacher's model (visual cue).
2.) Tell the child verbally to "Place a blue triangle to the right of an orange diamond" (auditory cue).
3.) Allow the child to visually inspect a pattern. Then blindfold his and ask him to reproduce the pattern (visual memory and tactual sense).

Balance

1. Progression of Balance Skills for Classroom Training Without Equipment
   a. Kneel on all fours and repeat all of the activities with your eyes open, then with your eyes closed.
      1.) Lift one leg off the floor. Lift the other leg off the floor.
      2.) Lift one arm, then the other arm off the floor.
      3.) Lift the left arm and the right leg off the floor at the same time.
      4.) Lift the left arm and the left leg off the floor at the same time.
   b. Kneel on your knees with your back straight.
      1.) Lift one knee off the ground and balance on the other knee. Do this with your eyes open and then with your eyes closed.
   c. Stand up straight.
      1.) Lift one leg and balance on the other.
      2.) Rise up on your tiptoes and walk about the room.
   d. Walk about the room on different parts of your feet (outside, inside, toes, heels).
   e. Perform jumping and hopping activities.
      1.) How far can the child jump? How high?
      2.) Hop on your feet using various patterns - 1/1, 2/2, 2/1, 1/2, and so forth.
      3.) Hop or jump while keeping time to an imposed rhythm.
2. Balance Skills with Equipment
   a. Balance Board - The following are only a few suggestions, you could do many more exercises.
      1.) Stand on two feet with eyes open, then closed.
      2.) Stand on one foot, then the other.
      3.) Touch various body parts such as your toes or knees.
      4.) Tip the outer sides down to the floor and return to an upright position.
      5.) Bounce and catch a ball while keeping your balance on the board.
   b. Balance Beam—The following are only a few suggestions, you could do many more exercises.
      1.) Walk forward, backward and sideways while keeping your eyes on a target.
      2.) Walk across the beam with an eraser on your head.
      3.) Walk over and under objects while crosing the beam.

Figure 12-6. Walking across the low balance beam with feet on alternating sides helps with balance and midline.

 4.) Use weighted objects on a broomstick to force the child to balance with one side or another.
 c. Ladder Activities
 1.) Walk on the rungs in a forward, backward, and sideways direction.
 2.) Jump and hop in between the rungs in various directions.
 3.) Walk on the sides of the ladder, one foot on each side.
 4.) With the ladder on its' side, have the child crawl in and out of the rungs.
 3. Exercises for Earthbound Children
 a. Have the child place both hands on a low table for support, palms flat. Raise one leg. Press down on the table while giving a little hop in the air. Repeat with the eyes closed.
 b. Without using the table, have the child try to touch or grasp an object in the teacher's outstretched hand as he tries to jump up.
 c. Jump over obstacles, first withone foot, then with both feet.
 1.) lines on the floor
 2.) a yardstick
 3.) ladder rungs
 4.) old tires

Hyperkinetic or Hyperactive Children

 1. Activities Designed to Help Pace a Child
 a. Keep time to a slow metranome beat.
 b. Jump and hop over ladder rungs.
 c. Swimming has a buoyant and relaxing effect.
 d. Keep slow "mood music" in the background while the child is in your room.
 e. Use progressive relaxation techniques by teaching children to recognize the differences between tense and relaxed muscle groups.

2. Eliminate Unnecessary Auditory and Visual Distractions in the Child's Environment.
3. Provide Routing (structure), Regularity, and Repetition (positive reinforcement) in the Child's Environment.

Visual Perception

1. Ocular Pursuits or Tracking
   a. Follow a moving target held 16-18 inches from the eyes as it moves in four directions (horizontal, vertical, diagonal, rotary). Exercise both eyes at the same time, then one eye at a time.
   b. Perform Marsden Ball activities. Suspend a small (tennis size) ball from a ceiling with a heavy piece of string or cord.
      1.) Have the child hold his head still and follow the ball as it swings in various directions (left, right, to, fro).
      2.) Using the index finger, have the child tap the ball with one or alternating hands as it swings toward him.
      3.) Hold one hand on each end of a waxpaper tube and hit the ball with the tube as it swings to and fro.
      4.) Tap the ball with your elbow, shoulder, forehead, ear, and so forth.
      5.) Have the child lie down under the Marsden Ball and follow the path of the ball with his eyes and/or hands (horizontal, vertical, diagonal, rotary).
   c. Marble track - Follow the marble with your eyes without moving your head. For eye-hand coordination, follow the marble with your eyes and hand at the same time.
   d. With a flashlight in a darkened room, project the light in various directions and have the child follow the target with his eyes.
   e. Follow the stem of a metranome with your eyes.

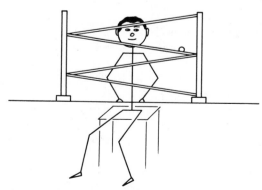

Figure 12-7. Tracking a marble helps children with ocular pursuits.

f. Trace a geometric pattern on the chalkboard, then follow the path with your eyes.

2. Convergence-Reconvergence
   a. Hold an object about four inches away from a child's nose. Have the child look at the target, look at you, look at the target, and the like.
   b. Place two different colored balloons on opposite ends of the chalk tray. On command, have the child look at the red balloon, look at the green balloon, repeating several times. Then add the ceiling, floor, clock, teacher, and so forth. The child should not move his head.
   c. Sit in front of a child and move a target in toward his nose. Have the child follow the target with his eyes as the object moves all the way in and back away from him again.
   d. At meal time ask the child to look at objects in the room without moving his head. For example, look at the table, stove, window, refrigerator, knife, daddy, spoon, and so forth.

Eye-Hand and Eye-Foot Coordination

1. Gross Motor and Fine Motor Coordination
   Ball, yarnball, or beanbag activities
   1.) Toss a ball into the air with both hands, catch it with both hands.
   2.) Toss the ball into the air with one hand, catch it with the same hand. Then catch it with the opposite hand.
   3.) Cut the bottom out of a large plastic bleach bottle. Hold on to the handle and toss a ball up in the air with your free hand. Catch the ball in the "scoop." Play catch with a partner using a ball and your "scoops."
   4.) Toss a bean bag in a waste basket while standing at various distances - three feet, four feet, five feet, and so on.
   b. Throw a ball into the air and catch it after a specific number of bounces.
   c. Keep a balloon in the air by hitting it with various body parts.
   d. Alternately touch or hit a suspended swinging ball with the right and left hands or feet.
   e. Roll a large ball while tossing a small one back and forth with a partner. Perform in a sitting or kneeling position.
   f. String beads or other small objects. If a sequence is repeated, this activity is also good for visual sequential memory.
   g. Make geometric shapes, numbers, or letters by placing pegs into a pegboard.
   h. Put various sized nuts and bolts together.
   i. Maneuver a toy car on a roadway drawn on the chalkboard.

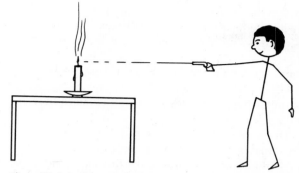

Figure 12-8. Putting out the flame of a candle is good for eye-hand coordination.

j. Pick up tiny objects such as coins or toothpicks with your fingers.
k. Flip things such as marbles, ping pong balls, tiddly winks, or other small objects with your fingers.
l. Wad up a piece of newspaper by using one hand only.
m. Cut paper with a scissors and paste the shapes on a background to make a picture.
n. Perform coloring and finger painting activities.
o. Use a squirt gun to put out the flame of a candle.
p. Play finger snapping and clapping games.
q. Allow a child to make toys such as boats and airplanes from lumber scraps by utilizing a hammer and nails or paste.
r. Have a child draw various geometric forms, numbers, letters, or pictures on a chalkboard.
s. Hoola hoops, balls, jump ropes, Footsies, ice skating, roller skating, hopscotch, swimming, and tree climbing are good for improving eye-hand and eye-foot coordination as well as body coordination in general.

Form Perception

1. Use of Kinesthetic or Tactual Sense
   a. Use templates to trace and copy forms.
   b. Form shapes, numbers, or letters with clay or play dough.
   c. Use a stylus to inscribe shapes, numbers, or letters into a soft material such as clay or dough.
   d. With your finger draw on a child's back and have him guess the shape, letter, or number that you have drawn.
   e. Have the child trace over sandpaper or felt letters and numbers with his fingers.

    f.   Draw forms in the air or on the floor with various body parts.

    g.   Use wooden matches with the heads cut off or toothpicks to make various geometric shapes, letters, numbers, and designs for children to copy.

    h.   Put objects in a box and let a child guess what they are through his sense of touch. Blindfolding works the same way.

    i.   Have the child copy various shapes and designs on a pegboard by placing pegs into appropriate holes.

2. Chalkboard Activities - Perform all of the activities with the child standing in one place to help a child with a midline problem if there is one.

    a.   Single circle - Have the child press his nose against the board and make a large "X" on top of the mark made by his nose. The child should then draw a circle around the "X" so that the circle is about 18-24 inches in diameter.

    b.   Double circles - Using a piece of chalk in each hand the child makes two large circles simultaneously while keeping his eyes on the "X".

        1.) Draw with the right hand moving clockwise, the left hand counter-clockwise. Reverse directions.

        2.) Draw with both hands moving counter-clockwise.

        3.) Draw with both hands moving clockwise.

    c.   Make horizontal lines with one or both hands at the forehead, shoulder, and waist levels. Draw from left to right and from right to left.

    d.   Make vertical lines with one or both hands from the forehead to the waist. Do one or both hands at the same time and draw from top to bottom or from bottom to top.

    e.   Draw "lazy eight" figures (∞) on the chalkboard with one or both hands and change directions of the drawing on command.

    f.   Clock game - Have the child place his hands on the numbers of a clock drawn on the board. Use unilateral, bilaterial, and contralateral activities.

    g.   Encourage a child to scribble, draw pictures, and draw letters, numbers, and geometric designs on the chalkboard. Encourage free flowing and rhythmical movement patterns.

    h.   Use templates to draw simple geometric forms on the chalkboard. Progress from tracing, to copying, to reproducing forms from memory.

    i.   Rainbow writing - Have the child trace lines with colored chalk. Use a different piece of colored chalk for each line to produce a rainbow effect.

    j.   Blind writing - Have a child dip his finger in a bowl of water and make letters and numbers with his wet finger on the chalkboard while his eyes are closed.

Figure-Ground Perception

1. Visual Perception Activities
   a. Have a child identify various pictures (figures) from an embedded background.
   b. Classify and sort a pile of buttons according to size, shape, color, number of holes, and so forth.
   c. Have the child identify or cross out with a pencil all of the letters of a given kind on a page. For example, cross out each "e" on the page.
   d. Have the child put puzzles together.
   e. Play catch with a ball.
2. Auditory Perception Activities
   a. Discriminate words from a background of distracting noises.
   b. Pick out the different types of musical instruments being played on a record.

Auditory and Rhythmic Patterning

1. Use of Hands—Adult sets the pattern and the child repeats it.
   a. Have the child clap his hands, snap his fingers, and tap his knees in the following sequences.
      1.) Clap, clap, snap, tap—repeat for a while and then reverse the pattern.
      2.) Clap, snap, snap, tap—repeat and then reverse the pattern.
      3.) Clap, snap, tap, tap—repeat and then reverse the pattern.
2. Use of Instruments - Adult sets the pattern and the child repeats it.
   a. Use innovative equipment such as sticks, cocoanut shells, spoons, tambourines, maracas, and pots and pans. Have the leader create a rhythmical sequence and the children repeat the sequence. Vary the sounds (loud, soft) and sequences.
   b. While using innovative instruments, have the children keep time to the rhythm on a record.
3. Use of Feet—Perform each pattern 5 to 10 times
   a. Jump, jump, stamp left foot, stamp right foot.
   b. Hop, hop, jump, jump.
   c. Step, step, step, leap.
4. Use of Hands and Feet
   a. Jump, clap, clap, jump, clap, clap.
   b. Step, step, step, clap, step, step, step, snap.
   c. Snap fingers, snap fingers, hop, hop.
5. Auditory Sequential Memory
   a. Give a child a list of three words and have him repeat them after you.

    b. Tell the child a sequence of three or four numbers and have him repeat them after you.

    c. Tell the child a story, and have him repeat the details back to you.

The activities that have been presented are only a sampling of experiences available in each of the specific areas of perceptual-motor development. For a more extensive background in both theory and activities, the reader is referred to the selection of references that follow.

SELECTED REFERENCES

1. AAHPER, *Perceptual-Motor Foundations: A Multidisciplinary Concern*. Washington, D.C., 1968.
2. AAHPER, *Foundations and Practices in Perceptual Motor Learning - A Quest for Understanding*. Washington, D.C., 1971.
3. AAHPER, *Annotated Bibliography on Perceptual-Motor Development*. Washington, D.C., 1973.
4. Barsch, Ray. *A Movigenic Curriculum*. Madison, Wisconsin: Bureau of Audiovisual Instruction, University of Wisconsin, 1965.
5. Chaney, Clara, and Kephart, N.C. *Motoric Aids to Perceptual Training*. Columbus, Ohio: Charles E. Merrill, 1968.
6. Cratty, Bryant. *Perceptual-Motor Behavior and Educational Processes*. Springfield, Illinois: Charles C. Thomas, 1970.
7. Cratty, Bryant, *Developmental Sequences of Perceptual-Motor Tasks*. Freeport, Long Island, New York: Educational Activities, Inc., 1967.
8. Cratty, Bryant, and Martin, Sister M. M. *Perceptual-Motor Efficiency in Children*. Philadelphia: Lea and Febiger, 1969.
9. Delacato, Carol. *The Diagnosis and Treatment of Speech and Reading Problems*. Springfield, Illinois: Charles C. Thomas, 1963.
10. Early, G. H. "Low Level Functional Deficits in Learning-Disabled Children," *Academic Therapy*. 8:231-34, Winter, 1972.
11. Estes, R. E., and Huizinga, R. J. "A Comparison of Visual and Auditory Presentations of a Paired-Associate Learning Task with Learning Disabled Children," *Journal of Learning Disabilities*. 7:44-51, January, 1974.
12. Frostig, Marianne, and Horne, D. *The Frostig Program for the Development of Visual Perception*. Chicago: Follett Educational Corporation, 1964.
13. Getman, G. N. and others. *Developing Learning Readiness*. St. Louis: Mc Graw-Hill Book Company, 1968.
14. Heath, Edward, and Early, G. H. "Intramodal and Intermodal Functioning of Normal and Learning Disabled Children," *Academic Therapy*. 9:133-49, Winter. 1973.
15. Kephart, Newell. *The Slow Learner in the Classroom*. Columbus, Ohio: Charles E. Merrill, 1971.
16. Lerner, J. W. *Children with Learning Disabilities*. Boston: Houghton Mifflin, 1971.
17. McCarthy, John, and McCarthy, J. F. *Learning Disabilities*. Boston: Allyn and Bacon, 1970.
18. Mourouzis, A., and others. *Body Management Activities: A Guide to Perceptual-Motor Training*. Cedar Rapids, Iowa: Nissen Company, 1970.
19. Myers, P. I., and Hammill, D. D. *Methods for Learning Disorders*. New York: John Wiley and Sons, 1969.
20. Radler, D. H., and Kephart, N. C. *Success Through Play*. New York: Harper and Row Publishers, 1960.

21. Saphier, J. D. "The Relation of Perceptual-Motor Skills to Learning and School Success." *Journal of Learning Disabilities*. 6:56-65, November, 1973.
22. Valett, Robert. *Programming Learning Disabilities*. Palo Alto, California: Fearon Publishers, 1969.
23. Vannier, Maryhelen, Foster, M., and Gallahue, D. L. *Teaching Physical Education in Elementary Schools*. Philadelphia: W. B. Saunders Company, 1973.
24. Williams, H. G. "Perceptual-Motor Development in Children," *A Textbook of Motor Development*. Dubuque, Iowa: Wm. C. Brown Company, Charles B. Corbin, Editor, 1973.
25. Wunderlich, R. C. *Kids, Brains, and Learning*. St. Petersburg, Florida: Johnny Reads, Inc., 1970.

SELECTED TESTS OF PERCEPTUAL-MOTOR FUNCTIONING

Ayres, Jean, *Southern California Perceptual-Motor Tests*, Western Psychological Services, Los Angeles, California.
Bender, Laura, *Bender Visual Motor Gestalt Test*, The Psychological Corporation, New York, New York.
Beery, K.E., *Developmental Test of Visual-Motor Integration*, Follett Educational Corporation, Chicago, Illinois.
Cheves, R., *Pupil Record of Educational Behavior*, Teaching Resources Corporation, Boston, Massachusetts.
Doll, E., *Oseretsky Motor Proficiency Tests*, American Guidance Service, Inc., Circle Pines, Minnesota.
Frostig, Marianne, and Horne, D., *The Marianne Frostig Developmental Test of Visual Perception*. Consulting Psychologists Press, Palo Alto, California.
Katz, J., *Kindergarten Auditory Screening Test*, Follett Educational Corporation, Chicago, Illinois.
Kirk, Samuel, et. al., *The Illinois Test of Psycholinguistic Abilities*, University of Illinois Press, Urbana, Illinois.
Perceptual Testing-Training Kit for Kindergarten Teachers, Winter Haven Lions Research Foundation, Inc., Winter Haven, Florida.
Perceptual Testing-Training Kit for First Grade Teachers, Winter Haven Lions Research Foundation, Inc., Winter Haven, Florida.
Roach, Edward and Kephart, N., *The Purdue Perceptual-Motor Survey*, Charles E. Merrill, Columbus, Ohio.
Semel, E., *Sound, Order, Sense*, Follett Educational Corporation, Chicago, Illinois.
Valett, Robert, *Valett Developmental Survey of Basic Learning Abilities*, Fearon Publishers, Palo Alto, California.
Wepman, J., *Auditory Discrimination Test*, Language Research Associates, Chicago, Illinois.

SUGGESTED FILMS ON PERCEPTUAL-MOTOR DEVELOPMENT

Bridges to Learning. (16mm, color, sd., 30 min.) Sale $125. Available Palmer Films, Inc., 611 Howard Street, San Francisco, California.
Illustrates the organization and administration of a K-6 physical education program with em-

phasis on perceptual training and innovative curriculum related to skills, games, and sports including evaluation techniques.

Creative Body Movements. (16mm, color, sd., 11 min.) Sale $125. Available Martin Moyer Productions, 900 Federal Avenue, East Seattle, Washington, 98102.

Shows how children can express themselves through movement using a perceptual-motor and problem solving approach (primary grade level).

Developmental Physical Education. (16mm, color, sd., 28 min.) Sale $225. Available Simensen & Johnson, Education Consultants, Box 34, College Park, Maryland, 20740.

A film developed by Dr. Louis Bowers, University of South Florida, depicting the development of balance, laterality, directionality, body image, spatial awareness, and visual perception among mentally retarded children.

Early Recognition of Learning Disability. (16mm, color, 30 min.) Available Churchwell Films, Department of HEW, Station K, Atlanta, Georgia 30324.

The film emphasizes the importance of early recognition and programming to help those children who have perceptual-motor problems.

Learning To Learn. (16mm, color, 24 min.) Available Wardell Associates, 49 Pinckney Street, Boston, Massachusetts.

The film identifies children who are having trouble learning in a normal school situation as unforthcoming or inconsequential. The film presents a behavioral modification approach through a Flying Start To Learning Program to help these children overcome their problems. Author - D.H. Stott.

Physical Education - Lever To Learning. (16mm, color, 24 min.) Available Stuart Finley Films, 3428 Mansfield Road, Falls Church, Virginia 22041.

The film shows educable mentally retarded boys and girls from a public school special education program taking part in a vigorous and varied program emphasizing the development of motor skills and physical fitness through the use of innovative equipment.

Sensorimotor Training. (16mm, color, 24 min.) Sale $135. Available Valdhere Films, 3060 Valleywood Drive, Kettering, Ohio.

Describes philosophy and training methods for helping preschool children develop sensory skills and physical coordination. Dayton Public Schools Program. Author - William Braley.

Thinking, Moving, Learning. (16mm, color, 30 min.) Available Bradley Wright Films, 309 North Duane Avenue, San Gabriel, California 91775.

A comprehensive movement program at the preschool and early elementary levels can help children develop a postiive self-concept, spatial awareness, visual perception and other concepts that help them achieve a readiness level for success in school. Author - Jack Capon.

Visual Perception and a Failure To Learn. (16mm, black and white, 30 min.) Available Indiana University Film Library, Bloomington, Indiana 47401.

The film focuses on the Frostig Developmental Test of Visual Perception. Eye-hand coordination, figure-ground perception, perceptual constancy, position in space, and spatial relationships are discussed.

Why Billie Couldn't Learn. (16mm, color, 40 min.) Sale $250. Available California Association for Neurologically Handicapped Children, Film Director, Box 604, Main Office, Los Angeles, California, 90053.

Focuses on the diagnosis and teaching techniques used in a special classroom for neurologically handicapped children.

Chapter 13
Developing Language Arts Concepts

Key Concept: Language arts is the teaching of language as a means of communication through speech, listening, writing, and reading. Physical education aids in the development of verbal and nonverbal communication through involving movement in the learning of language arts fundamentals.

Content: Introduction

Language Arts Experiences Through Physical Education
  Speaking and Listening
  Reading and Writing
  Nonverbal Communication

Language Arts and Physical Education at the Preschool Level

Examples Integrating Language Arts with Physical Education
  Speaking and Listening
  Nonverbal Communication
  Reading and Writing

Developing Language Arts Concepts

INTRODUCTION

Children learn to communicate through the use of language. The language arts program in the elementary school includes the areas of speaking, listening, writing, and reading. Nonverbal language or communication through actions is also learned directly or indirectly by the use of various bodily gestures.

All facets of the language arts program are interrelated and can be divided into two general categories, decoding and encoding. *Decoding messages is the receptive phase of language development.* Through this phase of development, a child learns to understand messages that come to him from an outside source. Receiving visual, auditory, tactile, olfactory, and gustatory cues help the child interpret incoming messages to the brain. Auditory and visual cues become the primary means to decode messages in the development of language.

Children learn to decode auditory messages by associating sounds with different people and objects (listening). Initially, the infant learns who "mama" is and what she does for him. Gradually, concrete objects such as a rattle or ball are associated with sounds or word cues given to the objects. Later, the child learns to associate abstract word cues such as right, left, in, on, and through with positions in his environment.

Refinement in the decoding process comes when the child is ready to decode visual, abstract symbols as the written word (reading). Initially, children read pictures. Gradually, abstract symbols (chair), when arranged in a certain order, come to be interpreted as meaning the same thing as a chair. Children learn to read words, phrases, sentences, and paragraphs as they learn to decode the written symbols from the left of the page to the right and from top to bottom.

Encoding is the expressive phase of language development. Through this phase of development, a child learns to make correct responses as a result of correctly interpreting incoming messages. Responses are in the form of verbal expression (speaking) and motor expression (writing and motor patterns). Children learn to make verbal responses to visual stimuli and to auditory stimuli. Books, toys, pictures, and games provide visual cues for verbal responses. Auditory stimuli such as "Tell me what you did," "What do you like to do best," and "Tell me the likenesses and differences of two different objects," provide cues for verbal responses. Completing a story and telling a story are other auditory cues for verbal responses.

Children learn to express themselves motorically in the form of pantomimes such as mirror actions, animal walks, and household actions. Manipulating materials such as blocks, cans, dowels, and number rods are other means in which children learn to express themselves. Dramatic play situations involving dress up materials, nursery rhymes, animal make believe, and adventure stories also provide opportunities for children to express themselves.

Motor expression moves from large muscle actions to fine motor responses (writing). Children learn to color, draw pictures, and construct geometric figures. Gradually, they learn to put various shapes together to form letters of the alphabet. Children learn to write letters, words, sentences, and eventually their own stories.

As children learn to decode and encode messages, the concepts of association, and sequential memory assist children in the development of language skills. The concept of *association* enables children to interpret likenesses and differences in material presented through auditory or visual means. Children learn to classify objects according to color, size, shape, and texture. The concept of *closure* enables a child to complete a message he is receiving even though the message is incomplete. For example, if a child sees or hears the partial word (airpla), he interprets the message to mean airplane. *Sequential Memory* enables children to interpret messages more effectively. Auditory and visual sequential processes enable a child to recreate the order of events in terms of time and/or space. Recall and reproduction of ordered number sequences, motor tasks, patterns or directions are examples of memory sequencing.

The different facets of language development are closely interrelated. Areas of study such as spelling, listening, reading, and the like should be considered as component parts of the broad area of communication. In the past, it was common practice to treat such areas of study as separate subjects. Subjects became isolated and unrelated. Their full potential as mediums of expression were never fully realized. Approaches to current language arts programs such as the Peabody REBUS Reading Program, the Sullivan Programmed Reading Series, the Science Research Associates Reading Program, Sesame Street, and the language program resulting from the Illinois Test of Psycholinguistic Abilities relate the various language areas to particular areas of interest. Language arts textbook series also teach the development of a unified program rather than teach each of the areas as separate entities. All facets of the language arts are utilized in the solution of problems in all curriculum areas.

Children who have difficulties in learning to communicate effectively with their environment are commonly referred to as being dyslexic, slow learners, or learning disabled. Various perceptual-motor problems such as body image, balance, laterality, directionality, form perception visual perception, time/space relationships, and figure-ground perception prevent these children from learning to cope successfully with language development. Experiences in physical education are often designed to aid such children in the development of readiness skills to prepare them for success in the communicative processes. However, since it is not the purpose of this book to develop a perceptual-motor program, the chapter will be restricted to physical education experiences that enhance the development of language arts skills in normal children.

Assuming that skill in communication should be developed in all areas of the curriculum, physical education offers many opportunities to enhance the development of language skills. Various activities in physical education can be designed to help children learn listening and speaking abilities, reading and writing abilities, and nonverbal communication.

LANGUAGE ARTS EXPERIENCES THROUGH PHYSICAL EDUCATION

Listening and Speaking

Although it is very often taken for granted, the listening and speaking abilities of children can be greatly enhanced through experiences specifically oriented toward improvement in these areas. With attention focused on decoding and encoding messages, specific practice is concentrated on (1) auditory directions with verbal responses, (2) verbal expressive abilities, (3) auditory association, (4) auditory closure, and (5) auditory memory. In each case the child must first listen to the message before speaking and making his verbal response. Other exercises concentrate on auditory cues with motor responses and visual cues with auditory and/or motor responses. Following are some experiences in physical education that develop the processes of listening and speaking.

The children can listen to the directions of the teacher (auditory decoding) and perform the required tasks. The directions may start with one task such as to do five sit-ups and move on to a sequence of tasks such as to do five sit-ups, four push-ups, and run around the gymnasium three times. This sequencing of activities (auditory memory) requires the children to memorize the order of events and to perform the exact number of repetitions. Auditory sequencing can be done rhythmically by having the teacher beat out a rhythmical sequence (auditory and visual cues) and having the children reproduce the sequence by whistling, snapping fingers, clapping hands, or stamping feet (auditory and motor responses). By having the children turn their backs to the teacher, the auditory and motor responses of the children become products of an auditory cue only.

Children Learn Through Acting Out Stories

By having the teacher silently beat out a rhythm in the air, the auditory and motor responses of the children become products of a visual cue only. Lummi sticks (small wooden sticks of wood used for tapping out rhythmical patterns) also provide many opportunities for auditory sequencing.

Poems, stories, myths, and fables either read aloud or spoken from memory can provide movement opportunities that allow children to develop listening and speaking abilities. Many works of children's literature contain actions or adventures that are particularly adaptable to movement in physical education. At the upper elementary level the children may become involved in dramatic plays with action themes. For example, a basketball theme could involve student coaches explaining strategy to players, referees explaining fouls to the players, and an announcer giving a play by play description of the action of the game. Other athletic events and circus shows enacted dramatically also provide children opportunities to learn about listening and speaking.

Children learn to associate words in their vocabulary with various movements (auditory association). Words that children "feel" and words for trips become creative movement experiences for children in physical education. Moving like splashing rain, a tree swaying in the wind, a jet plane or a motorcycle are movement experiences associated with words. Movement experiences through word association can also be initiated in physical education by having the teacher and children progressively create a movement story. For example, the teacher could have the children choose a word associated with the letter, "A." An apple grows from being small to being big and round. When the wind blows the apple falls to the ground. An animal whose name begins with a "B" comes along and eats the apple. The movement story could go on and on by having the teacher provide word cues through the introduction of other letters or words and having the children fill in the story with associated words and appropriate actions for their words.

The concept of auditory closure can be enhanced in physical education through other movement experiences. Familiar nursery rhymes can be started by the teacher. The children can then say the remaining part of the rhyme while enacting the movements. Roots of words, suffixes of words, and phonetic sounds of parts of words provide situations in which the children can anticipate hearing the whole word. The chasing and fleeing game of Crows and Cranes[8] allows the children a chance to anticipate the closure of the "CR" sound. Synonyms and antonyms of words also provide experiences in which the children learn about closure. In the game, In the Creek,[10] the synonyms for creek are pond, ocean, river, brook, and so forth. As the children hear the different commands from the teacher the only phrase that meets the conditions for movement is "In the Creek." As the children anticipate closure of the phrase movements are often incorrectly made to words that are synonyms to "creek."

Reading and Writing

As children enter school it is assumed that they are ready to learn to read and write. Work in the classroom leads children from reading pictures to recognizing abstract symbols. At the same time children learn to write various geometric forms on paper and chalkboard. Each child learns the letters of the alphabet. Each learns to combine groups of letters into phrases and words. Training proceeds in the direction of learning to read the written symbols on the page (decoding) and to write symbols on paper so as to send a message for someone else to read (encoding).

Experiences in physical education should be designed to enable a child to decode and encode written symbols more effectively. The following illustrations serve as means to implement the language concepts of reading and writing in physical education.

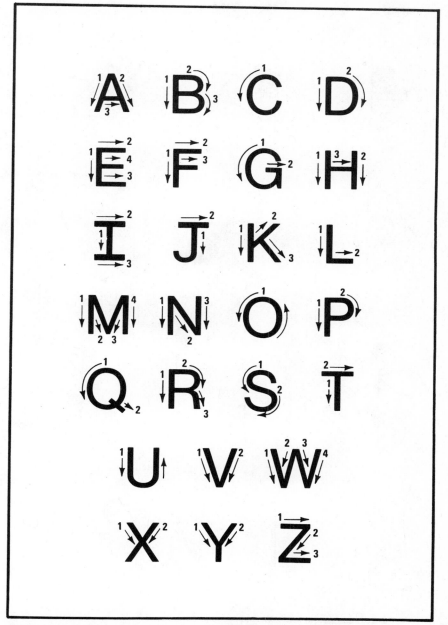

Figure 13-1. Children can make different letters of the alphabet through exercises.

Figure 13-2. Children can make different letters of the alphabet through different body poses.

Letters and Words

Exercises performed while shaping the body to form various letters of the alphabet (Figures 13-1 and 13-2) enable children to learn the abstract symbols in meaningful situations. Children can construct the letters in sequential parts as illustrated in the capital letters or form the shape of a letter in a single pose as is shown in the small letters. They can form the same letters with different body parts. For example, they could make an "O" with their arms, legs, fingers, mouth, and so forth. Jump ropes can also be utilized to enable children to form the letters of the alphabet. How many different ways can you form the letters of the alphabet?

Beanbags can be constructed in the shape of the different letters. Letters can be printed on balls with which the children play. While they throw and catch the objects they can identify the letters that they see.

Letters painted on both sides of twelve inch square blocks of wood can be utilized in several different ways. Eye-hand coordination exercises can be implemented by giving each of the children a block with which to work. They can toss the block into the air a short distance and catch it after allowing it to rotate half and whole turns in each of the three planes (horizontal, vertical, longitudinal). While manipulating the blocks the children are also learning to recognize letters of the alphabet regardless of the position in which they see them.

Letters can also be used to construct words. The physical education teacher can obtain the spelling list from the classroom teacher and have the children perform word relays. After the children are divided into teams, the teacher can call out a word. The children who are holding the letters in the word must run to a designated line in the gymnasium and form the word. Each child can sequentially call out their letter in the word and then as a group collectively say the word. The first group to complete the task and return to the line would win the relay. The same type of relay could be performed without the letter blocks by having the children pose in the different letter forms.

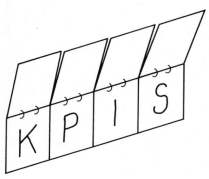

Figure 13-3. Games using word anagrams can be used to help children learn their spelling lists.

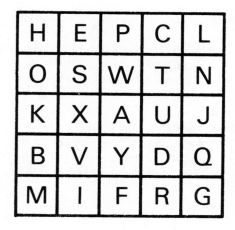

Figure 13-4. Children hop from square to square to spell words.

Teachers can also use spelling lists to play games involving word anagrams. The children should be arranged in small groups and instructed to play games involving the skills of kicking, striking, throwing and catching, or shooting baskets. As the game starts each group of children is given a word spelled in random fashion printed on a large chart (Figure 13-3). Each letter is covered up. As the group scores a point in whatever game they may be playing, they may uncover one of the letters. As all of the letters are uncovered, they must rearrange the order of the letters to make the word (SKIP). The first group to identify their word correctly wins the game.

The game of letter squares can be painted on the playground or gymnasium floor to help children spell various words (Figure 13-4). Children can hop or jump into the various squares to spell words they are learning in school.

Sentence Structure

As children learn about words in school they learn that various words perform different tasks in sentence structure. Some words act as nouns or as subjects in sentences. Nouns are names for different objects. Examples of nouns in physical education are balls, bats, rackets, and any other type of equipment used in the children's movement experiences. The names of games, rhythms and gymnastic activities are also nouns. Adjectives are words that help modify or explain nouns. Examples of adjectives used in physical education are large, small, wide, narrow, tall, short, and so on. Words such as on, above, below, through, and over are called prepositions. Prepositions are words that connect nouns to other words. For example, the ball is *above* the basket. The preposition, *above*, relates the position of the ball to the basket. Verbs are called predicates and are words that give action to sentences. Examples of action words in physical education are jump, kick, throw, and catch. Adverbs are words that modify or explain verbs, adjectives, or other adverbs. Examples of adverbs used in physical education are run *fast*, jump *high*, and dodge *quickly*. Conjunctions are words that are used to connect words, phrases, or clauses. Examples of words that are conjunctions are since, after, and, for, but, and so forth. In physical education the students may be told to do five sit-ups *and* five push-ups. The conjunction, *and*, indicates that both tasks are to be performed. Words such as either or neither, nor are called disjunctions. Disjunctions are words that are used to separate words, phrases, or clauses. In physical education the students may be told to do *either* five sit-ups *or* five push-ups. The disjunctions, *either* and *or*, indicate that the students may choose to do one of the tasks.

Reading

Regardless of the method used to teach reading, learning progresses from recognizing symbols, grouping symbols into words, reading words in sequence from left to right and from top to bottom, and comprehending thoughts contained in sentences or paragraphs. Physical education can enhance interest in reading and the development of reading skills through specially planned movement experiences. Initially, experiences may involve reading exercise cards specially prepared for the physical education class. Rather than using words and complicated directions, letters of the alphabet and pictures may be used to inform the children as to what to do (Figure 13-5). The children may be assigned to groups and asked to rotate from station to station until each group has performed the exercises at each station. As a group approaches a station they must read the designated exercises and perform the exercises assigned. In the example (Figure 13-5) Group 1 would hop on the left foot three times and then jump five times. Group 2 would do jumping jacks ten times and then sit-ups ten times.

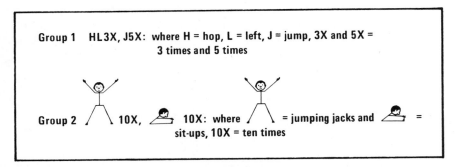

Figure 13-5. Exercise cards used around the third grade help children to read in physical education.

As children progress in their reading skills they could read about various activities, which they might play in physical education. Reading would progress from simple activities with few rules to more highly organized activities with many rules. As the children read about the activities, their reading comprehension could be tested by having them explain the rules of the activity to the class before participation begins.

Books, magazines, and newspapers often contain stories and articles about famous athletes, dancers, and sporting activities. Reading of this sort serves as a motivating factor in the developmental reading level of children. Used in this manner, physical education can make a fine contribution to the reading ability and interest of some children.

Composition

Physical education contributes to the development of writing skills in the same manner as it does to reading. Initially, the children can learn to write their own exercises such as is found in Figure 13.5. Later, in cooperation with the physical education teacher and classroom teacher, the children can compose stories about games they play, the rules of the games, and their enjoyment of games. Children may also be encouraged to invent a new game using various pieces of equipment and to write the rules to their game. During the upper elementary grades the children can compose their own sports stories and perhaps write a sports column for a school newspaper. Used in this manner, physical education can make a fine contribution to the writing ability of children.

Nonverbal Communication

Movement, like speaking and writing, is a means of expression. It is a universal language that helps us communicate with others. Greetings are accompanied by gestures such as the handshake and smile. Gestures are used in everyday speech to supplement words. Talking with the hands is characteristic of many people. Words in our language often suggest movement and action. Words such as swinging, swaying, falling, and splashing are examples of action words. Body postures or gestures reveal our feelings. Various movements tell others when we are angry, sad, happy, and the like. Specific types of actions characterize different tasks or occupations. Mixing a cake, dancing, sawing wood, and plowing a field are but a few of the tasks that can be conveyed through imitative actions.

Physical education offers many opportunities for children to learn to communicate through movement. They can create various moods through dance. They can dance the movements of nature such as swaying like a tree or splashing like the rain. They can dramatize a day at the zoo, a day on the farm, a day at sea, and other such action sequences. Pictures as well as other objects and themes can often be used to help children communicate through movement. Showing children pictures of birds in flight, kites in the spring wind, or balloons floating through the air as well as other action scenes is a means to help children learn to communicate through movement. Flying against the wind or gliding high with the wind swept clouds are suggestions to compare and contrast movements. Picking up on themes of action words is another means of expression through movement. Have the children make an "angry" body movement, facial expression or pose. Have them fight with another child in slow motion without touching to express anger. Have them introduce themselves to each other without talking or create a feeling of joy or happiness between friends at a party. Utilize streamers or scarves to express a feeling of lightness or to explore floor and air patterns. Other objects may be used to create a feeling of heaviness or other moods.

When using pictures, objects or themes for expression it is important to remember two factors for successful implementation. First, the stimulus (picture, object, or theme) is a means to an end—not an end in itself. The stimulus should be used for stimulation not imitation. We should help children move from using the stimulus in a literal sense, for example: copying a scene in a picture, waving a streamer, or making angry movements, to expressing the qualities of movement that the stimuli suggest such as the impression or mood of the picture, the color, shapes, lightness, and movement patterns of the streamer, or the strong, forceful, tense movements of a person when angry. When the children can draw relationships between what they see and feel and hear to how they move, they are using the process of abstraction. The intention, then, is to move away from the "doing the picture or streamer syndrome" toward utilizing the various stimuli to reinforce the qualities of movement and expression.

Secondly, when utilizing pictures, objects or themes for movement experiences, avoid having the children imitate something that they really cannot be such as an inanimate object (pumpkin). To move like a pumpkin is an impossible task that will create confusion and undesirable results from children. It would be better to ask the children to make their bodies into the shape of a pumpkin and then ask them how it would move if it could move.

Nonverbal communication through body postures, gestures, imitation, and dramatization helps people convey feelings and ideas. Actions become linguistic tools of alert teachers who are quick to seize upon a teachable moment. Movement helps us articulate our experiences, thoughts, and perceptions.

LANGUAGE ARTS AND PHYSICAL EDUCATION AT THE PRESCHOOL LEVEL

Movement is an important aspect of a child's language arts experiences at the preschool level in both the receptive and expressive phases of language development. The child living in a perceptual and motor world continually receives auditory and visual cues to help interpret the environment around him. Listening to directions or stories and then moving accordingly helps develop auditory discrimination and auditory perception. Beating out a specific rhythm done by the teacher or creating a rhythmical beat and then repeating it are further ways for children to develop auditory perception. In an educational movement setting special cues can be contrived to help children decode auditory and visual messages by following instructions properly. A drum beat might mean to move fast, a tambourine to move slow, a whistle to stop, an arrow drawn on a chart to move forward, backward or sideways, a color to start or stop movement (green and red), and a geometric shape drawn on a chart to move at a high or low level (Δ or ∇).

As children encounter their environment movement experiences help them understand words in their vocabulary. Learning to throw, catch, strike, and kick objects as well as developing other manipulative skills such as playing with blocks, trucks, or dolls helps children develop eye-hand coordination (perceptual-motor match). Children learn what a ball is and what they can do with it. They learn about blocks and how to stack them. They learn about objects in their environment, their names, and for what they are used through experiencing and manipulating them. They move around the table, under the chair, through the tunnel, and over the bench. Experiencing action words such as run, walk, hop, and jump as well as the qualifying adjectives and adverbs of high, low, round, fast, or slow give a child further background in language development. Other prepositional phrases such as in front of, in back of, on top of, and to the side of help children understand their position in space. Later, when they are ready to read they will fully understand and recognize the words in their vocabulary because they fully understand them.

Movement during the early years helps children learn their body parts, what they can do, and how they can move in space. Through successful movement experiences a child gains a positive self concept and begins to express himself both verbally and motorically. They often say, "I can." or "Watch me!", as they run, climb, color, or perform a wealth of other motor experiences. A variety of large and small muscle tasks should be provided each child through an enriched environment so that he can experience success in his drive toward expressive development. Experiences involving moving to a children's story, poem, or nursery rhyme help children interpret what they hear and express their moods and feelings. Prereading skills are encouraged by teaching children the letters of the alphabet through movement experiences in body alphabet, alphabet beanbags, and letter blocks (pages 306-311). Verbal expression is encouraged when teachers allow children to talk about their movements, make up their own stories, or tell the nursery rhymes that they have learned. Showing the children a picture of an action scene (a kite flying), asking them what is happening, followed by flying a kite, and then moving like a kite flying in the wind are other ways to encourage verbal and motoric expression. As children at this stage of development are quite egocentric, teachers should allow each child a chance to express himself.

EXAMPLES INTEGRATING LANGUAGE ARTS WITH PHYSICAL EDUCATION

As children learn language arts concepts in the classroom, they should have related learning experiences in physical education. This does not mean, however, that the objectives of physical education must be sacrificed in order to teach the children language arts. It does mean that the physical education teacher should be familiar with what is being taught in the classroom and be ready to emphasize and follow up subject matter when it applies to physical education.

Repeated examples have been illustrated that incorporate the concepts of language arts while maintaining an activity oriented program. Some movement

Acting Out Stories With Puppets Enhances Fundamental Concepts In The Language Arts

experiences help children learn how to listen and speak better. Other movement experiences help children learn how to read, write, and communicate non-verbally.

As children learn to communicate more effectively with their environment, the main factor to remember is to introduce the language arts concepts according to the ability level of the children. The following are some sample lessons of ways in which language arts and physical education can be integrated. Teachers should use their own ingenuity and creativeness in using these lessons and in adapting other language arts concepts to lessons in physical education. It must be remembered, however, that in any attempt to integrate language arts with physical education, the physical education class must remain activity oriented rather than become an academic class. The main point to consider is to follow the physical education curriculum as usual, but to use every *teachable moment* to integrate language arts with physical education in an effort to realize more meaningful instruction in both disciplines.

Concept: *Speaking and Listening*
Grade: *1 and 2*
Emphasis: *Auditory decoding, auditory memory and auditory sequencing activities in physical education help children to listen better.*
Organizing Center: *Manipulation*
Equipment: *Two lummi sticks for each child in class, record player, records containing various types of rhythms, tempos, and accents.*
Location: *Gymnasium*
Instructional Ideas:

During exercises the teacher should give several series of tasks to perform to see if the children can remember the correct sequence and the proper number of repetitions of each of the exercises. Following exercises the teacher will ask all of the children to sit down and face him. The teacher will tell the children that they are going to practice some listening games. First, the teacher will clap out some rhythms and have the children respond. Finger snapping and foot stamping exercises will follow. All of the activities will move from simple to more complex series of sounds. Snapping, clapping, and stamping may be combined in other sequence activities. Next, the children will be asked to turn their backs to the source of the sound. The above exercises will now be performed with an auditory cue only. After the activities are performed in this manner, each of the children will be given two lummi sticks. With their eyes watching the teacher and their ears listening, the children will learn several series of tasks to be performed with the sticks. They may hit them together over their head; hit them both on the floor to the right, left, front and back of their bodies; hit one on each side of the body (same side and cross pattern); hit the toe and heel of the stick on the floor alternately; and flip them into the air and catch them one or two at one time. The teacher may now show the children specific series of tasks to be performed to music. The music may vary in rhythm, tempo, and accent. The tasks may require performance on each beat of the measure for slower music and on the first beat of each measure for faster music. In each case the children have to combine listening skills and motor skills for correct performance. As time allows children can explore and make up their own rhythmical sequence with the lummi sticks.

Concept: *Nonverbal Communication*
Grade: *3 and 4*
Emphasis: *Nonverbal communication through body postures, gestures, imitation, and dramatization helps people convey feelings and ideas.*
Organizing Center: *Stability and Locomotion*
Equipment: *Record player, records*–Action Songs for Growing Up and Movement Fun *by Educational Activities, Inc.*
Location: *Gymnasium*
Instructional Ideas:

The initial movements during class will serve not only as a warm-up, but also as a means of creating an atmosphere of communicating feelings and ideas through movement. Initial tasks may be: make yourself round; make yourself tall as possible: move only one part of your body; move every part of your body; tremble like a leaf; chug like a train; slink like a cat; crawl like a snake; wriggle like a worm; walk like an elephant; and move like a grasshopper. Next, the children will interpret musical recordings of many moods and tempos. They will create a happy dance, a sad dance, an angry dance, and a calm dance. They will dance the movements of nature such as swaying trees, buzzing bees, falling snow, and splashing rain. The children will enjoy mimicking circus animals, throwing, swimming, golf swings, being a bulldozer, dump truck, and drawbridge. The records also give the children an opportunity to act out the movements of pilots, bus drivers, doctors, cowhands, repairmen, and other occupations with which they are familiar. The imitative movements and dramatizations to music help children to explore what the various pieces of equipment and occupations mean to them.

Concept: *Reading and Writing*
Grade: *5 and 6*
Emphasis: *Physical education can enhance interest in reading and the development of reading skills through specially planned movement experiences.*
Organizing Center: *Locomotion and Manipulation*
Equipment: *Two 4' x 6' gymnastics mats, four basketballs, and four jump ropes.*
Location: *Gymnasium*
Instructional Ideas:

The lesson will begin with a circuit training course. The students will be divided into eight different groups. The gymnasium will be divided into eight different stations. Each station will be provided with the proper equipment and a 4″ x 6″ card with typewritten directions for the exercises at that station. An example card follows:

Wall Pass

Choose a partner for a wall pass exercise. You are to stand 6 feet away from the wall (behind the black line). By using a chest pass or a bounce pass, pass the ball to yourself as many times as you can for 30 seconds. One partner will remain sitting while the second partner does the activity. The partner who is sitting will give the command to begin the activity. By watching the clock on the wall and the active partner, the observer will count the number of passes and give the command to stop at the end of 30 seconds. Each partner take two turns at the wall pass to see if you can better your first performance.

The remaining seven exercises will involve similar directions to the standing long jump, sit-ups, push-ups, jump rope, shuttle run, rope climb, and shooting baskets.

After every group has completed the circuit training course, the children will play a game about which one of them has read. The teacher should allow the students to take books out of his office or place game books in the school library under reference for students to read. The children could read about sporting activities and relays. If a unit on one of the team sports is the current physical education topic, the children could read about the lead-up games for that sport and choose a game appropriate for their level of skill. Perhaps the child who read about the game could even teach the others how to play the game.

SELECTED REFERENCES

1. Buchanan, Cynthia. *Programmed Reading*. St. Louis: McGraw-Hill Book Company, Sullivan Associates, 1966.
2. Bush, William, and Giles, M.T. *Aids to Psycholinguistic Teaching*. Columbus, Ohio: Charles E. Merrill.
3. Cratty, B.J. *Active Learning: Games to Enhance Academic Abilities*. Englewood Cliffs, New Jersey: Prentice-Hall, 1971.
4. Humphrey, James. *Child Learning Through Elementary School Physical Education*. Dubuque, Iowa: Wm. C. Brown Company, 1974.
5. Dravitz, Richard, and Shapiro, M. "Reading-Boxing Class," *Journal of Health, Physical Education, and Recreation*. 40:26-29, November, 1969.
6. Miller, Arthur, Cheffers, J.T., and Whitcomb, V. *Physical Education: Teaching Human Movement in the Elementary Schools*. Englewood Cliffs, New Jersey: Prentice-Hall, 1974.

7. Schiller, Andrew, et. al. *Language and How to Use It*. Glenview, Illinois: Scott, Foresman, and Company, 1969.
8. Schurr, Evelyn. *Movement Experiences for Children*. New York: Appleton-Century-Crofts, 1967.
9. Woodcock, Richard, Clark, C.R., and Davies, C.O. *The Peabody Rebus Reading Program*. Circle Pines, Minnesota: American Guidance Service, Inc., 1969.
10. Vannier, Maryhelen, Foster, N., and Gallahue, D.L. *Teaching Physical Education in Elementary Schools*. Philadelphia: W.B. Saunders, 1973.

Chapter 14
Developing Mathematic Concepts

Key Concept: Play experiences and game situations are utilized to enhance the presentation of mathematics in the classroom. Understanding and using mathematics concepts correctly can be as much a part of the physical education period as play experiences and game situations are a part of the mathematics lesson in the classroom.

Content: Introduction

Mathematics Experiences Through Physical Education
  Mathematical Sentences
  Sets
  The Whole Numbers
  The Field Properties of Mathematics
  Communication of Quantitative Ideas
  Geometry
  Measuring and Graphing
Mathematics and Physical Education at the Preschool Level
Examples Integrating Mathematics with Physical Education
  Communication of Quantitative Ideas
  Geometry
  The Field Properties of Mathematics
  The Whole Numbers
  Sets
  Measuring and Graphing

Developing Mathematic Concepts

INTRODUCTION

Upon reviewing mathematics textbook series it becomes evident that play experiences and game situations are utilized to enhance the presentation of mathematics concepts. Classroom teachers often use physical education activities such as team scores, measurement activities, and batting averages to teach mathematics more effectively to their children.

In many schools physical education is considered a subject separate from those subjects that are taught in the classroom. If we can agree, however, that the whole child comes to the physical education class, it is important that we incorporate all of his learning experiences with that which he will learn through physical education. Understanding and using mathematics concepts correctly can be as much a part of the physical education period as play experiences and game situations are a part of the mathematics lesson in the classroom.

If children are to be provided with learning experiences in mathematics, teachers should be aware of the mathematics concepts that are taught at the various grade levels. Review of several mathematics textbook series and current mathematics projects such as the School Mathematics Study Group, Greater Cleveland Mathematics Program, University of Illinois Arithmetic Project, Madison Project, Stanford Project and Minnesota Mathematics, and Science Teaching Project indicate that the following mathematics concepts are being taught in the elementary schools: the whole numbers, mathematical sentences, sets, field properties of mathematics, geometry, and measuring and graphing. In the primary grades children learn about counting, adding, subtracting, sets, geometry, number sentences, measuring, commutative and associative properties for addition, fractions, and word problems. In the intermediate grades children learn about sets, set operations, identity properties for addition and multiplication, commutative and associative properties for addition and multiplication, distributive properties for multiplication and division, geometry, measuring and graphing, mathematical sentences, fractions and decimals.

A number of studies have been conducted to determine the effectiveness of the integration of mathematics with physical education. Humphrey[2] studied the effects of the integration of mathematics with physical education by testing 20 first grade children on eight mathematics concepts. The children learned about

322

the eight mathematics concepts in physical education and were then retested. It was concluded from the results of this study that first grade children can learn mathematics concepts through the physical education medium.

Other studies advocating the integration of mathematics concepts with physical education evolved a series of lessons combining the two subjects. Memmel[4] illustrated lessons in which rope jumping, team games, throwing, kicking, marching, rhythms, and shooting baskets were integrated with mathematics lessons. Jensen[3] stressed the use of ropes in solving simple arithmetic problems and in designing geometrical patterns through physical education. Lessons for the teaching of number concepts, integers, rationals, addition, subtraction, multiplication, division, averages, linear measures, time, and geometric forms through physical education have also been presented by various other authors.

With the knowledge that mathematics experiences through physical education are numerous and that integration of mathematics and physical education helps children learn, let us turn to an examination of the possibilities of teaching mathematics experiences through physical education.

MATHEMATICS EXPERIENCES THROUGH PHYSICAL EDUCATION

Mathematical Sentences

Just as children learn to communicate with words and sentences in language arts, they also learn to communicate using mathematical sentences. Some of the symbols used in mathematical sentences are illustrated as follows.

1. Capital letters are generally used to denote sets.
2. Equal signs are used to denote equality on each side of the equation.
3. Braces, $\{\ \}$, (sometimes called brackets) are enclosures for members of a set.
4. Symbols or names enclosed in braces are understood to refer to members of sets.
5. Commas separate the symbols that represent the members of a set when the members are listed between braces.

An example of the symbols that have been illustrated to this point is demonstrated. $A = \{$forward, center, guard$\}$, which is read: "A is the set of basketball positions whose members are forward, center, and guard.

6. Three dots (. . .) mean follow on in the indicated pattern. For example: A = {2, 4, 6, . . .}, which is read: "A is the set of even whole numbers beginning with 2 and continuing to infinity."
7. Symbols used to denote individual members of sets are usually taken from the lower-case letters of the alphabet.
8. The Greek letter epsilon, ϵ, is used to abbreviate "is a member of," or "is an element of." For example: a ϵ A, which is read, "a is a member of the set A."
9. The slant bar, /, is frequently used as a negation symbol in mathematics. For example: a $\notin$ A, which is read, "a is not a member of the set A."
10. For sets A and B, the statement, A B, means that A is a subset of B and that B has at least one member that is not a member of A. For example: running locomotion, which is read, "running is a subset of locomotion."
11. The symbols, $<$ and $>$, denote "is less than" and "is greater than," respectively. For example: $3 < 5$, which is read, "3 is less than 5." $7 > 5$, which is read, "7 is greater than 5."
12. Set operations involving the union and intersection of sets are also capable of being represented through mathematical sentences as was shown in the discussion of sets.

The following examples illustrate further practical means to involve mathematical sentences in physical education.

U = Universal set of all movement patterns.
A = Set of Locomotion patterns.
B = Set of Stability patterns.
C = Set of Manipulative patterns.
C ϵ U, which is read, "manipulation is a subset of all movement patterns."
A = {walking, running, hopping . . . galloping}, which is read, "walking, running, hopping . . . galloping are elements of locomotion."
Balancing ϵ B, which is read, "balancing is an element of stability."
Skipping $\notin$ B, which is read, "skipping is not an element of stability."

By continuing this line of thought, mathematical sentences could be used to help children better understand mathematics and human movement. Other examples follow:

1. {1, 2, 3, 4} ϵ SD, which is read, "Couples 1, 2, 3, 4 are elements of a square dance set."
2. The terms "less than" ($<$) and "greater than" ($>$) may be used: in measuring play areas; in keeping scores of teams in games; in measuring the amount of work done in different play situations; and in calculating team batting averages in softball.

Sets

Set concepts are introduced in the first grade and taught throughout the elementary school grades. Set concepts constitute a solid foundation upon which to base the more advanced mathematical concepts the children will encounter in their later school years. Set theory may also be applied in physical education to help us gain a better understanding of human movement. A set is simply a collection of a particular kind or group of objects. For instance, there is a set of whole numbers, a set of tires on a car, or a set of balls used in physical education. The things that constitute a given set are called members or elements of a set. Elements of the set of balls used in physical education are baseballs, basketballs, footballs, and any other type of ball.

Any part of a set can be viewed as a subset. For example, the members of the set of children in a gymnasium at any one time may be divided into two other sets, the set of boys and the set of girls. Subsets may be divided into classifications according to color, size, weight, sex, age, and so forth. The use of sets and subsets thus provides a means of classifying the discipline of physical education into a hierarchical structure. One may attempt to classify physical education activities according to the type of equipment used, according to the sex of those participating, or according to the type of movement patterns being explored. For the moment let us explore the development of basic movement patterns through the involvement of set theory (Figure 14-1).

Many Principles Of Movement
May Be Demonstrated Through
Bicycle Activities

Development of Fundamental Movement Patterns

Body Handling Patterns		Object Handling Patterns	
Stability	Locomotion	Manipulation	
		Absorptive	Propulsive
balance	walking	trapping	lifting
rolling	running	catching	throwing
springing	hopping	carrying	kicking
bending	skipping		striking
twisting	galloping		pushing
sitting	sliding		pulling
rotation	jumping		blocking
swinging	dodging		bouncing
standing	vaulting		rolling
supports	combinations		
curling			

Qualities of Movement

Space	Force	Time	Flow
Levels	strong-weak	slow	free
high	heavy-light	medium	bound
medium	tight-loose	fast	sequential
low	hard-soft		
Ranges	Directions	Emphasis of Movement	
wide-narrow	forward-backward	sudden	
far-near	upward-downward	explosive	
long-short	sideways	sustained	
	direct path	staccato	
	circle pattern	relaxed	
	diagonal patterns		

Figure 14-1. Classification of the fundamental patterns of movement and the qualities of movement.

All movement in physical education may be classified as being part of the universal set of basic movement patterns. Movement patterns may be classified into subsets of body handling patterns and object handling patterns. Locomotion and stability are subsets of body handling patterns.

Locomotion may be classified into subsets of walking, running, hopping, skipping, and so on. Manipulation is a subset of object handling patterns. Absorptive and propulsive patterns are subsets of manipulation. The elements of movement are a subset of the universal set of basic movement patterns. Space, force, time, and flow are subsets of the elements of movement. A set with no elements in the set is an empty set. The set of people who are able to fly is an empty set. A set with a definite number of elements in the set is called a finite set. The number of children in a given classroom is a finite set. A set with an infinite number of elements is called an infinite set. The set of locomotor movements is an infinite set because we may vary the way in which we move through space in an infinite number of ways.

There is a schematic means of representing set concepts using what are called Venn diagrams. Figure 14-2 is such a diagram. In general, a closed geometric figure is used to represent the universal set, with the understanding that the region interior to the boundary line represents the universal set. Smaller closed geometric figures completely contained in U are then used to represent the subsets of the universal set. Subsets may often overlap or intersect. For example, if Figure 14-2 represents a class of boys and girls in a physical education class, we could designate the girls in subset A and the boys in subset B. The intersection of A and B could be the number of children who have black hair. Black hair is a common element of subset A and subset B.

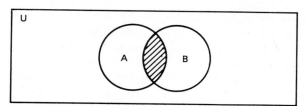

Figure 14-2. Venn diagram.

Operations on set concepts may be performed. The *first* operation that we will illustrate is the union of sets. If A and B are sets from Figure 14-3, the *union* of A and B (written AUB) is the set of all elements that belong to A or belong to B or belong to both A and B. The union of sets has great application in understanding movement in physical education. If we consider locomotor patterns as set A and manipulative patterns as set B, the union of A and B (AUB) incorporates all locomotive patterns, all manipulative patterns, and all movements where locomotion and manipulation are explored simultaneously. One can also consider the union of the subsets of basic movement patterns when we explore various movement combinations of stability, space, force, time, and flow.

The *second* operation that we will illustrate is the *intersection* of sets. If A and B are sets from Figure 14-4, the intersection of A and B (written A∩B) is the set of all elements that belong to A and that also belong to B. The intersection of sets also has great application in understanding movement in physical education.

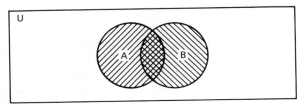

Figure 14-3. The union of sets.

Whereas the union of movement incorporated all patterns of locomotion, manipulation, or elements common to both locomotion and manipulation, the intersection of movements is more limiting in the sense that only elements common to both locomotion and manipulation form a subset. Thus, when a child is simultaneously running and bouncing a ball, he is moving while intersecting the patterns of locomotion and manipulation. This intersection of basic movement patterns is more commonly known as the skill of dribbling seen in the game of basketball.

If we consider locomotion as the universal set, specific combinations of the subset of running and the subset of hopping intersect to form the movement pattern of skipping. The intersection of stepping and leaping when one foot remains in front of the other foot is commonly known as galloping or sliding depending on the direction in which the feet move. The reader is encouraged to think of other intersecting movement patterns involving locomotion, manipulation, and stability. As children refine their movement patterns intersecting the qualities of space, force, time, and flow may also be explored. For example, which movement patterns evolve when children intersect a high level movement with a free flowing movement?

The hierarchical structure through classification of sets and subsets and the set operations of union and intersection provide a means through which physical educators can define and analyze human movement. By viewing basic movement patterns from a new outlook, we may come to understand movement more thoroughly. As we gain more insight, we become increasingly adept in teaching students how to move.

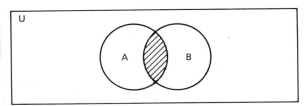

Figure 14-4. The intersection of sets.

The Whole Numbers

The set of whole numbers contains the set of counting numbers and zero—{0, 1, 2, 3, 4...}. This set of numbers has a least member, zero, but no greater member. This set is an infinite set because, no matter how many members of the set are listed, there are still other members of the set.

Early in a child's school experiences he begins various operations on the set of whole numbers. First experiences include counting, adding, and subtracting numbers. Gradually children move into multiplication, division, fractions, and decimals.

Here is a summary of the experiences that children should learn concerning the teaching of whole numbers in physical education.

1. Ropes can be utilized to construct numbers on the gymnasium floor. Following the construction of the numbers children can stand inside or outside, jump over, and straddle various parts of the numbers. Children can also perform simple addition, subtraction, multiplication, and division problems with ropes by forming the answer to a problem with a rope on the floor.

2. The game of number squares can be painted on the playground or gymnasium floor to help children solve simple mathematical problems (Figure 14-5). Children can hop or jump into the various squares to solve the mathematical problems. For example, $4 + 3 = 7$. The child would hop from the 4 to the 3 to the 7. Simple subtraction, multiplication, and division problems can also be solved in the same manner.

4	3	1	7	4
0	6	2	5	6
5	8	9	7	8
2	7	4	3	1
3	9	0	8	2

Figure 14-5. Children may hop from one number to another to solve mathematics problems.

Figure 14-6. Numbers may be combined for experiences in figure-ground perception.

3. Beanbags can be constructed in the shape of various numbers. When children throw and catch the beanbag numbers, they can identify the numbers they manipulate.

4. Whole numbers can be combined to form different animals and pictures on the gymnasium floor (Figure 14-6). The exercise becomes an experience in figure-ground perception as the child tries to draw and identify each number on the floor.

5. During warm-up exercises the children can try to assume body shapes of the whole numbers (Figure 14-7).

6. In certain types of games such as line games where a certain number of children are caught, the number of children caught can be counted. The number of children not caught and the total number of children in the class can be used to include addition and subtraction problems.

7. Children can count the number of times they bounce a ball during different time trials. Addition and subtraction problems can be used to compare differences between trials.

8. Children are often organized in number groups of twos, threes, fours, eights, and odd-numbered groups for purposes of dancing, gymnastics stunts, games, and relays. Further classification of children into groups can be made by having them divide into groups according to names of animals, vegetables, automobiles, and so forth. For example, the children could count off by bears, dogs, horses, and tigers. All children with the same animal name would become members of the same team.

9. Counting can be utilized in rhythms to count the number of beats or measures. Counting is also used in games of low organization such as Red Light, jump rope rhymes, and dodge ball.

10. Games in which players have numbers and go into action when their number is called can utilize operations on numbers by having the leader who calls the number give a problem that will have as its answer the number of the players who are to go into action. Problems in addition, subtraction, multiplication, and division can be used in such games as Steal the Bacon, Line Soccer, and relay games.

Figure 14-7. The body can assume the shapes of whole numbers through exercise.

11. In any type of activity that requires scoring, for example, the number of points scored in a basketball-type game, there are opportunities for counting, adding, and subtracting.
12. Children learn to understand number concepts in team sports through learning sports terminology such as outs, strikes, fouls, penalties, downs, innings, and batting order. In track and field children can count the number of trials, jumps, and throws.
13. Fractions can be learned by dividing the class members into groups consisting of halves, thirds, quarters, and so on. The physical education period may also be divided into fractions of time.
14. Team standings and batting averages are means to help children learn about division, fractions, and decimals.

The Field Properties of Mathematics

Most people think that learning arithmetic consists merely of learning to compute using the operations of addition, subtraction, multiplication, and division. Most of us learned methods for performing these operations very early in our lives and have completely forgotten how we learned them. We probably began this learning process by memorizing the basic sums and products:

$$1 + 1 = 2 \qquad\qquad 1 \times 1 = 1$$
$$1 + 2 = 3 \ldots, \qquad\qquad 1 \times 2 = 2 \ldots;$$

and we drilled until our response to 5×7 was automatically 35.

Ultimately we discovered that $2 + 4 = 4 + 2$, that $5 + 7 = 7 + 5$, and that the sum of any two numbers does not depend on the order of the addends. This important property of whole numbers is called the commutative property of addition. Similarly, most of us discovered that $(2 + 3) + 4 = 2 + (3 + 4)$. This associative property of addition tells us that we achieve the same sum no matter the order in which we add the numbers. These are some of the facts that form the basis of the structure of arithmetic. Arithmetic is built on these and other properties, some of which shall be discussed as follows.

1. Identity Element for Addition and Multiplication.
$$1 \quad 0 \quad 1 \qquad\qquad 1 \quad 1 \quad 1$$
$$2 \quad 0 \quad 2 \ldots, \qquad\qquad 2 \quad 1 \quad 2 \ldots;$$
The identity element for addition is the number zero (0). If we add zero to any number, the sum is still the number. The identity element for multiplication is the number one (1). If we multiply any number by one, the product is still the number. We have identity elements in all human movement in physical education. For example, we recognize certain mechanics of mo-

tion as a skill we term running. No matter how many variations of direction, level, space, time, and flow we explore, running has certain elements that identifies it as a specific skill separate from any other movement pattern. Thus, as we define all movement patterns whether they be running, hopping, throwing, and so forth, we are identifying elements that help us differentiate one movement pattern from another.

2. Commutative Property for Addition and Multiplication.

$2 + 4 = 4 + 2$ $5 \times 7 = 7 \times 5$

$3 + 9 = 9 + 3 \dots ,$ $8 \times 6 = 6 \times 8 \dots ;$

The commutative property of addition states that the order of the addends may be changed without changing the sum; that is, $2 + 4 = 4 + 2$, or in general, if a and b are any whole numbers, then $a + b = b + a$. The commutative property of multiplication states that the order of the two factors may be changed without changing the product; that is, $5 \times 7 = 7 \times 5$, or in general, if a and b are any whole numbers, then $a \times b = b \times a$. In physical education we may help children learn this concept by utilizing several practical examples. When working with partners in physical education and two partners are sharing a piece of equipment, the order in which the partners use the equipment makes no difference as the same quantative or qualitative results regardless of the order in which the activity was performed. The softball lead-up game of Run Around the Bases is another example of the commutative property. When two children run around the bases regardless of the order or direction they run, they will both return to home plate.

3. Associative Property for Addition and Multiplication.

$(2 + 3) + 5 = 2 + (3 + 5)$ $(2 \times 3) \times 4 = 2 \times (3 \times 4)$

$(1 + 5) + 3 = 1 + (5 + 3) \dots ,$ $(1 \times 6) \times 3 = 1 \times (6 \times 3) \dots ;$

The associative property for addition states that when three or more numbers are being added, the order in which the numbers are added may be changed without changing the sum; that is, $(2 + 3) + 5 = 2 + (3 + 5)$, or in general, if a, b, and c are any whole numbers, then $(a + b) + c = a + (b + c)$. The associative property for multiplication states that when three or more factors are multiplied, the order in which the factors are multiplied may be changed without changing the product; that is, $(2 \times 3) \times 4 = 2 \times (3 \times 4)$, or in general, if a, b, and c are any whole numbers, then $(a \times b) \times c = a \times (b \times c)$. In physical education we may help children learn this concept by utilizing several practical examples. When working in groups of three or more children in relays, the order in which the children perform results in the same performance. When performing a Grand Right and Left in square dance, the four males move counterclockwise and the four females move clockwise, but regardless of the direction they move, they finish with their partner and promenade to the home position.

Other field properties of mathematics such as the property of closure and the distributive property have little or no practical application in physical education. As a result, they will not be discussed in this text. The reader is encouraged to become familiar with those field properties that have been discussed and to be innovative in applying them to situations in physical education other than those cited in the examples.

Communication of Quantitative Ideas

Activities for children are often designed to utilize quantitative experiences to describe and compare things. The list below is a clue to the innumerable types of experiences through which teachers can build and extend quantitative concepts of young children. Experiences are initiated through preschool and nursery school activities and are clarified and refined throughout the elementary school years.

1. Size: little-big; small-large; half-whole; tiny-huge.
2. Length or distance: long-short; near-far; tall-short; wide-narrow; high-low.
3. Quantity: few; many; some; all; less than; greater than; shorter than; smaller than; taller than; faster than; slower than.
4. Weight: heavy-light.
5. Amount: full-empty; some; much; enough.
6. Position: up-down; right-left; first-last; above-below; between; in; through; beside; on; over; under.
7. Form: circle, line; straight; middle; end; round; square; triangle; diamond.
8. Time: year; month; week; day; hour; minute; second; season; today; tomorrow; yesterday; noon; early; late; day; night.
9. Speed: fast; slow; medium.
10. Climate: warm; cold; hot; snow; ice; rain; sleet; sunny; fog.

The gymnasium floor may serve as a medium to help primary age children relate to quantitative ideas (Figure 14-8). Children may line up for circle games, rhythmical activities, and the like by positioning themselves on a day of the week, month, season, or direction. They may stand inside, on or outside the circle or any other geometric form in the gymnasium. Different geometric shapes should be painted on the floors for form recognition. Some figures should be large and others small for comparison of size. Walls can be used to measure height (tall, short, etc.). Other gymnasium designs are left to the imagination of each individual for communication of quantitative ideas.

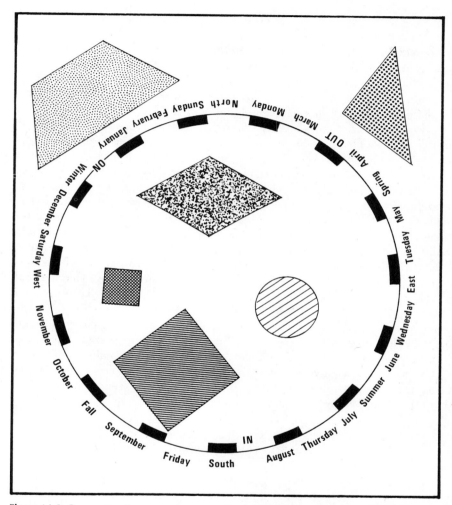

Figure 14-8. Gymnasium floors may be designed to help children learn quantitative ideas.

By relating to the qualities of movement (See Figure 11-1), it should be quite evident that physical education can also contribute to the development of quantitative ideas through movement. Movement experiences in physical education should include activities in which children can explore gradations of movement such as smaller than, faster than, up, down, right, left, near, and far. How many experiences can you create that involve the teaching of quantitative concepts through physical education?

Geometry

Until recent years there was very little attention given to the teaching of simple geometric concepts in the primary grades. In these grades the work in geometry should be informal. The emphasis should be placed on the study of form, space, points, lines, angles, shapes, sizes, patterns, and designs. In the intermediate grades work in geometry includes work with symmetry, open and closed curves, concave figures, convex figures, inside, outside, and on geometric forms. Children also perform more advanced work on topics from the primary grades. Geometry can be related to physical education activities through rhythms, movement exploration, and games and sports. Rhythmical experiences in physical education should include the learning of floor patterns: circles, lines, (horizontal, vertical, parallel, diagonal), squares, triangles, and diamonds. A combination of rhythmical and/or movement exploration experiences should include the learning of form, body shapes and angles, sizes, symmetry, concave and convex figures, and various designs through total body or floor pattern movement. Ropes can be utilized to construct geometric figures with which children can explore the above movement exploration experiences. Geometrical forms can be painted on the gymnasium floor or playground and utilized in many movement activities (Figure 14-8). Cutting geometrical shapes out of large appliance boxes and having the children crawl through the various openings and playing with geometrical shaped beanbags are other activities that help acquaint children with shapes and forms. Games and sports help teach children the shapes of the different playing areas. In various lead-up games to team sports children learn boundary lines and that points are awarded to teams according to whether the ball landed inside, outside, or on the boundary line.

Measuring and Graphing

To measure a quantity means to find how many times it contains a standard quantity of the same kind. The use of numbers in this way to present facts about aspects and properties of things enables us to describe them precisely and to understand them. Measurement makes it possible to define, to predict, and to control.

Children pass through several stages in learning to measure. At the lowest stage of premeasurement, the child describes things in indefinite terms such as large, heavy, short, and narrow. At a higher level he measures objects through comparison such as longer than, shorter than, and hotter than. At a still higher level the child learns to use one object to help describe another object. For example, he may say. "This ball is about two times as heavy as an apple," or "The teacher is almost two times as tall as John." Later the child will directly use standard units of measurement to compare height, weight, distance, and so

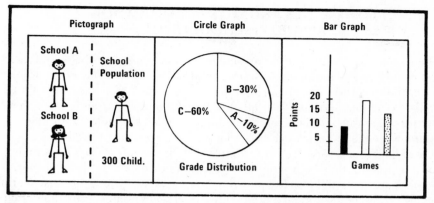

Figure 14-9. Graphs help children interpret experiences in physical education.

forth. At the highest level the child actually uses a measuring device to measure or describe an aspect of something with number. Thus, he may measure with a tape to see how far or high he can jump, measure how far he can throw a ball, or time how long it takes someone to run 100 yards.

As children enter the intermediate grades they become capable of using graphs to represent a collection of data. Types of graphs that children use depend on the kind of data to be presented and the competence level of the children. Types of graphs most commonly used are the pictograph, circle graph, and bar graph (Figure 14-9).

Here is a summary of ways to include measuring and graphing experiences in physical education.

1. Comparative measurement (faster, slower, etc.) in tag, running games, jumping activities, or rhythmical activities helps children learn about measurement.
2. Children can measure the number of minutes, hours, or weeks spent on various activities or units in physical education.
3. Bowling or similar target games enable children to learn about measurement through scoring experiences.
4. Children can make various graphs showing improvement in performances for different sports skills.
5. Various physical education activities require boundaries and certain dimensions for size of playing area. Pupils can measure, lay out the necessary boundaries and field dimensions, and make scale models of the playing areas (Cartography).
6. Height, distance, and time measures from track and field; team sport scores and field dimensions; and individual sport scores and court dimensions are other experiences that children can encounter.

MATHEMATICS AND PHYSICAL EDUCATION
AT THE PRESCHOOL LEVEL

Mathematical experiences at the preschool level concern the whole numbers, sets, geometry, and communication of quantitative ideas. In terms of the whole numbers, children form initial concepts of numeration. "3" means a group of three objects, rather than only a symbol to be recognized. Three is more than two, but less than four. Initial experiences in movement can help children learn these number concepts. Stacking three blocks, hopping two times, jumping four times, bouncing a ball once, and throwing four balls are a few examples among numerous activities that help children learn number concepts through movement experiences. As children learn the concepts of numeration, they also learn to recognize the symbols for each number. Making body numbers, manipulating ropes into the shapes of numbers, modeling clay into the shapes of numbers, hopping or jumping into number squares, or playing catch with number beanbags (pages 329-332) are experiences that help children recognize the shape of numbers. Experiences in counting also help children learn the whole numbers in sequence. Jumping four times, bouncing a ball six times, or tapping a rhythm stick to the floor ten times are examples of counting activities through movement.

Children learn fundamental concepts of sets through numerous experiences in classifying objects. Stacking all blue objects in one pile, finding all of the circles on a page, naming all four legged animals, and bouncing only the red playground balls are ways in which children learn about a sense of order through classification. Basically, objects can be classified according to color, shape, size, weight, texture, and temperature. Later, children become ready to learn about set terminology and operations on sets.

Geometrical concepts are learned by preschool children through several experiences involving movement activities. First, children learn to recognize forms by recognizing the elements of the form. A triangle is recognized as having three sides and three points. If a child is shown an incomplete form (<) or if the size, color, or angle of lines change, the child is apt not recognize the triangle. In essence, the young child is able to consider only one element at a time when trying to recognize a form. The same holds true for each of the other geometric forms. Later, the child learns form perception or form constancy. At this stage he will recognize an incomplete triangle, large or small triangle, various colored triangles, and acute and obtuse triangles. In other words, although some of the elements change, the form of "triangle" is still recognized. Making and playing with geometrical shaped beanbags, modeling clay into geometric shapes, painting geometric forms with shoe polish on the floor and playing games, posing with the body in different geometric shapes, and forming ropes into different geometric shapes are some experiences that help children learn about shapes. Cutting geometrical shapes out of large appliance boxes and crawling through the different openings and naming all of the objects in the room that are of a particular shape are other experiences that help children learn about geometrical forms.

Movement experiences can also be designed to help children learn about quantitative ideas (pages 334-335). Teachers should provide different situations in which children are encouraged to compare variations in size, length, quantity, amount, speed, weight, position, form, time, and climate. For example, running fast or slow, being as large or as small as you can, moving above or below an object, hopping straight or in a zig-zag pathway, and bouncing a ball higher than or lower than your waist should be an integral part of each child's experiences in learning about quantitative ideas.

EXAMPLES INTEGRATING MATHEMATICS WITH PHYSICAL EDUCATION

As children learn mathematics concepts in the classroom, they should have related learning experiences in physical education. This does not mean, however, that the objectives of physical education must be sacrificed in order to teach the children mathematics. It does mean that the physical education teacher should be familiar with what is being taught in the classroom and be

Learning About Shape Form
And Quantity Are Important
Early Learning Skills

ready to emphasize and follow up subject matter when it applies to physical education.

For example, if the fourth grade is learning the softball throw for distance, the primary goal is to teach proper throwing skills. The alert teacher, who knows that measurement is being taught in the classroom, will stretch out the tape measure and have each child learn how to measure the distance he has thrown the ball. Two phases of learning are thus integrated. Each discipline is made more effective because of the other.

We have learned that in the primary grades children learn about counting, adding, subtracting, sets, geometry, number sentences, measuring, commutative and associative properties for addition, fractions, and word problems. In the intermediate grades children learn about sets, set operations, identity properties for addition and multiplication, commutative and associative properties for addition and multiplication, distributive properties for multiplication and division, geometry, measuring and graphing, mathematical sentences, fractions and decimals. The main factor to remember is to introduce each concept according to the vocabulary and maturity level of the children. The following are some sample lessons of ways in which mathematics and physical education can be integrated. Teachers should use their own ingenuity and creativeness in using these lessons and in adapting other mathematics concepts to lessons in physical education. It must be remembered, however, that in any attempt to integrate mathematics with physical education, the physical education class must remain activity oriented rather than become an academic class. The main point to consider is to follow the physical education curriculum as usual, but to use every teachable moment to integrate mathematics with physical education in an effort to realize more meaningful instruction in both disciplines.

Concept: *Communication of Quantitative Ideas*
Grade: *1*
Emphasis: *Children learn about various gradations of size and length through movement experiences.*
Organizing Center: *Stability and Locomotion*
Equipment: *None*
Location: *Gymnasium*
Instructional Ideas:

During these lessons the children will experiment with various gradations of size and length through movement experiences. As the children come to class they should be instructed to go to a place in the gymnasium that no one else occupies so that they will not be in each other's way when they begin to move. In the beginning problems will be posed to the children that involve stability. How can you make your body fit into a small box? How many different ways can you change your body shape and still be as small as you can? Now become as large as you can. How many different ways can you change your body shape and still be as large as you can? Next the children can experiment with gradations of size. For example, make your body smaller than or larger than the last position.

The next topic for discovery will be with the dimension of length. How can you make your body be very tall or very short? How many positions can you make in which your body is wide or narrow? Now make your body taller than or shorter than the last position.

As children learn about the various dimensions of size and length, locomotor movements may also be included in the lesson. Can you walk, hop, skip, slide, or gallop while keeping your body very tall? Now move about the room and be as short as you can. Next, try to move about the room while you are in a wide position or a narrow position. As the children complete the various movements they should be encouraged to move in the various directions of forward, backward, and sideways.

Concept: *Communication of Quantitative Ideas*
Grade Level: *Intermediate*
Emphasis: *Selected experiences in compass cross country enhance the development of skills in map reading, compass reading, estimating distance and following directions in elementary school children.*
Organizing Center: *Locomotion*
Equipment: *Paper, pencils, and compasses*
Location: *Outdoor area*
Instructional Ideas:

The purpose of this lesson is to develop the skills of map reading, compass reading, estimating distance, and following directions in elementary school children through physical education activities emphasizing locomotor and physical fitness development. At the outset a cross country course should be organized by the teacher with various checkpoints at given distances. Each child or small group of children should be given a map, compass, and direction sheet. After some basic instruction, each child or small group can set out to complete the course in the shortest period of time possible. At the various checkpoints different tasks are to be performed such as identifying a rock, flower, or leaf; solving an arithmetic problem; singing a song; or any other cognitive task assigned by the teacher. As a matter of fact, any cognitive area can be stressed at the checkpoint areas.

In addition to running around, under, or through various obstacles on the course, the children are encouraged to learn to read and interpret a compass (arithmetic, science); study trees, leaves, flowers, and rocks (science); make and read a map (geography, art); follow directions (reading); and judge distance (arithmetic). As the children become more adept in the various skills involved, they can become a part of planning their own cross country courses. Courses for various areas can be developed such as the school grounds, locale, local park, or woods.

Concept: *Geometry*
Grade: *2*
Emphasis: *Circles, lines, triangles, and rectangles are four different kinds of geometric shapes.*
Organizing Center: *Stability and Locomotion*
Equipment: *An 8 foot jump rope for each child.*
Location: *Gymnasium*
Instructional Ideas:

During these lessons the children will explore four different geometric shapes with their body and with a jump rope. A line is a thin, threadlike mark on a surface that may be straight or curved. A circle is a curved line that has no beginning and no end. All points on a circle are equal distance from the center. A triangle is a geometric shape constructed from three intersecting lines that has three angles. A rectangle is a four sided geometric shape with four right angles.

To begin the lesson, the children may explore various body shapes in which their body forms different lines. How many different curved and straight lines can you make with your body? Next, how many ways can you make a circle with your body? Can you make a circle with just your fingers? Can you make a circle with your arms or legs? Can you use your whole body to make a circle? Now change and make your body into a triangle. How many different ways can you balance on the floor with three different points of contact? Can you make a triangle with your two arms and one leg touching the floor? How many other ways can you make a triangle? Can you make your body look like a box? How many different ways can you make your body look like a rectangle? Can you make a rectangle with four body parts touching the floor?

After exploring different body shapes without equipment, the children should begin using the rope. First, have the children stretch the rope out on the floor. The path of the rope may be straight or curved. How many different ways can you move along the line? Walking, hopping, skipping, crawling, and so forth may be explored at different levels and speeds. Now make the rope into a circle. How many different ways can you move from the outside of the circle to the inside and then back to the outside? Can you move from the outside of the circle to the other side without touching the inside? Can you walk around the circle while keeping your balance? Now make a triangle with your rope. How many different ways can you move along the triangle? Can you jump from the top to the bottom of the triangle? Next make a rectangle with your rope. Explore different ways to move around the rectangle.

Concept: *The Field Properties of Mathematics*

Grade: *3*

Emphasis: *The associative property of mathematics has practical application in physical education.*

Organizing Center: *Locomotion and Manipulation*

Equipment: *An 8½" playground ball for each child.*

Location: *Gymnasium*

Instructional Ideas:

After proper warm up the children will explore different manipulative patterns with the playground balls. For purposes of these lessons they will explore different dribbling patterns. They will explore dribbling fast or slow, high or low, and while in a stationary position or while moving about the room. As a culmination of the class period, several dribbling relay races will be held.

The children will be organized into several groups consisting of five or six children per group. The first type of relay will consist of having each child execute the same skill as it becomes his turn. Thus the children may hop, skip, gallop, or run while dribbling the ball over the relay course. If we give each child within a group a number from one through the total number in each group, we may change the order in which the children participate. Whether the children participate in the order of 1, 2, 3, 4, 5, and 6 or in the order of 2, 4, 6, 1, 3, and 5 makes no difference. The end result is still the same. This example illustrates the associative property of mathematics. A second type of relay will be held in which each child within the group is required to perform a different skill. One child may be asked to hop while dribbling. Another child may be asked to dribble while moving backwards. Other skills may be assigned to equal the number of children within the groups. As the children participate in the relay, the order in which the skills are performed may be varied. The end result that is the completion of the relay remains the same. This is a second example of the associative property of mathematics having practical application in physical education.

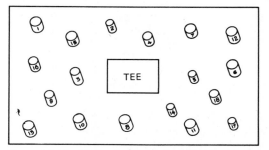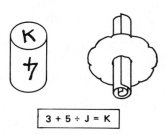

Figure 14-10. "Calcu-Cookie" helps children learn mathematics concepts as well as develop manipulative skills.

Concept: *The Whole Numbers*
Grade: *4*
Emphasis: *Selected experiences in physical education enhance the development of addition, subtraction, multiplication, and division concepts in elementary school children.*
Organizing Center: *Manipulation*
Equipment: *Tin Cans of various sizes and a yarnball or paper ball for each child.*
Location: *Gymnasium*
Instructional Ideas:

The purpose of this lesson is to focus on various ways of manipulating a ball into a can. The children will explore different ways to stroke the ball into a can by playing a game called "Calcu-Cookie." The cans of different sizes will be placed around the gymnasium in a miniature golf course (Figure 14-9), each with a number from 1-18 painted on the outside of the can. There will be one tee area in which the children are given a "Calcu-Cookie" - a mathematical problem on a small sheet of paper rolled up and placed in a butter cookie. Problems may be concerned with addition, subtraction, multiplication, division, or any combination according to the ability level of the children. The children may eat the cookie as they unroll the paper and solve the mathematical problem. Answers to problems will vary from 1-18. As problems are solved children are to move the balls from the tee to the hole number of their answer in as few strokes as possible. Each stroke must be made with a different body part (finger, hand, elbow, head, nose, toes, ankle, knee). Different types of manipulative patterns should be encouraged by the teacher as the children stroke the ball toward the hole. As the children get the ball into the hole, they are to turn over the can. The bottom of the can will contain an alphabet code (A-R). If the code matches the answer on their paper (K-K), the children may move back to the tee to solve a new "Calcu-Cookie" problem. A child making a mistake in his calculation must re-calculate his answer until he gets it correct before he moves on to a new problem. In addition to calculating answers to various problems, the children may also keep tract of their scores as they move from hole to hole.

Concept: *Sets*
Grade: *5*
Emphasis: *The intersection of sets helps children understand movement in physical education.*
Organizing Center: *Stability and Locomotion*
Equipment: *Record player, several records that provide for change in tempo, flow, mood, and even and uneven rhythmical patterns.*
Location: *Gymnasium*
Instructional Ideas:

It is common for children to combine the elements of movement in their exploratory experiences in physical education. It is often done in the early grades, but by the fifth grade the children are capable of understanding combinations of movements in terms of the intersection of sets. If the elements of movement are considered the universal set, space, force, time and flow may be considered subsets. Within the set of space movements, the subsets are moving at different levels, ranges, and directions. Within the set of force movements, the subsets are comparisons of hard and soft, strong and weak, heavy and light, and tight and loose. Within the set of time movements, the subsets are moving at different speeds. The set of flow movements also has a subset of movements. During these lessons the children will explore the intersection of two or more elements of movement. Music will be provided to vary the tempo, flow, mood, and even and uneven rhythmical patterns that the children will explore. Stability and locomotor movements will be explored. The teacher will stimulate the children's movement by posing stimulating problems. What types of movement occur when the set of space movements intersects with the set of force movements? What types of movement occur when range movements are intersected with time movements? After intersecting movements from two elements, the children may be asked to explore the intersection of three movements. What types of movement occur when children are asked to intersect the sets of flow movements, force movements, and space movements at the same time? How many different variations can the children think of in which the elements of movement are intersected?

Concept: *Measuring and Graphing*
Grade: *6*
Emphasis: *Children can learn to measure the height or distance of their jump and to graph their improvement in jumping over a period of time.*
Organizing Center: *Locomotion*
Equipment: *Two measuring tapes and standards for a high jump pit.*
Location: *Playground*
Instructional Ideas:

The learning experience intended for these lessons will be extended over a series of lessons. During the first lesson the details of measurement can be shown. In the high jump the measurement is made from the top of the high jump bar to the ground. The measurement is made in feet and inches. In the long jump the measurement is made from the board to the nearest point of impact when landing. The measurement is made in feet and inches. The children should also be instructed as to the number of trials in each of the events and how a foul is committed in each of the events. After the children understand the details of measurement, they can be taught the essentials of graphing. The bar graph will be most appropriate for measuring improvement in jumping skills.

During this first lesson an example bar graph for each of the events should be provided for the children. In the bar graph for the high jump, the horizontal scale will represent the number of the trial. The vertical scale will represent the height in feet and inches. In the bar graph for the long jump, the horizontal scale will represent the number of the trial. The vertical scale will represent the distance in feet and inches. In both of the graphs the children will be taught how to illustrate the height or distance of the jump in succeeding jumps.

As the children begin jumping they will be divided into two groups. One group will work on high jumping skills and the other group will work on long jumping skills. The groups will be subdivided to include some children who are measuring, some children who are recording the bar graphs, some children who are taking care of the pits, and some children who are jumping. Children will rotate positions within the group and will change jumping events at an appropriate time to allow all children a chance to perform at each station.

During succeeding lessons the children can learn how to construct their own bar graphs as measuring devices. As children improve in each of the skills, the bar graphs will indicate the amount of improvement for each child.

SELECTED REFERENCES

1. Grossnickle, Foster E., and Brueckner, L. J. *Discovering Means in Elementary School Mathematics*. New York: Holt, Rinehart, and Winston, 1973.
2. Humphrey, James H. *Child Learning Through Elementary School Physical Education*. Dubuque, Iowa: Wm. C. Brown Company Publishers, 1974.
3. Jensen, Terry M. "Creative Ropes." *Journal of Health, Physical Education, Recreation*, 32 May 1971, pp. 56-57.
4. Memmel, Rudolph L. "Arithmetic Through Play." *Journal of Health, Physical Education, Recreation*, 24 June 1953, p. 31.
5. Miller, Arthur G., Cheffert, J. T., and Whitcomb, V. *Physical Education in the Elementary School Curriculum*, Englewood Cliffs, New Jersey: Prentice-Hall, 1974.
6. National Council of Teachers of Mathematics, *An Analysis of New Mathematics Programs*, Washington, D.C.: National Council of Teachers of Mathematics, 1965.
7. ____*Sets*. Washington, D.C.: National Council of Teachers of Mathematics, 1965.
8. ____*The Whole Numbers*. Washington, D.C.: National Council of Teachers of Mathematics, 1965.
9. School Mathematics Study Group. *Mathematics for the Elementary School*. Grades 1-6. New Haven: Yale University Press, 1963.
10. Smith, Eugene P., *et al*. *Discoveries in Modern Mathematics*. Columbus, Ohio: Charles E. Merrill Company, 1968.

Chapter 15
Developing Science Concepts

Key Concept: The curriculum areas of elementary school science and elementary school physical education are closely related and mutually dependent. Through a variety of science experiences in physical education, children will learn to better understand themselves and the world about them.

Content: Introduction
Science Experiences Through Physical Education
  Stability
  Newton's Laws of Motion
  Factors Affecting Man and His Motion
  Types of Motion
  Levers
  The Production, Application, and Absorption of Force
  Projectiles
  Buoyancy
  Sound
Implications of Science Projects with Relation to Physical Education
Science and Physical Education at the Preschool Level
Examples Integrating Science with Physical Education
  Archimedes' Principle of Buoyancy
  Newton's First Law of Motion
  Newton's Third Law of Motion
  Work
  Sound
  Levers

Developing Science Concepts

INTRODUCTION

The age and culture in which we live demand that children in the elementary schools have a variety of meaningful science experiences that lead them to an understanding of the world about them. Through a variety of science experiences in physical education, it is hoped that children will learn to better understand themselves and the world about them.

Science experiences through physical education are numerous. The application of science to physical education is almost unlimited. Classroom teachers and physical education specialists often overlook these many possibilities. Most classroom teachers would be interested in utilizing physical education in every situation where it would help to broaden the experiences within the school life of the pupil. The desire has been frustrated because of the difficulty in obtaining the necessary material that although available, is to be found in such limited sources that it takes more time to procure than the teacher can afford.

If children are to be provided with learning experiences in science, teachers should be aware of problems that are of real concern to children in their daily lives. Several science series as well as science supplement textbooks for teachers and children were reviewed to discover with science concepts: (1) could be related to physical education, (2) were included as science concepts in the current science curriculum, and thus, (3) are of real concern to children in their daily lives. Books concerned with subject matter to be presented in grades one through six were reviewed. It was found that science concepts were based on and taught through units on the biological, physical, and earth sciences. Concepts in the physical sciences were most applicable to physical education. Concepts that were related to physical education and mentioned most often in the science textbook series and science supplement books are machines, levers, Newton's laws of motion, work, resistance, friction, gravity, centrifugal force, sound, buoyancy, energy, inertia, and momentum.

To test the effectiveness of the integration of science with physical education an investigation of the effects of the integration of physical education with selected science concepts upon science knowledge and selected physical performance skills of fourth, fifth, and sixth grade children was carried out. One-hundred-eighty children in the fourth, fifth, and sixth grade served as subjects in

348

the study, Initial tests were administered to all subjects on nine criterion variables. The variables were the softball throw for distance test, the soccer kick for distance test, the playground ball wall pass test, the McDonald Soccer Test, the standing long jump test, and the written science knowledge test. The subjects then took part in a learning program for a period of seven weeks that involved teaching four selected science concepts in the classroom and in physical education. The four science concepts selected for study were levers, Newton's First Law of Motion, Newton's Third Law of Motion, and work. The subjects were taught science in the classroom three days per week for 40 minutes each class period. The subjects were taught physical education two days per week for 40 minutes each class period. The control group received instruction in the selected science concepts from the classroom teachers. Physical education was taught without integration of the selected science concepts. The experimental group received instruction in the selected science concepts from the classroom teachers. The physical education teacher integrated the selected science concepts with the physical education instruction. At the conclusion of the period of seven weeks, all subjects were given a final test on the nine criterion variables. Conclusions resulted in a significant difference between groups that favored the method of integrating science and physical education.[13]

With the knowledge that science experiences through physical education are numerous and that integration of science and physical education helps children learn, let us turn to an examination of the possibilities of teaching science experiences through physical education.

SCIENCE EXPERIENCES THROUGH PHYSICAL EDUCATION

Stability

Stability is an important factor in all movement skills. A stable position is important for maintaining balance, regaining balance, and producing force.

In order to maintain balance or produce force while in a stable position, one must understand the concepts of gravity and base of support. Gravity is a force pulling downward toward the center of the earth. A center of gravity exists within all masses that pulls each mass toward the earth. Gravity is the reason that all objects projected into the air return to the earth. The center of gravity for a geometric shape is in the center of the object. The center of gravity in asymetrical masses (our bodies) may be determined by a system of balancing and weighing. A line of gravity is established to extending an imaginary line vertically through the center of gravity to the earth. The base of support is that part of the body that is in contact with the supporting surface. Usually the feet act as the base of support but, there are times when other points of contact act as the base of support such as when we are lying down, performing a headstand, or a handstand. The interrelationship of the center of gravity and the line of gravity to the base of support will determine the degree of stability or instability. If the line of gravity falls within the base of support the object will balance. If it falls outside the base of support the object will fall. Thus the body is balanced when the center of gravity is directly over the base of support (Figure 15-1).

The sensory organs are important in the maintenance of stability. The semicircular canal in the inner ear is the center for dynamic balance. The otoliths in the inner ear is the center for static balance. Proprioceptive-end organs are found in muscles, tendons, and ligaments. They contribute to the development of kinesthetic sense; (i.e., the feel that one has concerning his position in space). Visual perception also plays a part in maintaining balance. In general, the eyes should be focused in the direction of the intended movement. The eyes help determine the relative position of the body. An individual can usually control his position better if he focuses them on a fixed target than if the eyes are closed or allowed to wander randomly.

Here are some general principles of stability.

1. A body is most stable when the center of gravity is directly over the base of support.
2. When receiving or applying force, widen the base of support in the direction of the force.
3. In order to stop quickly, bend the knees and place the feet in a forward stride position. This action will lower the center of gravity and keep it over the base of support.
4. The closer the center of gravity is to the base of support, the greater will be the stability.

Figure 15-1. The body remains balanced when the center of gravity and line of gravity fall within the base of support.

5. When regaining balance, raise the arms or legs on the side of the body opposite the direction in which the balance is lost.
6. When carrying of lifting a heavy object, keep the object close to the body.
7. When moving in rotary motion, keep the eyes focused on one spot straight ahead.

NEWTON'S LAWS OF MOTION

When an object is changing its position, it is said to be in motion. A force is required to start a body in motion, to slow it down, or stop it, to change the direction of its motion, or to make it move faster. All of these types of motion are influenced by three laws that were described by Sir Isaac Newton. Examples of Newton's laws of motion are in evidence in daily living. Anything movable always follows these laws, which describe how things move and make it possible to predict the motion of any object.

Newton's First Law

A ball that is placed on the floor will remain in the same place unless someone causes it to move by picking it up or kicking it. Once the ball is in motion, it will remain in motion at the same speed and will keep moving in the same direction unless it is acted on by some other force, such as friction, gravity, or muscular action. This example illustrates Newton's first law of motion: an object at rest tends to remain at rest, and an object in motion tends to remain in motion at the same speed and in the same direction. Another example illustrating Newton's first law of motion is when a car starts or stops quickly. When a car starts suddenly, the people in it are pressed back against their seats. When a car that is traveling fast stops suddenly, the people in it are thrown forward against the

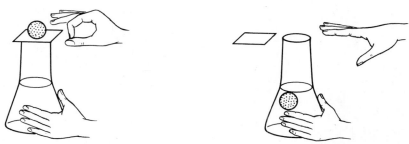

Figure 15-2. Inertia causes the ball to drop down into the flask when the card is "shot" out from underneath the ball.

dashboard. This is the result of inertia. Inertia is the tendency of the body to remain at rest or to remain in motion until it is acted upon by an outside force. In this case, the outside force was when the car started or stopped suddenly. Seat belts are used to keep people in their seats against the tendency of inertia to keep the people moving forward when a car stops.

Momentum is another factor that helps children understand Newton's first law of motion. Momentum is the quantity of stored up energy of a moving body. Momentum is less for a great mass with little speed than for a great mass with great speed. Momentum tends to cause an object or mass to remain in motion. For example, a girl who is roller skating discovers that the tendency to continue rolling will be much greater if she is moving at a high speed than if she is moving at a low speed (see figure 15-3).

If a person is running fast and is told to stop, is it harder for him to halt than if he had been walking? Why? Why does a long jumper run to build up as much speed as he can before he jumps? Why does a ski jumper go down a long, steep hill before leaving the jumping platform? Inertia and momentum account for the answers.

Newton's Second Law

An object, when acted upon by an external force, will experience a change in speed that will be proportional to the force applied and inversely proportional to the object's mass. This is a statement of Newton's second law of motion and means that for a given object, application of greater force will result in greater speed. If the same amount of force is applied to two objects of different mass, the object with the smaller mass will move faster. This law has great application

Figure 15-3. Momentum causes the girl on the roller skates to remain in motion after she has stopped her skating movements.

in the different sports where balls of different mass are manipulated with equipment of different lengths, shapes, and masses.

Newton's Third Law

Most children have at some time inflated a balloon and released it without having the end tied. The result is that the air rushes out the the opening in one direction and the balloon flies away in the opposite direction. This is a very simple example of the concept of action and reaction, which is referred to in Newton's third law of motion: for every action, there is an equal and opposite reaction. The statement may seem puzzling at first until some common activities are observed. For example, when you row a boat, the oars dip in the water and their blades are put into backward action by the force on the handles. This exerts a

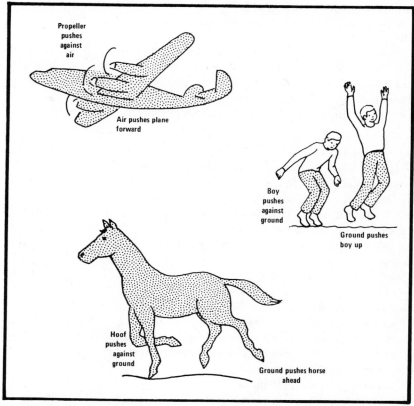

Figure 15-4. The law of action-reaction enables movement through space.

forward reaction on the boat, causing it to glide through the water. If a person steps from a rowboat to the dock, the boat moves away from him and away from the dock. Why? If a boy turns on a water hose so that the water comes out with great force he will have to hold the hose tightly or it will leap from his hands. Why? What causes a gun to recoil when fired? Why is it harder to stop a ball that is thrown very fast than one that is thrown more slowly?

The principle of action-reaction means that whenever one body exerts a force on a second body, the second body will exert an equal force, in the opposite direction to the first force, upon the first body. If there were not an equal and opposite reaction for every action, we would be unable to walk, boats could not be propelled through water and vehicles would be unable to move. In fact, all motion is dependent on the action-reaction principle.

Even bodies that are at rest have equal but opposite forces acting upon them. A book lying on a table is at rest because the table provides an upward force equal to the downward force of gravity. Children can see this more readily if a heavy weight is placed in a child's hand. He can see that the object exerts a force downward in his hand and that he must use his muscles as an opposite force to counteract it.

Another activity is to draw pictures on the blackboard similar to the ones in Figure 15-4. Ask the children to point out the action-reaction forces. Then ask them to think of other moving objects. Try to show them that all movement in physical education is based on the action-reaction principle.

The following is a summary of Newton's laws that children should learn.

1. A body at rest tends to remain at rest.
2. A body in motion tends to continue in motion in a straight line and at the same speed unless an outside force acts on it.
3. The tendency of a body to remain at rest is called inertia.
4. Momentum is the tendency of an object to stay in motion.
5. Momentum is directly proportional to the mass of the object and to the speed with which the object is moving.
6. For objects that have equal mass, the greater the speed, the greater the momentum.
7. For bodies moving at equal speed, the greater the mass, the greater the momentum.
8. If unequal forces are applied to objects of equal mass, the greatest force will cause the greatest acceleration; if equal forces are applied to objects of unequal mass, the greatest mass will have the smallest acceleration.
9. For every action, there is an equal and opposite reaction.
10. A moving body exerts a force against something else, which in turn exerts a force against the body, pushing it.
11. Every force causes another force to be exerted in the opposite direction.
12. Without action-reaction, there would be no motion.

Factors Affecting Man and His Movement

Mass

Mass is the measure of quantity of matter in an object. Mass is anything that has weight or takes up space. Although mass is sometimes thought of as being the same as weight, it is not true, as weight is the gravitational pull on the mass of an object. Objects on earth have the same mass as they do when they are in outer space, but they are weightless in space as there is no pull exerted by gravity in space. Baseballs and tennis balls are much the same size, but one has greater mass than the other and appears to be heavier. A balloon may be much larger but have less mass than a golf ball. Mass may be the same, but shape may differ. A football has about the same mass as a soccer ball. The mass of an object affects an object's motion. It is more difficult to move an object with a great amount of mass than is to move an object with less mass.

Force and Work

A force is a push or a pull exerted against an object. Everything one does is subject to one or more forces that affect the motion or stability of an object. Work is a force acting on mass through a distance. In simpler terms, work means the ability to push or pull something over a distance. Work may also mean the ability to complete a task. Many times children think of work as a chore or any unpleasant task. Under our definition, work may be a chore or any task that requires movement of an object. Thus, even the games or playful activities of children can be considered work. As children learn about work, several points must be considered.

How is work measured? Initially, the children should learn that work equals force times distance moved. $W = F \times D$. Once this concept is grasped, the concept of work per unit of time can be introduced. $W = \dfrac{F \times D}{T}$. Work equals force times distance moved divided by the time needed to complete the task. Other points to be considered are as follows: (1.) How much force is required to do the work? (2.) Where should the application of force be made on an object? and (3.) How do friction and resistance affect work?

Energy

Energy is required to move matter from one place to another. For an object to move, the forces acting on it must be unbalanced. A heavy object will need a great force to move it. A light object will need less force to move it. If an object is moved a great distance, a great deal of energy is needed to do the work. It takes more force to propel an object fast than it does to propel an object slow.

Application of Force

When doing work, the point of application of force is a necessary consideration. The intention is to exert the applied force in the direction you want to move so that efficient motion is possible (Figure 15-5). When moving an object up or down, a person should stand as close to the object as possible so that motion can be in a vertical direction. When pushing an object in a horizontal direction, several factors should be considered. Most of the work should be done by the legs as they contain our strongest muscles. As was explained when referring to stability, one should have a wide base of support with the legs spread in the direction of motion. One can better control the object if his hands are spread apart and placed in line with the center of gravity. If the hands are close together he may get a rotary motion of the object. If the hands are placed too far above or below the center of gravity the object may tip over because of the rotary motion. A person should contact the object to be moved and set the muscles for the task before exerting the pushing force. The same rules apply for pulling an object.

Friction and Resistance

Resistance is an opposing force that makes it difficult to move an object. Friction is a resistance to the motion of the surface of one object over the surface of another object. The force resulting from the friction between two surfaces depends on the type of surfaces and the force pushing them together. Friction is necessary to start and stop an object's motion.

There must be some friction between the surface of shoes and the walking surface. Tennis shoes help give us traction to help us move in the gymnasium. In some instances it is desirable to reduce the amount of friction. Ice skates and roller skates are examples.

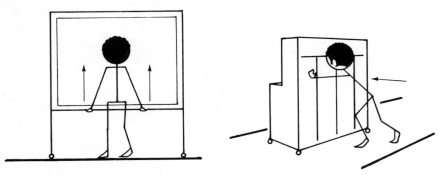

Figure 15-5. Exert the applied force in the direction of the intended movement.

There are three circumstances when friction is present: (1) starting friction (2) sliding friction and (3) rolling friction. Starting friction is present when we start to move an object. This type of friction causes greatest resistance and is the hardest to overcome. Sliding friction is demonstrated when we drag or slide one object over another. Rolling friction is evident when one object rolls over another. Rolling friction is easier to overcome. Children will find that a heavy object that is put on wheels will be easier to move than if it is resting flat on the floor. Other aspects to consider about friction are the less surface area in contact with another object the easier it will be to move and the heavier an object the more friction there is to overcome.

Air Resistance

Air resistance is a force that is always present and slows the fall of moving objects. The effects of air resistance on objects is dependent on the size, shape, and form of the objects. The velocity of an object also is a factor in the amount of air resistance. A light object with a large surface area falls more slowly than a small object with great mass. This is why a badminton shuttle and a golf ball when dropped from a height do not fall to the earth at the same rate of speed. They also have a different flight pattern when they are hit.

Centripetal and Centrifugal Force

Centrifugal force is the name given to any force directed toward the center of a circular path of motion. There is an opposing force that works against this inward pull called centrifugal force. Centrifugal force is the inertia tendency of a body in motion to travel in a straight line and is the reaction to centripetal force. For example, if a person were to use a "windmill" motion before releasing a softball pitch, the muscles of the forearm and hand would serve as the centripetal force in pulling the ball inward and in keeping the ball in contact with the hand as it travels in a circular pathway before release. Upon release, centrifugal force will cause the ball to move in a straight line, tangent to the point of release.

The following is a summary of factors that affect man and his motion.

1. Mass is anything that has weight or takes up space.
2. Two objects may be the same size but have different masses.
3. Two objects may have different shapes but have the same mass.
4. More force is needed to move objects with great mass than is needed to move objects with less mass.
5. A force is a push or a pull on an object.
6. Work equals force moved over a distance divided by a period of time.

7. It takes more energy to do work fast than it does to do work slow.
8. For an object to move, the forces acting on it must be unbalanced.
9. A heavy object that is put on wheels will be easier to move than if it is resting on the floor.
10. Resistance is an opposing force that makes it difficult to move an object.
11. Friction is a resistance to the motion of the surface of one object over the surface of another object.
12. Friction is necessary to start and stop the movement of an object.
13. Starting, sliding, and rolling friction are the three different circumstances when friction is present.
14. Air resistance pushes against an object and slows down its flight through the air.
15. The larger the surface area of an object the more air resistance will affect its movement.
16. An object that moves in a circle has a force on it that pushes the object to the outside of the circle (centrifugal force).
17. If an object that is moving in a circular path is released, it will go off in a straight line from the point where it was released.

Types of Motion

Linear Motion

There are two types of motion, linear and rotary. Linear motion is motion in a straight line. A person uses linear motion when he moves in a straight line at a constant speed over a given distance. Sometimes a person is carried by another object such as a car, horse, or scooter. Under these conditions the body acquires the same motion as the object that carries it. An object that is carried by the hand acquires the same motion and speed as the hand. Thus a ball acquires the same speed as the hand at the time of release. After it is released, it continues to move at the same speed until it is acted upon by another force.

Rotary Motion

Rotary motion is movement of a body around an axis. In rotary motion the shorter the radius of the circle of rotation, the greater will be the rotary speed. The longer the radius, the lesser the speed. In tumbling forward and backward rolls or sommersaults are executed more quickly and efficiently by shortening the radius through tightening the tuck. Skaters are able to turn or spin faster by

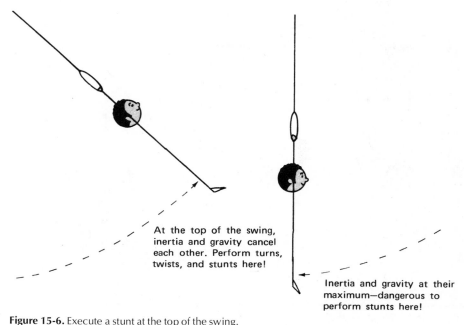

At the top of the swing, inertia and gravity cancel each other. Perform turns, twists, and stunts here!

Inertia and gravity at their maximum—dangerous to perform stunts here!

Figure 15-6. Execute a stunt at the top of the swing.

pulling the arms toward the body. When a skater wishes to stop the spinning action, he can extend the arms out to the side.

In a pendulum type of rotary motion where an object rotates around a fixed point, the critical time in swinging movements occurs at a time when the effects of the inertia of the swing are cancelled out by the effect of gravity (Figure 15-6). Thus, the time to execute a stunt on the swinging rings or ropes is at the top of the swing at the time when motion is cancelled. The most dangerous time of the swing is at the bottom when the force of inertia and gravity are at their maximum.

To accomplish the pumping action in swinging in a pendulum, while working with gravity increase the radius of rotation. When working against gravity shorten the radius of rotation (Figure 15-7). The radius of rotation is the distance (force arm) between the center of gravity and the axis of rotation. A longer radius with a low center of gravity helps the body gain momentum on the down phase of the swing. A shorter radius with a high center of gravity helps reduce resistance on the up phase of the swing. Thus, when children learn to pump a swing, they learn to bend the knees on the down phase of the swing, and to stand up straight on the up phase of the swing.

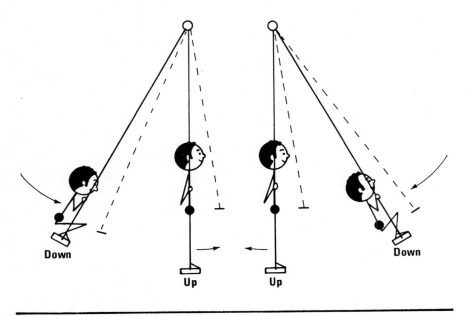

Figure 15-7. Children learn to pump a swing.

Levers

Children learn about levers throughout their elementary school years. They learn about the inclined plane, lever, screw, wedge, and pulley. Perhaps most important to physical education is the knowledge of levers. Levers are used many times a day while playing, eating, and working. A person moves through the use of a lever system. Leverage is involved when a person throws a ball, uses a bottle opener to pry off the top of a bottle. uses a nutcracker to crack the shell of a nut, or moves any part of his body.

A lever is defined as a rigid bar that turns around an axis or fulcrum. In the human body the bones represent the rigid bars and the joints represent the fulcrums. Levers are of three different types according to the relationship between the fulcrum and the point of application of force and resistance.

First Class Levers

A first class lever has the fulcrum located between the resistance and the force. Some examples of this type of lever are the seesaw, crowbar, scissors, and arm extension at the elbow (Figure 15-8).

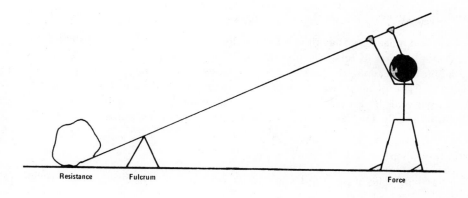

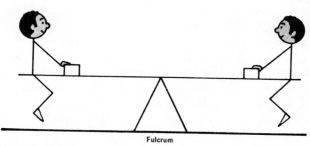

Figure 15-8. First class levers.

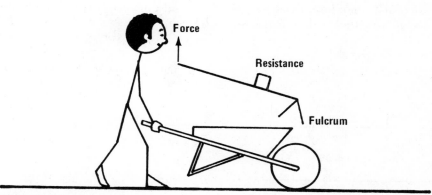

Figure 15-9. Second class lever.

Second Class Levers

The second class lever has the resistance located between the fulcrum and the point of application of force (Figure 15-9). This type of lever favors force. This force advantage is gained at the expense of speed and range of motion. Examples of this type of lever are the wheelbarrow, nutcracker, and door when it is opened by use of the knob. There are very few examples of a second class lever in the human body. One example is the foot when it is supporting weight.

Third Class Levers

The third class lever has the force application between the fulcrum and resistance. This type of lever favors speed and range of motion at the expense of force. Examples of third class levers are a door closing with a spring device and throwing a ball. In fact, most athletic skills involve the use of a third class lever (Figure 15-10).

Mechanical advantage is the number of times a force is multiplied by a machine. A lever converts a small force exerted over a great distance into a larger force operating over a lesser distance or utilizes speed to gain mechanical advantage. Mechanical advantage is the ratio of the load to the applied force that allows a machine to multiply force and do work. Thus, speed and range of motion are critical to the application of force. If two levers (Figure 15-11) move through an angle of 40 degrees at the same velocity, the tip of the longer lever (AB), travels much farther than the tip of the shorter lever (AC), and because it covers this longer distance (BD) in the same time that the shorter lever covers the shorter distance (CE), it must travel faster. When a lever moves about its fulcrum the distance that all points on the lever move is proportional to their distance from the fulcrum. If a point is twice as far from the fulcrum, it will move twice as far and, therefore, twice as fast. As a result, mechanical advantage allows a ball to be batted farther than it can be thrown.

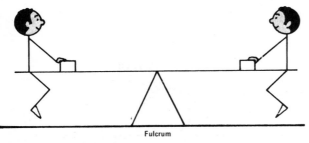

Fulcrum

Figure 15-10. Third class levers.

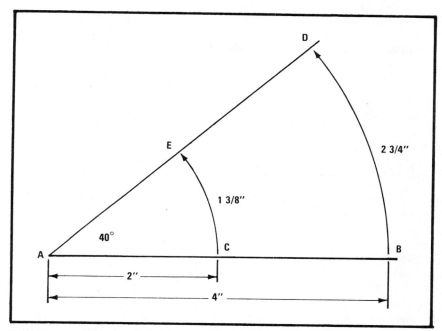

Figure 15-11. Mechanical advantage is gained through the use of levers.

The term "moment of force" is used to describe the effective force producing motion. The moment of force is determined by multiplying the magnitude of the force by the distance between the point at which the force is applied and the fulcrum (length of the force arm). When a lever is in equilibrium, the moment of force is equal for the force arm and the resistance arm. Any additional force either from the force arm or the resistance arm will produce motion. For this reason, the formula (F × FA   R × RA) is used to calcualte the amount of force or resistance and the length of the force arm or resistance arm needed to produce motion. When any three of the quantities are known the fourth can be calculated. If a person were trying to move a 300 pound rock (Figure 15-12) with a crow bar that was seven feet long, how much force would he have to use to move the rock. If the fulcrum was placed one foot from the rock, the resistance arm would be one foot and the force arm would be six feet.

$$F \times FA = R \times RA$$
$$F \times 6 \quad = 300 \times 1$$
$$6F \quad = 300$$
$$F \quad = 50$$

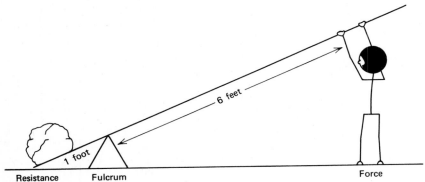

Figure 15-12. The moment of force may be calculated to find the amount of force needed to produce motion.

Thus, a force of fifty or more pounds would be needed to move the rock. Other examples such as the seesaw or throwing a ball could be used to help children understand this concept.

The reaction of a lever is proportional to its length. A slight movement at the end of a long lever causes a reaction at the other end. This is the principle applied by use of the crow bar. The longer the force arm, the greater the amount of force about the fulcrum.

The longer the force arm the less energy it takes to balance the lever, and the longer the weight or resistance arm the more force necesary to balance it. Thus, for strength tasks a lever with a long force arm in relation to the resistance arm should be used; and when movements requiring speed, range of motion or light weights are desired the resistance arm should be lengthened.

Children will learn that the human body uses predominantly a third class lever. Thus, the body is build for speed and range of motion at the expense of using great force. From a practical point of view, this means that children's muscles should be developed to be strong in order to supply the necessary force for body movements, especially in strenuous activities.

In addition to being utilized during the application of force, the lever system may operate to absorb force from external objects. For example, when catching a ball that is moving fast an individual uses a lever system to diminish the shock of the catch by sequentially reducing the speed of the ball until it comes to rest. This is sometimes called giving with the ball.

A lever system is also used to absorb force during a fall. The shock of the body striking the ground should be spread to the more padded segments of the body. By keeping the arms flexed and taking the shock of the fall on the forearm, upper arm, shoulder, and back in sequence many serious accidents could be avoided.

The lever system incorporates an increase in distance and time of the fall in order to absorb force during a fall.

The following is a summary of lever concepts that children should learn.

1. A lever is composed of a fulcrum, a force, and a resistance arm.
2. A first class lever has the fulcrum located between the resistance arm and the force arm.
3. A second class lever has the resistance located between the fulcrum and the point of application of force.
4. A third class lever has the force application between the fulcrum and resistance.
5. A lever is a rigid bar that turns around a fixed point or fulcrum.
6. The human body uses a third class lever predominantly.
7. A third class lever gains speed and range of motion at the expense of using a great force.
8. Mechanical advantage is the ratio of the load to the applied force that allows a machine to multiply force and do work.
9. The longer the force arm the greater the force produced.
10. The longer the resistance arm at the time of release the faster the action can be. Throwing with a straight arm or using a racket as an extension of the arm enables a person to throw or propel an object faster and farther than when the arm is bent or no racket is used.
11. When receiving force from an external object as in catching, landing from a jump, or recovering from a fall, the center of mass moves in the direction of the force and gradually diminishes the force.

The Production, Application and Absorption of Force

Since force initiates motion, it is obvious that force and motion are closely associated. As a result, it is important for the teacher to understand how force is produced and how it is used. The source of force in the human body is strength derived from muscle action. Force is needed to move the body as well as to move other objects with one's own body. The following is a summary of the factors concerned with the production, application, and absorption of force that children should learn.

1. As more muscles are used, more force is produced.
2. As the muscles act faster, more force is produced.
3. Muscles exert more force when they are placed in a stretch position before they contract. This is the reason for a windup before throwing any ball.

4. The most effective total force is developed when the force from each contributing part of the body is applied in a single direction in a sequential order.
5. The greater the length and the number of levers that are brought into action in successive fashion, the greater the amount of time will be provided for force to develop.
6. There is a summation of forces as each body part contributes its share until momentum reaches its maximum at the point of application of force or the release of the ball.
7. If a heavy object is to be moved, force should be exerted directly on the object by all of the large muscles of the legs, hips, thighs, shoulders, and arms simultaneously in the direction the object is to go.
8. Application of force should be as even as possible so that all the force is used to overcome resistance, not to overcome inertia.
9. To move an object upward, all force must be directed upward.
10. To move an object forward, the force should be applied through the center of the weight of the object in the desired direction.
11. If force is applied away from the center of weight, a rotary motion will result.
12. The direction an object takes is a line tangent to that which the arm or implement is moving at the point of release or impact (centrifugal force).
13. To accomplish a continuous turn in the air, a person must establish the turning force before leaving the support.
14. When absorbing or receiving the force of an object, there should be a gradual reduction of force over as large a surface area as possible and over as long a period of time as possible.
15. When receiving a force a person should get in line with the oncoming force and assume a stride position in the direction of the force with the body weight low and over the base of support.
16. A follow through in all hitting, throwing, and kicking activities ensures maximum application of force and allows time for gradual reduction of momentum.

Projectiles

A projectile is any object that is sent in motion into space. Many activities in physical education require projection of the body or objects into space. The body is a projectile as it moves through space in a jump, dive, or a rebound on a trampoline. Any ball, hoop, or object becomes a projectile as it is thrown or hit. The flight of a projectile in space is affected by gravity, air resistance, angle of release, spin, and degree of initial force that launched it. The following are some mechanical principles related to projectiles that children should learn.

1. The amount of force imparted to an object is dependent on the mass of an object and the distance and speed necessary for the purpose of the flight.
2. A sport implement (bat, racket, or club) becomes a part of the body.
3. A sport implement enables a person to contact a ball with more momentum and range of motion at the expense of using more force to generate the motion.
4. More velocity can be achieved with a long lever, but a long lever is often difficult to control.
5. Gravity will exert a downward pull on an object.
6. A ball that is projected at a large angle at the time of release will travel high in the air for a short distance and be in the air longer than a ball released at a small angle.
7. To project the body or an object into the air and over as great a distance as possible the angle of takeoff or release should be a forty-five degree angle.
8. The linear motion of a projectile can often be increased if the person develops rotary motion prior to throwing or hitting the object. This is why we rotate the hips and shoulders in a throwing motion and why a shot putter rotates the whole body prior to putting the shot.
9. The flight of large light objects is affected by air resistance by decreasing the height and distance that the objects travel.
10. A ball that spins to the left will curve to the left and bounce to the left as it comes in contact with the floor.
11. A ball that spins to the right will curve to the right and bounce to the right as it comes in contact with the floor.
12. A ball with top spin will drop fast and have a long and low bounce.
13. A ball with back spin will rise in the air, travel farther, and have a high short bounce.
14. For greatest throwing or kicking accuracy, the eyes should be kept on the target, motion should be in a straight line with the target, and release of the ball should be at a point tangent to the target.
15. A ball will bounce back from the floor, wall, racket, bat, paddle, or club at the same angle at which it hit (angle of refraction).

Buoyancy

Stated briefly, Archimedes' principle of buoyancy says that a fluid such as water or gas exerts a buoyant force upon a body placed in it. When a body is placed in a fluid, the fluid exerts a buoyant force equal to the weight of the fluid the body displaces. Stated in terms that a child in the elementary school can more easily understand, things which are heavy for their size will sink when placed in a liquid; things that are light for their size will float when placed in a liquid. Locomotor, stability, and manipulative activities can readily be utilized in physical education to teach children about buoyancy through the action of their bodies in the water.

Sound

A sound represents something that is heard. It results from stimulation of auditory nerves by vibrations in the air. The source of the vibrations may be our vocal chords, a ball hitting a bat, a ball being kicked, or one of thousands of other vibrating objects. Objects vibrate at different rates. Objects that vibrate at a fast speed produce high pitch sounds. Objects that vibrate at a slow speed produce low pitch sounds. The word pitch describes how high or low a sound is. Objects that are dense vibrate rapidly and produce a high pitch. Objects that are not dense vibrate slowly and produce a low pitch. Children can compare the pitch of different objects. Does wood when struck with an object have a higher pitch than steel when struck with an object? Does a golf ball have a higher pitch than a basketball when each is bounced?

Listening to sounds is a very important way of learning about one's environment. A study of sounds can help children become aware of observing as a conscious process. Good listening habits are useful in learning to read and in learning about any subject. The whole area of dance is rich with experiences through which children can learn about sound. Children can learn about underlying beat, echoes, rhythmic pattern, measures, accents, tempo, phrases, and intensity through various experiences in rhythms. Children should come to recognize that it is possible to make distinctions among the various types of sounds, and that it is possible to learn to identify events and objects in the environment and the sounds associated with them. Children should also be able to recognize sounds at night as well as in daylight to relieve the fear of darkness or night. Children can learn about sounds in physical education through various activities in classification of objects as to density or pitch of sound when bounced or struck. They can also make various rhythmical interpretations of different sounds. Children can experiment with learning to recognize sounds at night by participating in activities involved while they are blindfolded. Following a summary of sound concepts that children should learn in physical education.

1. A sound is that which is heard, resulting from stimulation of auditory nerves by vibrations in the air.
2. The pitch of sound is determined by the rate of vibration.

3. The pitch of sound is affected by the surface area, the density, and the velocity of an object.
4. An echo is made when sound is reflected from an object.
5. Noises are sounds that come from objects that produce irregular sound vibrations.
6. Music is made from sounds that come from regular sound vibrations.
7. You can recognize sounds at night.
8. Some sounds that are made are not heard.

SCIENCE AND PHYSICAL EDUCATION AT THE PRESCHOOL LEVEL

Science experiences at the preschool level should involve everyday activities in the lives of young children. Rather than highly structured experiences, activities should evolve from teachable moments in loosely structured situations. Rather than having all children involved in the same activity, it is usually better to work with small groups of interested youngsters on individual projects. When approached in this manner, we have often seen the attention span of a small child held for a long period of time (ten minutes to an hour). One time we were playing out on the playground after a brief shower and one child discovered an earth worm crawling on the ground. Three or four other boys and girls gathered around and watched the worm crawl until it finally disappeared into a hole in the ground. Once involved, many types of inquiring questions were asked. "How do they crawl?" "Do they have legs?" "What do they eat?" "Where do they live?" A whole unit evolved by capturing the interests of children at a teachable moment.

Children at the preschool level are engrossed in the observation and exploration of their environment. They look at, pick up, manipulate, smell and taste almost everything with which they come into contact. Many of these experiences involve the earth, biological, and physical sciences. Picking up and collecting rocks, playing with water, watching insects crawl, gazing at butterflies, planting a flower or garden, driving a car or truck (role playing), and watching a huge digger clear the earth in preparation for a house are all experiences in the lives of young children that involve each of the sciences. In each instance, movement experiences through physical education could be related in meaningful ways to help the children learn basic science concepts.

For example, the children could explore the qualities of movement involved with crawling slowly and close to the ground like a worm or catepillar, flying freely through space at a high level like a bird or butterfly, or moving slowly but forcefully like a digger carrying or pushing a mound of dirt. These are but a few of the many everyday movement experiences that involve science concepts through role playing activities in physical education.

In addition to imitative movement experiences, children at the preschool level should be encouraged to observe, compare, classify, rank, and measure various aspects of their movement patterns and skills. For example, they could observe a pattern of movement or rhythmical pattern demonstrated by the teacher or another child and then try to duplicate it. Comparative movements could be made by exploring the qualities of movement such as higher, lower, faster, slower, near, far, and soon. The children could learn about classification and rank order through experiences such as stacking similar colored blocks or by grouping objects according to amount (more than, less than). They can also learn basic concepts of measuring through counting the number of times they can jump a rope or measuring the distance they can long jump with a stick. The measurement does not have to be in feet and inches, but perhaps by a system of the child's own choosing such as a hand, foot, forearm, or toy. The children can then measure whether a jump was longer or shorter than a previous one, or perform other such measurements.

As children become more and more curious about their environment through experiences involving observation, comparison, classification, ranking, and measuring, they become ready to learn about some of the basic mechanical principles and science concepts described previously in the chapter. Science concepts taught to children during the preschool level should be explained in elementary terms rather than going into detail. However, we should not refrain from teaching a concept because it is too difficult. As Bruner has said, *a child can learn anything provided it is presented at his/her level*. For example, children can learn about some of their body systems. They can learn that the bones serve as the foundation of their bodies. The muscles provide the force that allows them to move. As muscles exert effort, the arms, legs, and trunk flex and extend in order to perform work. Simple aspects of base of support and center of gravity can be taught through balance activities. Children can learn that they can roll better and faster if they are tucked into the shape of a ball. They also can learn about simple machines through classifying objects in their environment or pictures into machines that operate through a system of wheels, levers, screws, pulleys, and inclined planes. Playing on a see-saw teaches a child about balance and levers. Pounding a nail into a piece of wood teaches a child about leverage. Riding a tricycle teaches a child about wheels. Children can learn about action-reaction by learning that they have to push straight down on a ball if they expect it to come straight up. Various aspects of receipt and propulsion can be taught through having children jump and land from a height or in throwing and catching activities. Any concept can be presented to preschool children provided that it is broken down into terms that the child may understand. The main goal is to teach children to explore and become curious about their environment.

IMPLICATIONS OF SCIENCE PROJECTS WITH RELATION TO PHYSICAL EDUCATION

By drawing from the materials of current educational projects concerned with elementary school science, other science experiences can be integrated with physical education. Trends from projects such as the Science Curriculum Improvement Study directed by Karplus, the University of Illinois Elementary School Science Project directed by Atkin and Wyatt, the Inquiry Training Project directed by Suchman, the Elementary School Science Improvement Project directed by Wood, and the American Association for the Advancement of Science Project directed by Mayor and Livermore are highly related to physical education. Children are learning about problem solving in science and in physical education as well as other areas of the curriculum. School experiences in science include activities dealing with classification of objects, observation, comparison of objects, ranking information in order of importance, measuring, recognizing space/time relationships, and the ability to plan and carry out experiments. Children in physical education can classify balls, implements, and large equipment according to size, shape, sound, and use. Children can observe a group of different balls, compare those that are larger or smaller than an object of a given size, and rank them according to the sport for which each ball is appropriate. Many situations occur in physical education where there are possibilities to measure. Children measure how far they can throw or kick a ball, how high they can jump, how far they run, and the size of different fields for different sports. Space/time relationships occur often in physical education and are especially evident in rhythmical experiences. Children can also plan and carry out experiments in physical education. For example, children could learn how to measure their pulse rate by counting their pulse rates at the carotid artery for a minute. The children could then jump rope at different speeds or for varying durations of time after which they would measure their pulse rates. Children would learn that the faster or longer they jump rope or do work the faster their pulse rates, and as a result, the harder their heart has to work.

EXAMPLES OF INTEGRATING SCIENCE WITH PHYSICAL EDUCATION

The mechanical principles presented here are those that are most essential to basic movement patterns and movement skill development. The main purpose of the presentation of mechanical principles in this text is twofold. First, the teacher should be able to help the children understand the mechanical principles as the movement patterns and movement skills of locomotion, stability, and manipulation are learned. Knowledge of fundamental mechanical principles will help children develop efficient patterns and skills of movement in all areas of physical education. Secondly, every effort should be made to integrate these science principles with physical education. As children learn these science principles in the classroom, they should have related learning experiences in physical education. There is no way these scientific principles of human movement can be divorced from physical education. First graders can learn basic concepts of stability, machines, work, and force. Thereafter, concepts of levers, force, motion, projectiles, sound, buoyancy, and factors that affect motion are introduced in subsequent years. The main factor to remember is to introduce each concept according to the vocabulary and maturity level of the children. The following are some sample lessons of ways in which science and physical education can be integrated at each grade level. Teachers should use their own ingenuity and creativeness in using these lessons and in adapting other science concepts to lessons in physical education. It must be remembered, however, that in any attempt to integrate science with physical education, the physical education class must remain activity oriented rather than become an academic class. The main point to consider is to follow the physical education curriculum as usual, but to use every *teachable movement* to integrate science with physical education in an effort to realize more meaningful instruction in both disciplines.

Concept: *Archimedes' Principle of Buoyancy*
Grade: *1*
Emphasis: *Things that are heavy for their size will sink in water, things that are light for their size will float in water.*
Organizing Center: *Manipulation*
Equipment: *Balloons, small rubber ball, marbles, chewing gum, and a sink or small area with a container of water.*
Space: *Classroom or small science lab area*
Instructional Ideas:

The purpose of these lessons is to teach the children the action of small objects in water. The balloon is a rather large object but it is filled with air and floats easily. The rubber ball will float also. The rubber ball is smaller than the balloon but it is rather spongy and light for its' size. Therefore, the ball will float. The marble is dense. The children will not understand density but they can be told that there are no air spaces in the construction of the glass ball. Without air spaces the marble is heavy and will not float. The chewing gum will be fun for the children. They will guess whether the gum will float. They can experiment whether it will float. Different kinds of gum can be used to vary the experiment. Some boys and girls can blow bubbles to see if the gum will float with air inside it. The gum chewed and unchewed will not float. When a bubble is blown, the gum is full of air, large for its' size, and will float.

As the children learn that objects heavy for their size will sink and that objects light for their size will float, they will learn an understanding of objects in the water. The teacher can emphasize to the children that when we breathe air into our lungs we make ourselves light for our size and we will float also.

Concept: *Newton's First Law of Motion*
Grade: *2*
Emphasis: *A push or a pull must be exerted for an object to be set in motion.*
Organizing Center: *Manipulation*
Equipment: *Soccer-kick balls and bowling pins.*
Space: *Playground or gymnasium*
Instructional Ideas:

The purpose of these lessons is to teach children about Newton's First Law. A push or a pull must be exerted for an object to be set in motion. The push or pull can be supplied by muscles, air, magnets, and other types of machines. Starting from rest, an object will move in the direction of the applied force. The children will be divided into two groups. They will line up in two parallel lines about ten feet apart. One line of children will receive a ball. They will face the children across from them. They will place the ball on the floor. The ball will stay in one place. The teacher will pose several problems. How can the ball be made to travel? What type of forces can be supplied by the children? How can the ball be made to go to the left, right, straight ahead? A push or a pull is needed to start something moving. The children can throw, roll, or kick the ball. The ball will move in the direction of the push or the pull.

The children will then play the game of Pinball Soccer. They will stay in the same lines, but will move apart until they are twenty feet apart. A number of bowling pins will be placed between the two lines. The objective of the game is to kick the balls and knock the bowling pins over. The balls are placed on the floor. They will not move unless they are kicked. Once they are kicked, they will travel in the direction of the applied force. The bowling pins will stand until pushed over by the force of the balls. When the bowling pins are hit, they will fall in the direction of the push.

Concept: *Newton's Third Law of Motion*
Grade: *3*
Emphasis: *For every action, there is an equal and opposite reaction.*
Organizing Center: *Locomotion and Manipulation*
Equipment: *Playground balls or basketballs.*
Space: *Gymnasium or playground*
Instructional Ideas:

The purpose of these lessons is to teach the children a practical application of Newton's Third Law of Motion through the use of dribbling relays. The children will be divided into groups of five or six boys and girls to each group. The groups will line up parallel. The boys and girls within each group will line up one behind the other. The relays will begin at a starting line. The first person will dribble the ball thirty feet, stop, turn around, and return to the starting line. Then the second, third, fourth, fifth, and sixth people will receive their turns. To vary the relay the children may dribble with the right, left, or both hands. They may also try to hop, skip, or gallop while they are trying to dribble the ball.

The emphasis will be placed on the dribbling. As the child pushes the ball, he sends it toward the floor. As the ball hits the floor, it bounces up and begins its rebound off the floor. The floor pushes the ball up in the opposite direction. The rebound is the reaction. The push against the floor is the action. The rebound is the equal and opposite reaction. One dribble leads to another. This produces motion. As the child runs down the floor, the feet push back against the floor. The floor pushes the child ahead and movement is achieved. This is another example of an equal and opposite reaction.

Concept: *Work*

Grade: *4*

Emphasis: *Work is a force acting on mass through a distance. It takes more energy to do work fast than it does to do work slow.*

Organizing Center: *Locomotion and Manipulation*

Equipment: *Record player, record: one of the several records available containing rope jumping rhythms, sixteen eight foot jumping ropes, and eight sixteen foot jumping ropes.*

Location: *Gymnasium*

Instructional Ideas:

During these lessons the children will jump rope to the rhythm of the music. Some of the music will have a slow tempo and the boys and girls will jump with a slow pace. Other music will be faster and will require a faster jumping rate. As the children jump fast it will require a lot of force and energy. The slower jumping rate will require less force and energy. A good way for the children to measure the amount of force and energy that they use while jumping rope is to teach them how to count their pulse rate. The children can take their pulse rates by feeling their carotid artery on the side of their neck just under the jaw. The children can count their pulse rates for a half of a minute and multiply by two to get their heart rates for one minute. The children can take their resting heart rate, heart rate after jumping to a slow tempo, and heart rate after a fast jumping rate. The faster a child jumps the more force and energy required to do the work.

Work is a force acting on mass through a distance. While jumping rope the child is the mass, the force is provided by the leg muscles, and the distance is the jumping into the air. The faster a child jumps or the higher a child jumps, the greater the rate and amount of work done.

Concept: *Sound*

Grade: *5*

Emphasis: *The pitch of sound depends on the rate of vibration, the density of an object and the velocity of an object.*

Organizing Center: *Manipulation*

Equipment: *Set of tuning forks, a basketball, a softball, a golf ball, table tennis ball, soccer ball, and playground balls of six inch, eight and one-half, and 13 inch diameter.*

Space: *Gymnasium*

Instructional Ideas:

The pitch of sound of an object depends on the rate of vibration. In general, a large surface area or a long surface will have a low pitch. A short surface or a small surface area will have a high pitch. Density also plays a part in the pitch of sound. An object of high density will have a high pitch. An object of low density will have a low pitch. Important to physical educators, the velocity of an object upon impact determines the pitch of sound. For example, baseball players can tell how far a ball will travel from the "crack" of the bat. The greater the velocity of an object the higher the pitch of sound. In science there is a table of classification of elements. Everything we do can be classified. The set of tuning forks is classified. The children can be shown the classification from high to low pitch. Present the children with a set of balls, one of each kind available in the gymnasium. One way to classify the balls is to the type of game played with them. The purpose of this lesson is to classify the balls according to pitch as they bounce on the floor. A good way to vary this experiment is to change air pressure in the inflatable balls to see if air pressure changes the pitch of sound of the balls.

Concept: *Levers*

Grade: *6*

Emphasis: *The human body uses a third class lever predominantly.*

Organizing Center: *Manipulation*

Equipment: *Four softballs, four playground balls, four basketballs, four volleyballs, and four soccer balls.*

Location: *Gymnasium or playground*

Instructional Ideas:

During these lessons the children will throw different kinds of balls. As the children throw a ball the body utilizes a third class lever system. The ball is the resistance. The muscles of the arm are the force and the fulcrum is the shoulder joint. The force arm is between the fulcrum and the resistance arm making the action a third class lever.

The children should become aware that all racket or batting sports involve the use of third class levers. Tennis, golf, badminton, and hockey involve the use of third class levers. The teacher should challenge the children to figure out some examples of third class levers used in every day life. Some examples of third class levers may be peddling a bicycle and pushing a grocery cart. Even such locomotor movements as jumping and hopping involve the use of third class levers.

After the children understand this concept, the class may begin doing different kinds of throwing activities. They may throw the ball underhand or overhand. They may throw for distance or accuracy. They may throw chest passes, bounce passes, or baseball passes with the basketballs or playground balls. The volleyballs may be served or volleyed.

To structure the class more, the teacher can select one type of throwing and emphasize it. For example, in throwing for accuracy the teacher may set up targets that are three feet in diameter and placed three feet high against a wall. The children should stand 40 feet away from the target and see how many times they can hit the target in ten throws.

SELECTED REFERENCES

1. Anderson, Marion, Elliot, M.E., and LaBerge, J. *Play with a Purpose*, New York: Harper and Row Publishers, 1972.
2. Barr, George. *Here's Why: Science in Sports*, New York: Scholastic Book Services, Division of Scholastic Magazines, Inc., 1965.
3. Bruner, Jerome. *The Process of Education*, Cambridge, Massachusetts: President and Fellows of Harvard College, 1960.
4. Corbin, Charles, *Becoming Physically Educated in the Elementary School*. Philadelphia: Lea and Febiger, 1971.
5. Dauer, Victor. *Dynamic Physical Education for Elementary School Children*. Minneapolis: Burgess Publishing Company, 1971.
6. Dunn, Lois. *Motion: Investigating Science with Children*. Darien, Connecticut: Vol. 4, National Science Teachers' Association, Teachers' Publishing Corporation, 1968.
7. Humphrey, James. *Child Learning Through Elementary School Physical Education*. Dubuque, Iowa: W. C. Brown Company, 1974
8. _____. *Elementary School Physical Education*. New York: Harper and Row Publishers, 1958.
9. Kirchner, Glenn. *Physical Education for Elementary School Children*. Dubuque, Iowa: W. C. Brown Company, 1974.
10. Miller, Arthus, Cheffers, J. T., and Whitcomb, V. *Physical Education: Teaching Human Movement in the Elementary Schools*. Englewood Cliffs, New Jersey: Prentice-Hall, 1974.
11. Schurr, Evelyn. *Movement Experiences for Children*. New York: Appleton-Century-Crofts, 1967.
12. Ubell, Earl, and Strong, A. *The World of Push and Pull*. New York: Atheneum, 1964.
13. Werner, Peter. *Effects of the Integration of Physical Education with Selected Science Concepts Upon Science Knowledge and Selected Physical Performance Skills of Boys and Girls at the Fourth, Fifth, and Sixth Grade Levels*. Bloomington, Indiana: Indiana University, Unpublished Doctoral Dissertation, 1971.

Chapter 16
Developing Social Studies Concepts

Key Concept: The integration of physical education and social studies should be conducive to the development of a sense of rights and responsibilities in children in relation to themselves and to others. Cross-cultural similarities and differences between families, ethnic groups, nations, and people during different periods of history may be studied and enriched through participation in physical education activities.

Content: Introduction

Social Studies Experiences Through Physical Education
People and Families at Home
Communities and Social Needs
Regions and Social Needs
Our Country
The World
Social Studies and Physical Education at the Preschool Level

Examples Integrating Social Studies with Physical Education
People and Families at Home
Communities and Social Needs
Regions and Social Needs
Our Country
The World

Developing Social Studies Concepts

INTRODUCTION

As children are thrust from the home into a school environment, they become involved in an increasing number of relationships with others throughout life. Initial experiences through social interaction bring children toward an understanding of the family, home, and neighborhood. As their world expands, they come to know the community, region, state, nation, and world. The social studies curriculum in the elementary school enables children to understand the sequential levels of social development through topics such as sociology, economics, history, geography, civics, and anthropology. In many instances concepts in the social studies may be integrated with experiences in physical education to enable the learning situation to be more meaningful in both disciplines. Cross-cultural similarities and differences between families, ethnic groups, nations, and people during different periods of history may be studied and enriched through participation in physical education activities.

The integration of physical education and social studies should be conducive to the development of a sense of rights and responsibilities in children in relation to themselves and to others. Movement experiences should be designed to compare and contrast cultures of different people around the world. As boys and girls learn more about the history, geography, economic conditions, political background, and sports of other countries, they will come to understand that there are more similarities than differences among the peoples of the world. Our main goals should be to develop in children an awareness of the environment and a willingness to receive new information even though it may be contrary to our present beliefs. Then, gradually, the children will progress along the scale of the affective domain toward responding, valuing, and developing an organized value system. As children learn about their expanding environment, they will be more able to cope with the problems of today's society.

The social studies units that follow lend themselves to integration with physical education through movement experiences involving locomotion, stability, and manipulation.

378

SOCIAL STUDIES EXPERIENCES THROUGH PHYSICAL EDUCATION

People and Families at Home

As the child comes to school the most logical place to initiate experiences in social studies is through an increased awareness of the family and home from which he comes. To assist the child in increasing his knowledge of the family and home, experiences are designed to help him learn about the responsibilities of family members, equipment in the home, pets in the home, and toys in the home.

Responsibilities of family members often lend to imitative and creative rhythmical experiences for children in physical education. Children enjoy role playing experiences when they can make believe they are a spaceman, fireman, policeman, ballerina, or athlete. Responsibilities such as cleaning house, washing clothes, raking leaves, shoveling snow, and chopping wood are other experiences that children enact through movement. Situations can also be created in which children recreate a story play from times past. Riding horses, protecting the fort, sword fighting, cowboys and Indians, and dinosaur expeditions are typical situations in which children become involved through physical education.

Equipment which may be found in the home is another source of ideas for movement in physical education. Pendulum movements of the clock can be enacted through rhymes such as Hickory, Dickory, Dock. Rhythmical activities such as I'm a Little Teapot or the Shoemaker's Dance often depict types of equipment or articles of clothing that may be found in the home. Stability or fitness exercises can be designed to illustrate the movements of other types of equipment found in the home. As children move their bodies as if they are using an ax, egg beater, saw, hammer, typewriter, scissors, or rocking chair, they learn about simple machines, movement principles and social studies while enjoying and increasing their movement repertoire.

As children learn about pets in the home through their social studies experiences, physical education lessons should be designed to allow for exploration of various animal walks. The movements of dogs, cats, rabbits, ducks, birds, ponies, or even less common varieties of pet animals such as monkeys or frogs can be explored by children. At times children may be given specific directions as to how different animals walk. In other situations they may explore various ways in which they imagine animals to move.

Movement experiences that involve toys in the home can be explored in much the same manner in physical education. On occasion the children might imitate the movements of traditional toys such as a toy soldier, ball, yo-yo, doll, scooter or bicycle. Other situations might call for children to create a new innovative toy and to explore the movements that they imagine the toy to make.

Communities and Social Needs

The child's world expands from the home to the community. The child becomes more aware of his expanding environment through school experiences, going to the store, visits to the zoo, playing with neighbors, and circus parades. Children also learn about urban and rural communities.

School experiences, running errands, and playing with neighbors offer children many opportunities to learn more mature processes of social interaction. Opportunities for leadership, followership, friendliness, group consciousness, group planning, group cooperation, and solving group problems abound. Physical education experiences offer numerous situations through which children learn the same qualities. Problem solving techniques through movement experiences and small group games such as Follow the Leader are examples when children learn these important social qualities.

Visits to the zoo and circus parades become ideas for movement experiences in physical education. The movements of seals, elephants, giraffes, ostriches, and bears can be explored by children. At times children may be given specific directions as to how different animals walk. In other situations they may explore various ways in which they imagine animals to walk. Circus parades afford children opportunities to explore the movements of clowns, acrobats, swinging on the trapeze, balancing on the tightrope, and riding a unicycle through physical education. Rhythmical experiences that create the happy and sad moods of clowns or folk dance records are also used to enhance the circus atmosphere in physical education.

The life of people and families in rural and urban situations may also be compared and contrasted through related physical education activities. Activities such as Red Light, Green Light can be used to illustrate city traffic. Other movement experiences can be designed to illustrate traffic jams, hectic shopping expeditions, and other urban situations. The children may imitate the movements of trucks, airplanes, and trains. In contrast, rural and farm life may be illustrated in physical education through farm chores, farm animal walks, and various rhythmical experiences such as Old MacDonald, Farmer in the Dell, and Oats, Peas, Beans, and Barley. Children may also compare urban playground experiences to natural play situations in rural areas involving tree climbing, balancing on fence rails and swinging down from the haymow.

Regions and Social Needs

Children's knowledge of their environment expands from communities to regions of the world. Experiences in social studies increase knowledge of the types of lives people live in regions of coastal lands, deserts, tropical rain forests, plains and mountains. Meaningful physical education experiences can be designed to enhance children's knowledge of regions of the world.

Various rhythmical experiences can be explored to compare climatic and geographical conditions in different regions. Children can explore the movements: (1) of being tossed about on a ship in a stormy sea; (2) of being sand blown about in a desert wind; (3) of rain splashing down in a tropical forest; (4) of roaming about the grassy plains; and (5) of snow on a wind swept mountain side.

Games of various regions may also be taught to children. Winter games such as ice skating, skiing, curling, sledding, and making snow forts are popular games enjoyed in northern regions. Coastal regions enjoy water sports such as boating, water skiing, swimming, and surfing.

Our Country

The United States has a rich heritage about which children learn in the intermediate grades. Experiences in social studies increase children's knowledge of early America, the development of a new nation, and the relationship of our country to other nations of the world. Meaningful physical education experiences can be designed to enhance a child's knowledge of the development of our nation, geography in the United States, our cultural heritage, and minority groups.

Children learn about the development of our country through learning about events such as the discovery of America, the Boston Tea Party, the midnight ride of Paul Revere, the development of the West, the pony express, the laying of our railroad system, the Civil War, and the invention of the automobile and airplane. Various rhythmical experiences in physical education can be enacted to depict each of the above situations. For example, children could rhythmically act out the development of the railroad through clearing trees and rocks to prepare for laying the rail, pounding the sledge, and Engine No. 99 rolling down the tracks.

The geography of the United States can be learned through several map experiences in physical education. A map of the United States can be painted on the playground or gymnasium floor on which children can long jump from state to state, lake to river, or mountain to plains. Children can be taught to recognize states and their relative location when they are asked to jump from Wisconsin to Ohio, or Texas to California. They can also learn to recognize bodies of water and regions of the United States by asking them to jump from the Mississippi River to the Atlantic Ocean or from the Rocky Mountains to the Midwest (Figure 16-1). Other map experiences in physical education involve the vertical jump. The map of a state or region can be painted on the wall of the gymnasium. Children can then try to vertical jump to a city, county, or lake (Figure 16-2).

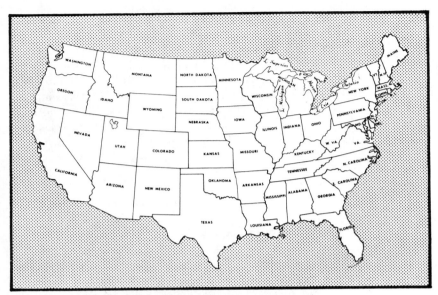

Figure 16-1. Children can learn to long jump from one state to another.

᠂ As children learn about games, sports, and rhythmical activities through various movement experiences, they learn that the United States has a rich cultural heritage. Square dancing and various contras (line dances) such as the Virginia Reel have their origin in the United States. The Hokey Pokey originated from taking a bath on a Saturday night. The game of baseball invented by Abner Doubleday and the game of basketball invented by James Naismith were originated in the United States. These and other experiences can and should be related to what children are learning in social studies in the classroom.

The contributions of various minority groups to our cultural heritage should also be emphasized in physical education. The American Indian, Black, Polynesian, and Eskimo in particular have contributed much to the culture of the United States. The rain dance, sun dance, war dance, and other dances of the American Indian should be learned as children study about Indians in the classroom. Archery, throwing spears, and hoop and running games that Indian children learned as they became braves or warriors are all a part of the Indian culture that children should learn. The contributions of the Black subculture to folk dancing and the contributions of the Black athlete to sports in the United States should be taught to our children. Tinikling from the Philippine Islands and hula dancing from the Hawaiian Islands as well as the surfing, skin diving, and boating of our Polynesian neighbors should be related to our children

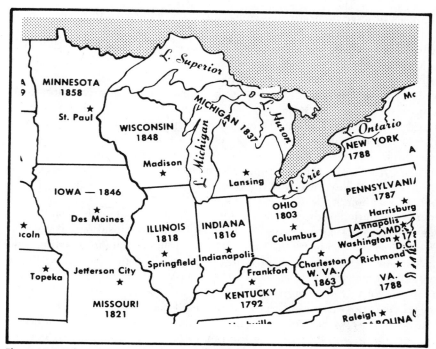

Figure 16-2. When maps are placed on walls, children can try to vertical jump to a city, county or lake.

through physical education. The Eskimos from Alaska also have various ice and snow games such as Shinny, a form of ice hockey, which should be related in physical education.

The World

As a child enters the intermediate grades, the social studies expand to learning about the world. At different times during the intermediate years all children learn about man before history, ancient civilizations, Eastern and Western societies, man in the middle ages, the world from 1500 to 1850, and the world from 1850 to present. Units in social studies also discuss various countries around the world. Meaningful physical education experiences can be designed to enhance a child's knowledge of man before history, early civilizations, man in the middle ages, different countries throughout the world, travel in space, life on other planets, and life in the future.

Adventures of cave men intrigue young children. They can imagine being a prehistoric animal such as a dinosaur or large bird. Story plays involving living in a cave, hunting for food, and killing a wild beast are other experiences that children enjoy in physical education. These experiences can be taught through the use of rhythm or an exploratory approach.

Units in the social studies delve into early civilizations. Children learn about the Egyptians, Greeks, and Romans as well as other civilizations. The pyramids of the Egyptians may stimulate discussion about pyramid building in gymnastics. The Olympics and the Spartan way of life are major contributions of the Greeks. Children enjoy learning about Olympic events such as track events, field events, gymnastics, and wrestling. The Romans' military way of life and the gladiators prior to the overthrow of the Roman Empire are also interesting topics in physical education.

Although the period of the middle ages is best known for the stress on the development of the mind at the expense of the body, the medieval period contributed to physical education through the skills of archery, fencing, jousting, and staffing. Upper elementary school children learn the fundamental skills of archery and playing the role of Robin Hood. D'Artanian and the three musketeers are favorite roles children like to play as they learn the fundamental skills in fencing. Boys and girls enjoy being one of King Arthur's knights of the round table as they learn about jousting and staffing. Being King George and slaying a dragon in an effort to save the fair young maiden in distress may be another role playing situation in physical education.

Experiences in physical education also provide situations for boys and girls to learn about various countries of the world. While children learn about different countries in the classroom, they may learn about the games, sports, and folk dances of the countries to enhance their knowledge and make it more meaningful. The following are some examples of games and rhythms that children from other countries play:

Bolivia

La Thunkuna—hopscotch
La Pollerita—hopscotch
Bailecito Estilizado—folk dance

Canada

Goodminton—lead-up game to volleyball and badminton
Skinny—hockey game
Dog Dance—folk dance

Congo

Nsunsa—combative game

Czechoslovakia

Nations—ball tag game
Black Peter—line tag game
Mak—folk dance

Denmark

Little Man in a Fix—folk dance
Crested Hen—folk dance
Seven Jumps—folk dance
Shoemaker's Dance—folk dance
Dance of Greeting—folk dance
Three Man High-3 Deep—tag game

England

A Hunting We Will Go—folk dance
Greensleeves—folk dance
Jacks—fine motor and eye-hand
coordination
Cricket—baseball game
Rounders—baseball game
Hopscotch—hopping game

France

Minuet—folk dance

Germany

At the Inn—folk dance
Hansel and Gretel—folk dance
Bavarian Landler—folk dance
Come Let Us Be Joyful—folk dance
Polka Zu Dreien—folk dance
Heel and Toe Polka—folk dance
Gymnastics
Hinkspiel—hopscotch

Holland

Greppel—Jump the Ditch game
Ambachten—Dutch charade game
Leak in the Dike—tag game
Verlos—tag game
Dutch Couples Dance—folk dance
Ice Skating

Ireland

Waves of Tory—folk dance
Irish Step Dance—folk dance
Curling—baseball game
Irish Washerwomen—folk dance

Italy

La Solitudine—folk dance
Bocchi Ball—bowling game
Imprisoned Ball—dodgeball game
Angels and Demons—tag game

Japan

Kagome—folk dance
Sumo—combative game

Mexico

Arrema—Mexican target game
Pipas y Gallos—fighting cocks
Pinata—Mexican Christmas game
Los Colores—tag game
La Raspa—folk dance
Chapenecas—Mexican clap dance
Empezamos a Bailar—folk dance
similar to Virginia Reel

Norway

Norwegian Polka—folk dance
Tretur—folk dance
Norwegian Ball—soccer lead-up game

Russia

Troika—folk dance
Kohanochka—folk dance
Korobushka—folk dance

Scotland

Highland Schottische—folk dance
Highland Fling—folk dance

Sweden

Gustaf's Skoal—folk dance
Carrousel—folk dance
Bleking—folk dance
Tantoli—folk dance
North Winds and South Winds—tag
game
Skiing—all Scandinavian countries

Switzerland

Drei Lederne Stromph—folk dance
Der Lauter Bach—folk dance
Swiss Changing Dance—folk dance
Weggis—folk dance
Drei Mann Hoch-3 Deep—tag game

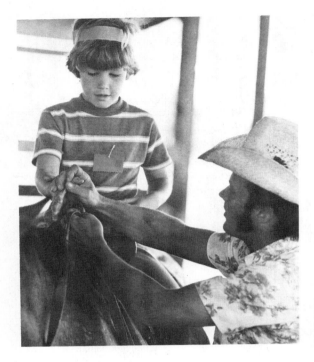

Basic Horsemanship Can Be A
Part Of The Movement Program
In Some Areas

In addition, a child's knowledge of the world may be expanded through the study of space travel, life on other planets, and life in the future. In physical education the children can take an imaginary walk in space, pretend they are weightless, and perform all of the routines associated with space travel. They can take a walk on the moon and bound about as if they were under the reduced gravitational pull of the moon. As they travel to other planets they can discover the animals, toys, machines, transportation vehicles, and the like through creative movement. In a similar fashion, children can create movement situations to predict life in the future. Machines, toys, games, and jobs are examples where children would enjoy predicting the future through movement.

SOCIAL STUDIES AND PHYSICAL EDUCATION AT THE PRESCHOOL LEVEL

Social studies experiences at the preschool level should be directed at helping children learn more about families at home as well as people and social needs in the community. In an effort to achieve this goal experiences should be designed to make children more aware of animals, birds, fish, toys, transportation, occupations, and lifestyles of people in various cultures. Experiences should move from the immediate environment to comparison and contrast with other cultures. In this way children will learn that the basic family unit consists of a mother, father, siblings, and relatives. Gradually, the environment expands to significant others (friends) and to the community.

Animals, birds, and fish with which the children are familiar can be used as an introductory theme to learn more about these creatures. Children can learn where they live, what they eat, and whether they are domestic (pets) or wild. Animals on the farm may be one specific theme. Another may be animals from other lands. A trip to the farm or zoo or film and film strips may accompany such a theme. In relation to physical education, the children may observe the animals, birds, or fish in movement, and then try to move as the animals do. They can climb, fly, land, run fast, change directions quickly, crawl, swim, and participate in all other forms of animal movement.

Locomotion, stability, and manipulative movement patterns are an innate part of a child's play with toys. Building with blocks, playing house with dolls, riding a tricycle, playing with trucks, and all other forms of play with toys involve the exploration and development of various movement patterns. The environment of children is expanded as they are introduced to and are allowed to play with different toys and toys from other cultures.

Transportation is another theme that suggests other movement experiences in the lives of children as it expands their awareness of their environment. Boats,

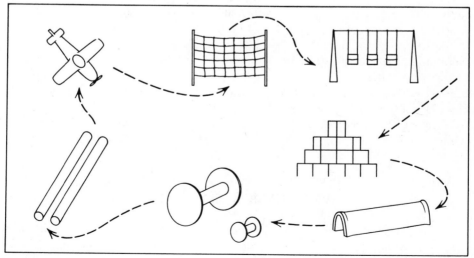

Figure 16-3. Nursery school children can learn to read the map of the playground.

planes, trains, cars, tractors, trucks, elevators, escalators, motorcycles, tricycles, and other mechanical pieces of equipment may be explored through movement experiences. Children may stop and go with the signals, move fast or slow, move as if they were carrying a heavy load, move uphill, and so forth. Old boats, train cars, planes, trucks, tractors, diggers, catepillars, tanks, fire engines, and the like may also be placed on playgrounds on which children may explore and role play. In other instances animals may be used for transportation. Children may pretend they are riding horses, burros, elephants, or even ride imaginary objects like Puff, the magic dragon, or the cyclone in Pecos Bill.

In relation to transportation, simple map reading experiences may become a part of a child's experiences in social studies. A map of the room or playground could be constructed (Figure 16-3). The children could then follow the map to go from one place to another. Perhaps a map of a grocery store or zoo, which the children have visited, could be constructed and recreated in the classroom with the aid of the teacher.

In terms of occupations the children may learn about the responsibilities of various family members. Children can role play "going to" and "being at" work. Washing dishes, sawing wood, cutting the grass, raking leaves, shoveling snow, farming chores, typewriting, and operating a machine are all experiences that can be interpreted through movement. Other occupations such as nurse, doctor, candlemaker, fireman, policeman, shoemaker, forest ranger, cowboy, sailor, and spaceman can be interpreted through movement as a result of a field trip, film, poem, or story. Occupations of people from other cultures also can be introduced to children.

Lifestyles of people are affected by their history, culture, climate and geography. Children may learn about different lifestyles by being introduced to the way in which people live when they are in the Arctic or northern regions, Tropics or southern regions, near the sea or any body of water, in the desert, and in the mountains. Movement experiences should accompany these themes. In terms of history and culture children may learn about some of the special holidays celebrated by different people. For example, Christmas may be compared with Hanukka of the Jews and with the breaking of the Pinãta by the Mexicans. Other national and foreign celebrations may be introduced to the children. In addition, games and toys of children from other lands may be introduced to the children.

EXAMPLES INTEGRATING SOCIAL STUDIES
WITH PHYSICAL EDUCATION

As children learn social studies concepts in the classroom, they should have related learning experiences in physical education. This does not mean, however, that the objectives of physical education must be sacrificed in order to teach the children social studies. It does mean that the physical education teacher should be familiar with what is being taught in the classroom and be ready to emphasize and follow up subject matter when it applies to physical education.

Repeated examples have been illustrated that incorporate the concepts of social studies while maintaining an activity oriented program. Some movement experiences help children gain an insight into the way of life of our own people and people of other lands by learning dances, stunts, and games in which various people engage. Other movement experiences help children to learn about the values of cooperation, competition, friendliness, group consciousness, and leadership and following abilities.

As children advance from a knowledge about the home and family toward an understanding of the world about them, the main factor to remember is to introduce each concept according to the vocabulary and maturity level of the children. The following are some sample lessons of ways in which social studies and physical education can be integrated. Teachers should use their own ingenuity and creativeness in using these lessons and in adapting other social studies concepts to lessons in physical education. It must be remembered, however, that in any attempt to integrate social studies with physical education, the physical education class must remain activity oriented rather than become an academic class. The main point to consider is to follow the physical education curriculum as usual, but to use every teachable movement to integrate social studies with physical education in an effort to realize more meaningful instruction in both disciplines.

Concept: *People and Families at Home*
Grade: 1
Emphasis: *Movement experiences in physical education help children learn about equipment in the home and the various responsibilities of family members.*
Organizing Center: *Stability and Locomotion*
Equipment: *None*
Location: *Gymnasium*
Instructional Ideas:

During these lessons the children will explore the movements of stretching, bending, twisting, and rotating along with various locomotor patterns in an effort to learn about equipment in the home and job responsibilities of family members. Qualities of movement such as space, force, time, and flow will also be utilized. First the children will explore the concepts of stretching and bending. Words such as repeating, yawning, and extending can be used to help children understand stretching. Curl, close, and small are words to signify bending. The children should be asked to move like equipment in the home or jobs that require stretching and bending. They should also be asked to name their responses. Some possible answers may be a jacknife, scissors, eye glasses, sawing wood, hammering a nail, and washing or hanging clothes. Next the children will explore the concepts of twisting and rotating. Words such as around, turn and circle may be used to signify twisting and rotating. The fact that twisting involves turning around an axis while holding a stationary base of support may be compared to the fact that rotating involves turning around an axis while changing the base of support. Again the children should be asked to move like equipment in the home or jobs that require twisting and rotating. They should be asked to name their responses. Some possible answers may be a clock, drill, egg beater, mix master, wash machine, or record player. At the end of the lesson the teacher may conclude by having the children play a game such as Twister to reemphasize the concepts of bending, stretching, twisting, and rotating.

Concept: *Communities and Social Needs*
Grade: 2
Emphasis: *The life of people and families in rural and urban situations may be compared and contrasted through related physical education activities.*
Organizing Center: *Stability and Locomotion*
Equipment: *Record player, any of several records available that contain rhythms for various animal walks and machines.*
Location: *Gymnasium*
Instructional Ideas:

During the introduction to these lessons, the children will perform various animal walks to the rhythm of the music. To make the learning situation more meaningful the teacher should question the children about the different animals that are found in the city as compared to the rural setting. Except for the dog, cat, and pet bird or goldfish, the urban situation does not present many situations for children to relate to animals. The rural setting on the other hand allows children to learn about many animals such as the horse, rabbit, frog, and ducks. The zoo is a contrived situation that permits children from all cultural settings to become acquainted with animals from other lands. During the lesson the children may attempt to move like an elephant, ostrich, bear, or kangaroo. After the introduction to the lesson, the children will explore the movements that machines from urban and rural areas make. The children may explore springing, bending, rotating, twisting, and stretching movements that they imagine large machines in the factory to make. They may become a plow or tractor in relation to the rural setting. The movements may be directed or left to exploration depending on the teaching situation. To conclude the class, the children may play two games of low organization such as Red Light, Green Light and In the Creek so that urban and rural situations may again be compared.

Concept: *Regions and Social Needs*
Grade: 3
Emphasis: *A child's knowledge of the environment expands from communities to regions of the world. Experiences in social studies increase his knowledge of the types of lives people live in northern regions of the world. Meaningful physical education experiences can be designed to enhance a child's knowledge of the types of games people play in northern regions of the world.*
Organizing Center: *Manipulation and Locomotion*
Equipment: *24 plastic hockey sticks and pucks or appropriate similar equipment, 24 cones to be used as obstacles and goal markers.*
Location: *Gymnasium*
Instructional Ideas:

After a brief warm-up, the teacher will discuss with the children several types of games people might play in northern regions. Some of the possible responses might be skiing, sledding, throwing snow balls, and playing ice hockey. Discussion might continue an the class could talk about northern climates, animals that may be found in the north, or winter sports. In summary, the teacher will introduce ice hockey skills that the children will do during the period. The first activity will involve having the children explore manipulation skills involving the hockey stick and puck. Partners might take turns dribbling the puck or they may pass the puck back and forth to one another. After practicing these skills, the teacher should set up some goals to have the children practice making goals. A final activity for the period will involve a lead-up game in the form of a relay.

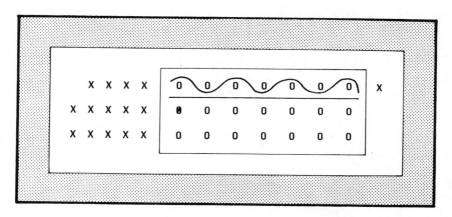

The children will be divided into five equal groups. The objective of the game is to have each child dribble the puck around the cones to the end of the playing area. At the end of the playing area the children are to stop the puck and shoot it back to the next member of the team. After all members of the team are finished they will be seated at the end of the playing area. The first team to finish will be the winner.

Concept: *Our Country*
Grade: 4 or 5
Emphasis: *The American Indian contributed a great deal to the cultural heritage of our country. Various dances of the different Indian tribes portrayed significant events in their life styles.*
Organizing Center: *Locomotion*
Equipment: *Record player, record album—Music of American Indians, RCA Victor Records for Elementary Schools, Album WE-89.*
Location: *Gymnasium*
Instructional Ideas:

The Indians had many songs, dances, and ceremonies to celebrate various occasions. For example, they had dances to celebrate the growing corn, harvest season, and hunting trips. They had similar dances for seasons of the year, rain, sun, baby lullabies, love songs, wisdom, evil spirits, war, and death. It is the purpose of this lesson to introduce the children to two of the basic Indian dance steps. The first dance the children will learn is the war dance. As Indians performed the war dance, dancers were usually divided into four groups of braves in full war regalia, carrying clubs, bows and arrows, lances, and sometimes

The "Indianapolis 500" Race May Be Reinacted On The Parking Lot

shields, At a signaled drum beat they gave a yell and rushed together, waving their weapons as though attacking the enemy. Then they spread out in a large, irregular circle and dramatized ways of stealthily stalking a foe, hunting him down, and preparing to attack. Suddenly each dancer separated himself from the group and pantomimed his own war experiences—charging the enemy, dodging arrows, drawing the bow string, and raising the war club to strike. After a struggle lone dancers from each of the four groups emerged victorious. This symbolized the bravery of individual members of the war party, and anticipated the tribe's triumph in battle. Steps used for war dances included the slow toe and heel step; rapid hop with body bent forward, arms and legs lifted high and angularly; and fast step-hop, knees lifted, "skipping" with two short hops on the ball of each foot, heels never touching the ground.

The second dance that the children will learn is the eagle dance. The Thunder Bird of the Indian and the American Eagle of our present civilization are both symbolic of the power of this mighty bird who knew no fear. The dance began in a ceremonial circle. The entire dance is done with body bent forward and "wings" moving up and down in imitation of the eagle in flight. One dancer enters and slowly walks around the circle. He is soon joined by a second dancer who moves in the opposite direction. They meet and circle around each other with caution, dipping and bending. Flapping their "wings" menacingly, they hop first to one side, then to the other. Finally, they circle cautiously once again and disappear, stepping side by side, with wing tips touching.

Concept: *The World*
Grade: 6
Emphasis: *As children learn about the people, geography, climate, culture, and social and economic systems of various nations of the world, they will learn to understand and accept the similarities and differences that exist among people and nations.*
Organizing Center: *Locomotion*
Equipment: *Record player, record—Weggis, Folk Dancer, MH1046.*
Location: *Gymnasium*
Instructional Ideas:

During this lesson the children will learn Weggis, a Swiss folk dance. This lesson would be appropriate as the children are studying a social studies unit about the Scandinavian countries. Weggis is the name of a village in the canton of Lucerne, Switzerland. The words of the song tell of a favorite trip between two villages, Weggis and Lucerne. The steps are characteristic of Swiss folk dance patterns as the dance utilizes the polka, and schottische steps. The formation for the dance is a double circle.

Figure 1. Heel Toe Polka
Measure 1—Beginning left, place left heel forward, touch toe in front of right toe.

Measure 2—Take one polka step forward.
Measures 3-4—Beginning right, repeat action of measures 1-2.
Measures 5-8—Repeat action of measures 1-4.

Chorus
Measure 9—Hands on hips, man beginning left, lady right, take one schottische step moving away from each other diagonally forward.
Measure 10—Take one schottische step diagonally forward toward partner.
Measures 11-12—Shoulder-waist position. Take four step hops, turning clockwise.
Measures 13-16—Repeat actions of measures 9-12.

Figure 2. Center and Back
Measures 1-2—Man beginning left, lady right, repeat action of measures 1-2, Figure 1. Take polka step toward center of circle.
Measures 3-4—Repeat action of measures 1-2, Figure 2, moving away from center of circle.
Measures 5-8—Repeat action of measures 1-4, Figure 2.
Measures 9-16—Repeat action of measures 9-16, Chorus.

SELECTED REFERENCES

1. AAHPER. *Learning About the World Through Games and Dances*. Washington, D.C., 1964.
2. Bell, R.C. *Board and Table Games from Many Civilizations*. New York: Oxford University Press, 1968.
3. Bird, James. "Exploring the Middle Ages Through Physical Education." *Journal of Health, Physical Education, Recreation*, 43 January 1972, p. 31.
4. Harbin, E.O. *Games of Many Nations*. Nashville: Abington Press, 1954.
5. Hofsinde, Robert. *Indian Games and Crafts*. New York: William Morrow and Company, Inc., 1957.
6. Humphrey, James. *Child Learning Through Elementary School Physical Education*. Dubuque, Iowa: W.C. Brown, 1974.
7. Hunt, Sarah. *Games and Sports of the World Around*. New York: The Ronald Press, Inc., 1964.
8. International Council on Health, Physical Education, and Recreation. *Book of Worldwide Games and Dances*. Washington, D.C., 1967.
9. Krathwohl, D.R., Bloom, B.S., and Masia, B.B. *Taxonomy of Educational Objectives, Handbook II: Affective Domain*. New York: David McKay, Inc., 1964.
10. MacFarlan, Allan. *Book of American Indian Games*. New York: Association Press, 1958.
11. Miller, Arthus, Cheffers, J.T., and Whitcomb, V. *Physical Education: Teaching Human Movement in the Elementary Schools*. Englewood Cliffs, New Jersey: Prentice-Hall, 1974.
12. Young, Vera, "Correlation-Physical Education (Rhythms) with Social Studies," *North Carolina Association of Health, Physical Education, and Recreation*. 5:10, May, 1969.
13. Werner, Peter, and Simmons, R.A. *Do It Yourself: Innovative Physical Education Equipment for Creative Movement Experience*. Dubuque, Iowa: Kendall/Hunt, 1973.

CHAPTER 17
Developing Art and Music Concepts

Key Concept: The arts are a means through which man learns to express himself. Music is expression through rhythm, melody, and harmony. Paintings, statues, and beautiful buildings integrate space and form concepts with color, rhythm, and design. The dancer uses space, form, and design with rhythm to interpret concepts through movement. Experiences in physical education should offer children ample opportunities to express themselves through an integrated arts approach.

Content: Introduction
Art Experiences Through Physical Education
   Drawing and Painting
   Cutting, Tearing, and Fastening
   Constructing and Arranging
   Modeling and Sculpting
Music Experiences Through Physical Education
   Listening
   Singing
   Reading and Playing
   Dancing and Creating
Art, Music, and Physical Education at the Preschool Level
Examples Integrating Art and Music With Physical Education
   Singing
   Drawing and Painting
   Listening
   Playing
   Dancing and Creating

Developing Art and Music Concepts

INTRODUCTION

The arts are a means through which man learns to express himself. Music is expression through rhythm, melody, and harmony. Paintings, statues, and beautiful buildings integrate space and form concepts with color, rhythm, and design. The dancer uses space, form, and design with rhythm to interpret concepts through movement.

Each art has its own materials or medium that the artist manipulates through creative expression in an attempt to interpret his feelings, moods, or concepts. The musician arranges musical sounds. The poet works with the sounds and meanings of words. The sculptor models in clay, wood, or stone. The painter uses oils, chalk, or water color. The dancer uses the medium of movement to express creative, aesthetic, and humanistic aspects of the environment. Experiences in the arts through these materials and mediums should be an integral part of every school curriculum to help children better express themselves through their work and play.

As children learn more about the arts, they discover that the arts are a part of their heritage, a vital part of life, and a means of personal expression. The history of man can be found in his art, music, and dance. Woven into the art, music, and dance fabric of the centuries is the tale of man striving toward a richer life. As children learn about the art, music, and dance of people, they will become aware of the place of the arts in the past and present life of man. As they explore the arts, they will realize that art, music, and dance have played an important part in the rituals of primitive and sophisticated cultures. As a child learns about art, music, and dance from many countries and periods in history, he will discover that the arts reflect the culture from which it springs. Each child will come to know and value the arts in his own society. Through involvement in a variety of art, music, and dance activities, he will find ways to participate in that life.

396

The arts also provide each child an avenue for personal expression in a way that language does not. The arts are not bound, as are words, by specific meanings. Through the arts, each individual can communicate his own ideas or reflect the ideas of others. The child will discover his own potential for expression as he is given the opportunity to explore many different areas of artistic performance and response. The arts take a humanistic approach toward allowing each child to express himself freely and creatively in an aesthetic approach.

In turn, providing experiences in the arts helps children develop a knowledge of the literature of the arts, an understanding of the structure of the arts, and skills of artistic performance and response. While discovering their heritage, children should have an opportunity to explore many kinds of literature concerning the arts. As children study the literature, they will become aware of the infinite variety of creative expression (paintings, sculpture, opera, folk song, jazz, ballet, folk dance, etc.) and of the many different media through which it may be communicated. Children will come to realize that exploration of the arts can be a lifetime pursuit.

Perhaps more important than the acquisition of a knowledge of the literature involved in the arts is the active participation required in learning about the structure of the arts and the skills required in performance and response. Although anyone may enjoy the arts on a limited level without knowledge of its structure, independence of expression is contingent upon an understanding of the organization of the arts. Teachers should move beyond the obvious to help children become aware of the principles that govern rhythm, melody, harmony, color, design, space, and form. Such understanding results in deeper enjoyment and more complete participation in the arts.

Every child should have an opportunity to explore the activities through which the arts can be an expressive medium for him. Skills in art should involve drawing, painting, cutting, tearing, fastening, printing, weaving, stitching, modeling, sculpting, constructing, dyeing, enameling, selecting, and arranging. Skills in music should involve singing, playing, listening, dancing, and creating. Skills in dance should involve fundamental locomotor patterns, folk dance, square dance, social dance, and creative dance. Each skill contributes in a different way to the total development of the child. As the child develops skills of performance and response, he will find greater satisfaction in his feelings and ideas through the arts.

As children learn to express themselves through the arts, physical education offers many opportunities for children to integrate movement experiences with art, music, and dance. Because dance experiences are normally considered to be an integral part of the physical education program and have been described in previous chapters, efforts in the remainder of this chapter will be limited to ways in which art and music can be integrated with physical education.

ART EXPERIENCES THROUGH PHYSICAL EDUCATION

Drawing and Painting

During the primary school years children use chalk, crayon, opaque, transparent or finger paint freely and spontaneously in various drawing and painting experiences. Children learn to recognize the basic colors of red, yellow, blue, black, and white and experiment with combining the colors to produce green, orange, and violet. Children use the blackboard and various types of large paper such as construction paper and newspaper as surfaces for their drawing and painting experiences. Various size brushes are used as well as painting and drawing with the fingers. In relation to physical education, drawing and painting experiences should encourage large free rhythmical patterns of movement that are gradually refined into small muscle, eye-hand coordination tasks. Through drawing children should be encouraged to compare the patterns of angular lines that change direction abruptly to percussive music with the patterns of free flowinglines of soft gentle string music that are smooth and curved. Children can listen to the music, then draw or paint the pattern, and finally recreate the pattern through movement Children also should react to the way different colors invite movement. Some colors suggest vigorous movement while others suggest movement that may be more serene. Colors also may be suggestive of moods such as the bright colors being of a happy festive nature while the darker colors are more gloomy. These moods can be acted out through movement experiences.

As children progress through the grades, drawing and painting activities are used to express reactions to their environment. Children draw and paint realistic or abstract impressions about people, play experiences, the home, the school, the neighborhood, and the world. In relation to physical education children should be encouraged to draw and paint pictures of the games they play, skills they learn, and how they feel while they play. In addition to drawing their own pictures, children should be introduced to the art of others that involves people at play in various activities. The scenes, lines, and designs in movement pictures will help children develop an appreciation of the aesthetic and humanistic nature of the integration of art with movement.

Cutting, Tearing, and Fastening

In the first four grades children learn to cut and tear paper and other materials of various colors and textures into free shapes. These shapes are arranged into various designs and fastened onto objects or backgrounds to make artistic products such as pictures, booklets, puppets, bulletin board decorations, murals, and mobiles. In addition, experiences with cutting, tearing, and fastening enable children to develop the small muscles of the hands and allow for the development of eye-hand coordination—a perceptual-motor skill.

As art and movement are integrated as experiences, children should be encouraged to cut and tear materials of various textures. Thick, thin, smooth, and rough materials should be manipulated. In addition to free form, children should be encouraged to cut and tear materials into geometric designs to help with the development of form perception. After arranging the materials into the desired form or design, children should learn to fasten one object to another in different ways. Paste, glue, velcro, hook, pin, staple, string, yarn, and hammer and nail are some suggestions for materials to use as fastening devices. Children should be allowed to make their own creations out of raw materials as much as possible. Just as they are encouraged to cut and tear materials of various textures into their own designs, so also should they be allowed to work with raw materials for fastening devices. Children should make their own paste, for example. Much is gained from the texturizing experience of making paste in the way of tactile and kinesthetic experience. Children should also perform their own actions of hooking, nailing, typing, and the like to fasten objects rather than allow the adults to perform the task. Children delight in performing these tasks. The "sloppy" mess created or time lost in using raw materials is gained when the child can look at a product and say "that's mine!"

Constructing and Arranging

Experiences involving constructing and arranging range from various small muscle activities to gross motor activities. Children are taught to create paper forms for holiday ornaments and party favors. They learn to make simple booklets, folios, envelopes, dolls, jewelry, marionettes, collages, and mobiles. They learn to build and manipulate play articles from boards, blocks, cartons, plastics, wires, cans, boxes, spools, and other available materials. These articles may range from small pieces of equipment for individual use to large pieces of apparatus on an environmental playground.[13] Saws, files, hammers, nails, and glues are used to construct with wood and other raw materials. Sewing, stitching, and lacing may be used to make masks, puppets, and costume accessories. Children can construct their own beanbags, musical instruments, badminton rackets, scoops, balls, targets, model airplanes, and the like for individual use in physical education. They can arrange automobile tires, inner tubes, appliance boxes, barrels, and other large apparatus such as the Lind Climber in designing an obstacle course or environmental playground. Designs can be painted by the children on large apparatus and playground equipment such as swings, telephone poles, and cement culvert tiles to make the equipment more attractive and inviting for play.

Modeling and Sculpting

Young children learn to mold and sculpt forms with composition clay, plastic dough, papier mache, wire, soap, wax, and the like. Children should be encouraged to model simple geometric forms as well as to make free forms such as masks, animals, toys, the human body, and pottery. Modeling and sculpting experiences also should include work with sand, soil, snow, and other raw materials. For example, children can build sand castles and snow men. These experiences involve activities that include the use of large muscles as well as the small muscles.

When guiding children through modeling and sculpting experiences, it is important to stress the haptic experience that allows them to discover variation in texture, medium, temperature, shape, smell, and color. Playing with tactile materials thus should involve comparative modeling experiences with course wet sand, cold slippery snow, warm pliable clay, and the like. It is very important for children to learn the "feel" of their environment.

MUSIC EXPERIENCES THROUGH PHYSICAL EDUCATION

Listening

As children learn about music during the elementary grades, they develop better skills in auditory perception concerning auditory reception, auditory association, auditory discrimination, auditory figure-ground perception, and auditory sequential memory. Specific listening experiences in music help children learn about the concepts of melody, rhythm, harmony, form, and expression. Many experiences in physical education can be integrated with the musical concepts to help children refine their listening skills. For example, when children learn to listen for the melody and rhythm of music, they learn how to discriminate between even and uneven rhythms as well as how to distinguish between the beat, accent, and rhythmical pattern of the music. In physical education children should be taught to listen to music and tell whether they would use an even pattern (walk, run, hop) or uneven rhythm (skip, gallop) to move to the music. With regard to beat and accent, the children could clap their hands, snap their fingers or tap their feet to designated beats or accents.

When learning additional skills in auditory discrimination and figure-ground perception, the children should be taught how to discriminate between the various musical instruments. Children's symphony music such as Peter and the Wolf and the Nutcracker Suite are good selections for such activities. Then, when the children know what each instrument sounds like, they can be divided into small groups for each instrument and asked to move creatively whenever they hear their instrument. The sounds of jet planes, fire engines, wind blowing, motorcycles, and the like can be utilized by having the children listen for the sound, tell what the sound is, and move however the sound makes them feel.

Auditory association can be enhanced by having children learn about musical phrases, tempo, chord changes, or changes in pitch. At each new phrase and change in chord, tempo, or pitch the children could explore various aspects of space, force, time, and flow. With a change in pitch the children might associate moving at a high or low level. With a change in chord the children might associate free flowing movements or bound percussive movements. With a change in tempo a child might associate fast and slow movements.

Auditory sequencing and memory may be enhanced through various finger snapping, hand clapping, and foot tapping exercises in physical education. As children learn about beat, accent and pattern, the teacher could create a rhythm (clap, clap, snap, tap) and expect the children to repeat it. Patterns can be of any length - 4 beats, 8 beats, 16 beats. Patterns should be repeated in sequence several times and then reversed (tap, snap, clap, clap) or new patterns created. At first the teacher should direct the sequence and then gradually allow the children to create their own auditory sequence patterns involving the above skills as well as locomotor or manipulative patterns.

Singing

During their elementary school years children develop the ability to sing on pitch while improving their vocal range, tone production, and diction. Specific singing experiences enhance the concepts of melody, rhythm, harmony, form, and expression as children sing music for various seasons; from different countries; about the past, present and future; and concerning special themes. Again, experiences in physical education can be integrated with musical concepts to help children refine their singing skills.

At the early primary level children often learn to sing rhymes that accompany finger plays and nursery rhymes. As children learn to sing the words to Insy Winsy Spider, or Heads Shoulders Knees and Toes they learn the associated hand or body movements to accompany the words. Other finger plays and nursery rhymes to which children may sing and move are as follows[6,11,12].

1. Here Is the Church	11. Two Little Blackbirds
2. Ten Little Indians	12. Old MacDonald
3. Open, Shut Them	13. Gay Musician
4. Where Is Thumbkin	14. Humpty Dumpty
5. Hands	15. Farmer in the Dell
6. Ten Little Gentlemen	16. Jack and Jill
7. Five Little Mice	17. Baa, Baa Black Sheep
8. Ten Galloping Horses	18. Mary Had a Little Lamb
9. Looby Loo	19. Bingo
10. The Duke of York	20. Long Legged Sailor

Additional finger plays and singing games may be found in the selected readings section of this chapter.

Singing experiences in physical education can be associated with nonsense syllables, names and word sequences as children progress through the grades. Dum Dum, Da Da is a clapping and singing song using nonsense syllables and is commonly learned in girl scouting. Children sit in a circle and sing the song while clapping their hands, tapping their knees, tapping their partner's knees on either side, or touching their various body parts to the rhythm of the melody. Children can also learn to sing their name or sing and chant word sequences while performing clapping or locomotor sequences. Familiar rhymes (ibbety bibbety, hippety hop), nonsense phrases (hey nonny nonny), children's names (David Lee Gallahue, Billie Joe McCalister), cities, rivers, states (Minneapolis, Mississippi River, Maryland-Delaware), work chants (yeo heave ho, whoopee ti yi yo), days (Monday, Tuesday), and colors (red, blue, and white) are possible ideas for chanting and movement sequences. For example, Da-vid Lee Galla-hue would involve a singing and clapping sequence of long and short beats. "I live on Chest-nut Street," may involve a short, short, short, long, long, long sequence to which children may run, run, run, jump, jump, jump.

Singing rhymes to jump rope rhythms have always been a popular activity for children learning to jump rope. In addition, folk songs that accompany the many folk dances that the children learn in physical education may be taught. Examples of jump rope rhythms, folk songs, and dances may be found by referring to the books on the selected reading list at the end of the chapter.[2,6,12]

Reading and Playing

When learning how to read or play music, children learn that any grouping of beats around an accent is called a measure. A measure is a musical sentence. By grouping beats into measures more complex and extended movement patterns can be created. With the beginning of each new measure, children in physical education settings may be asked to change their body shape, level, direction, and so forth. When measures are formed into larger rhythmic structures, they are called phrases. A phrase is of greater duration than a measure and is a means by which children learn to respond to larger groupings of time. In physical education children can make up a rhythmical sequence and repeat it over and over with the beginning of each new phrase. Tempo is the rate of speed of the music or the rate at which one movement follows another. Tempo is continuous and repetitive and defines the intervals of the unit by which time is measured. Thus, although tempo may be fast, slow, or moderate, it acts as the steady underlying line against that beats form a pattern.

As children are learning about beats, accents, measures, phrases, tempo and other concepts, they are also learning about meter. Children learn about the

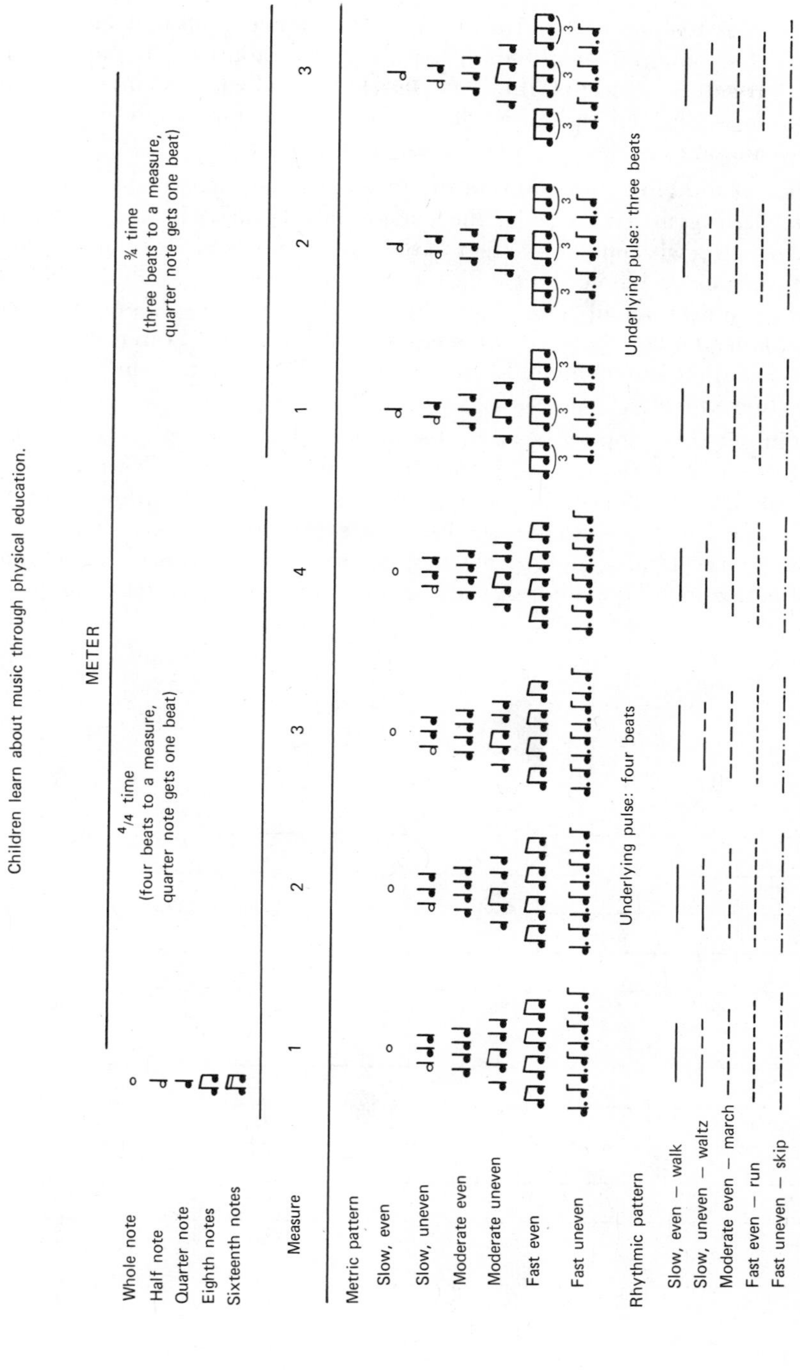

Children learn about music through physical education.

Figure 17-1. Children learn about music through physical education.

time value of notes and how to read measures with even and uneven beats (Figure 17-1). The children should learn that they can walk, run, hop and jump to even rhythm patterns and that they can skip, slide, and gallop to uneven rhythm patterns. Depending on the note value movement patterns may be slow and even, slow and uneven, fast and even, and fast and uneven.

In an effort to help teach children the musical scale, lines may be drawn on the floor in the gymnasium or on the playground (Figure 17-2). Children may then hop or jump with one or two feet to the various notes (do, re, me, fa, so, la, ti, do) on the scale. Whole, half, quarter, and eighth notes should be varied to help teach children about tempo and rhythm. Rubber discs or painted plastic lids may be used as the notes. Sequences should be changed often. Recordings or piano accompaniment should be included as well as encouraging the children to sing as they move.

When initiated in cooperation with the music and art teachers, a whole unit of integrative experiences concerning playing music can evolve. Instruments can be made in art class. Percussive instruments will predominate although it is possible to make some string instruments. The elements of music such as beat, measure, accent, tempo, and the like can be taught by the music teacher and in physical education. The children can learn to play their instruments and move

Figure 17-2. Children can learn to hop the musical scale.

creatively to the rhythm of their own modern rhythm band tunes[13:35-36]. Records such as Clap, Snap and Tap and Modern Rhythm Band Tunes* as well as rounds such as Row, Row, Row Your Boat and Ferre Jacques are most adaptable to playing and movement sequences.

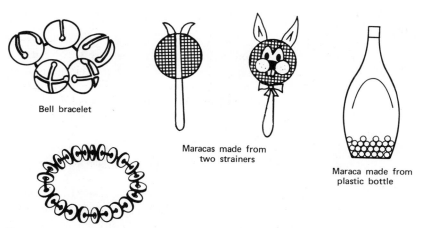

Bell bracelet

Maracas made from two strainers

Maraca made from plastic bottle

Figure 17-3. Musical instruments can be made for use in physical education.

In an effort to make equipment, strainers, cans, coat hangers, sand paper, bottle caps, pots and pans, spoons, mason caps, drum sticks, cardboard boxes, beans, peas, bells, TV dinner trays, plastic bottles, and other throw away items can be brought from home to make musical instruments for use in physical education (Figure 17-3). Bells can be attached together on a string and placed around the head, arm, or leg for various rhythmical experiences. Two strainers can be attached together with wire. Beans are placed on the inside to make a maraca. Faces or designs can be painted on the outside for effect. Two TV dinner trays attached together in the same way with beans on the inside elicit the same sound. Other hollow cardboard boxes or plastic bottles can be partially filled and shook to elicit the same sound. Hollow cardboard boxes or plastic bottles may also be used as drums. Spoons, sticks, cans, pots and pans, and pieces of metal or wood can be struck together to achieve various percussive sounds. Sand paper or other abrasive materials can be rubbed together for other percussive sounds. Washers, bottle caps, or mason caps can be strung on a coat hanger to make a tambourine. Monofilament fishing line of various pound tests or rubber bands can be stretched between nails of varying distances to achieve musi-

*Brazelton, Ambrose, *Clap, Snap and Tap*, Educational Activities, Inc. 1973. Palmer, Hap, *Modern Rhythm Band Tunes*, Educational Activities, Inc. 1969.

cal notes of different pitches. Various size glass jars may be filled with water to different levels and struck with objects to achieve musical notes of different pitch also. A xylophone may be constructed out of pieces of wood or ceramics by attaching and suspending different length pieces in order of size or density on a string.

Dancing and Creating

As it is not the purpose of this section to develop dance as a unit, the authors would simply like to emphasize the importance of dance as a movement experience in the music and physical education curriculum. When approaching dance from a creative movement aspect, children should be allowed to explore the various qualities of movement such as space, force, time and flow. Gradually, children can combine movements together into sequences. At times they should work individually, and at other times small group work should be emphasized. Finally, efforts at creative movement in dance should reach the selection and performance stages.

Children in the elementary schools should also be taught some of the more traditional and structured forms of dance. At an early elementary level, there are many folk dance records as well as exercises and locomotor movement patterns to music available to teach children. Later, additional folk dances, square dances, and simple social dances should be taught to children. Jump rope and ball bouncing routines to music can also be considered as dance experiences.

ART, MUSIC, AND PHYSICAL EDUCATION AT THE PRESCHOOL LEVEL

Several research studies have been conducted that concern the child's ability to make contact with and conceptualize about his environment.[9] One way to accomplish this is through "haptics;" that is, through the active manual exploration of objects in his environment. Principle components or mediating dimensions of space that have been identified through the study of haptics are resistence (force), rough-smooth (texture), thick-thin (dimension), open-closed (closure), wet-dry (medium), warm-cold (temperature), round-square (shape), and sharp-dull (edge). These components describe the dimensionality of the total psychological realm called "haptic space." One can readily see that these components are similar to the qualities of movement alluded to earlier in this book. Statistical evidence supports the existence of a highly differentiated multidimensional object system in children by the time they reach the age of eight.

In an effort to provide for the development and refinement of this differential system, experiences in art and physical education should be implemented at the preschool level. Children should be encouraged to explore the qualities of space, force, time, and flow through an integration of art and movement experiences. Experiences in painting, drawing, cutting, tearing, fastening, and the like should provide for the development of the large and small muscles of the body as the children work with various textures, shapes, implements, colors, materials, and so forth.

As haptic art and play experiences at the preschool level expand a child's knowledge of space (visual) and environment, experiences integrating music and physical education should expand a child's knowledge of rhythm (time/space), song, dance, and creativity. Children at the preschool level should be provided an atmosphere in which they are encouraged to sing and dance freely for this is the time at which they are most uninhibited and free to express themselves. Simple songs, nursery rhymes, finger plays, and the like allow children to develop their singing abilities as well as large and small muscle development. Children can move creatively to story plays and nursery rhymes to develop large muscles. Singing while performing the movements in finger plays will help develop small muscles. Dancing creatively to folk dance and symphony music for children such as The Ball, Leap Frog, Dance of the Little Swans, and Parade* will help develop a sense of rhythm and dance ability. Children should be encouraged to clap, tap, step, hop, jump, twirl, and perform other movements as they interpret the beat of the music. They should make their whole body a musical instrument. They should be given scarves, paper strip streamers, and large pieces of cloth for capes or old flowing dresses to discover swinging and swishing movements. They should use sticks (lummi) and home made instruments (maracas, drums, bells) to beat out rhythmical patterns to music. As a result they will develop initial playing abilities as they learn about the fundamentals of music.

EXAMPLES INTEGRATING ART AND MUSIC WITH PHYSICAL EDUCATION

At present there are several federally funded programs jointly sponsored by the American Association for Health, Physical Education, and Recreation such as Interdisciplinary Model Programs in the Arts for Children and Teachers and the Alliance for Arts Education that are making an attempt at the local, state, and national levels to integrate experiences in the performing and visual arts with the elementary school curriculum. As children learn about art, music, and dance in the classroom, we as physical educators should be prepared to teach them related learning experiences in physical education. This does not mean, however, that the objectives of physical education must be sacrificed in order to

*Tipton, Gladys, *Adventures in Music*, Volumes 1 to 6, RCA Victor.

teach the children about art and music. It does mean that the physical education teacher should be familiar with what is being taught in the classroom and be ready to emphasize and follow up subject matter when it applies or can be reinforced through movement experiences.

Repeated examples have been illustrated that incorporate the concepts of art and music with physical education while maintaining an activity oriented program. Some movement experiences help children develop their art skills in drawing, painting, modeling, sculpting, cutting, pasting, fastening, constructing, and arranging to a more refined degree. Other movement experiences help children develop more proficient musical skills concerning singing, reading, playing, listening, dancing, and creating.

As children learn more about art and music through physical education, the main factor to remember is to introduce each concept according to the ability level of the children. The following are some examples of ways in which art and

Experiences With Art Can Be Integrated With Music And Movement

music can be integrated with physical education. Teachers should use their own ingenuity and creativeness in using these lessons and in adapting other art and music concepts to lessons in physical education. It must be remembered, however, that in any attempt to integrate art and music with physical education, the physical education class must remain activity oriented rather than become an academic class. The main point to consider is to follow the physical education curriculum as usual, but to use every teachable moment to integrate art and music with physical education in an effort to realize more meaningful instruction in each discipline.

Concept: *Singing*
Grade: *1*
Emphasis: *Singing abilities of children can be enhanced through experiences in physical education that encourage auditory responses while playing.*
Organizing Center: *Stability and Locomotion*
Equipment: *Record player and records that provide music to which children can jump more.*
Space: *Gymnasium or playground*
Instructional Ideas:

During this lesson the children will practice jumping the long rope. The children will take turns being the rope turner and rope jumper. Jumping skill may be developed through continued practice of jumping. They may want to start jumping in the middle or try to enter the turning rope through the front or back door. One jump with two feet, rebounding and hopping on alternating feet should be encouraged as variable responses. The children should also attempt to jump to the rhythm of the music being played. While jumping the children can practice singing some of the jump rope rhymes they have learned.*

1. Bubble gum, bubble gum,
   Chew and blow,
   Bubble gum, bubble gum,
   Scrape your toe,
   Bubble gum, bubble gum,
   Tastes so sweet,
   Get that bubble gum off your feet. (Runs out)

2. Down in the valley where the green grass grows
   There sat *(name)* as sweet as a rose.
   She sang and she sang and she sang so sweet.
   Along came *(name)* and kissed her on the cheek.
   How many kisses did she get? (Count)

*Other jump rope rhymes and finger plays may be found in Vannier, Foster, and Gallahue, *Teaching Physical Education in Elementary Schools*, W.B. Saunders: Philadelphia, 1973.

3. Teddie Bear, Teddie Bear turn around (Appropriate action)
   Teddie Bear, Teddie Bear touch the ground (Appropriate action)
   Teddie Bear, Teddie Bear go upstairs (Jumps toward the head of the rope)
   Teddie Bear, Teddie Bear say your prayers (Fold the hands)
   Teddie Bear, Teddie Bear turn out the light (Appropriate action)
   Teddie Bear, Teddie Bear say good night (Runs out)

4. The Jackson Five went to France
   To teach the children how to dance
   A heel and a toe and around you go (Appropriate action)
   A heel and a toe and around you go (Appropriate action)
   Salute to the Captain (Appropriate action)
   Bow to the King (Appropriate action)
   Turn your back on the ugle ole Queen (Runs out the back door)

For a quiet activity to end the class period, the children may choose to perform and sing any of the finger plays that they have learned.

1. Where is Thumbkin? Where is Thumbkin? (Hide thumb inside fist)
   Here I am. Here I am. (One thumb pops up at a time)
   How are you today sir? How are you today sir? (Thumb of one hand wiggles as if talking to the other thumb.)
   Very well, I thank you. Very well, I thank you. (Opposite thumb repeats action)
   Now run away, run away (Both thumbs run off together as hands disappear behind the back)
   > Repeat using: Pointer—index finger
   > Biggie—middle finger
   > Ringer—ring finger
   > Pinky—little finger

Concept: *Drawing and Painting*
Grade: *2*
Emphasis: *Children can be made aware of texture, directional change, flow of movement, and design through integrated experiences in art and physical education.*
Organizing Center: *Locomotion and Manipulation*
Equipment: *Large sheets of paper or newspaper on which to draw, tempra paints, shaving cream, spices, scents, record player, records.*
Space: *Art room or gymnasium*
Instructional Ideas:

After the paper is distributed and arranged, the children can begin finger painting. Commercial finger paints may be used, but we have found that shaving cream works just as well. To add to the color of the paints, it is suggested that various colors of tempra powder be sprinkled into the paint or shaving cream so that the children can experiment with color combinations. To vary the texture, add talcum powder, sand, oil, and the like to the paints. To vary the scent, add banana, peppermint, spice, and similar scents to the paints. It is very intriguing for the child to compare finger painting experiences in a blue-red, talcum powder (slippery), peppermint base paint with a yellow-blue, oil (greasy), spice base paint. Children are quick to learn various colors, textures, and scents through haptic experiences in a multisensory approach.

While the children are experimenting with the paints, records with varying tempos, pitch, and flow may be played in the background. Have the children pay specific attention to the music and draw finger painting patterns according to the tempo, pitch and flow of the music. A record with a fast tempo might suggest gaiety, excitement, and danger, while a slower tempo might suggest solitude, tranquility, and calmness. A record with a percussive beat would indicate sharp, angular changes of direction, while a smooth flowing sound would indicate free, smooth, gradual changes of direction. Drawing at different levels may reflect changes in pitch. After comparing painting experiences with records, the children should take their drawings to the gymnasium and dance their movement patterns on the floor showing similar changes of tempo, direction, level, and flow.

Figure 17- 4. Children can learn to dance to the patterns that they paint to music.

Concept: *Listening*
Grade: *3*
Emphasis: *Selected physical education experiences offer opportunities for children to develop listening skills through rhythmical activities involving eye-hand and gross motor coordination.*
Organizing Center: *Stability and Manipulation*
Equipment: *Record player and an even tempo (4/4) record.*
Stage: *Gymnasium*
Instructional Ideas:

During this lesson the children will use finger snapping, hand clapping, knee slapping, and foot stamping activities to develop their skills in listening along with eye-hand and gross motor coordination. At the beginning of the class, the children will be blindfolded, close their eyes, or sit with their backs to the teacher. Without musical accompaniment, the teacher will perform a sequence while the children listen (snap, clap, snap, stamp, snap, slap). The children will then perform the sequence they heard. Work from simple short sequences to longer more complex sequences. Several sequences should be developed to allow the children time to develop their skills. As children learn to listen better, they will develop better skills in auditory discrimination and auditory sequential memory. To develop skills in auditory closure or association, a sequence can be established (snap, clap, stamp, snap, clap, . . .) with part of the sequence not completed. The children should be expected to tell you which sound was missing.

After a while the children can learn to perform sequences to music. Teach the children a sequence that can be repeated (snap, snap, clap, clap, stamp, stamp). Repeat it over and over to the beat of the music. Reverse the sequence or change the order of the sequence while still keeping time to the music. Change levels or body positions while performing the sequence (clap high, snap low, clap right, snap left). As children perform these skills they are learning about beat, accent, tempo, rhythm, eye-hand coordination, and gross motor coordination as well as developing more efficient listening skills.

Concept: *Playing*
Grade: *4 or 5*
Emphasis: *Children can learn to make and play their own musical instruments, and then move to the music that they play.*
Organizing Center: *Manipulation and Stability*
Equipment: *Materials from home to make musical instruments, a record player, and several records such as "Ferre Jacques."* *
Space: *Gymnasium or classroom*

---

*Ferre Jacques, *Modern Rhythm Band Tunes*, Educational Activities, Inc., 1969.

Instructional Ideas:

When initiated in cooperation with the music and art teachers, a whole unit of integrative experiences can evolve. Instruments can be made in art class (page). The elements of music such as beat, measure, accent, tempo, and the like can be taught by the music teacher and in physical education. The children can learn to play their instruments and more creatively to the rhythm of their own modern rhythm band tunes.

As the children learn to play their instruments, they should keep time to the beat or tempo. As most instruments will be percussive in nature, the children will be shaking, beating, or drumming in time to the music. They should also be encouraged to move about the room while playing their instruments by changing body positions, relationships, levels, and directions. To extend the experience, the children may be divided into small groups. Each person in the group should select a movement sequence while playing their instrument to the rhythm of the music. Each member of the group should relate their movement sequence to each others as if they were a machine with interrelated cogs and levers working together.

In addition to playing together as machines, the children may be divided into groups and play rounds with each group playing a different sequence. An example of implementation of this experience can be done to the record "Ferre Jacques." The record is played in 4/4 time. One group of children (drums) will play the sequence—rest, beat, rest, beat to the background music (z♩z♩). A second group (tambourines) will play the sequence - rest, beat, beat, rest, beat to the music (z♫z♩). The third group (bells) will play the sequence - beat, beat, beat, beat, beat to the music (♩♩♫♩). Again the children should be encouraged to move to the music while they are playing their sequences.

Concept: *Creating and Dancing*
Grade: *5 or 6*
Emphasis: *Children can use the basic locomotor patterns to create their own dances.*
Organizing Center: *Locomotion and Stability*
Equipment: *Record player and any modern record with an even 4/4 beat.*
Space: *Gymnasium*
Instructional Ideas:

During this lesson the children will learn to combine various locomotor patterns to create a dance of their own. To begin the lesson the teacher may demonstrate one dance sequence (Hully Gully) that may be repeated. The steps are as follows.

Count 1 - 4	Step Left, Right (Grapevine), Left, Kick
Count 5 - 8	Step Right, Left (Grapevine), Right, Kick
Count 9 - 10	Step Left, Kick Right

Count 11 - 12 Step Right, Kick Left
Count 13 - 16 Walk Ahead 4 Steps, LRLR
Count 17 - 19 Walk Back 3 Steps, LRL
Count 20   Step Right with a quarter Turn to the Left.

Go over this dance until the children have mastered the steps and feel rather comfortable in performing it. Then ask them to create their own dance by combining walking, hopping, jumping, and kicking movements. Divide the children into groups with three to five children per group. As they develop their dance encourage them to change directions, pathways, and levels. Where appropriate, also encourage them to add finger snapping or hand clapping gestures. The dance should involve from 16 to 32 counts and should be repeated in sequence. After the children create their own dances, allow each group to teach the other groups their dances.

SELECTED REFERENCES

1. AAHPER *Children's Dance,* Washington, D.C., 1973.
2. Anderson, Marian H., Elliot, M.E., and LaBerge, J., *Play With A Purpose,* Harper and Row, New York, 1972.
3. Boardman, Eunice and Landis, B., *Exploring Music,* Grades 1 to 6, Holt, Rinehart and Winston, Inc., New York, 1966.
4. Boorman, Joyce, *Creative Dance in the First Three Grades,* McKay Company, Inc., New York, 1969.
5. Cherry, Clare, *Creative Movement for the Developing Child,* Lear Siegler, Inc., Belmont, California, 1971.
6. Dauer, Victor, *Essential Movement Experiences for Preschool and Primary Children,* Burgess Publishing Company, Minneapolis, 1972.

12. Vannier, Maryhelen, Foster, M., and Gallahue, D.L., *Teaching Physical Education in Elementary Schools,* W.B. Saunders Company, Philadelphia, 1973.
13. Werner, Peter H. and Simmons, R.A., *Do It Yourself: Creative Movement with Innovative Physical Education Equipment,* Kendall/Hunt, Dubuque, Iowa, 1973.
14. Willis, Benjamin C., *Teaching Guide for Art,* Chicago Public Schools, 1961.

Index